Decisions, Decisions

*Case Studies and Discussion Problems
in Communication Ethics*

Second Edition • *Revised Printing*

Randy Bobbitt

University of West Florida

Kendall Hunt
publishing company

Cover image © Shutterstock, Inc.

www.kendallhunt.com
Send all inquiries to:
4050 Westmark Drive
Dubuque, IA 52004-1840

Contents

PREFACE   xi

ABOUT THE AUTHOR   xii

CHAPTER 1   Why a Book About Communication Ethics?   1

Defining Communication Ethics   1

Sources of Ethical Guidance   2
    Personal Standards   2
    Employer Standards   3
    Industry Standards   3
    Combining the Three Sources   3

The Changing Nature of the Media   4
    American Journalism Tradition: The First Amendment
        and the Free Press   4
    American Media Today   6
    What this Means for Ethics and Decision-Making   7

Americans' Cynical View of the Media   9

Cynicism is Not Aimed Only at Journalists   11

Perception of Honesty and Ethical Standards of
    Employment Fields   14

For Discussion   16
    Case Study 1: James Frey and *A Million Little Pieces*   16
    Discussion Questions   17

Notes   18

**CHAPTER 2   Philosophical and Critical Perspectives   19
on Communication Ethics**

Greek Influences   19
    Socrates and Plato   19
    Aristotle and the Golden Mean   21

European Influences   22
    Abelard: Focus on Intent Rather Than Consequences   23
    Aquinas, the Natural Law Doctrine, and "Jocose Lies"   23
    Machiavelli: Results More Important Than the Process   24

Bacon and Rational Decision-Making 24
Hobbes and the Social Contract 25
Milton, Libertarianism, and the Marketplace of Ideas 26
Rousseau and Compassionate Decision-Making 27
Blackstone and the Blackstonian Doctrine 27
Kant and the Categorical Imperative 28
Bentham, Mill, and Utilitarianism 29
Kierkegaard, Multiple Motives, and Avoiding
    Procrastination 30
Durkheim and Cultural Relativism 30
Sartre and Individual Responsibility 31
Baudrillard and Hyper-reality 32

American Influences 33
Dewey and Pragmatism 34
Rand and Objectivism 34
Meiklejohn and Absolutism 35
Fletcher and Situational Ethics 36
Rawls and the Veil of Ignorance 36
Bok and the Principle of Veracity 38
Lippmann and the Imperfect System 39
Boorstin and Pseudo-Events 40
Bagdikian and the Media Monopoly 40
Postman and the Study of Humor 41

For Discussion 41
Case Study 2: Football Player's Field of Dreams is a Hoax 41
Discussion Questions 43

Notes 45

CHAPTER 3   Journalism, Broadcasting, and Entertainment: Content Issues   47

Background 47
Academic Studies 48
Government Intervention 48
Professional Codes of Ethics 48

Current Issues and Controversies 50
The Debate over Public Service Journalism 50
The Debate over Sponsored News 51
The Danger of Stereotypes 52
Does the News Media Show a Bias Toward
    Liberal Views? 54
Knowing When to Be Afraid 56
Parody and Ridicule 56
Covering Tragedies: How Much is Too Much? 60
Political Correctness: Who Can Say What? 61
Are Television and Movies Obligated to Be Realistic? 65
The Debate Over Video News Releases 66

(Alleged) Over-Dependence on News Releases	67
The Debate Over Television Indecency	67
The Debate Over Citizen Journalism	70
For Discussion	71
Case Study 3-A: The Lesser of Two Evils	71
Case Study 3-B: Amtrak Tries to Derail Leno	73
Case Study 3-C: Tragedy at Virginia Tech	74
Case Study 3-D: The World According to Don Imus	75
Case Study 3-E: The CSI Effect	76
Discussion Problem 3-A: Ghost Walk	78
Discussion Problem 3-B: Tell Me More	79
Discussion Problem 3-C: Big Problems in Brookwood	80
Discussion Questions	81
Notes	82

CHAPTER 4

Journalism, Broadcasting, and Entertainment: Personnel Issues — 83

Background	83
Current Issues and Controversies	85
Conflicts of Interest	85
Diversity as a Personnel Issue	91
The Problems of Plagiarism and Unlabeled Fiction	93
The Debate Over Immersion Journalism	95
For Discussion	97
Case Study 4-A: A Case of Drunk Driving	97
Case Study 4-B: Bamberger Blows the Whistle	98
Case Study 4-C: The Unlikely Disciple	100
Discussion Problem 4-A: Plugging the Zoo	101
Discussion Problem 4-B: The Award-Winning Environmental Reporter	102
Discussion Questions	103
Notes	104

CHAPTER 5

Journalism, Broadcasting, and Entertainment: Policy Issues — 105

Background	105
Current Issues and Controversies	107
The Private Lives of Public People	107
The Private Lives of Private People	110
Dealing with Sexual Assault Victims	111
Harassment and the Paparazzi	113

Dealing with Suicide 114
The Debate Over Confidential Sources 117
Issues in Interviewing 119
Deception, Misrepresentation, and Hidden Recording
Devices 122
Media Ride-Alongs 125
Checkbook Journalism 126
Junkets and Freebies 127
To Report or Not Report 129
Staging Photographs and Video 131
Correction Policies 131
Digital Manipulation of Photographs 135

For Discussion 138
Case Study 5-A: Arthur Ashe Has AIDS 138
Case Study 5-B: No One Asked You to Leave, But
No One Invited You In 140
Case Study 5-C: Is Nancy Grace to Blame for
Melinda Duckett's Suicide? 141
Case Study 5-D: To Err is Human, to Correct Divine 142
Case Study 5-E: Naming Names 144
Case Study 5-F: A Ryder Truck Outside the Federal
Building: Déjà vu All Over Again 145
Discussion Problem 5-A: The Senator and the Tattoo 146
Discussion Problem 5-B: The Mayor and the Missing Kid 147

Discussion Questions 148

Notes 149

CHAPTER 6   **Ethical Issues in Advertising**   **151**

Background 151
Legal and Ethical Framework 152
Government Regulation 153

Current Issues and Controversies 154
False and Deceptive Advertising 154
The Debate Over Product Placements 156
Advertising of Controversial Products and Services 158
Advertising Aimed at Children 159
Advertising Boycotts 159
Advertisers' Influence on News and Reviews 160
Portrayals of Women 162
The Influence of Advertising on Consumer Spending 163
The Myth of "Suggested Retail Price" 163

For Discussion 164
Case Study 6-A: Lottery Advertising: What are the Odds? 165
Case Study 6-B: Campaign for a Commercial-Free
Childhood 167

Case Study 6-C: What Time Does the Movie Really Start? 168
Case Study 6-D: Aggressive Fund-Raising, or Deceptive
    Advertising? 169
Case Study 6-E: Academic Bait and Switch 171
Case Study 6-F: Joseph Lister and the Product That
    Bears His Name 173
Discussion Problem 6-A: The Case of the Cable
    Descrambler 174
Discussion Problem 6-B: Is This Ad Too Good to
    Be True? 175
Discussion Problem 6-C: Advertising Agencies and
    Competing Proposals 176
Discussion Questions 177

Notes 178

CHAPTER 7   **Ethical Issues in Public Relations**   **179**

Background 179
    What is Public Relations? 179
    Legal and Ethical Limitations on the Public
        Relations Profession 181
    Some General Rules 181
    Public Relations and the First Amendment 182
    Differentiating Between Advertising and Public Relations 183
    Public Relations Representatives Working as Lobbyists 184
    Legal and Ethical Problems in Investor Relations 184
    Professional Codes of Ethics 185

Current Issues and Controversies 192
    The Challenge of Media Relations 192
    The Debate over Licensing 194
    Ethical Dilemmas on the Job 194
    Unethical Practices of Some Public Relations Agencies 195
    News Releases and Manufactured Quotes 196
    Dealing with Inaccurate or Misleading Media Coverage 196
    The Debate over Confidentiality and Privilege 197
    Litigation PR 198

For Discussion 199
    Case Study 7-A: When a PR Firm Could Use a PR Firm 199
    Case Study 7-B: PR for PR 201
    Case Study 7-C: Another Bad Day at the Office for FEMA 203
    Discussion Problem 7-A: Was That Focus Group Really
        Confidential? 204
    Discussion Problem 7-B: Get Your Can to the Game 205
    Discussion Problem 7-C: The Golf Weekend 206
    Discussion Problem 7-D: Go Quietly or Else 207
    Discussion Problem 7-E: College Degrees for Sale 208
    Discussion Questions 210

Notes 211

CHAPTER 8   **Ethical Issues in Political Communication**   **213**

Background   213

Current Issues and Controversies   215
 The Science of Shaping Opinions   215
 The Difference Between Persuasion and Propaganda   215
 Other Propaganda Techniques   219
 Disinformation   221
 Problems with Polls   221
 Associated Press Guidelines for Reporting
  Research Results   213
 Federal Laws and Supreme Court Cases on Political
  Advertising   224
 Funding of Government Communication Activities   226
 The Influence of Talk Radio   227

For Discussion   228
 Case Study 8-A: Cindy Watson vs. the Hog Farmers   228
 Case Study 8-B: Taking License with Free Speech   230
 Case Study 8-C: Violating the Law, or a Series of
  Honest Mistakes?   231
 Case Study 8-D: Mixing Entertainment with Politics   232
 Case Study 8-E: Stop Using Our Song!   233
 Discussion Problem 8: All or Nothing   234
 Discussion Questions   235

Notes   236

CHAPTER 9   **Ethical Issues in Workplace Communication**   **237**

Background   237

Current Issues and Controversies   238
 Sexual Harassment in the Workplace   238
 Race, Religion, and Politics in the Workplace   240
 Honesty in the Workplace and at School   240
 Employee Evaluations and Letters of Recommendation   243
 Salary Negotiations   244
 Which Forms of Workplace Communication Should
  be Privileged?   245
 Communicating with Disabled Co-Workers and Customers   246
 Employer Monitoring of Employee Email and
  Web Activity   247

For Discussion   248
 Case Study 9-A: The (Bad) Luck of the Irish   248
 Case Study 9-B: Riley Weston's Little White Lie   250
 Discussion Problem 9-A: Competing Loyalties   251
 Discussion Problem 9-B: Harry and Sally's Letters of
  Recommendation   252

Discussion Problem 9-C: Traveling on Company Business   253
Discussion Problem 9-D: The Reverse Reference Call   254
Discussion Problem 9-E: Overheard at the Coffee Shop   255
Discussion Problem 9-F: At the Mall, No News is
      Good News   256

Discussion Questions   257

Notes   258

CHAPTER 10   **When Ethical Issues Become Legal Issues**   **259**

The First Amendment and Political Speech   259
    What the Amendment Says (and Doesn't Say)   259
    Levels of Speech   261
    What Does the First Amendment Really Mean?   261
    The Hierarchy of First Amendment Protection   262
    Clarification on the First Amendment Hierarchy   263
    The Supreme Court and Political Speech   264
    Prior Restraint vs. Punishment After the Fact   267

Copyrights and Trademarks   268
    Copyright Basics   269
    Recent and Ongoing Issues in Copyright Law   273
    Trademarks   274
    Intellectual Property Issues in the International
      Marketplace   275

Libel and Privacy   276
    The Basics of Libel Law   276
    Categories of Libel   277
    Components of Libel   278
    The Nature of Libel Plaintiffs   279
    Defenses Against Libel Claims   280
    Private Figures vs. Public Figures   281
    Limitations and Clarifications Regarding the
      "Fair Comment" Defense   282
    SLAPP Suits   283
    The Basics of Privacy Law   284
    Libel and Privacy Law Applied to Non-Journalistic
      Products   286

Access to Information   288
    Who Owns Information?   288
    Access to News Events and Locations   289
    Access to Public Meetings   290
    Access to Public Records   291
    The Freedom of Information Act and Its Amendments   292
    State Public Records Laws   293

For Discussion 295

Discussion Problem 10-A: Roadside Memorials 295

Discussion Problem 10-B: Who Owns What the Professor
Says . . . or What the Students Write Down? 296

Discussion Problem 10-C: Libel in the Student Newspaper 296

Discussion Questions 297

Notes 299

APPENDIX A Codes of Ethics 301

American Advertising Federation Code of Ethics 301

American Society of Newspaper Editors Statement 302
of Principles

Associated Press Sports Editors Ethical Guidelines 304

College Media Advisors Code of Ethical Behavior 306

International Association of Business Communicators 308
Code of Ethics

Online News Association Mission Statement 311

Public Radio News Directors Inc. Code of Ethics 312

Public Relations Society of America Member Code of Ethics 313

Rebecca Blood's Code of Weblog Ethics 319

Society of American Business Editors and Writers 323
Revised Code of Ethics

Society of Professional Journalists Principles and 324
Standards of Practice

APPENDIX B Sources / For Further Reading 327

SUBJECT INDEX 339

BOOKS BY RANDY BOBBITT 355

Preface

Decisions, Decisions is the culmination of a decade's worth of work in researching, teaching, and writing about communication ethics. It is based on my teaching style, which has changed dramatically since I began as a graduate teaching assistant.

For the first 10 years or so of my teaching career, I used the traditional lecture/note-taking model of instruction. While I enjoyed the process of preparing lecture notes, and students seemed to enjoy my classes, I always believed there might be a better way to use our class time. While I was in my doctoral program I took a number of courses in communication law and ethics that were taught by professors who had taught in law schools in addition to communication programs. I was intrigued with their Socratic dialogue approach to teaching — one that required students to thoroughly prepare for each class meeting and challenged them to think about controversial issues, develop positions, and then publicly defend them.

I have been very pleased with the students' reactions to this teaching method. I can tell from their comments made to me directly, as well as those on student evaluations, that they agree that it leads to a more thorough learning of the material, as opposed to just memorizing definitions for a test. While some students are initially uncomfortable speaking about controversial subjects in front of their peers, most of them warm up to it eventually. Much of the positive reinforcement for this teaching method comes from transfer and transient students, who are quick to compare it to the lecture/note-taking model they have encountered at other institutions.

Communication ethics is often a difficult subject for students to grasp, but it is important for those who plan on careers in journalism, broadcasting, advertising, and public relations. Basic knowledge of decision-making processes will often help you to operate in the best interests of yourself or your employer. Other times it involves respecting the rights and feelings of others.

Nearly all aspects of communication ethics are complex, in part because of the rapidly changing nature of the technology with which professional communicators work. That means encountering many questions for which there are no simple answers. As one of my favorite graduate school professors often told his Constitutional Law classes, sometimes the safest answer to legal and ethical questions is "sometimes . . . maybe . . . it depends."

Like many textbooks written by college professors, this book began as a collection of lecture notes and handouts. The biggest thanks go out to Kendall-Hunt representatives for their patience in getting this second edition into print: Katie Wendler, assistant editor, and Brenda Rowles, project coordinator.

Many of those lecture notes and handouts came from five professors who were influential in my teaching career: Donna Dickerson, former director of the School of Mass Communications at the University of South Florida (USF), now dean of the College of Arts and Sciences at the University of Texas at Tyler; Barbara Petersen, professor of media law at USF; and three professors at Bowling Green State University: Dennis Hale (who passed away before seeing the finished product) and Jim Foust in the School of Communication Studies, and Steven Ludd in the Department of Political Science.

In addition to those professors, I thank Bruce Swain, my former department chair at the University of West Florida, whose 1978 book, *Reporters' Ethics,* was one of the first on the subject. I also thank hundreds of students who have taken my classes over the last decade and provided valuable feedback.

About the Author

Dr. Randy Bobbitt is visiting lecturer in the Department of Communication Arts at the University of West Florida, where he teaches courses in journalism, public relations, communication law, communication ethics, and communication management. Prior to joining the faculty at UWF, he taught at the University of North Carolina at Wilmington, Marshall University, and the University of South Florida.

His research interests include public relations, political communication, popular culture, and communication law and ethics. Prior to college teaching, he worked professionally in both journalism and public relations. He is a past president of the West Virginia Chapter of the Public Relations Society of America and is a frequent speaker at professional and student public relations conferences. He holds a Ph.D. in communication law and policy from Bowling Green State University.

In addition to *Decisions Decisions*, he has published six other books on topics including public relations, communication law and ethics, journalism history, and political communication: *A Big Idea and a Shirt-Tail Full of Type: The Life and Work of Wallace F. Stovall* (1995), *Developing the Public Relations Campaign* (co-authored with Ruth Sullivan, 2004, 2009, and 2013), *Who Owns What's Inside the Professor's Head* (2006), *Lottery Wars: Case Studies in Bible Belt Politics* (2007), *Exploring Communication Law* (2007), and *Us Against Them: The Political Culture of Talk Radio* (2010). He is currently working on a new book, *From Barnette to Blaine,* which tracks major court cases involving student speech and press rights at high schools and colleges. It will be published in 2016.

CHAPTER 1

Why a Book About Communication Ethics?

Defining Communication Ethics

In 1964, a major obscenity case reached the United States Supreme Court that required the justices to develop a definition for what was obscene and what was not. Justice Potter Stewart, one of the most quotable justices in the history of the Court, told his colleagues, "I cannot give you a definition for obscenity, but I know it when I see it."

Many professional communicators feel the same way about ethics. Most have not looked at their profession's ethical codes or even thought about ethics since taking their last final exams in college, so if someone were to ask them to explain the ethical rules involved in their work, most could not give them a formal answer. But all of them know — or at least claim to know — right and wrong when they see it.

Nearly every textbook about communication ethics begins with a discussion of definitions, and this one is no exception. One accepted definition of ethics (in general) is "the study of what constitutes right or wrong, or good and bad, human behavior." Another common definition says that "ethics is what you do when no one else is looking." Another rule simply says that "a clear conscience makes a very soft pillow."

To establish a more formal definition for *communication ethics*, perhaps the best starting point is to distinguish the field from its cousin, *communication law*. That is appropriate because in many communication programs, courses in ethics and law are taught by the same instructors, are found on the same page of the university catalog, and have similar course titles and numbers. At some institutions, the two topics are even combined into one course.

There are some important differences, however. While communication law deals mostly with rigid rules and guidelines that are established by federal, state, or local governments, communication ethics deals with voluntary decisions made by individual professional communicators and media organizations. Put another way, the law tells you what you *can and cannot do,* while ethics tells you what you *should and should not do.*

Justice Stewart once defined ethics as "knowing the difference between what you have a right to do and what is the right thing to do." A journalism professor paraphrased Stewart when he explained his opinion that print and broadcast journalists should not publish or broadcast the names of rape victims, even though the law allows them to do so. "Just because you can," he told student journalists and students taking his ethics class, "doesn't mean that you have to."

Sources of Ethical Guidance

Successful journalists need to earn and then maintain their credibility, not only with their audiences, but also with the people they work with on a regular basis — their superiors, subordinates, and peers. Reporters and editors who lose their jobs because of ethical breaches will find it difficult to find subsequent jobs if the reasons for their dismissal are known.

Professional communicators vary greatly in their approach to decision-making on the job, drawing guidance from three sources: personal standards, employer standards, and industry standards.

Personal Standards

Some professional communicators make their decisions based solely on their own personal beliefs that are often influenced by their family or religious upbringing. Davis Young, a communication educator and expert on the issue of communication ethics, says that, "Our personal ethics are based on our system of values and believes . . . You cannot be forced to lose your values; they are only lost if you choose to relinquish them."

One example of personal beliefs or family upbringing affecting students as they make the transition from college student to professional communicator can be found in the reluctance of young journalists to ask difficult questions when interviewing authority figures they are assigned to interview. Many professors who teach in journalism programs in the southeastern United States report that their students, who were raised by their parents to always respect and show deference to authority figures, are not comfortable in interview situations that call for them to question authority and to be skeptical of the information they are provided. While it is unlikely that any professor (or editor) would expect a student or professional journalist to be rude or disrespectful to government officials, professional communicators who are easily intimidated or cannot be assertive in gathering information will not be successful in investigative reporting and similar fields.

Employer Standards

Nearly every newspaper, television or radio station, or advertising or public relations agency has an employee policy manual that explains the ethical guidelines that employees are expected to follow. The degree to which companies enforce those guidelines, of course, varies greatly.

Ron F. Smith, a journalism professor at the University of Central Florida, contends that placing too much emphasis on ethics may create a "chilling effect" on journalists' work. Much like excessive concern for the legal results of their work may cause them to shy away from aggressive or investigative journalism due to the fear of libel suits, some reporters worry that too much concern for ethics may result in "wishy-washy" journalism that is based too much on trying to please ethicists and not enough on reporting the news.

Industry Standards

Many professional communicators base their decisions on ethical guidelines of the profession in which they are employed.

The Society of Professional Journalists is believed to be the first professional organization to develop a code of ethics for journalists, doing so in 1923. At the time, the American government was plagued by a series of political scandals — most of them associated with the presidency of Warren G. Harding — and SPJ announced that if the profession was going to scrutinize the ethical misdeeds of politicians, it must first make sure its own house was in order. The best way to accomplish that, SPJ leaders believed, was to establish and enforce a code of ethics that placed journalists on a higher ethical plane than politicians and persons in other employment fields.

In addition to SPJ's guidelines for individual print and broadcast reporters, the American Society of Newspaper Editors and the Radio Television Digital News Association provide guidelines for media organizations as a whole. These industry-wide codes deal with issues such as conflicts of interest, correcting errors, respect for the privacy of persons in the news, and the use of confidential sources. The Public Relations Society of America, International Association of Business Communicators, and the American Advertising Federation have established similar guidelines for those fields. Those codes deal with issues such as conflicts of interest, confidentiality, and fair competition. Many are provided in their entirety in the appendices.

The professional associations listed above have one thing in common: If you skim their publications, survey their World Wide Web sites, and look at the agendas from their conferences, you will see that ethics and professional standards is one of the most talked-about topics among those professions in the past 20 years — perhaps second only to the impact of technology.

Many observers believe that strong ethical codes within the communication-related professions will enhance credibility in fields that have lost public confidence. They believe that even though most reporters should have a natural sense of right and wrong, formal ethical guidelines are still necessary and useful. Part of the reason for that is the high rate of turnover among professional communicators; newspaper editors and television news directors cannot assume that newcomers will know the guidelines. Not only should those guidelines be provided to newcomers and then enforced, critics say, but also ethical behavior should be ingrained into the workplace culture.

Combining the Three Sources

In some cases, professional communicators may draw upon all three sources for help in decision-making. But what happens when a professional communicator's personal beliefs are in conflict with the standards of their employer or industry? Most communicators would tend to follow their personal beliefs rather than industry standards, especially for the long term. Those who place loyalty to their employer or industry above adherence to their personal standards for conduct would likely do so only in short-term circumstances.

The late Mike Wallace, a veteran reporter for CBS News and one of several featured interviewers on the long-running program *60 Minutes,* says that when the three sources of guidance are in conflict, it is up to individual journalists to "find their own moral compass," which he defined as a friend, family member, or co-worker whose opinion the journalist trusts. Wallace cited the example of former CBS colleague Bernard Kalb, who admired legendary anchor Edward R. Murrow so much that he often asked himself, when faced with an ethical dilemma and conflicting opinions about how to resolve it, "What would Murrow do?"

The Changing Nature of the Media

American Journalism Tradition: The First Amendment and the Free Press

Almost any discussion of the American journalism begins with the First Amendment. Passed in 1791, it included clauses dealing with freedom of religion, speech, press, assembly, and petition. The two clauses of most interest to journalists (and students studying journalism) are those dealing with speech and press. Over the years, legal scholars have established five values to explain the need for the First Amendment's free speech and free press clauses:

Search for the truth. This concept has been a common theme of legal and philosophical literature for centuries. Today, free-speech advocates contend that the First Amendment gives us the right to hear all sides of every issue and to make our own judgments without governmental interference or control. Other defenders of freedom of expression worry that even the slightest limitation on such rights might lead to more dangerous restrictions in the future, an argumentative technique called the **slippery slope.**

An informed electorate. Free speech and a free press are necessary, scholars claim, in order to help citizens make informed decisions about which candidates and issues to vote for and against. Journalists and broadcasters need First Amendment protections in order to effectively investigate the qualifications and backgrounds of political candidates and gather background information on critical public issues.

Limitations on government power. The media need a free press guarantee in order to fulfill their role of "watchdogs" of government. Effective investigative journalism is necessary to prevent and uncover government corruption. When explaining the importance of this function of the media, free press advocates often point to the Watergate scandal of the early 1970s. Without First Amendment protections, they claim, the political corruption of that era might not have been uncovered.

Orderly societal change. Free speech represents a "safety valve" through which ideas can be debated and evaluated, and conflicts can be resolved peacefully rather than violently. Examples include the opportunity to "blow off steam" by participating in displays of hate speech, writing letters to the editor of a newspaper, making public speeches or debates, or staging peaceful demonstrations — instead of choosing more violent and less constructive alternatives. Observers point to countries without free speech protection, where change takes place only as a result of the violent overthrow of a repressive government, as evidence to support the need for free speech protections.

Personal fulfillment and artistic expression. This value refers to providing an outlet for forms of creative expression, even those that may be controversial in nature, such as pornography. Although this value was likely not part of the founding fathers' discussion of the First Amendment more than two centuries ago, it is often cited today.

Once the First Amendment was passed, the American journalism industry began to grow in size and influence. The groundwork for much of American journalism tradition was established by Thomas Jefferson, who among the founding fathers was perhaps the strongest proponent of free speech. Much like the outspoken free-speech advocates in England — among them John Milton and John Stuart Mill — Jefferson believed that freedom of speech and press were essential components of a successful society.

Libertarianism was the prevailing philosophy guiding the American media through the 1800s and early 1900s. Although they stopped somewhat short of an "anything goes" philosophy of disseminating information, most journalists of the day felt free to publish anything they pleased, and in some cases even libel went unpunished.

The powerful newspaper publishers of the time had considerable influence in social and political trends. The advent of the "penny press" allowed newspaper circulation to expand beyond the small circle of intellectual and privileged business leaders and outward to less-educated, lower-income audiences. Publishers became successful and wealthy by lowering production costs, increasing circulation, and expanding their advertising bases. The philosophy of that time was that newspapers could succeed in their role as "watchdogs" on the government and major corporations while still returning a profit to their owners and shareholders.

In the early 1900s, American media shifted away from the libertarian philosophy and toward a newer approach called **social responsibility,** a philosophy still followed today. In short, the social responsibility approach says that just as in the libertarian model, the media should be free to disseminate any information it considers important. But instead of stopping there and expecting the audience to interpret the information to judge its truth and value, the media take the additional step of helping the audience to interpret the information and make judgments about its value and importance.

The social responsibility model continues to emphasize the "watchdog" role of the media. A group of journalists called the "muckrakers" believed that the accumulation of wealth and economic power de-emphasized choice among members of the audience, and therefore endangered democracy. Ida Tarbell, Upton Sinclair, and other muckrakers used the tools of a free press to serve as a watchdog on large corporations that they believed to be exploiting their employees, unduly influencing politicians, and misleading or neglecting consumers. Joseph Pulitzer's *New York World* was one of the first newspapers to give the muckrakers a venue to perform their watchdog role.

The term "social responsibility" was first used by the Hutchins Commission, a think tank formed in 1947 by the University of Chicago and the ownership of *Time* Magazine. It was named after Robert M. Hutchins, then chancellor at the university. The commission's task was to study the impact of the news media on American society and determine what role the media should play. After several years of work, the commission issued its findings that are still looked at today as guidelines for journalism schools and media organizations. According to the commission, the news media should (1) place the news of the day in context, (2) provide a realistic picture of society, (3) provide an outlet for diverse viewpoints, and most importantly, (4) perform their watchdog function on government and big business. Today, that latter idea has been encapsulated into the journalism buzz-phrase "the people have a right to know."

While sometimes erroneously attributed to the First Amendment (which says nothing about the people having the right to know), the phrase is more accurately attributed to the Hutchins Commission findings, as well as to the Society of Professional Journalist's Code of Ethics, which cites the "people's right to know" as one of the cornerstones of the journalism business.

American Media Today

Today, many historians believe that American society is facing a good news/bad news scenario in terms of the future of freedom of speech and press.

On the negative side is the concern over deregulation of traditional media. Interpreting the results of the Hutchins Commission and the work of social scientists studying media effects, Congress and the Federal Communications Commission created rules concerning how many television stations or radio stations an individual or company could own in one market and what percentage of the American people could be included in the audience of any given television or radio network. The Justice Department, which began in the 1950s to limit the growth of corporate giants and break up monopolies in a number of industries, expanded the scope of its scrutiny to include newspaper chains.

In the 1980s, the deregulation of the broadcasting industry dissolved or weakened many of the FCC rules. Similarly, the Justice Department loosened its regulations regarding the ownership of newspaper chains. As a result, media critics such as Ben Bagdikian and consumer advocates such as Dean Alger and John Stauber today write and lecture today about the pitfalls of the government's hands-off philosophy: higher prices (for the media we pay for), less competition, less choice, and less diversity in viewpoints.

On the positive side, the inability to regulate the Internet* is evidence that libertarianism and the marketplace of ideas are making a comeback. In their popular media law textbook, Kent Middleton and William E. Lee wrote that, "Just as shoppers in the commercial marketplace are said to seek the best products, participants in the marketplace of ideas are said to seek the most original, truthful, or useful information."

Despite its historical significance, the marketplace of ideas is not a concept that has been universally accepted in the United States. Many American presidents have been reluctant to release information about the inner workings of their administrations, and public officials at the state and local level have similarly limited public access to information and proceedings. In addition, feminist scholar Catharine MacKinnon argues that the "marketplace of ideas" metaphor is abstraction of little value to women as they

---

*Early in 2015, the Federal Communications Commission instituted a principle known as "net neutrality" that would treat the Internet as a regulated utility. The primary purpose was to maintain the status of all Internet services and service providers being treated equally and to prevent ISPs from creating "fast lanes" that would allow companies to pay more for faster delivery of their content. The principle is expected to be challenged by ISPs on First Amendment grounds.

have less access than men to the marketplace. Citing pornography as an example, MacKinnon contends that women are more likely to be the victims of speech rather than the benefactors. The pornography industry, MacKinnon suggests, is one in which the "free speech of men silences the free speech of women." Similarly, law school professor Jerome Barron argues that minorities also lack access, especially to such critical forums such as the newspaper editorial page.

What This Means for Ethics and Decision-Making

The starting point for studying communication ethics is to look at how trends in the field affect both veteran communicators and newcomers to the profession. Here are some of the most significant trends that have either direct or indirect effects on how journalists and their editors make ethical decisions.

Technology. As it has in most areas of society, the Internet has created both opportunities and challenges for professional communicators and the companies that employ them. For newspapers, magazines, and television stations and networks, the Web — as well as other delivery devices such as smartphones and tablet computers — represent an opportunity to reach larger audiences, including individuals who may not subscribe to the hard copy of the newspaper or watch the traditional television newscast. From an employment standpoint, the Web creates more opportunity for journalists, as newspaper and television stations need larger and more technology-oriented news staffs capable of quickly adapting to new methods of gathering and presenting the news. Many college journalism programs are teaching future journalists to prepare news stories in three formats — print, broadcast, and Web. The two terms that have emerged from this trend are **media convergence** and the **common newsroom.**

While the World Wide Web provides another outlet for established media organizations to reach their audiences, it has also turned out to be a competitor for those same organizations. Upstart news organizations that produce Web-only content, as well as individual bloggers who seek the same professional status and privileges as traditional journalists, have a built-in advantage in terms of the speed with which they can get information to their audiences.

As of 2014, many established media organizations still look at media convergence as either "experimental" or a "work in progress." Among individual reporters and editors, those attitudes don't always fall along generational lines — younger journalists in favor and older veterans opposed — but that is the impression one gets when reading about the issue in traditional journalism publications. "When I started in this business, journalists required two basic skills: reporting and writing," wrote *Washington Post* executive Robert J. Samuelson in a 2007 opinion piece in *Newsweek.* "Now journalists are expected to be utility players, feeding Web sites, posting videos, and doing TV. Up to a point, this is valuable; we're finding new ways to engage and inform. But it's also time-consuming, and it detracts from reporting. What constitutes 'journalism' is less clear . . . the skills that are rewarded are shifting from diligent, curious, and clear to tech-savvy, quick, and edgy."

The late Mike Wallace is one of numerous observers who believe that some day in the future, traditional hard-copy newspapers and magazines will be hard to find, and that younger members of the audience will think it's completely normal for such publications to exist only online. But Wallace wrote in a 2010 book that while "the transition will take much longer than most people think, it is inevitable." *Washington Post* editor Marcus Brauchli added that "it doesn't ultimately matter whether newspapers survive or not . . .

what matters is that journalisms survives . . . that it remains independent and continues to hold the state and the powerful accountable."

Here are the numbers: In 1965, 67 percent of adults between the ages of 21 to 35 had read a daily newspaper the day before responding to the survey. By 1990, that number had fallen to 30 percent, and by 2010, it was less than 25 percent. A 2011 study by the Pew Research Center found that the number of Americans getting their news from online sources surpassed the number who get theirs from newspapers, that nearly half of readers get some portion of their news from cellphones or similar hand-held devices, and that in the previous year, the number of new hires in online journalism surpassed the number of layoffs in traditional news organizations.

Prior to the mid-1990s, the generalization among media researchers was that Americans with high levels of education and income preferred daily newspapers over television, while those with relatively lower levels of education and income preferred television over newspapers. Since the mid-1990s, however, the popularity of the Internet has affected those numbers. The latter category still prefers television, but the former is now dividing its attention between the traditional daily newspaper and online sources.

The advertising industry has also taken advantage of the new technology in the form of banner advertising and other forms of direct-response advertising that many Internet users find intrusive. Despite the negative connotation, many advertisers have found the World Wide Web to be an effective way to execute either Web-only campaigns or Web-based promotions that complement other forms of advertising.

For the public relations industry, the Internet presents both benefits and drawbacks. The benefits include more opportunities to communicate more effectively with employees, stockholders, potential stockholders, customers, potential customers, and the media. But the technology also presents a number of challenges, as organizations and their public relations staffs must deal with angry consumers and advocacy groups that launch their criticisms using a variety of non-traditional media such as Web sites, chat rooms, on-line discussion groups, and blogs.

Competition and clutter. In the early days of the mass media, competition for news and advertising was constructive and generally beneficial for both media organizations and their audiences. Many large cities had two or more newspapers, and their friendly rivalries produced a higher quality of journalism than that found in smaller towns with only one newspaper.

With the advent of television news in the 1950s, those broadcast programs became the newspapers' chief rivals, as they competed against newspapers (in addition to competing against each other). In the 1980s, the growth of cable television networks provided even more competition, and in the 1990s the growth of the Internet raised the competitive stakes yet again. The latter two developments have increased the size of the potential news audience exponentially, but the results have not been all positive. The competition for news and advertising revenue among newspapers, broadcast networks, cable networks, and Internet news services results in more cases of bad decision-making, carelessness, sloppy reporting, and clutter. As many media critics are fond of saying, the competition among media outlets often spins out of control as journalists and their employers place too much importance on being first with a news story and not enough emphasis on being accurate.

Speed. An issue closely associated with competition is that of the speed with which journalists gather and report news. In the early days of print journalism, a daily newspaper was faced with only two deadlines per day — late morning for an afternoon newspaper and early evening for the next day's morning newspaper. The early days of television news did not change the deadlines significantly, as producing only one newscast per day meant having only one deadline per day. But in the 1960s, local television stations began to offer late evening newscasts, and in 1980s they added newscasts at mid-day and again in the late afternoon — in effect increasing the number of daily newscasts from one to as many as four. Another development of the 1980s was the emergence of 24-hour cable news channels. The result of the latter two phenomena is the creation of nearly round-the-clock deadlines. The growth of Internet news services only compounds the deadline problem.

Americans' Cynical View of the Media

While most Americans appreciate freedom of speech and press as abstract concepts, most hold cynical views about the state of American media in respect to specific media behaviors. One common complaint is that the media tends to over-report the negative and under-report the positive. "Millions of Social Security checks worth billions of dollars are delivered accurately and on time each month," wrote Gannett News columnist Richard Benedetto. "But let one recipient run into a bureaucratic snafu and the news media stand ready to paint the entire system as a hopeless boondoggle." The media defend themselves against such criticism by claiming that their job is to report the unusual and point out the problems, not to praise government agencies and companies for the routine performance of their jobs. Speaking to a group of college journalists, a newspaper publisher once said that "when we pick up the telephone and get a dial tone, we're not going to celebrate that because it's what we expect . . . but when phone service is disrupted city-wide, it's something that we need to write about."

On a similar note, another complaint of consumers is that the media sometimes go beyond simply reporting on conflict, and often create conflict — in effect; creating news stories where no news stories previously existed. A few years ago, a sportswriter for a daily newspaper was on the receiving end of that criticism while a guest on a radio call-in show. In order to describe how sportswriters worked with their sources, he used an example from a story he had written about the chilly relationship between the coach of the local professional football team and its former quarterback who had left several years earlier to play for another team. On a slow Monday afternoon, he called the quarterback and asked him if he still held hard feelings toward his former coach. He told the sportswriter that he did and provided some colorful quotes. Those quotes appeared in Tuesday morning's newspaper. On Tuesday afternoon, the sportswriter called the coach to ask him for his reaction, which generated another story for Wednesday's paper. On Wednesday afternoon, the sportswriter called the quarterback again to tell him what the coach has said, and that conversation generated a story for Thursday's paper. At that point, the sports editor stepped in and put a stop to the sportswriter's "he said/he said" approach to generating news stories.

When a caller to the radio show accused the sportswriter of artificially creating a news story where no news story previously existed, the writer's defense was that he was simply "reporting a conflict between a coach and one of his former players that was of interest to the readers . . . it was news."

"Yes," the caller responded. "But it *wasn't* news until you *made it* news."

While some Americans are simply predisposed to hold negative attitudes toward the media based on their family upbringing, education level, or socio-economic status, others cite examples of media mistakes or missteps to support their attitudes. Media researchers cite the following as examples:

- In 1981, *Washington Post* reporter Janet Cooke was found to have made up characters and events for a series of stories about ghetto life in Washington, D.C. The series won a Pulitzer Prize and Cooke was celebrated as a rising star, but after the story was exposed as fiction, Cooke was fired and the newspaper returned the prize and apologized to its readers. In the early 2000s, *New York Times* reporter Jayson Blair and *New Republic* writer Stephen Glass were fired from their respective publications after it was revealed they had made up people, organizations, events, and quotes in their stories for several years.

- In 1988, CBS News anchor Dan Rather engaged presidential candidate George H. W. Bush in a confrontational interview that was broadcast live on the network's evening news program. Rather's defenders believe that Bush may have orchestrated the confrontation in order to address criticisms that he wasn't "tough enough" to be president, but the majority of Americans (according to polls) believed that Rather came across as a bully and reinforced the stereotype of journalists being overly aggressive and arrogant. Almost two decades later, Rather left the anchor chair after admitting numerous errors in a story he reported about President George W. Bush's service in the National Guard. His admission provided further evidence for critics of the news media to assert that journalists sometimes behave recklessly and often demonstrate a bias against conservatives and republicans holding public office.

- In the late 1990s, the town of Grand Forks, North Dakota was devastated by weeks of rain that produced record flooding. More than 7,000 families were homeless, and hundreds of businesses closed down. Despite its own building and employees being affected by flood, the town's daily newspaper continued to keep its readers informed, distributing papers for free for several weeks. When an individual donated $15 million to help the town rebuild, the newspaper disregarded her request for anonymity, deciding that her identity was newsworthy and that its readers deserved to know who it was. The donor turned out to be Joan Kroc, widow of McDonald's founder Ray Kroc. Much of the goodwill the newspaper had earned with its readers through its coverage of the tragedy was lost with one story. The paper's own poll indicated that 85 percent of respondents thought Kroc's name should not have been published.

- In 2007, the news media were heavily criticized for their reporting on the massacre of 32 students and faculty at Virginia Polytechnic Institute (Virginia Tech). NBC received the majority of the criticism after airing in its entirety a "video manifesto" the killer had mailed to the network before carrying out his crime.

- In 2014 and 2015, some media critics accused both print and broadcast journalists of "over-covering" civil unrest in St. Louis and Baltimore after accusations of excessive force against local police in the killings of black citizens. The critics believed that coverage of the cases and the protests that followed added to the problems and demonstrated the media's lack of understanding of racial issues.

A lack of respect for the journalist profession is nothing new. As far back as the mid-1970s, opinion polls showed that the majority of Americans labeled the press — both individual reporters and media organizations — as arrogant, criticized the media for invading individuals' privacy, and believed that media organizations cover up their mistakes. The chair of the journalism program at a major university recently suggested in a journal article that his friends and colleagues should feel sorry for him because he was teaching an undergraduate course in media ethics at a time when ethics seems to matter less and less in the conduct of professional journalists.

Despite that skeptical view, the number of ethics courses taught in journalism programs has grown exponentially in the last decade, and in most programs, such courses are requirements to complete a journalism degree program. That follows a similar trend found in business schools, where the downturn in public perception of American businesses has prompted business educators to offer more courses in business ethics and make them requirements rather than electives.

Cynicism Is Not Aimed Only at Journalists

While Americans may be more cynical about the institution of journalism, some observers contend that nearly every aspect of society is subject to cynicism. Despite all of the talk about the importance of ethical behavior, ethics in journalism as well as other facets of society continues to be treated much like the weather in the classic Mark Twain quote: "Everyone talks about the weather, but no one does anything about it."

In society in general, some business travelers continue to falsify travel reports, some employees take home office supplies, some politicians make campaign promises they know they will be unable to fulfill, some students plagiarize term papers, some used car dealers turn back odometers, and some welfare recipients lie about their eligibility for government assistance. In the world of professional communications, some journalists resort to borderline or clearly unethical newsgathering tactics to get "the story." Some advertising agencies produce ads that are misleading and sometimes false. Some public relations departments distribute news releases that don't include false information, but intentionally leave out information that would give reporters a more complete understanding of the issues.

Historians and social scientists point to the 1963 assassination of President John F. Kennedy, the government deception surrounding the Vietnam War in the late 1960s, and the Watergate scandal of the early 1970s as factors contributing to a decline in trust and an increase in cynicism regarding the government. In the 1990s, scandals involving American oil companies and other corporate giants caused Americans to become cynical of the business environment as well, as did the Wall Street scandals of the early 2000s.

What is the result of Americans' growing level of dissatisfaction with their government and business institutions? According to William Bennett, a former Secretary of Education and now a social critic and political commentator, the result is the inability of citizens to be shocked or angered by the behavior of government or business. In his 1998 book, *The Death of Outrage*, Bennett claimed that political scandals from Watergate to Iran-Contra (the exchange of weapons for political hostages during the Reagan administration of the 1980s) to President Clinton's affair with a White House intern have created a culture in which people simply accept scandal and misbehavior by public officials as routine.

Although not mentioned in Bennett's book, one could also point to the 2001 incident involving college football coach George O'Leary as evidence of citizen's growing cynicism and acceptance of wrongdoing. O'Leary was a popular and successful coach at Georgia Tech, but left the school for what he described as his "dream job" — head coach at Notre Dame. But after only five days at his new job, O'Leary was asked to resign after Notre Dame officials discovered inaccuracies on his resume concerning his educational background and previous coaching positions. While many Americans responding to polls indicated the O'Leary story simply validated or increased their already negative perception of big-time college athletics, others simply said it was "no big deal" because "everyone lies on their resume."

Another reason for the rise of cynicism in America is the tendency of politicians and celebrities to lie about their personal and professional behavior, even after considerable evidence comes to light to indicate their guilt. "It amazes me that people can do that stuff with a straight face and get away with it," wrote *Miami Herald* columnist Leonard Pitts Jr., in a 2007 column. "I suspect that public figures spew so many lies, alibis, and rationalizations that we become desensitized. When controversy arises, they pretend to apologize or explain, and you and I continue to believe . . . it's a spin doctors' world, and we're just living in it."

In addition to the problem of cynicism, sociologists and other researchers have found that Americans are simply taking issues such as ethics and decision-making less seriously. Examples:

- In the early 1990s, United Way President William Aramony lost his job and later faced criminal charges after internal audits and media reports uncovered years of financial mismanagement. In hindsight, members of the organization's board of directors concluded that the problems stemmed not only from Aramony's dishonesty, but also from their own failure to evaluate his work and scrutinize annual reports and other financial documents.

- One recent survey reported that prospective employers found that more than 80 percent of resumes they received included inaccuracies ranging from "minor exaggerations" to "outright falsehoods." Management journals reporting the results did not condone the falsehoods, but claimed that sorting through the deceptions has become a routine part of the recruiting process.

- A study of student cheating at prestigious universities, including military academies (which administer some of the most severe punishment of any institution) found that more than 75 percent of seniors admitted having committed some form of academic misconduct during their college careers — ranging from cheating on exams to plagiarism on term papers. While the 75 percent figure in itself is alarming, what is even more troubling is that those are *just the ones who admitted it.* In 2007, officials at Duke University announced that 34 students in its prestigious Masters of Business Administration (MBA) program had been caught cheating on an exam.

- In 2014, evidence emerged that the cheating culture in education had trickled down to the K-12 level, but ironically, the cheating was done by teachers and administrators rather than students. In response to "high-stakes" testing programs that not only determined student progress but also salary increases for employees, teachers and administrators in the Atlanta public school system allegedly changed answers and artificially inflated student test results. Similar cases were subsequently found in other school districts around the country.

- A survey of public relations professionals found that more than 35 percent admit to having "exaggerated" when providing information to a boss, client, or journalist; and another 25 percent admit to telling outright falsehoods. While that 60 percent total might cause concern, keep in mind that, like the students in the above-mentioned survey, those are *just the ones who admitted it.*

For a frame of reference, it may be helpful to examine the chart on the following page, which illustrates how communications-related professions compare to other fields. Three of the four professional fields covered in most communication classes are shown in boldface (figures for public relations professionals were not available).

Perception of Honesty and Ethical Standards of Employment Fields

Each year since 1976, the Gallup organization has conducted a survey in which respondents were asked to rate various professions on their honesty and ethical standards.* Some professions are included every year, while others are included on a rotating basis. The far-right column indicates the most recent year that profession was included in the survey. Communication professions are shown in **boldface.**

Profession	very high	high	average	low	very low	year
Accountants	7	36	49	6	1	2011
Advertising professionals	**2**	**8**	**44**	**31**	**11**	**2014**
Auto mechanics	5	24	53	12	4	2013
Bankers	4	19	49	20	66	2014
Building contractors	4	22	58	12	3	2011
Business executives	2	15	50	23	9	2014
Car sales	2	6	46	31	14	2014
Chiropractors	6	32	46	8	3	2012
Clergy	11	35	35	8	5	2014
College instructors	12	41	34	7	3	2012
Day care workers	11	35	43	6	1	2013
Dentists	11	51	33	3	1	2012
Firefighters	40	50	10	-	-	2001
Funeral directors	9	35	43	7	2	2011
Grade school teachers	25	45	23	5	1	2013
High school teachers	13	49	29	6	2	2011
HMO managers	2	10	52	22	5	2012
Insurance sales	2	13	49	28	8	2012
Journalists	**5**	**19**	**45**	**21**	**9**	**2012**
Judges	10	35	37	12	4	2013
Labor union leaders	1	16	37	28	13	2011
Lawyers	5	16	45	22	12	2014
Lobbyists	1	5	31	30	26	2013
Local officeholders	4	19	49	18	8	2013
Members of Congress	1	6	30	37	24	2014

Profession	very high	high	average	low	very low	year
Military service	38	43	17	1	-	2001
Newspaper reporters	3	18	47	20	10	2013
Nurses	25	55	17	1	1	2014
Nursing home operators	8	24	42	17	5	2013
Pharmacists	15	50	28	4	3	2014
Physicians	14	51	29	4	3	2014
Police officers	14	34	31	12	8	2014
Psychiatrists	6	35	43	8	3	2012
Real estate agents	3	17	57	18	4	2011
Senators	2	12	39	33	12	2012
State governors	3	17	48	24	7	2012
State officeholders	2	12	46	24	13	2013
Stockbrokers	2	9	48	30	9	2012
Telemarketers	2	6	38	37	16	2011
Television reporters	**2**	**18**	**47**	**20**	**11**	**2013**
Veterinarians	16	55	23	2	1	2006

*These are the results of telephone surveys conducted each fall with sample sizes of approximately 1,000 individuals aged 18 and older. The margin for error was plus or minus three points. Copyright © 2006-2014 Gallup Inc. Used by permission.

For Discussion

Case Study 1   **James Frey and *A Million Little Pieces***

In 2005, little-known author James Frey pulled off what is believed to be the biggest literary hoax in history. Frey's book, *A Million Little Pieces,* was marketed as a true-life story of how the author fell into a constant cycle of drug and alcohol addiction, recovery, and relapse. The book, published by Random House, was destined for mediocrity until it came to the attention of talk show host Oprah Winfrey, who included it on her "book club" list and featured Frey on her show. Within weeks, more than 3.5 million copies of the book were sold, putting it on the *New York Times'* list of best-sellers. It was heralded by literary critics as an excellent example of autobiography and by addiction counselors who said it was an inspirational work that could help many of their clients.

Much of the book, however, turned out to be exaggerated. Although based loosely on Frey's real struggles with addiction, he also took considerable "literary license" in describing his time in rehabilitation clinics, criminal activities, altercations with police, and encounters with other addicts. The deceptions came to light after a website called The Smoking Gun used public records searches in an attempt to obtain his mug shot and arrest record. When the official record of Frey's criminal past turned out to be far less serious than what was portrayed in the book, TSG posted a lengthy expose titled, "The Man Who Conned Oprah."

Random House defended the book and claimed the deception was overshadowed by the fact that the book had likely helped thousands of other alcoholics and drug addicts change their lives. Frey attempted to defend his work by pointing out that his embellishments accounted for only 18 pages — less than 5 percent of the book. But critics responded that the problem was not one of proportion, but one of intent, as the parts of the book that were embellished were also those that made it so powerful.

At first, Winfrey said the controversy amounted to "much ado about nothing" because there were "hundreds of thousands of lives changed by the book." But later, she said that Frey had betrayed her because he had originally denied the accusations of exaggeration in private conversations and on her show. A guest columnist added in *USA Today* that "the good that Frey might do for addicts with his book is outweighed by the damage he has done to future authors' abilities to convince readers of stories that will change their lives."

- Does Frey's objective of inspiring others to improve their lives justify his deception? Is this a case of the ends justifying the means?

- Did Frey's action to a disservice to other self-help authors, who may now see their work questioned by potential readers?

Discussion Questions

101. Consider the chart on pages 14-15 that describes public perception of various professions. Which of the entries surprise you? Which ones merely confirm your previously held beliefs?

102. This chapter included some alarming statistics about the phenomenon of job applicants lying on resumes and college students cheating. Do those statistics surprise you? What do those trends say about our society and how we look at honesty and ethics?

103. This chapter discusses the growth of media ethics courses in colleges and universities. Some skeptics of such courses believe that college students preparing for careers as professional communicators should already have a sense of right and wrong before entering college, and that such efforts at "ethics education" come too late. Agree or disagree?

Notes

1   **"but I know it when I see it":** from the Supreme Court case, *Jacobellis v. Ohio*, 378 U.S. 184 (1964).

1   **a clear conscience:** This quote is attributed to playwright George Bernard Shaw (occasion unknown).

1   **ethics is what you do:** This quotation is attributed to college basketball coach John Wooden, politician Ross Perot, and an old French proverb.

1   **"knowing the difference":** Kathleen Parker, "Is Technology Killing Our Decency?" Syndicated newspaper column, October 10, 2010.

2   **"Our personal ethics":** Quoted in *Strategic Communications Planning* by Laurie Wilson and Joseph Ogden. Dubuque, IA: Kendall-Hunt. 2010, p. 174.

3   **"wishy-washy journalism":** Ron F. Smith, *Ethics in Journalism*. Malden, MA: Black-well Publishing, p. 9.

4   **"What would Murrow do?":** Mike Wallace and Beth Knobel, *Heat and Light: Advice for the Next Generation of Journalists*. New York: Three Rivers Press, 2010, p. 235.

6   **"Just as shoppers":** Kent R. Middleton and William E. Lee, *The Law of Public Communication*. Boston: Allyn & Bacon, 2004, p. 27.

7   **"free speech of men":** Catharine MacKinnon, *Feminism Unmodified: Discourses on Life and Law*. Cambridge, MA: Harvard University Press, 1988, p. 244.

7   **minorities also lack access:** Jerome Barron, "Access to the Press — A New First Amendment Right." *Harvard Law Review*, Vol. 80 (1967), pp. 1641-1655.

7   **Now journalists are expected":** Robert J. Samuelson, "Long Live the News Business." *Newsweek*, May 28, 2007, p. 40.

7   **"the transition will take longer than expected":** Wallace and Knobel, p. 220.

8   **"hold the state and the powerful accountable":** Ibid.

8   **the number of layoffs in traditional news organizations:** Yolanda Young, "Online News Staffs: Where's the Diversity?" *USA Today*, April 1, 2011, p. 13-A.

8   **traditional daily newspaper and online sources:** Michael Schudson, *The Sociology of News*. New York: W.W. Norton and Company, 2003, p. 175.

9   **"hopeless boondoggle":** Richard Benedetto, "What Readers Don't Understand About Daily Newspapers." Syndicated newspaper column, January 5, 1993.

12   **"spin doctors' world":** Leonard Pitts, "Celebrities and Politicos Take the Truth Out for a Spin." Syndicated newspaper column, May 30, 2007.

16   **"hundreds of thousands of lives":** Laura Vanderkam, "When Truth Masquerades as Fiction." *USA Today*, January 17, 2006, p. 12-A.

16   **"the good that Frey might do":** Ibid.

CHAPTER 2

Philosophical and Critical Perspectives on Communication Ethics

Greek Influences

According to the ancient Greeks, who provided the foundation for most philosophical thought in the western world, ethics was one of the fundamental branches of philosophy. In their way of thinking, there were three such branches: aesthetics was the study of beauty, epistemology was the study of knowledge, and ethics was the study of what was good and virtuous. In all three branches, the goal was to base an argument on logic more than emotion, and on tangible facts and evidence rather than intangibles such as intuition and assumptions. Statements such as "I conclude that . . . " and "the weight of the evidence indicates that . . . " were far more valuable than those such as "I just think that . . ." and "It seems to me that . . . "

The Greeks also believed that curiosity was an important trait in human development and that it was the responsibility of a society's intellectuals to pursue knowledge and seek wisdom and virtue by reflection, inquiry, argumentation, and (eventually) consensus.

The three dominant philosophers in the Greek tradition were Socrates, Plato, and Aristotle. In addition to their study of decision-making, all three taught the principles of **rhetoric**, a term used to describe the art of attempting to influence others through the written and spoken word. Rhetoric is derived from the Greek word *rhetors,* the equivalent of today's politicians.

Socrates and Plato

Socrates (470-399 B.C.) was a Greek philosopher and educator who believed that right and wrong were concepts that could be, and should be, identified and practiced in everyday life. In his public commentary, he exposed ignorance, hypocrisy, and incompetence in governmental matters. He was also known for his fondness for bringing out into the open controversial ideas that individuals would otherwise be reluctant to discuss in public. He believed that society was best served when its citizens put aside their fear of

19

ridicule and were instead willing to openly debate and evaluate controversial issues (more than 2,000 years later, English poet and essayist John Milton would advocate a similar view, and even later, the United States Supreme Court referred to the concept as the "marketplace of ideas").

Plato (427 to 347 B.C.) was a student of Socrates and a teacher and mentor to Aristotle. Many modern-day philosophers believe that Plato may have been the most influential of the Greek philosophers, and perhaps the most influential of all time. One modern philosopher, Alfred North Whitehead, claims that nearly all important material in the field is either the direct work of Plato or the result of someone commenting on his work.

Plato's writings and teachings dealt mainly with political persuasion. He treated the concept of political persuasion as if it consisted of speaking in superficial terms and relying on euphemisms and misleading comparisons — what modern-day critics would call *spin*. More than 2,000 years after his death, Plato's principles are standard part of undergraduate and graduate classes in rhetoric, debate, and argumentation.

In his writings and teachings, Plato encouraged moral conduct even when it might be inconsistent with current social norms. He wrote that one should avoid wrongdoing regardless of the consequences. Even though the expressions did not exist in his time, it is likely that Plato would agree with the principles that "two wrongs do not make a right" and that "the ends do not justify the means." But Plato was far from an absolutist. Instead of suggesting hard-and-fast rules, he preferred that decisions be made based on personal experience and judgment, what American philosopher Joseph Fletcher, 14 centuries later, would call "situational ethics."

Plato criticized other teachers for encouraging their students to look for shortcuts in decision-making. The prevailing attitude of the time was that most political issues were too complex for the average citizen to thoroughly understand, and therefore it was acceptable to persuade an audience toward the desired thought or action through shortcuts such as assumptions, oversimplifications, and stereotypes. Using the example of voting on public matters or jurors deliberating the fate of a defendant in a criminal trial, that way of thinking meant that it was acceptable for decision-makers to arrive at conclusions based on what was *probably true* rather than what was *actually true*. Plato, however, believed audiences should be given more credit than that, and that they were capable of processing complex ideas if the facts were laid out clearly. He also believed that it was important that audience members not only agree with the point of view presented by the speaker, but also thoroughly understand why they agreed with it.

Plato contended that the goal of political communication should be to enhance the well-being of the audience, not to advance the agenda of the person or organization speaking. The essence of many of his writing was that people should always seek, rather than fear, new knowledge. In one essay, he wrote that, "We can easily forgive a child who is afraid of the dark; the real tragedy of life is when men are afraid of the light."

Critics of modern-day political or advertising campaigns say those efforts are aimed clearly at promoting the agendas of the speakers rather than the audience, while idealists such as Plato would likely say that in a perfect world, a communication campaign or other persuasive effort could be aimed at producing benefits for both. Today, leaders of the public relations industry claim just that, contending that "mutually beneficial outcomes" are always the goal of any persuasive campaign.

Plato's teaching method included dialogues, which were fictional conversations in which two or more characters argued various sides of an issue. In many of the dialogues, the protagonist was his mentor, Socrates, and the method became known as Socratic dialogues.

Aristotle and the Golden Mean

Unlike his predecessors Socrates and Plato, **Aristotle** (384 to 322 B.C.) did not believe that everything in the world could be explained in precise and finite terms. In politics and government, for example, there could be no concrete laws or rules, such as those governing the sciences. Aristotle believed that political persuasion was a high calling and should be carried out honestly and ethically.

Aristotle also believed that "you get a good adult by teaching a good child to do the right things." Centuries later, modern child psychologists paraphrase this idea when they claim that children "learn ethics at home, not in school classrooms."

Like his predecessors, Aristotle used the term *rhetoric* to refer to the art of persuasive communication, and it was not until the late twentieth century that the term took on its negative connotation (as in "that's just rhetoric.") But in Aristotle's time, the term was used to refer to fairly presenting a point of view to an audience to achieve a legitimate objective.

He believed that it was seldom possible to convince an audience based on proof that was absolute; therefore, the best a speaker or persuader could do was present the *best possible evidence*. Today, in that spirit, many social scientists avoid using the term *proof* (which implies absoluteness) and instead refer to *supporting evidence* (which implies something short of absoluteness).

Aristotle spoke and wrote of three rules for ethical decision-making. First, the decision-maker must understand the facts and conditions surrounding the decision, rather than taking action based on accident, chance, or assumptions. Second, the decision-maker must be free to choose without being coerced or inappropriately influenced by others. And third, the decision made must be consistent with the character of the person making the decision.

He also believed that mediation was a virtue, and his primary contribution to modern philosophical thought was a principle he called the **Golden Mean**, which referred to making decisions by finding the "just right" mid-point between two extremes, which he claimed would be the ideal place to find virtue and wisdom.

Aristotle did not, however, intend for individuals to determine where the extremes were in a situation and then determine what position would fall at the mathematical center mark. Instead of such an artificial position, Aristotle suggested that a virtuous person would naturally be drawn to the mid-point without considering where the extremes would be found. He further stated that the mid-way point was not a fixed point that would be the same for each individual. Instead, that point could be any one of a number of points that fit the perspectives of individuals while still avoiding the extremes.

Today, professors introducing the Golden Mean to journalism ethics classes use the following example to illustrate its applications to decision-making in newsrooms: A newspaper editor must decide whether or not to publish one or more photographs showing a badly burnt victim being removed from a collapsed building by paramedics. The two extremes would be clear: (1) choose a photograph or photographs that illustrate the drama of the situation, without taking into consideration the privacy of the individual or the feelings of the family, or (2) do not use any of the photographs in any form. A logical middle point between the two extremes (i.e., a compromise) would be to choose a photograph that illustrates the drama of the rescue without showing the victim's face.

European Influences

Many of the great European philosophers share some common characteristics — not all of them positive. All were brilliant thinkers and highly educated, and many of them at an early age spoke and wrote in multiple languages, including Greek and Latin — two of the most difficult languages to learn. Many also earned advanced degrees in philosophy, theology, or mathematics.

But many also had sad and lonely childhoods, either living with abusive parents or spending their early years in orphanages or boarding schools. As a result, despite their brilliance and success in professional careers, they suffered from severe depression or schizophrenia in adulthood. Philosophy scholars also note a degree of hypocrisy in how their scholarly work was inconsistent with how they lived their personal lives. While they wrote, spoke, and taught about virtue and moral living, many were serial adulterers and carried on multiple affairs with married women and in some cases, underage girls. And while many earned degrees in theology when they were quite young, in their later years they declared themselves to be either atheists, agnostics, or otherwise critical or skeptical of organized religion.

Unlike the ancient Greeks, who clearly preferred to make decisions on logic rather than emotion, many Europeans philosophers tended to recommend factoring into decision-making intangible factors such as emotion and intuition. This is evident in the writings of nineteenth century philosophers such as Soren Kierkegaard of Denmark and Immanuel Kant of Germany. Their time period is often referred to as the Romantic Period, with the term being used not to refer to emotional relationships between people, but to describe a way of thinking about the past, making decisions about the present, and dreaming about the future. This tendency continued into the twentieth century, earning a new name — New Age — with notable French philosophers such as Jean-Paul Sartre and Jean Baudrillard writing and teaching about ethics and decision-making from a variety of perspectives. An oversimplified view of European ethicists is that one should always choose courses of actions that maximize benefit and minimize harm. Others refer to this as "seeking pleasure while avoiding pain."

Abelard: Focus on Intent Rather Than Consequences

Peter Abelard (1079-1142) may have been the earliest of the French philosophers to achieve international recognition.

He believed that it was man's nature to constantly question and challenge authority, but one should do so not to serve one's self-interest, but rather to serve and improve society. Centuries later, American writer Henry David Thoreau expressed similar ideas in his work on political philosophy, *Civil Disobedience,* and throughout the American civil rights movement, leaders such as Dr. Martin Luther King Jr., advocated similar behavior.

Abelard's philosophy centered largely on the notion of intention, with little regard for the consequences. A media application of that decision-making philosophy is found in the case of a newspaper editor who must decide how much of a criminal suspect's background should be included in a reporter's accounts of the investigation. An editor following the journalism axiom of "the people have a right to know" might decide to publish details of the suspect's life and facts uncovered in the investigation, without regard to the effect such revelations might have on the family of the defendant or the pool of perspective jurors for a criminal trial.

Aquinas, the Natural Law Doctrine, and "Jocose Lies"

St. Thomas Aquinas (1225-1274) was an Italian monk who earned his master's degree in theology and began a long career of university teaching and service to the Catholic Church.

Aquinas wrote more than 40 volumes about philosophy, and more than seven centuries after his death, his theories are still taught in Catholic schools around the world. He is most famous for his **Natural Law Doctrine**, which states that universal laws of human nature are determined by reason and take priority over artificially created customs and laws created by governments.

Aquinas taught that natural law is derived from divine law, and should therefore serve as the basis for people's moral decision-making.

As a devoutly religious man, Aquinas obviously chose to advocate a Christian view of ethics and advocate intellectual virtue as being more important than material things. Aquinas believed the best source of guidance for moral decisions is a combination of divine guidance and rational argument.

Some of Aquinas' more interesting writings dealt with the issue of deception. His philosophy allowed for **jocose lies** (the Latin term for "joking") and lies that do no harm, what in modern times we would refer to as "white lies." In other words, Aquinas said, there are degrees of falsehood — on one extreme are those that are potentially harmful and based on illegitimate motives of the speaker; and on the other extremes, those minor falsehoods that serve some valid short-term purpose. But in the latter case, Aquinas said, the perpetrator of a falsehood must be prepared to justify the falsehood once it is exposed.

Here's a simple, modern-day example: Suppose a boss, friend, roommate, spouse, romantic partner, or sibling asks for your opinion on a new article of clothing he or she has purchased. If you were to say that you liked it, even though you did not, that's a white lie that Aquinas would likely have no problem with. No harm is done, the other person's feelings are spared, and a potential argument is avoided. A day later, neither you nor the other person is likely to remember the conversation.

But what if you believed that the article of clothing was so ugly that you feared the other person might be ridiculed or embarrassed when wearing it in public? You would then be faced with a choice: telling a lie that spares someone's hurt feelings but subjects him or her to ridicule; or tell the truth, risk the hurt feelings, but spare the person from a fashion faux pas.

A good example of applying Aquinas' philosophy of deception to the newsgathering process is the decision to use deception to uncover wrongdoing on the part of businesses or government agencies. In such cases, followers of Aquinas would claim, a journalist could justify deception because (1) it serves a greater purpose, and (2) the media organization participating in the deception would be prepared to explain it once it is detected.

Machiavelli: Results More Important Than the Process

Niccolo Machiavelli (1469-1527) was an Italian philosopher. In contrast to other philosophers of the day, Machiavelli believed in quick action preceded by a minimum of thought, reflection, or information-gathering. Excessive consultation with others was a form of procrastination, he believed, and it seldom contributed to effective decision-making.

Machiavelli believed that the results of an action are far more important than the action itself, and it was acceptable to break or bend the rules in order to achieve a result that is a greater positive than the negative value assigned to the behavior. Today, that belief is paraphrased by the expression, "the ends justify the means."

Machiavelli also believed that in evaluating the lives of politicians, it was possible to separate a person's professional performance from his personal ethics. In short, he wrote that one could be an ethical person in his or her private life while being a dishonest politician; and conversely, one could be an ethical and honorable public official while living a scandalous personal life.

Machiavelli contended that one should avoid procrastination and indecisiveness and instead take bold and rapid action whenever possible. While other philosophers might suggest that journalists not make a decision concerning newsgathering techniques until considering the issue from all angles and possibly consulting legal counsel or other experts, Machiavelli would likely suggest making the decision quickly and avoiding the unnecessary deliberation that might result in the failure to complete the investigation in a timely manner.

A possible media application of this principle is found in the case of a television news producer who must decide whether to authorize a team of reporters to use hidden cameras while investigating alleged wrongdoing at a local business. If he or she decided to allow the reporters to use that newsgathering technique, he or she is going along with Machiavelli's belief that the results of an activity are more important than the process of conducting that activity.

A similar issue involves checkbook journalism. By Machiavelli's reasoning, a modern-day television network newspaper could vary from its policy of not paying sources for interviews if (1) the positive of attaining the interview outweighed the negative of violating its own ethical policy, and (2) if the payment could be done secretly. Critics of that approach might agree with the first idea while rejecting the second; they might change the two-part test to say that paying a source for an interview might be acceptable in the rare instance that the interview would be valuable enough to justify violation of the policy, but only if the television network or newspaper publicly acknowledged the payment.

Bacon and Rational Decision-Making

Sir Francis Bacon (1561-1626) was an English philosopher and politician who grew up in a wealthy and very religious family. He believed in scientific inquiry and was an advocate and defender of a process of fact-finding known as the **scientific method**. However, his work came at a time when political leaders considered science to be unimportant, and scientists were generally distrusted.

One of Bacon's philosophies on decision-making was that no decision should be made in haste, and that decisions are best made after a careful review of the facts and seeking of input from all interested parties. He also wrote that individuals were constantly subject to internal and external pressures and that it was the responsibility of the individual to keep his or her passions under control and to make decisions in a rational manner.

An example of applying Bacon's philosophies in the journalism business includes the function of newspaper editorial boards, which gather information from interested parties prior to determining the newspaper's editorial policy, and reporters' consultation with social service agencies when developing stories about issues such as hunger, poverty, and homelessness.

Hobbes and the Social Contract

Thomas Hobbes (1588-1679) was born in London and was considered to be one of the great thinkers of his time, but he was also labeled an eccentric.

Hobbes derived his income from serving in a number of positions in service to the king and queen, including financial advisor, political advisor, secretary, and tutor to their children. Such employment provided him the opportunity to travel across Europe, and those travels provided much of the basis for the works of political philosophy he would later write. In short, he believed that one should rise above self-interest in personal and professional decision-making, strive for mutually beneficial outcomes in all decisions, and follow through on commitments made.

Hobbes is best known for his 1651 book, *The Leviathan,* which was published during a period of civil war in England and today is considered a staple in the study of political philosophy. In that book, Hobbes wrote that individuals were selfish by nature, and left to themselves, would naturally act in their own self-interest. As Hobbes believed that individuals could not be trusted to govern themselves, a strong central government was necessary to provide for social harmony and to avoid future wars. In later works, he suggested that loyalty to God did not have to be sole driving principle governing one's life. He claimed that is was natural for individuals to have a number of loyalties — including loyalties to God, to their country, to their family, and to themselves — and that it was not uncommon for these loyalties to be in conflict.

Hobbes believed that the natural state of human beings was one of competition and conflict, and any attempts to bring about total harmony in society would be futile. Humans were destined to be constantly at odds with their environment and with each other. But while absolute harmony was unobtainable, humans were naturally inclined to make some effort at self-government, and in doing so could advance their own interests while improving the lives of others. Hobbes referred to that tendency as **the social contract.**

Hobbes also believed that there should be no universally true or valid standards for moral behavior and that one should rise above self-interest and do things for the greater good of society.

Hobbes' work was so controversial that the Catholic Church and Oxford University attempted to burn his books, and a century later his biographer claimed that if given the chance, they would have burned Hobbes as well.

Applied to journalism, Hobbes' principles that call for individuals to rise above self-interest would require media professionals to make decisions based on the welfare of the individuals affected, the journalism profession, and society as a whole. Other parts of his philosophy might be difficult to apply, however. Hobbes believed that the interests of the government were more important than individual liberties — a philosophy in direct conflict with the First Amendment and many of the other important concepts that govern professional and personal communication.

Milton, Libertarianism, and the Marketplace of Ideas

John Milton (1608-1674) was an English poet and essayist who is famous for his epic poem "Paradise Lost," a 10-volume work about the temptation of Adam and Eve and their expulsion from the Garden of Eden.

One of his first jobs was writing propaganda for the English government, but he would later become a critic of the government and an advocate of free speech — an unusual idea for the time. He published an essay suggesting that English divorce laws should be loosened so he could dissolve an unpleasant marriage. He did so without a publishing license (a legal requirement at the time), however, and he was prosecuted for doing so. He responded with a lengthy work titled *Areopagitica,* in which he argued that licensing of the written word deprives citizens of knowledge and ideas that could improve their lives. He further argued that efforts at limiting the individual's access to information were futile because the most important information would always find its way to the audience. In addition, Milton feared that individuals carrying out the task of censorship would likely be the least qualified to do so because those most qualified would not want such a boring task. And lastly, Milton wrote, there was considerable value in the intellectual exercise of processing large quantities of information and deciding what was valuable and what was not.

John Milton was the first true libertarian, but the term was not used in the same way as it is today. In Milton's time, the term **libertarianism** had a narrower meaning and it referred mainly to a philosophy regarding free speech. Rather than attempting to censor an individual's controversial writings, Milton and other libertarians of the time argued, a better philosophy was to allow the greatest possible access to the greatest diversity of ideas. They believed that everyone should be free to openly discuss controversial social and political issues, even if it meant challenging the views of authority figures or anyone else. In the battle between truth and falsity, Milton believed, truth would always win if the audience carefully evaluated the competing ideas. Three centuries later, the U.S. Supreme Court paraphrased the idea when it coined the term, "marketplace of ideas."

Milton and other libertarians of the day believed that individuals should have absolute rights of free expression, and that it was the responsibility of the populace to determine what was true and what was false, and what was important and what was trivial. That belief ran counter to the prevailing authoritarian philosophy of the time, which held that only the English monarchy and other government officials were qualified to determine the value of ideas and who would be allowed to express them.

In the early 1800s, the libertarian philosophy of free expression was advocated by Thomas Jefferson, the third president of the United States, who believed that education and journalism went hand-in-hand. Journalism was necessary to inform people about important issues, Jefferson believed, but in order to read the newspaper and make sense of the information they process, individuals needed a broad, liberal arts education. Toward that end, Jefferson spent much of his later years advocating the inter-related topics of education, literacy, and free speech and press.

Today, the "marketplace of ideas" principle first espoused by Milton and John Stuart Mill is often cited by critics of mergers among media companies. Such mergers, the critics contend, is inconsistent with the spirit of the marketplace principle because it limits the number of voices that can reach prospective audiences.

In contrast, many social commentators contend that libertarianism is alive and well on the Internet, as bloggers and other non-traditional journalists are free to express whatever outrageous opinions and falsehoods they choose, but are not responsible for how the information is processed or interpreted.

How would Milton feel about today's methods of political discourse, such as Internet discussion groups, blogs, and various forms of social media? It's likely he would go along with the Supreme Court's "marketplace of ideas" principle, saying that while much of the information one finds in such venues is inaccurate (and often distasteful and objectionable), it would be inappropriate to prohibit it or legally punish the individuals who post it. Instead, Milton might say, it is more appropriate to offer competing information and let the audience make decisions as to its accuracy and value.

Rousseau and Compassionate Decision-Making

Jean-Jacques Rousseau (1712-1778) was a French philosopher who wrote and taught that society is analogous to a living being, and even the smallest part (such as an individual) is essential to the well-being of the larger organism. Individuals are equally important to the social good as they try to make social contacts and work for the most benefit to society as possible, with values assigned to the interests of the poor and less powerful being equal to the interests of the rich and powerful. Rousseau believed that individuals should use conscience and compassion to make ethical decisions that promote harmony among all concerned.

Thousands of years earlier, the same concept was found in the African word *ubuntu*. The word is found in the Zulu, Xhosa, and other African languages and translates approximately as "humanity toward others." Another term associated with the idea of compassion is *communitarianism*, which refers to the interdependence of all constituent groups within a culture (i.e, "we're all in this together").

Applied to the world of journalism, Rousseau's philosophy would require that newspaper editors and television news directors to make the extra effort to protect the privacy and dignity of individuals in the news, without sacrificing their news judgments.

Blackstone and the Blackstonian Doctrine

William Blackstone (1723-1780) was an English legal scholar who wrote a number of important works that helped shaped the English legal system as well as that of the United States. He is best known for being an advocate of free speech while warning that those taking advantage of the privilege were also required to accept the consequences of such speech. Blackstone believed that expression should never be suppressed (such as in the case of government censorship), but that the government has the right to punish the source of harmful speech after it takes place under the appropriate laws such as those involving copyrights, libel, or obscenity. Writing in 1769, Blackstone stated that, "The liberty of the press is indeed essential to the nature of a free state; but this consists in laying no previous restraints upon publication, and not in freedom from censure for criminal matter when published. Every free man has an undoubted right to lay what sentiments he pleases before the public; to forbid this is to destroy the freedom of the press, but if he published what is improper, mischievous, or illegal, he must take the consequences of his own temerity." Today, the principle of not allowing for government censorship, but allowing instead for punishment after the fact, is known as the **Blackstonian Doctrine.**

Kant and the Categorical Imperative

Immanuel Kant (1724-1804) was a German philosopher and one of the great thinkers of the eighteenth century. Unlike his contemporaries, who moved from one university to another, Kant spent his entire career at the University of Konigsberg, one of the great liberal arts institutions of the time period.

Kant wrote and taught that individuals and organizations should make decisions based on moral duty rather than self-interest. The focus of decision-making is on the behavior or action itself, with little or no attention paid to the result. Instead of a philosophy of "the ends justifying the means," Kant would suggest focusing entirely on the means and paying no attention to the ends. One modern-day ethicist who paraphrases the "ends do not justify the means" concept is Bruce Weinstein, author of a weekly newspaper column on ethics in the workplace. Weinstein is fond of quoting one of his graduate school professors, who told his classes that "evil must not be done so that good may come of it."

Kant is best known for a rule known he called the **Categorical Imperative**, which states that once created, a society's rules and laws must be followed to the letter and are not subject to interpretation or exception. Put simply, the Categorical Imperative is based on Kant's belief that the process of making a decision was more important than the results. If one uses the correct procedure or process in making a decision (i.e. following established rules or guidelines), what happens as a result of that decision is not important.

He further stated that unlike other philosophical concepts of the time period, the categorical imperative had no connection to God, as right and wrong should not be limited to religious connotations.

Loosely interpreted, the Categorical Imperative has been interpreted with expressions such as "rules are rules" and "rules are set in concrete." Under the Categorical Imperative, rules cannot be set aside or bent, even when some short-term benefit may result. According to Kant, the long-term benefit of following the rules outweighs any short-term benefit that may result from breaking or bending them. Other interpretations of the Categorical Imperative include rules such as "always tell the truth and always keep promises" and "do your duty whether you want to or not."

In modern times, the Categorical Imperative has been used by liberals in arguing against capital punishment, based on their belief that killing a human being is wrong, regardless of the crime of which the person has been convicted; and by conservatives arguing against abortion, based on their belief that life begins at conception and therefore abortion is the equivalent of murder.

Today, an example of the Categorical Imperative in action is found in the issue of mandatory prison sentences being imposed for certain crimes, as opposed to allowing judges to determine sentences based on several factors, including the age and previous behavior of the guilty party, severity of the crime, and other factors. Another example: A neighbor who hides an abused wife from her husband might believe he or she was acting out of a sense of duty (to protect the wife), but a more strict interpretation of the Categorical Imperative would indicate the individual's first duty was to tell the truth, even if it jeopardized the woman's safety.

Another aspect of the Categorical Imperative is that one should not make any decision or take any action in one case unless he or she were prepared to make a similar decision or take a similar action in all other similar cases — either that day or at any point in the future. Today, many people in a position of authority decline to help others based on their contention that "if I do it for one person, I will have to do it for everyone else."

An example of applying the Categorical Imperative in journalism is the decision to identify rape victims by name in published or broadcast news stories. While most media organizations have a policy of not identifying victims, the few that do claim that part of their rationale was the need for consistency — because they identify the victims of other types of crimes, they believe they are obligated to also identify rape victims.

Bentham, Mill, and Utilitarianism

In the early 1800s, Europe was seeing the beginnings of the industrial age, and many countries saw their populations migrate from rural areas to growing cities to work for low wages at low-skill factory jobs. Poverty, labor abuses, and unsafe working conditions were common. Exploitation of workers and the widening gap between social classes prompted the intellectuals of the day to muse about economic disparity in their writings and teachings.

Against this backdrop, philosophers **Jeremy Bentham** (1748-1832) and **John Stuart Mill** (1806-1873) worked as reformers — social activists who wanted to improve the condition of British citizens and workers, many of whom lived and worked in appalling economic conditions, similar to those portrayed in the novels of Charles Dickens. Bentham was a friend of James Mill, father of John Stuart Mill, and Bentham became the younger Mill's teacher and mentor.

Bentham and Mill developed the concept of **utilitarianism**, which has been loosely translated as "the greatest good for the greatest number of people."

According to utilitarianism, the consequences of actions are the most important factor in deciding whether those actions are ethical, and the more people who benefit from a decision, the more likely it is to be the appropriate choice. Utilitarianism is one of several philosophies based on the assumption that one's ethical behavior should be based on the outcome of the behavior rather than the person's intent (i.e., the ends justify the means). Under utilitarianism, one's actions are always judged by the results, and ends often justify the means because the utility of the ends outweighs the disutility of the means.

Bentham's definition of utilitarianism provided that "an action is right from an ethical point of view if and only if the sum total of utilities (results) produced by that act is greater than the sum total of utilities produced by another other act the agent (decision-maker) could have performed in its place." In short, utilitarianism suggests that faced with the choice of two or more courses of action, one should choose the action that creates the greatest benefit (or lowest costs) for the greatest number of people.

Outliving his mentor by more than 40 years, Mill refined the principle of utilitarianism to put more emphasis on long-term results than on the short-term results. For example, a person might receive greater pleasure in spending an evening eating a fine meal than in reading great literature, but the literature will be of a higher quality and the benefit will be more for the long-term.

In his 1859 essay *On Liberty,* Mill wrote that he supported free expression because he believed people should always be open to new ideas instead of being inclined to reject them without a fair hearing. He added that people need to be exposed to false ideas in order to value those that are true. Mill was not as optimistic as Milton concerning the ability of truth to win out over falsity, pointing out that history was littered with "instances of truth put down by persecution," such as the tendency of European governments to imprison scientists who espoused ideas that were inconsistent with religious doctrine. But he also believed that the only way truth could win in its battle against falsity was through true freedom of speech and press — ideas that would later be reflected in the constitutions of the United States and several other countries.

Mill believed that people should be allowed to engage in whatever behavior gave them pleasure as long as it did not harm others. Mill was one of the few male authors of his time to advocate equal rights for women — a radical idea for the nineteenth century. He believed that the oppression of women was a holdover from ancient times and impeded the overall progress of society. In addition to writing a book on the subject, *The Subjection of Women* (1869), Mill authored numerous newspaper articles and speeches on the issue. He was a controversial figure not only for that idea, but also for his suggestion that better-educated individuals should get more votes in elections; whereas at the time the prevailing philosophy was to distribute voting rights based on ownership of property.

A modern-day example of utilitarianism in journalism is found in decisions regarding investigative reporting. While a few people may be hurt by the publication or broadcast of a news story, in most cases it is the proper thing to do because far more people will benefit from the story than will be harmed by it.

Kierkegaard, Multiple Motives, and Avoiding Procrastination

Soren Kierkegaard (1813-1855) was a Danish philosopher who became one of the most famous intellectual figures of his time. The majority of his work dealt with the benefit of living a virtuous life and the importance of thoughtful decision-making.

Because of the difficulty of translating Danish into other languages, few scholars were interested in the assignment, and as a result his writings remained out of reach for audiences outside his home country for decades after his death.

Kierkegaard believed that most problems facing society or individuals might be addressed in different but equally effective ways. Using the example of man's desire to help the poor, Kierkegaard wrote that while two men might have honorable intentions in wanting to help the poor, they may choose to do so in different ways, with neither method necessarily better than the other.

Kierkegaard also believed that the most effective way to make decisions is to consider all the possible options or choices, then consider the motives connected to each. While motives should not the sole basis for choosing one option over another and the decision-maker should not feel compelled to always choose the course of action associated with the most honorable motive, he believed that motives should be given considerable weight in the decision-making process. Unlike Francis Bacon and other philosophers who spoke and wrote about the value of seeking consensus in decision-making, Kierkegaard believed in making decisions quickly and independently. Much like Machiavelli, Kierkegaard believed that excessive consultation and assigning too much value to the opinions of others was a form of procrastination and simply a way to avoid taking responsibility for one's own decisions.

Durkheim and Cultural Relativism

Emile Durkheim (1858-1917) was a French sociologist. What may have been his most important work was unpublished, and the world lost an opportunity to gain access to it posthumously when his unpublished manuscripts and papers were left behind when his daughter fled France during the Nazi occupation at the beginning of World War II.

But work published before his death provided some interesting ethical principles for discussion. One of those principles which he wrote about and taught was that of collective rule-making. According to Durkheim, any proposed solution to a problem should be rejected if the benefit to society would be absent or difficult to measure, while proposed solutions that offered clear and tangible benefits should be quickly adopted.

Durkheim was an advocate of relativism — a philosophical concept that says that many ideas cannot be identified as universally right or wrong, as what is right for one person may be wrong for another, and vice-versa. Relativism is often described in terms of clichés such as "one man's meat is another man's poison," "what is pornography to some is art to others," and "one man's vulgarity is another man's lyric." The later cliché is attributed to Supreme Court Justice John Harlan, who included that comment in writing the majority opinion in a case in which a man protesting the Vietnam War walked through a public building with a profane word on the back of his jacket and was charged with public indecency.

While often applied to differences of opinion between individuals, relativism was originally applied to differences between cultures. Using the term **cultural relativism,** anthropologists and other social scientists studying differences between cultures often refrain from saying that one culture's way of personal or professional decision-making is better than another. One example is found in the working relationships between the public relations representatives and journalists. American public relations professionals representing their companies in foreign countries are often aghast to find the bribing of journalists is commonplace in those cultures, while in this country, both the public relations and journalism professions would find such conduct unethical. While communication researchers might also label it as such, anthropologists and other social scientists, applying the concept of relativism, would avoid using labels such as "right and wrong," preferring instead to refer to them as "different."

Sartre and Individual Responsibility

Jean-Paul Sartre (1905-1980) was a French philosopher and one of the great thinkers of the twentieth century. His mother was the cousin of humanitarian Albert Schweitzer.

While teaching at several French universities in the 1950s, Sartre became involved in many of the political controversies of the time. His political positions earned him labels such as "liberal" and "radical," and while he publicly sympathized with the Communist Party, he never joined. Later in his life, he was one of a number of European intellectuals who gathered in Paris cafes to eat extravagant food, drink wine, and discuss the events of the day. Sartre was awarded the Nobel Prize for Literature in 1964, but declined it in order to protest the values of the wealth and privilege society that was common in France at the time. Late in life, Sartre because active in international humanitarian causes and chaired the International War Crimes Tribunal that investigated charges of American military misconduct during the Vietnam War.

The principle underlying much of Sartre's written work was that of individual responsibility. Instead of uniform rules to determine right and wrong, Sartre believed that nearly any decision made or action taken by an individual was acceptable as long as he or she was prepared to accept the consequences for it. There were only a few concrete limits to human behavior, among those being the prohibition against intentionally harming another person or squandering one's personal wealth while not taking the opportunity to use one's resources to help others. Sartre believed that almost all of an individual's ideas and decisions are the products of his or her real-world experiences.

In one of his brief written works, titled "The Case of the Lying Husband," Sartre offered a common ethical dilemma. A man learns that his wife is dying of cancer and has only a year to live, yet the wife is not aware of the diagnosis. Even though the couple made a promise to always be honest with each other, he considers the possibility that not telling her might be the best course of action. On one hand, he could tell her, which would fulfill his promise to always be honest and provide her the opportunity to live the last year of her life to the fullest. But on the other hand, by not telling her, he spares her the pain of the prognosis and serves his own self-interest by sparing himself the difficult task of delivering the bad news. Like most other parables of this nature, Sartre never took a position on which course of action he believed the husband should take. As a result, the "lying husband" scenario has been a standard discussion-starter in philosophy and ethics classes for decades.

The applicability of Sartre's ideas to ethical issues in journalism, broadcasting, advertising, and public relations is obvious. Journalists and broadcasters, for example, often struggle with issues that are not addressed in the ethical codes of the organizations to which they belong; therefore they may feel justified in basing their decisions solely on their willingness to defend them if criticized.

Professional communicators are also faced with dilemmas such as whether or not to release information to groups at risk. Should a government agency or television network warn the public about the possibility of contaminated food being on the grocery store shelves and in their refrigerators, thus providing the opportunity to avoid such dangers? Or keep the information secret until a more definite determination can be made, thus avoiding public panic?

Baudrillard and Hyper-reality

Jean Baudrillard (1929-2007) was born in France and was the first member of his family to earn a university education. After receiving his degree, he taught at the University of Paris, became a Marxist, and supported rioting students who attempted to overthrow the French government and President Charles de Gaulle. He was a frequent visitor to the United States, where he became both fascinated and repulsed by American culture. His criticism of American entertainment and mass media was based on a theory he called **hyper-reality**. In short, the theory stated that people were more interested in spectacle than substance and were so absorbed in popular culture that they are incapable of seeing it for what it is — a distraction from what was important.

Although he published more than 50 books, Baudrillard was best known for *Simulacra and Simulation*, published in 1981, and *America*, published in 1986. In *Simulacra and Simulation*, he explained his theory of hyperreality, which claimed that individuals were so absorbed in technology, entertainment, and retail consumption that they no longer enjoyed the simple things in life, and in some cases, could no longer distinguish between the real world and the artificial world that corporations and the mass media had created for them. In *America*, Baudrillard identified American culture as the primary example of a society that had fallen victim to hyperreality and called the U.S. the "only remaining primitive society" in the world.

Baudrillard believed that the media — especially those found in America — had the potential to be both intrusive and manipulative. He also claimed that modern technology had "turned society into a video game" and that most Americans could no longer distinguish what was real and what was not. In 1991, for example, Baudrillard published a book titled *The Gulf War Did Not Happen*. In it, he claimed that the first Gulf War (1990-91) did not actually take place, but was instead a fictional event created entirely by the federal government in cooperation with the television networks. That premise was illustrated in the 1997 movie, *Wag the Dog,* in which the U.S. government hired a Hollywood film director to create a fictional war to district the population from a political sex scandal.

His hyper-reality theory was spoofed in a scene in the 1999 film *The Matrix*, which told the story of a futuristic world in which most people had lost the ability to distinguish reality from hallucinations. In the scene, the main character opens a copy of *Simulacra and Simulation* to reveal a collection of pirated computer disks. Baudrillard claimed the film misinterpreted his theories, but it nonetheless motivated moviegoers to learn more about him and his work.

While supposedly repulsed by popular culture, Baudrillard was also absorbed in it. He reportedly subscribed to hundreds of American newspapers and magazines and in his home had more than 50 televisions simultaneously tuned to different cable channels.

Baudrillard died on March 6, 2007, after a long battle with cancer. Upon hearing of his death, his followers paid tribute to him by posting messages on the Internet that "Jean Baudrillard's death did not actually take place."

American Influences

One of the simplest guidelines for decision-making in American society does not come from the code of ethics of a professional organization, but rather a fraternal one. In 1932, Rotarian Herbert J. Taylor was the owner of an aluminum supplier in Chicago on the edge of bankruptcy. Concerned over the potential for misconduct on the part of well-meaning employees attempting to save the company from financial ruin, he issued a list of four simple rules to guide their decision-making. Those four rules have since been incorporated into the Rotary Club's formal operating policy. Instead of do's and don'ts, the rules take the form of questions:

1. Is it the *Truth*?
2. Is it *Fair* to all concerned?
3. Will in build *Goodwill* and better *Friendships*?
4. Will it be *Beneficial* to all concerned?

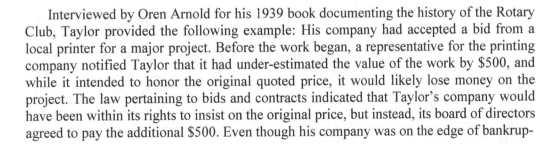

Interviewed by Oren Arnold for his 1939 book documenting the history of the Rotary Club, Taylor provided the following example: His company had accepted a bid from a local printer for a major project. Before the work began, a representative for the printing company notified Taylor that it had under-estimated the value of the work by $500, and while it intended to honor the original quoted price, it would likely lose money on the project. The law pertaining to bids and contracts indicated that Taylor's company would have been within its rights to insist on the original price, but instead, its board of directors agreed to pay the additional $500. Even though his company was on the edge of bankruptcy and was looking to save money wherever it could, Taylor believed that questions 2 and 3 mandated the extra cost; the decision would be fair to both companies and would result in goodwill and better friendships. Although the cause-and-effect relationship could not be proven, Taylor believes that making decisions such as that was at least partially responsible for his company eventually surviving its financial challenges.

After noticing the brevity of this section compared to the two that preceded it, the reader might infer that Americans have not contributed as much to the field of communication ethics as their counterparts in Greece and Europe. But that is far from the case. However, it is fair to say that Americans simply have not been doing it as long.

Dewey and Pragmatism

John Dewey (1859-1952) was an American philosopher who expanded Emile Durkheim's notion of relativism and applied it to his work in the field of education.

He is best known for a concept he called **pragmatism**, which called for every profession or government agency to stay within its traditional or assigned role: police investigate crime, teachers teach children, and the military protects the country. One example was his admonition to school administrators that it was not appropriate for schools to attempt to teach values, as those were better learned in the home. While Dewey was advocating such ideas in the United States, his counterpart in England, Bertrand Russell (1872-1970), was making similar claims in that country.

Applying the concept to the field of journalism, one could contend that it is not appropriate for the media to advocate for or against public issues, but instead concentrate on reporting on those issues in a neutral fashion. America's newspaper publishers, however, counter with their belief that a competent newspaper can "walk and chew gum at the same time" — having reporters cover the news without taking sides while also employing editorial writers whose job it is to advocate only one side of an issue. Nevertheless, Dewey would likely express concern over public journalism (discussed in more detail in Chapter 3), a trend in which media organizations step outside of their traditional roles in order to take the lead in the development of their communities.

Rand and Objectivism

Ayn Rand (1905-1982) was born Alissa Zinovievna Rosenbaum in St. Petersburg, Russia. Raised in the economic depression of pre-revolutionary Russia, she became enthralled by literature that described life in other countries and, while still a child, she decided to become a writer. She changed her name to Ayn Rand (the first name rhymes with "dine") in order to honor a Finnish writer she admired.

Throughout her adult life, Rand identified herself as an American, even though it is not known if she ever sought formal citizenship. She considered herself a novelist rather than a philosopher, but her work is studied in philosophy classes around the world, and graduate students have written masters' theses and doctoral dissertations dealing with the philosophical implications of her work. Her novels are treated by social critics, economists, and political scientists as treatises on the role of government in society. Her first work, *The Fountainhead*, was published in 1943, and her most famous, *Atlas Shrugged*, followed in 1957. Late in her life, Rand was a visiting lecturer at a number of universities in the Northeast and Midwest.

Her novels espoused her belief in the virtues of capitalism and the preeminence of the individual, a philosophy she later called **objectivism.** At the core of objectivism was the notion of self-interest, which allowed individuals to disregard service to or concern for others and make decisions that benefited their own interests without regard to the impact on society. According to Rand, humans were predisposed to make decisions based on what was best for them, and they should not feel guilty or be criticized for doing so. "The pursuit of his own rational self-interest and of his own happiness is the highest moral purpose of his life," she wrote in "Introducing Objectivism," one of her few works of non-fiction.

Some modern-day political philosophers believe that Rand's work is misunderstood and has been treated unfairly. At the core of her objectivism philosophy was not that individuals should *always* make decisions based on self-interest, but only that is was *acceptable* to do so.

Many of Rand's novels were parables running 700 pages or more. While presented as works of fiction, they were based in part on her childhood experiences in Russia and dealt with themes such as political oppression and economic depression. But upon deeper examination, readers could see the dominant themes in Rand's works were individualism and self-reliance — the ability of individuals to rise above their circumstances and improve their lives.

Economist Milton Friedman cites Rand's work in his writings about economic trends, and Alan Greenspan, former chairman of the Federal Reserve Board, often referred to her work in announcing his policy decisions.

While few media organizations would overtly cite Rand's philosophy of self-interest in justifying their need to make a profit, defenders of the business side of journalism claim they can simultaneously serve the public interest by reporting the news and serving as government watchdogs and their own interests by generating profits for their owners and shareholders.

Meiklejohn and Absolutism

Alexander Meiklejohn (1872-1964) was born in England, but he was educated in two Ivy League schools (Brown and Cornell) and spent much of his adult life in the United States. He taught philosophy and social studies at Brown, then went into university administration, serving as president at Amherst and the University of Wisconsin. He also held numerous leadership positions in the American Civil Liberties Union.

When speaking or writing about free speech, Meiklejohn identified himself as an **absolutist,** meaning that there should be absolutely no limitations of personal expression. Those views were in line with Kant's categorical imperative, and he often took positions that would inflame co-workers, superiors, and subordinates.

Meiklejohn said that the purpose of the First Amendment was to aid citizens in understanding the "issues which bear upon our common life" and that "no idea, no opinion, no doubt, no belief, no counterbelief, no relevant information" should be withheld from the people, and in order to be appropriately knowledgeable, there must be no constraints on the free flow of information and ideas.

Fletcher and Situational Ethics

Joseph Fletcher (1905-1991) was an American professor, sociologist, and bioethicist who was best-known for coining the term **situational ethics** to refer to the concept of making decisions based on the merits of individual cases and not according to rigid or inflexible sets of rules. That idea was the opposite of Immanuel Kant's Categorical Imperative. Instead of following an inflexible set of rules, as Kant would have advocated, Fletcher recommended flexibility in the application of rules based on the merits of specific cases. In other words, while Kant believed that following the correct process in decision-making was more important than the results, Fletcher believed that results were more important than the process.

His view of ethics and decision-making was grounded in his Christian beliefs, one of which was the premise that important decisions should always be made based on the merits of the situation at hand, and not on some inflexible set of rules or standards. In 1966, he published these ideas in his controversial book, *Situation Ethics: The New Morality.*

Many readers may consider this as another way of saying that the "ends justify the means," but that might be a bit too extreme, as Fletcher would not agree with the principle that *any* behavior is acceptable if it produces a good result. Instead, Fletcher is simply claiming that instead of following rigid sets of rules (the means), a decision-maker should be flexible and consider both the ends and the means.

Nearly all of the professional codes, such as those of the Society of Professional Journalists, National Association of Broadcasters, Public Relations Society of America, and American Advertising Federation, are based on situational ethics. While purists in those professions may claim to base their decisions on Kant's Categorical Imperative (rules are rules; they're carved in stone), a more practical view is that the ethical codes can only provide a framework; decisions made in the real world must always be based on the merits of specific cases.

The logic of such a philosophy is obvious, but its critics say that a set of rules that is subject to an excess of exceptions means there are no rules at all. Philosophy professor Bert Bradley criticizes situational ethics because it offers the opportunity to justify more than one correct response to an ethical question and that some decision-makers might use that approach to justify choices that are in their self-interest rather than the interests of others.

An example of situational ethics applied in law enforcement involves the use of deception to lure criminal suspects to a place at which they could be easily apprehended. In such a case, the importance of apprehending the criminals outweighs any concern over the original deception — an extension of the idea of the ends justifying the means.

Similarly, many controversial forms of newsgathering such as misrepresentation or hidden cameras and microphones could easily be justified by claiming that the ends (of uncovering illegal or ethical business practices) made it acceptable to use those means (of newsgathering).

Rawls and the Veil of Ignorance

John Rawls (1921-2002), a Harvard University professor and author of dozens of books on ethics, decision-making, and political philosophy, is one of the few American philosophers to achieve international recognition. He is best known for his 1971 book, *A Theory of Justice.* He is widely regarded one of the most important English-language political philosophers of the twentieth century, and in some circles is considered the American equivalent of John Stuart Mill.

Rawls is best known for his theory of decision-making he called the **veil of ignorance**. In short, he contended that a person faced with making a difficult decision should do so without considering his own interests in the outcome or the identity of the persons affected. Some decision-makers believe it is easier to make difficult decisions if the people affected by those decisions "don't have names or faces."

In the original version of the veil of ignorance, the decision-maker is temporarily stripped of identity and forced to make his or decision without knowing whether his race, gender, financial status, education level, or any other demographic or psychographic factors that might create a bias. The decision-maker is encouraged to make the decision solely on general facts about human psychology, economics, history, and other factors. Once the veil is lifted, the decision-maker is expected to stick to whatever decision he or she made before.

In a recent television political drama, a government official applied the veil of ignorance concept when he instructed a group of subordinates that were discussing tax policy. "Suppose that on the day you were born you had no idea what your income level would be later in life," he told the staffers. "Now, design a tax plan."

Professors teaching classes in sociology and criminal justice often use the veil of ignorance as part of a two-part exercise. In the first part of the exercise, students debate the appropriate punishment for a hypothetical defendant in a criminal trial without knowing who he or she is. In the second part of the exercise, which takes place after the class makes its decision, students draw from an envelope slips of paper that assign them roles such as "judge," "defendant," "spouse of defendant," "victim," "family member of victim," "prosecutor," and "defense attorney." Students then discuss the decision from the perspective of the newly assigned roles.

In revised versions of the veil or ignorance concept, the veil is applied not to the decision-maker, but to those affected by the decisions. One example involves the responsibility of individuals serving on a jury. In deciding the fate of the defendant, the jury is required to consider only the facts of the case, not what effect the verdict may have on members of the defendant's family.

Professors grading essay exams or term papers sometimes use a variation of the veil of ignorance based on a self-imposed honor system. They require students to include only student identification numbers on their written work in order to allow the professor to grade the paper without knowing which student wrote it, supposedly to avoid reading the work while picturing the student's face or with preconceptions in their mind such as "good student" or "poor student." The professor does not match student identification numbers to names until after a grade is assigned.

The veil of ignorance concept also requires authority figures to make decisions based on the merits of the respective arguments involved, rather than the personalities of the individuals involved. In the 2010-11 Supreme Court session, for example, the justices reviewed a conflict between the family of a U.S. marine who died in Iraq and a group of protestors who chose the man's funeral as the site of a protest against U.S. military policy. The majority of Americans listening to the two parties being interviewed by the media identified the family as more deserving of sympathy and the protestors less deserving (or not deserving at all), but legal scholars predicted the justices on the Court would put aside the emotional nature of the conflict and make their rulings based solely on the merits of the arguments and not on the personalities involved.

A more simplistic example of the veil of ignorance is the often-told parable about the mother who taught her two small children a lesson in fairness by serving them a piece of cake that was large enough for both of them. Instead of cutting the cake and having the children argue about who got which piece, she simply told them that one would be allowed to cut the cake, but the other would choose his piece first.

When applied to journalism decisions, the veil of ignorance is more practical when the veil is not used to conceal the identity of the decision-maker, but instead, the identity of those individuals or groups affected by those decisions. One example involves the decision over how far a news story should go in revealing potentially embarrassing details regarding the life of a crime victim or suspect. A reporter or editor applying the veil of ignorance would reach the decision without regard to the identity of the person; that is, giving no consideration to how the decision might be different if the person in question was his or her spouse, child, parent, or friend. A few years ago, a newspaper publisher addressing the privacy issue while speaking to a college journalists said that he instructs his reporters and editors to "remember that everyone we write about in the newspaper has a mother" — an attitude clearly inconsistent with the veil of ignorance.

Bok and the Principle of Veracity

Sissela Bok (1934-) is a Swedish-born philosopher who has spent much of her adult life in the United States. She earned her doctorate at Harvard and subsequently taught at a number of American universities, including Radcliffe and Brandeis. In 1992 her career brought her full-circle as she became a senior visiting fellow at Harvard.

Bok's entire career has focused on various forms of deception in human communication — from the "white lies" individuals tell each other to the more harmful types of deception found in corporate advertising and public relations campaigns and information released by government agencies and officials. Her 1978 book, *Lying: Moral Choice in Public and Private Life*, is considered the starting point for any serious study of deception.

Bok explains her philosophy about deception with a concept she calls the **principle of veracity**. The principle refers to telling falsehoods only under the following conditions: (1) it is done as a last resort after all other alternatives have been considered, and (2) the person speaking is prepared to justify the need for the deception once it is exposed Bok's principle places the burden of justifying the lie solely on the liar — it is up to him or her to justify the reason for the lie, as opposed to the potential victim of a lie having to explain why it is harmful. In addition, Bok's principle requires that any time a practical and truthful alternative action is available to the potential liar, the more truthful alternative must be given priority.

In illustrating the virtue of the occasional lie, Bok cites the hypothetical example of a ship captain responsible for safely transporting refugees from Nazi Germany. When the ship is boarded by Nazis, the captain is asked if there are any Jews on board. While Immanuel Kant would likely suggest that because lying was unacceptable in all forms (based on the Categorical Imperative), Bok would suggest that lying in this case serves a higher good. While a ship captain following Kant's rule would tell the truth about the Jews on board, in effect sacrificing their lives, Bok would see a higher purpose in telling a lie. Bok clarifies that lies are still lies, and such exceptions should be rare and told only when the higher result (in this case, saving the lives of the passengers) could not be achieved without telling the falsehood.

Bok rejects the ends-justify-the-means justification for lying and believes that liars tend to *underestimate* the potential harm of their lies and *overestimate* the possible benefits. In the workplace, for example, a father may call in sick at work in order to attend a child's softball game under the assumption that his employer may not approve of a request for time off based on its true purpose. What he may not realize is that because of the value the company places on family, the employer may have approved the time off under the condition that the man compensate by working late the next day. Likewise, if the employer had learned later that the calling-in-sick claim was false, the man would have been subject to disciplinary action for not simply making a truthful request instead.

Contemporary philosopher Charles Fried has expanded on Bok's work, arguing that lying is never acceptable because it demonstrates a lack of respect for others by assuming they are incapable of reaching the desired decision based on the truth. Carl Wellman, professor of philosophy at Washington University in St. Louis, generally agrees, but adds one exception — that lying is acceptable in cases in which it is necessary to save human life or to spare hurt feelings over unimportant matters.

Bella DePaulo, professor of psychology at the University of California at Santa Barbara, takes a more flexible approach, contending that lying is almost a necessity for survival in a polite society. "Imagine how it would be if you couldn't tell little white lies such as telling someone on the phone that you're too busy to talk to them," DePaulo said in a 2004 television interview. "Or that you don't want to go to someone's party because it's always so boring."

Lippmann and the Imperfect System

Walter Lippmann (1889-1974) spent much of his career as a working journalist and was co-founder and editor of *The New Republic*. He did not become famous, however, until becoming a university professor and lecturer in his later years.

He did his most important work in the early 1900s, as American businesses began to embrace the persuasion business on a large scale, and the advertising and public relations industries began to apply new and sometimes manipulative persuasive techniques while simultaneously mastering new communications technologies capable of spreading their messages to larger and larger audiences. Lippmann was concerned about the vulnerability of unsuspecting audiences to such messages, and while he urged the media to play a bigger role in consumer protection, he was skeptical as to whether they were capable of doing so. In his 1922 book, *Public Opinion,* he described journalism as "a searchlight, moving here and there across the night sky, illuminating one small section and then the other, but never providing the broad, even light needed to conduct the public's business."

Lippmann coined the term "the pictures inside our heads" to refer to how the media use stereotypes and other literary shortcuts to persuade the audience. Lippmann claimed that by receiving information packaged in the form of stereotypes, audiences would be conditioned to "defining first and seeing second," resulting in audiences "expecting reality to imitate art." Lippmann was also one of the first media critics to be concerned with the growth of the mass media (through expansion and mergers) and its effect on the audience.

Lippmann believed that at best, American media operate in an "imperfect system" and that despite their skill and desire for accuracy and objectivity, they will always present a picture of reality that is a bit misleading in one direction or another. In crime stories, for example, newspapers and television news programs may both cover trends in local crime working from the same set of facts gleaned from police reports and other government sources. Because they choose different words and approaches to presenting the story, television stories might make the crime problem seem worse than it actually is, while newspapers might make it appear less serious. He stopped short of claiming that such differing results cancel each out or combine to give the audience an accurate picture. Instead, he emphasized the need for audience members to be skeptical of the information they receive from the media and make decisions based on information from a diversity of news sources.

Lippmann based that view on his claim that news and truth could be expected to coincide only when the results of an event were definite and measurable, such as the final scores of athletic competitions or final vote counts of elections. He added that the role of the press was to describe events rather than provide a true picture of reality upon which readers could act.

Boorstin and Pseudo-Events

Daniel Boorstin (1914-2004) was a professor, historian, and attorney who was best known for his criticism of the public relations and advertising industries. He coined the term **pseudo-events** to refer to activities that appeared to be important news events but were really just thinly disguised efforts at free publicity. Boorstin applied the term to any planned news event, implying that only spontaneous or unforeseen events could be truly newsworthy, and anything else was either propaganda or other form of "fake news."

Boorstin may have been the first to use the term *photo op* (short for "photo opportunity") to refer to the artificial photography sessions that political strategists arrange. While a standard part of a modern political campaign, such events were considered innovative during the early-to-mid 1900s. Boorstin criticized both the campaign strategists for arranging such photographs — typically the candidate kissing babies, walking through a flag factory, or greeting foreign dignitaries — as well as the media for publishing them under the guise of legitimate news. "We (Americans) are the most illusioned people on earth," Boorstin wrote. "Yet we dare not become disillusioned, because our illusions are the very house in which we live."

Today, while other critics continue such criticism, politicians continue to be seen posing for photographs with veterans or senior citizens, reading to children at elementary schools, or visiting soldiers in military hospitals. Newspapers continue to publish the photographs, and television networks continue to broadcast the video.

Bagdikian and the Media Monopoly

Ben Bagdikian (1920-) was born in Turkey but has spent much of his adult life in the U.S. He is a retired journalist, political commentator, and editor. Early in his journalism career, he posed as an inmate in the Pennsylvania prison system in order to investigate living conditions of the inmates.

Many years later, he became a full-time educator and author, teaching at the University of California at Berkeley and writing a number of books that were critical of the American media. His most famous work is *The Media Monopoly* (1983), in which he expressed his concern that mergers and consolidation in the news business created the potential for too much of the news to be controlled by too few media companies.

Bagdikian disputes the claim of media owners that they don't exercise influence over how their reporters cover issues that directly affect the media organization or the industry in which it operates. "Many media corporations claim to permit great freedom to the journalists, producers, and writers they employ," Bagdikian wrote. "Some do grant great freedom. But when their sensitive economic interests are at stake, the parent corporations seldom refrain from using their power over public information."

Postman and the Study of Humor

Neil Postman (1931-2003) was a media critic and author who was best known by for his 1985 book about the history of television, titled *Amusing Ourselves to Death*. Postman described himself as a "humanist" and often claimed that "new technology can never substitute for human values." Much like Jean Baudrillard, Postman was highly critical of American media and popular culture, especially television. In his book, Postman admonished the television industry for over-simplifying complex ideas and placing more emphasis on image than on substance. Targets of his criticisms also included television's claim that it was an educational medium. Postman said that television was a one-way form of communication, but true education requires a two-way exchange of information.

For Discussion

Case Study 2   **Football Player's "Field of Dreams" Is a Hoax**

For several days in the spring of 2008, few people could blame Kevin Hart for not answering his home telephone. "I don't mean to be impolite," the high school senior told journalists the few times he did answer. "I'm just going to hang up the phone."

Just a few days earlier, Hart was a celebrity in his small town of Fernley, Nevada. The 6-5, 290-pound offensive lineman — clearly the best player on his high school football team in Fernley — staged a news conference in the school gymnasium with caps from the University of Oregon and University of California on the table in front of him. The purpose of the event was to announce that after several months of deliberation, he had chosen to attend California over Oregon.

For months before the event and several days afterward, Hart told his parents, friends, classmates, coaches, school administrators, and local sports journalists that Oregon and California had offered him full scholarships and emerged from a long list of potential college football programs competing for his services.

There was only one problem: Neither California nor Oregon had offered him anything. He had attended football camps at Oregon and the University of Nevada, but both schools — and several others on his fictional list — had evaluated him as an athlete who was "average at best" and unlikely to compete at the Division I level.

"I wanted to play Division I ball more than anything," Hart said in an apologetic statement released to local media. "When I realized that wasn't going to happen, I made up what I wanted to be reality."

While local reporters were angry at being victims of Hart's deception, their editors were angry at the reporters for not being more skeptical. In covering the story, all had swallowed the deception in its entirety. If they had called the college coaches for comment, they would have known about the falsity of the story immediately. They should have also been aware of other red flags associated with the story: No college coaches had visited Hart's home, met his parents, or contacted his high school coach — all standard steps in the recruiting process.

When the inconsistencies in his story were uncovered, Hart attempted to explain them away with another lie — that a man claiming to be a talent scout working on behalf of several universities had duped him into believing the recruitment offers were real. In order to make that story sound plausible, he reported the fictional man to local police.

When that part of the story was also exposed as a lie, Hart found himself facing charges of filing a false police report. The county school system also investigated to determine if Hart should be held responsible for the expenses associated with the fake news conference in the school gymnasium.

Meanwhile, national sports journalists used the story to illustrate their contention that the business of recruiting high school athletes to play at the college level was largely "hype," and that the problem was not the original lie told by Hart, but the willingness of local journalists to ignore inconsistencies in the situation and other "red flags" in order to write a good story.

- Do you agree with the opinion of the national sports journalists, who used the story to illustrate their contention that the business of athletic recruiting is largely "hype"?

- While Hart had little justification for his deception, how much responsibility for the hoax lies with the media who covered the event (for not being more thorough in their fact-checking)? If you were the sports editor of one of the local newspapers involved, what punishment would you apply to your reporters who wrote the inaccurate stories?

- Which philosophers or philosophies discussed in this chapter would help you with this matter?

Discussion Questions

201. What have you learned from reading about the philosophers discussed in this chapter that you can apply to decision-making in your own life, either inside or outside of the workplace?

202. Baudrillard was highly critical of American media of the 1950s and 1960s, and Postman was equally critical of media of the 1970s and 1980s. Do those criticisms have more or less application today than during those decades?

203. In the section about St. Thomas Aquinas is a hypothetical scenario about ugly clothing. How do you believe Aquinas would have approached that dilemma? How would you have approached that dilemma and which other philosophers from this chapter do you believe would have the best advice for handling that scenario?

204. Do you agree with the media critics and historians who claim that John Milton's libertarian philosophy of media regulation (or lack of it) applies to cyberspace?

205. Working either individually or in groups, describe a scenario — either recalling one from your working experience or creating one that is entirely fictional — in which you believe it is either acceptable (or possibly acceptable) to lie. The audience for the lie should be an individual in one of the following categories:

     (a) your boss or other superior
     (b) a co-worker
     (c) a subordinate
     (d) a client or customer
     (e) a vendor, supplier, or other business contact.

Summarize the scenario in a paragraph of 5-10 sentences, and be prepared to discuss with the class.

Notes

20   **"men are afraid of the light":** The original source of this quote is unknown, but it appears in nearly every list of quotations attributed to Plato.

23   **"people's moral decision-making":** Today, many religious leaders and other persons claiming to make decisions based on religious principles believe that acts such as abortion, contraception to prevent pregnancy, or homosexuality are immoral simply because they are unnatural. More recently, the same argument has been made against cloning and stem-cell research; while not condemning all science, many religious leaders claim that advances in science that are inconsistent with the natural life cycle should not be allowed.

26   **"the same way as it is today":** In contemporary political discussions, the term "libertarian" is used to refer to a political philosophy that rejects the democrat-republican and liberal-conservative dichotomies and instead offers an alternative political philosophy that at times resembles one end of the spectrum and at other times resembles the other end. In the modern-day interpretation of libertarianism, the emphasis is on personal freedom and individual responsibility in decision-making.

27   **"consequences of his own temerity":** Robert Trager, Joseph Russomanno, and Susan Dente Ross, *The Law of Journalism and Mass Communication.* Boston: McGraw-Hill, 2007, p. 99.

27   **"marketplace of ideas":** The first Supreme Court case in which this phrase was used was the 1919 case of *Abrams v. United States*, in which Justice Oliver Wendell Holmes wrote that "the best test of truth is the power of a thought to get itself accepted in the competition of the market."

28   **"so that good may come of it":** Bruce Weinstein, "Lawful, Ethical Behavior Don't Always Correlate." *Northwest Florida Daily News*, August 19, 2006, p. 3-D.

29   **"could have been performed in its place":** Jeremy Bentham, *The Principles of Morals and Legislation.* London: Platt Press, 2007, p. 11.

31   **"one man's vulgarity is another man's lyric":** This metaphor comes from the 1971 Supreme Court case of *Cohen v. California.*

33   **"Baudrillard's death did not actually take place":** Elaine Woo, "Baudrillard Kept a Sharp Eye on Reality." *Los Angeles Times*, March 11, 2007, p. 15-B.

33   **Rotary Club operating policy:** Rotary International website, http://www. rotary. org.

35   **"the highest moral purpose in his life:"** "Introducing Objectivism," *The Objectivist Newsletter*, Vol. 1 No. 8, (August 1962), p. 35)

35   **"acceptable to do so":** Mark Sanford, "Atlas Hugged." Newsweek, November 2, 2009, p. 54-55.

35   **"free flow of information and ideas":** Alexander Meiklejohn, *Political Freedom, the Constitutional Powers of the People.* Oxford: Oxford University Press, 1965, p. 189.

37   **"Now, design a tax plan":** "Red Haven's On Fire." *The West Wing*, season 4, episode 17. Air date February 26, 2003.

38   **"the more truthful alternative":** Sissela Bok, *Lying: Moral Choices in Public and Private Life*. New York: Pantheon Books, 1978, pp. 30-31.

39   **"because it's always so boring":** "The Truth About Lying," *CBS Sunday Morning*, September 23, 2004.

39   **"to conduct the public's business":** Walter Lippmann, *Public Opinion*. New York: MacMillan, 1961, p. 358.

40   **"the very house in which we live":** Daniel Boorstin, *The Image: A Guide to Pseudo-Events in America*. New York: Atheneum, 1961, p. 241.

41   **"using their power over public information":** Ben Bagdikian, *The Media Monopoly*. Boston: Beacon Press, 1992, p. xxxi.

41   **"I'm just going to hang up the phone":** Gene Wojciechowski, "College Recruit's Lie a Tale Gone Horribly Wrong." ESPN.com, February 8, 2008.

41   **"what I wanted to be reality":** Ibid.

CHAPTER 3

Journalism, Broadcasting, and Entertainment: Content Issues

Background

- An author is told by his agent that his new novel is too dull, so he revises the manuscript to include a rape and torture scene that is unrelated to the main story.

- A reporter for a local daily newspaper opens a package that arrives at the station with no return address. Inside he finds a diary, allegedly written by a prostitute who is now in jail and awaiting trial on charges that she killed more than a dozen of her customers. Before turning it over to prosecutors, the reporter makes a photocopy, and the newspaper publishes portions of the diary entries in a five-part series, over the objections of the woman's defense lawyers.

- A movie critic for a major daily newspaper has a large readership but is also known for occasionally including offensive comments in his reviews, many of them slipping past his editors. Criticizing one movie for its choppy editing, he writes that the movie "appears to have been edited by an epileptic." In his review of a documentary tracing the history of a national chain of discount retail stores, he writes that the stores are "gathering places for the southern white trash subculture." In writing a review of a biopic about the life of a recently deceased rap singer, he writes that movie's soundtrack would "appeal mostly to the watermelon and fried chicken crowd."

Many issues related to media content have their origins in theoretical studies of the impact of the mass media on society. Early in the twentieth century, as politicians and media researchers began to consider the potential impact that news and entertainment media might have on the public, they began to study those issues in a number of forms. In addition, the federal government addressed the potential impact of the media by establishing a regulatory agency (the Federal Radio Commission, later to become the Federal Communications Commission), and professional associations did so by developing voluntary codes of ethics.

Academic Studies

In the previous century, media scholars developed a variety of theories concerning the impact of the media, and those theories fell into two categories. The category called **powerful effects theories** described the potential for the media to influence and manipulate their audiences. One of the theories, known as the **magic bullet theory**, contended that the media were so powerful that society might one day be at the mercy of those persons or companies that controlled the media. Even though the magic bullet theory and most other powerful effects theories have since been discounted, they were credible enough at the time that the federal government established rules to limit the size of media conglomerates and encourage competition.

In response to the powerful effects theories, media researchers who believed the media had considerably less impact on their audiences developed a group of alternative theories known as **minimal effects theories**. Among these was the **cumulative effects theory**, which stated that while the media had some potential to affect public opinion and consumer behavior, that effect was realized only after the audience's repeated exposure to those messages over long periods of time.

Government Intervention

In the 1920s, with radio expanding in popularity for both news and entertainment, Congress saw the need to regulate the rapidly growing industry. The result was the Radio Act of 1927, which created the Federal Radio Commission and charged it with developing a licensing procedure. The FRC was the first federal government agency to have any responsibility for media regulation (the Federal Trade Commission was created more than a decade before, but it did not assume responsibility for regulation of advertising until much later).

There was little concern for content; at the time the major concern was ensuring that radio frequencies were assigned in an orderly fashion and that entertainment programming did not overshadow more important applications of radio, such as communication during local and national emergencies. The following decade, even before the invention of television, Congress expanded the scope of the FRC and renamed it the Federal Communications Commission.

Today, the FCC remains the main source of media regulation within the federal government. It is charged with ensuring that broadcasters operate with regard to the "public interest, convenience, and necessity." The vague term "in the public interest" is often used to justify the FCC's regulatory and licensing procedures, which are often sources of controversy and public debate.

Professional Codes of Ethics

The major professional organizations serving communications professions include the Society of Professional Journalists and the Radio Television Digital News Association (formerly the Radio Television News Directors Association). When the NAB passed its first Code of Good Practice in 1929, part of its rationale was to avoid excessive governmental regulation in the industry. According to NAB officials, the code showed the organization's "desire to do our own housecleaning without waiting for regulation by the government."

While the SPJ Code of Ethics deals mainly with issues of policy — mostly the methods by which the reporters gather information — it also addresses a number of issues related to content. The most significant items are found within the first section titled, "Seek Truth and Report It." The complete text of the code is provided in Appendix A, but here are the most significant clauses related to content.

According to the code, journalists should:

- avoid stereotyping by race, gender, age, religion, ethnicity, geography, sexual orientation, disability, physical appearance, or social status;

- support the open exchange of views, even views they find repugnant;

- give voice to the voiceless; official and unofficial sources of information can be equally valid;

- distinguish between advocacy and news reporting; analysis and commentary should be labeled and not misrepresent fact or context;

- distinguish news from advertising and shun hybrids that blur the lines between the two.

In the section titled, "Minimize Harm," the code requires that journalists:

- be sensitive when seeking or using interviews or photographs of those affected by tragedy or grief;

- recognize that gathering and reporting information may cause harm or discomfort; pursuit of the news is not a license for arrogance;

- show good taste; avoid pandering to lurid curiosity.

The Radio Television Digital News Association Code of Broadcast News Ethics requires that broadcasters:

- strive to present the source or nature of broadcast news materials in a way that is balanced, accurate, and fair;

- evaluate information solely on its merits as news, rejecting sensationalism or misleading emphasis in any form;

- clearly label opinion and commentary.

Current Issues and Controversies

The Debate over Public Service Journalism

The concept of "public service journalism" (sometimes called "civic journalism") began in the early 1990s when newspapers and television stations decided to go beyond just reporting the news and took leadership roles in community improvement projects. Working either together or independently, newspapers and television stations began taking on a number of attention-getting projects. Examples:

- In many communities, media organizations sponsor holiday toy drives during which they invite their audiences to bring toys to the newspaper or TV station. Employees dress for the events as Santa Claus, elves, or other holiday characters. In other communities, media organizations sponsor litter-pickups, for which they supply volunteers with garbage bags, gloves, and refreshments. In both cases, the newspapers and television stations that organized the events then cover them as new stories.

- In other communities, television stations work with the American Red Cross or other nonprofit blood banks to promote blood donation drives and often host the events in their studios. During live newscasts, reporters interview blood donors and blood bank personnel.

- In Charlotte, North Carolina, the *Charlotte Observer* worked with a local television station to organize a number of community improvement projects, including having their employees work as volunteers for various nonprofit organizations.

- In Huntington, West Virginia, the daily newspaper worked with a local television station to organize a series of "town hall" meetings at which citizens could express opinions on the city's most pressing needs. The newspaper staff organized volunteers into committees to address issues such as health care, education, law enforcement, and the environment. The newspaper and television station then covered the committee meetings as news stories.

- Perhaps the best-known example of public service journalism is NBC's "To Catch a Predator" series that it incorporated into its popular *Dateline* series. Working with police and a nonprofit group called Perverted Justice, NBC personnel set up a sting operation that lured suspects, believing they would be meeting underage children for sex, to a home equipped with hidden cameras (this series is addressed in more detail in Chapter 5).

On the surface, such endeavors appear to produce win-win results: the communities receive much-needed help in a variety of areas, and the newspapers and television stations, while they deny that ratings and economics play a role, draw larger audiences and sell more advertising.

Many supporters of public journalism dispute the theoretical concept of detachment and contend that journalists cannot function as "social hermits" and retreat from all involvement in the communities. Instead, they believe that reporters should become more involved in their communities because doing so makes them more aware of problems and opportunities that might otherwise be missed.

Critics of public service journalism, however, have two main problems with such projects. One criticism, typically expressed by those who believe in the traditional values of journalism, is that when media organizations "adopt" nonprofit organizations and get involved in addressing community problems that are ordinarily the responsibility of local government, they are going beyond their conventional roles. The job of the media, they say, is to report on such projects, not organize them. Some use the metaphor of "marching in the parade rather than just reporting on the parade." One journalist phrased it this way: "If I'm a journalist responsible for covering the parade, I need to ask a lot of questions: Who is paying for the parade? Was that money well spent? Was the parade conducted safely and efficiently? Because of my newspaper's interest in diversity, I want to know if anyone was left out of the parade. Those are all important questions to ask, but I can't ask the questions about the parade and march in the parade at the same time."

Another criticism is that a newspaper or television station cannot simultaneously organize an event and then cover it as a news story — without creating a conflict of interest. Critics are uncomfortable reading or watching a news story about volunteers spending a weekend afternoon picking up trash on the highway when they know the newspapers or television station organized the event, recruited the volunteers, and provided the trash bags and refreshments. Likewise, they're uncomfortable reading or watching a news story about a holiday toy drive when members of the audience are encouraged to bring donations to the newspaper or television station.

In addition to metaphorically patting themselves on the back as they report on the success of the events, critics say, a bigger problem occurs when something goes wrong. Will journalists responsible for reporting on the success or failure of other community projects apply the same scrutiny to problems with an event that was organized by their own employer?

Although the term "public service journalism" has its roots in America, examples of the concept have been found on nearly every continent. In India, for example, journalists and educators have worked together for decades on projects to improve the quality of life in the country, with little concern being expressed about the appropriateness of those professions playing such roles. Since the late 1990s, broadcasters in Australia have developed "special projects" to closely examine issues such as politics, race relations, education, healthcare, and crime. In the early 2000s, journalism researchers found similar journalistic programs spreading across Asia, Latin America, and Africa.

The Debate over Sponsored News

One recent trend at local newspapers and television stations is to negotiate special rates for major advertisers who pay to sponsor, and often provide content for, special pages (and sometimes entire sections) in the newspaper or segments on evening news broadcasts. Called "sponsored news" or "news look-alikes," these pages, sections, or television segments are popular and effective communication tactics for advertisers who want to do more than just purchase traditional advertising space and time.

One example involves hospitals, which sponsor and provide content for newspaper features and television segments about health topics while indirectly promoting their services.

Newspapers often publish "special sections" to promote community events, and offer major advertisers the opportunity to sponsor the sections and generate community goodwill by associating themselves with the event. Other newspaper advertisers are invited to sponsor weekly "theme pages" such as those targeted at children or seniors.

Traditionalists in the newsroom or newspaper management often criticize this form of promotion because it blurs the lines between news and advertising. There is less concern at television stations, however.

In the SPJ Code section titled, "Seek the Truth and Report It," the code requires that journalists "distinguish news from advertising and shun hybrids that blur the lines between the two." In its section titled "Act Independently," the code requires journalists to "deny favored treatment to advertisers and special interests and resist their pressure to influence news coverage."

In 1999, the *Los Angeles Times* created controversy when it published a special section to celebrate the opening of the Staples Center, a new multi-million dollar sports arena built partially by taxpayer money as the new home of the Los Angeles Clippers of the National Basketball Association and Los Angeles Kings of the National Hockey League. While presented as news, the section was actually an advertisement paid for by Staples, a leading office supply retailer, which had also paid for the naming rights to the facility. Criticism came from both traditionalists working in the newsroom as well as media critics working for other publications. The management and ownership of the newspaper later apologized for the "lapse in judgment," but more than a decade later, the case remains a popular one for discussion in media ethics classes at colleges and universities.

What troubled media ethicists was not just the blurring of the lines between advertising and news, but the fact that money was flowing in both directions. While Staples was paying for the production of the newspaper supplement, the *Times* had agreed to pay the company $1.6 million over five years for the rights to be a "founding partner" of the new facility. Other founding partners included McDonalds, Anheuser-Busch, United Airlines, and Bank of America. After the financial arrangements were uncovered by the newspaper's own media critic, the publisher claimed that while she did not see any ethical conflicts in the situation, it was a mistake not to disclose the arrangement to all concerned, including newsroom personnel. The idea of keeping the relationship secret, she claimed, was to avoid influencing how the newsroom covered the opening of the facility.

The Danger of Stereotypes

The print and broadcast media are often accused of **stereotyping**, which is the portrayal of members of racial or ethnic groups in an unflattering and often offensive manner based on generalizations or outdated perceptions. Such offenses can be found in the content of news stories, entertainment programming, or advertisements. Professional communicators should always avoid stereotyping in their own work — whether intentional or not — and not allow it to appear in any printed, broadcast, or online material for which they are responsible.

Stereotyping in news stories was the topic of a study by the Center for Integration and Improvement of Journalism at San Francisco State University, which described stereotypes as "journalistic shortcuts" that are "frequently used to denigrate individuals based on race or ethnicity. Broad generalizations about a racial or ethnic population rob individuals of their uniqueness . . . To report with accuracy and comprehensiveness, journalists must be aware of, and avoid the use of, stereotypes."

One of the most recent examples of stereotypes in news stories were seen in the aftermath of Hurricane Katrina, which devastated the city of New Orleans and parts of southern Mississippi in late summer of 2005. Print and broadcast media from all over the country mobilized to cover the largest natural disaster in American history. In hindsight, many critics who examined the work of the media found that in their coverage of the storm's aftermath, television networks inadvertently resorted to stereotypes as they described the people whose lives were disrupted by the storm. While showing images of people taking food from abandoned stores in the days and weeks following the storm, for example, representatives of a variety of ethnic groups were included. But when photographs and video clips were accompanied by narration and commentary, a disturbing double-standard was applied. When visuals showed white individuals taking food from grocery stores, the commentary portrayed them as "desperate individuals gathering food for their families." But when African American individuals were shown taking food, they were described as "looters."

In entertainment programming, stereotypes have been an issue almost since the beginning of the television age. In 1951 — while television was still in its infancy — the National Association for the Advancement of Colored People (NAACP) executed a campaign to get the program *Amos n' Andy* off the air because of its negative stereotypes of African Americans. Ever since, advocacy organizations representing women, gays, Asians, Hispanics, and other audiences have executed similar campaigns aimed at canceling programs or altering their content based on what they perceive as negative portrayals. While some production companies and networks give in to the demands either in whole or in part, many others hold their ground, perhaps out of concern for the "slippery slope" that may result from altering their programming in reaction to the demands of special-interest groups. In doing so, some attempt to discredit the campaigns or the organizations that sponsor them, decry the idea of censorship or political correctness, and point out the weaknesses in the groups' monitoring systems.

Many examples of stereotyping were found in crime dramas of the 1970s and 1980s. African American men were shown as criminals more often than they were shown as teachers, doctors, lawyers, or other professionals. One television critic recalling that era joked that "black men on television were only shown in two positions — handcuffs in front or handcuffs in back." Until recently, other African American characters were depicted mainly in menial occupations such as janitors or bus drivers. Other common stereotypes included those portraying Mexicans as illegal immigrants, Italians being involved in organized crime, Asians being good at mathematics and technical jobs, blond women being inarticulate, old people being forgetful and doddering, northerners being rude to outsiders, southerners having bad teeth and being obsessed with guns, and gay men being concerned mostly with fashion and personal appearance.

Most such stereotypes have been eliminated in entertainment programming, but they occasionally surface in advertising. In the early 1990s, for example, Irish-Americans objected the beer companies — specifically Coors, Budweiser, and Miller Brewing — producing television commercials that portrayed their ancestors as heavy drinkers. Letter-writing campaigns organized by advocacy groups resulted in many of the ads being withdrawn.

In 1993, Taco Bell produced a series of television advertisements urging consumers to "run for the border." Mexican Americans called the series insulting because it added to the stereotype of Mexicans being responsible for illegal immigration and unemployment. As a result, many of the chain's restaurants were targets of consumer boycotts.

When advocates of a proposed state lottery in South Carolina wanted to play on the rivalry between that state and Georgia, they created a southern "white trash" character named Bubba, complete with bad teeth and an exaggerated southern accent.

The television commercials angered individuals and groups on both sides of the lottery debate, but the advocates refused to withdraw the ads or apologize to those claiming they were offended.

Does the News Media Show a Bias Toward Liberal Views?

Accusations of the alleged "liberal bias of the press" go back to the 1960s and the work of Edith Efron, a journalist and media critic. Writing a series of columns for *TV Guide* and a 1971 book titled *The News Twisters*, Efron based her theories largely on anecdotal evidence from the 1968 presidential election campaign, in which the news media, according to her, conspired to support liberal democrat Hubert H. Humphrey and oppose conservative republican Richard Nixon, the eventual winner. Much of her methodology was later found to be flawed, but the book was popular among republicans and conservatives. In order to artificially create "buzz" for the book, a member of Nixon's White House staff bought $8,000 worth of books in order to vault it into the *New York Times* best-seller list.

In the 1960s, many conservative politicians accused media organizations of being anti-American because they opposed against the Vietnam War on their editorial pages and because individual reporters appeared to second-guess military leaders on the execution of the war. David Shaw, media critic for the *Los Angeles Times*, claims that phenomenon was seen again following the terrorist attacks of September 11, 2001. Conservative politicians and radio talk show hosts, already predisposed to be critical of what they referred to as the "mainstream media," blasted major newspapers and television networks for pointing out the vulnerabilities in homeland security or strategic errors in the execution of the subsequent wars in Afghanistan and Iraq. In many cases, conservatives — especially radio talk show hosts such as Rush Limbaugh and Sean Hannity — use the term "mainstream media" as a derogatory label.

"Being cynical and pessimistic is not the same as being unpatriotic," Shaw wrote in his defense of the media. "Journalists are not being unpatriotic or treasonous when they ask tough questions or challenge official pronouncements or try to show the impact of the war on enemies or noncombatants. Quite the opposite. They're being loyal not just to this country, but also to the ideals on which it was founded and for which our troops are fighting."

One of the earliest academic studies of the bias issue took place in 1986, when researchers Robert Lichter and Stanley Rothman concluded that journalists were "predominately liberal" in their own political beliefs and that bias offered showed in their reporting. Specifically, they found that 54 percent of journalists in their sample admitted to being liberal and 17 percent identified themselves as conservative. In terms of party affiliation, a similar study showed that journalists' party affiliations were 45 percent democrat, 30 percent independent, and 25 percent republican. In both studies, however, nearly all denied that their political leanings or party affiliations affected their work.

In the late 1990s, the Washington, D.C.-based Media Research Center spent $2.8 million on a campaign to "expose for the American electorate the blatant left-wing agenda that has made a mockery out of the term 'objective journalism.' " The campaign included the publication of a book promoting its point of view, the exposure of examples of media basis via a newsletter and web site, and "blast faxes" to respond to media bias when detected.

The most recent entries into the media-bias debate include two books by CBS News reporter Bernard Goldberg. The first, simply titled *Bias,* was a 2003 work that documented dozens of examples of media allegedly showing favoritism toward democratic politicians and bias against their republican opponents. In his follow-up book, titled *Arrogance: Rescuing America from the Media Elite,* Goldberg claimed that the traditional media's liberal bias and concern for political correctness are at least partially responsible for the industry's decline. If they continue down that path, Goldberg wrote, "they will cease to be serious players in the national conversation and will become the journalistic equivalent of the leisure suit — harmless enough, but hopelessly out of date."

But Goldberg also clarifies that he is not suggesting there is a "vast liberal conspiracy" to slant the news toward the liberal point of view. Instead, he claims, the liberal slant results from thousands of print and broadcast journalists acting independently and allowing their personal political views to influence their reporting.

Despite persistent criticisms of bias, media executives continue to claim that while most journalists have a variety of political leanings, those leanings seldom show up in their work. "At our paper, we don't ask reporters to take a political litmus test," wrote Pat Rice, editor of the *Northwest Florida Daily News*, in a 2007 column. "But we do insist that they leave their own political slant out of their stories."

While accusations of liberal bias have focused mostly on privately owned media, those that are publicly owned have been the targets of similar criticism. The two national media outlets — Public Broadcasting Service (PBS) and National Public Radio (NPR) — have been criticized for decades as being biased against large corporations and republican officeholders.

In 2005, the chairman of the Corporation for Public Broadcasting (CPB), the federal government agency that operates PBS and NPR, hired consultants to monitor those broadcast outlets for signs of anti-Bush, anti-business, and anti-military slants in their reporting. As a result of the consultants' report, CPB established two news and business programs with a conservative slant and hired two ombudsmen — one conservative and one liberal — to "bring balance" to PBS and NPR programming, despite public opinion surveys that indicated that the audience did not believe the programming was biased in one direction or the other.

The criticism of PBS and NPR continued, however, and in 2011 Congress voted to dramatically reduce federal funding for those networks.

Today, conservative groups such as Accuracy in Media (AIM) and the Media Research Center have taken up where Efron left off. While it remains a popular belief among many political conservatives, the idea is not fully supported by that group. Some political observers claiming to be "moderate conservatives" believe the issue is largely overstated, and in many cases conservatives use the "liberal bias of the press" allegation as an excuse for the failings of the Republican Party and other conservative groups.

Knowing When to Be Afraid

The media's health warnings have forced many Americans toward the extremes in their attitudes toward their own health and mortality. On one extreme are those who accept as absolute truth every piece of health-related news gleaned from newspapers, television, and other media. As a result, they cut back on their consumption of beef, butter, cheese, cream, and eggs; opting for healthier (or so they believe) alternatives. They also practice safer sex, monitor their blood pressure and cholesterol, and examine themselves for early signs of breast cancer or skin cancer.

On the opposite extreme are those who reject health warnings from the media (and likely from their physician as well), often with the attitude of "I'm going die of something sooner or later anyway, so I might as well enjoy life in the meantime." Some individuals cite anecdotal evidence to support their beliefs, such as a family member who ate unhealthily throughout a lifetime but lived into his or her 90s. Psychologists refer to such attitudes with the term **cognitive dissonance,** which is the tendency of individuals to "explain away" information they receive that is inconsistent with previously held beliefs.

Beyond its implication for citizens, health-related news also tends to influence policy makers. Many state legislatures have changed their laws regarding indoor smoking, seat belt usage, and tobacco and alcohol sales, based on university studies they learn about through the media rather than directly from the sources. In addition, federal government agencies such as the Food and Drug Administration (which regulates the manufacturing and distribution of food and pharmaceuticals) and Federal Trade Commission (which regulates the advertising of those products) often make policy decisions based on university studies and news reports.

In the 1970s, media researchers Max McCombs and Donald Shaw developed a theory that is applicable here. They coined the term **agenda-setting** to describe how the media determine which critical issues are discussed in public and in the government. While social and political issues were the first application, health-related matters became subjects of agenda-setting in the 1980s, beginning with those related to AIDS, the effect of second-hand smoke, and drunk driving.

Television journalism and consumer advocate John Stossel blames the phenomenon of fear stories on political activists, governmental bureaucrats, and trial lawyers — three groups of people who, according to Stossel, "profit by scaring people." He also criticizes his fellow journalists for not being more skeptical in checking out the claims of their sources, especially those that appear to be dubious to the average audience member. He points to the example of the alleged "cancer epidemic" the media has been reporting for more than a decade. Television viewers have been exposed to a dramatic increase in the number of stories about various forms of cancer since the mid-1990s, but during the same time period, the death rates for those cancers has stayed the same or fallen slightly.

Parody and Ridicule

While celebrities often file lawsuits based on damage to their reputations, other public figures complain — sometimes in court and sometimes by other means — over matters of taste.

New York Mayor Rudolph Giuliani was involved in two such cases in the late 1990s. The first occurred when *New York Magazine* sponsored advertising on the sides of New York City buses that read, "*New York Magazine* — possibly the only good thing in New

York that Rudy hasn't taken credit for." Using his authority as mayor, Giuliani ordered the advertisements removed. The magazine filed suit against the city, claiming that the removal of the ad was a form of censorship. In its response, the magazine claimed its use of the mayor's name was a legitimate parody because he was the city's leading public official and the ad was based on his reputation for self-aggrandizement. The court ruled in favor of the magazine and ordered the city's transit authority to accept the advertisement.

A few years later, Giuliani was the target of a more questionable ad, this time on a billboard sponsored by the People for the Ethical Treatment of Animals (PETA). As part of its advertising campaign claiming that milk contributes to prostate cancer, PETA used a photograph of the mayor with a "milk mustache" that parodied the dairy industry's more famous "Got Milk?" campaign. Next to Giuliani's photograph was the question, "Got Prostate Cancer?" Giuliani, who had recently dropped out of the race for the U.S. Senate after being diagnosed with prostate cancer, threatened to sue, but PETA withdrew the ad and issued a formal apology.

In 1994, the *Minneapolis Star-Tribune* generated similar controversy when it accepted an ad from a company selling a self-defense device it called the "Tonya Tapper." The device was similar to the baton that assailants had used to injure Olympic skater Nancy Kerrigan, an attack allegedly orchestrated by rival skater Tonya Harding. The slogan, "You've seen how it works, now get one for your protection," prompted numerous complaints from readers, but the newspaper claimed "the ad met its in-house standards because it dealt with a legal product."

Much like other public figures, the late evangelist Jerry Falwell was often the target of newspaper editorial cartoonists and other forms of parody. But in the late 1980s he accused *Hustler* magazine, and flamboyant publisher Larry Flynt, of crossing the line from comedy into bad taste. At first glance, the full-page item appeared to be part of a series of advertisements in which celebrities talked about their first time drinking Campari Liqueur. But the Falwell piece was actually a parody that suggested that the reverend had sex (i.e. his "first time") with his mother and addressed his congregation while drunk. At the bottom of the page, in tiny print, was a disclaimer that read, "ad parody — not to be taken seriously."

Falwell sued Flynt for both libel and intentional infliction of emotional distress. Lower courts ruled that Falwell had no grounds for a libel case because they determined that the ad was "so outrageous that no reasonable person would have believed it," but he was initially awarded him $200,000 on his emotional distress claim. The Supreme Court eventually overturned that award, however, ruling that the item was protected speech because it was a parody of a public figure and was analogous to a political cartoon or caricature.

In 2006, American astronaut Lisa Nowak was caught in a love triangle with two other astronauts and was accused of stalking her female rival and driving non-stop from Houston to Orlando to confront her at Orlando International Airport. As the case unfolded, print and broadcast media labeled the story "Lust in Space" and focused on the more bizarre details of the story. Among those details were reports that during the long drive, Nowak wore an adult diaper in order to avoid having to make bathroom stops. For weeks that followed, the news media repeated that detail and late-night television comedians focused on it. Nowak's attorney denied that aspect of the news reports and pleaded with the media to stop reporting it, but most continued.

While media personnel are often responsible for providing the background material on which much parody and ridicule are based, at other times they find themselves on the other side of the issue — as targets of ridicule. In 2003, for example, a popular sports director for a television station in Tampa, Florida, was arrested for drunk driving (see Case Study 4-A). Compounding his legal problems were the public comments generated by the fact that the offense took place in a part of town known for drug-dealing and prostitution.

Local radio disk jockeys, while admiring the man for his humility in admitting and apologizing for his offense, couldn't resist the opportunity to poke fun. "Everyone knows that if you go into that part of town late at night, you're looking for one of two things," one early-morning disk-jockey said.

A decade earlier, a news anchor for a competing station in Tampa was arrested after being caught soliciting sex from a 15-year-old prostitute. One radio disc-jockey joked that a local sandwich shop that was well-known for naming its sandwiches after well-known local personalities should offer a new hot dog named after the newscaster; it would consist of a "tiny little wiener on 15-year-old buns."

The pain and embarrassment of being ridiculed in and by the media may be worse when it affects private individuals who place themselves in the public spotlight without considering the humiliation that may result. In the early 1970s, a young California surfer named Mike Virgil was interviewed by *Sports Illustrated* for its story about the surfing culture of which he was a part. Virgil admitted to a number of unusual behaviors, including putting out lit cigarettes inside his mouth, eating live insects, diving head-first off staircases in order to impress women, and faking work-related injuries so he could collect worker's compensation and spend more time surfing. Virgil originally consented to the interview, but later called the reporter and asked him to leave out some of the embarrassing details. The magazine refused to alter the story, and after its publication, Virgil filed a lawsuit, claiming the article invaded his privacy. *Sports Illustrated* claimed it was only trying to make a connection between Virgil's unusual lifestyle and his surfing style, but Virgil claimed the article ridiculed him. After years of legal proceedings, a civil court ruled in favor of the magazine, largely because Virgil had consented to the interview.

One of the most famous cases of a private person being exposed to public ridicule as a result of media exposure began with a March 6, 1995 taping of an episode of *The Jenny Jones Show* to be titled "Same-Sex Secret Crushes." Jones' production staff invited automobile mechanic Jonathan Schmitz to be part of the program and told him he would be meeting his "secret crush" — but did not tell him the title of the episode. When he finally met his crush in front of a studio audience, it turned out to be one of his customers, Scott Amedure. Schmitz reacted with laughter while on the show, but became disturbed by the incident later. He had a history of mental illness and alcohol/drug abuse. Three days after the show's taping, after enduring ridicule by family members and friends, Schmitz shot and killed Amedure. Schmitz was later convicted of second degree murder and was sentenced to prison for 25 to 50 years, and the episode was never aired.

In 2007, a contestant in the Miss Teenage America Pageant was the victim of not only an embarrassing moment on stage, but also months of ridicule that followed. Seventeen-year-old Lauren Caitlin Upton, representing South Carolina in the pageant, was asked by a judge on the panel for her opinion on weaknesses of the American education system. She responded with a rambling, 45-second answer that not only failed to address the question, but made little sense at all. The following day, radio talk shows across the country used the sound byte to ridicule the young woman based on the stereotype of blond women being inarticulate. Others used the sound byte as part of their tirade against the quality of public schools and what they believed was the superficial nature of beauty pageants.

In other cases, ridicule is aimed at news events rather than individuals — but it is often the individuals associated with the news events who feel the pain. A few weeks before Christmas 2004, for example, newspapers across the country published a syndicated editorial cartoon originally drawn by *Milwaukee Journal-Sentinel* cartoonist Gary Markstein. The cartoon depicted caskets covered by American flags coming back from the war in Iraq, and above them were the lyrics to the song, "I'll Be Home for Christmas." Nearly every newspaper that published it reported receiving complaints from its readers. Most were from readers identifying themselves as conservative and in favor of the war, but many also came from those identifying themselves as liberal and anti-war.

Regardless of their political leanings, readers' complaints centered on the issue of taste, claiming that it was disrespectful of the troops serving in Iraq as well as those who had already died — and the family members of both groups. The county commission of Iredell County, North Carolina passed a resolution denouncing the publication of the cartoon in the community's daily newspaper. Many newspaper editors apologized to their readers and regretted using it, but many others stood by it on the principles of press freedom. Markstein said he was caught off guard by the controversy, but defended his work by saying, "Sure, the cartoon was raw and unpleasant . . . but so is the environment our brave troops are working in."

In yet another case of an editorial cartoon creating controversy, the *New York Post* published a cartoon in 2009 that likened President Obama to a violent chimpanzee shot to death by police. A week earlier, the chimp had escaped from a local zoo and attacked a woman, prompting police to kill it after they are unable to capture it. In the cartoon depiction of the event, two police officers are shown standing over the bullet-riddled body of a chimp, with one officer saying to the other, "I guess they'll have to find someone else to write the next stimulus bill." After a week of public criticism, publisher Rupert Murdoch apologized for the cartoon and explained that it was not intended to play on a racial stereotype, but rather to "mock a badly written piece of federal legislation."

One of the most recent controversial cases involving the parody of a public figure occurred during the 2008 presidential election campaign. In July of that year, *The New Yorker* magazine chose a cover illustration portraying democratic candidate Barack Obama and his wife, Michelle. Barack Obama, who had repeatedly denied rumors that he was Muslim, was shown in Muslim garb, while his wife, who had been criticized for her aggressive demeanor in television interviews, was shown wearing military camouflage, combat boots, and an assault rifle. In the background of the Oval Office setting, an American flag was burning in the fireplace.

While Obama and his wife dismissed the cover art as simply an annoying part of life as a public figure, his supporters were not so forgiving. Many observers — including republicans who had also felt the sting of editorial cartoons and other forms of parody — criticized the cover as offensive and distasteful. The staff of the magazine, known for its generally liberal stance and advocacy of democratic candidates, defended the artwork by claiming it was simply trying to use hyperbole and exaggeration to illustrate how Obama's opponents were describing the democratic candidate in venues such as political talk radio and the newspaper editorial page.

Even after Sarah Palin's notoriety began to level off following her unsuccessful vice presidential campaign in 2008, the news media and late-night comedians continued to focus on her daughter, 16-year-old Bristol.

Late-night host David Letterman may have taken the cheapest shot, suggesting that the daughter's pregnancy may have been the result of a tryst with New York Yankees third baseman Alex Rodriguez, who had a reputation for dating Hollywood actresses and other famous women.

In the weeks leading up to the joke, Letterman had been criticized for comparing Sarah Palin's wardrobe to that of a "slutty flight attendant." Letterman refused to apologize for the remark, claiming that by becoming a voluntary public figure, she had opened the door for such comments. Most media ethicists and political observers agreed, but when Letterman made the remark about Bristol, many said he had crossed the line.

Letterman's apologized for the latter remark, but the controversy continued for weeks, raising the issue of to what extent, if any, the children of public figures should be considered fair targets for parody and ridicule. The incident followed a 16-year-period in which comedians and talk radio hosts routinely joked about Chelsea Clinton, the only daughter of President Bill Clinton, and Barbara and Jenna Bush, the twin daughters of President George W. Bush. During the early days of the Clinton presidency, for example, radio host Rush Limbaugh referred to Chelsea as the "White House dog." In commenting on how poised and well-spoken Jenna Bush appeared in television interviews, comedian Jay Leno, playing on her father's reputation for sometimes appearing inarticulate, quipped that it "must have been a very windy day when that apple fell from the tree."

Covering Tragedies: How Much Is Too Much?

For much of the twentieth century, the news media covered mass murders and other tragedies involving the loss of human life very much after the fact. Limitations in technology meant that the details of those stories, and the photographs and video used to illustrate them, were at best presented to the audience on the following day.

Beginning in the 1980s, however, advances in technology such as smaller, lighter cameras and mobile news vans and helicopters meant that news crews could provide same-day coverage of tragedies and in some cases even provide live coverage of events as they unfolded.

Many such tragedies took place on high school and college campuses. The first of such cases happened at the University of Florida in 1990. During the first week of fall semester, five UF students were murdered in their off-campus apartments over a span of three days. The crimes attracted media from all over the country, and the media struggled with issues such as (1) balancing the public's right to know with the potential for creating unnecessary panic, (2) sorting through rumors and unsubstantiated information from questionable sources, (3) avoiding the release of information that might harm the law enforcement investigation, and (4) showing concern for the privacy of the families affected. While there was some criticism of print and broadcast journalists in the aftermath, most critics gave the media high marks for covering the tragedy in a thoughtful and sensitive manner.

The media was challenged again in 1999, when two students at Columbine High School in Littleton, Colorado killed 12 of their classmates, a teacher, and themselves. Television stations in nearby Denver broke into their morning programming to cover the tragedy live, and one station stayed on the air to provide non-stop and commercial-free coverage for 13 hours.

Two daily newspapers serving the area published late-afternoon special editions. The following day, newspapers across the state each provided more than 20 pages of coverage that included gruesome details of how the students died and photographs showing bodies as they were removed from the building.

In the weeks that followed the killings, media critics scrutinized the coverage. While none objected to the amount of coverage, many found problems with the degree to which the images of the dead and wounded were shown. More importantly, both print and broadcast media were criticized for numerous factual errors that resulted from their desire to upstage their competitors. For example, early media reports indicated that more than 25 students had been killed — almost twice the number who actually died. One television station attempting to show photographs of the killers showed the yearbook photograph of the wrong student, and that photograph also appeared briefly on the station's website.

Perhaps the most egregious error, however, was one television station's broadcasting of details that could have affected the outcome of the tragedy if the killers had access to a television (which they did not). The station broadcast live telephone interviews with students trapped inside the building, during which students revealed the locations of other students hiding in adjacent classrooms. While such information would have been helpful to rescuers attempting to reach the students, to broadcast it was considered inappropriate because it was possible that the killers may have had access to the media coverage. The same station also reported the speculation of one helicopter pilot concerning which emergency exits the students would use.

On April 16, 2007, a student at Virginia Polytechnic Institute (Virginia Tech) carried out a similar massacre on that campus, resulting in the deaths of 32 students and faculty members and eventually the killer himself. The reviews of the media coverage were mixed. In the first two days after the tragedy, the media were praised for demonstrating restraint, good taste, and sensitivity. But much of that goodwill was lost two days later when television networks aired excerpts from a video prepared by the killer and mailed to NBC News (see Case Study 3-C).

Political Correctness: Who Can Say What?

The issue of political correctness can be traced back to two incidents involving sports commentators and unfortunate choices of words.

In 1983, ABC Sports announcer Howard Cosell was criticized following a *Monday Night Football* telecast in which he referred to an African American player as that "little monkey." Civil rights leaders called the comment "racist" and demanded an apology, but Cosell refused, claiming that he also used the term to refer to small white athletes, as well as to his own grandson.

Five years later, CBS Sports was forced to fire football commentator Jimmy "The Greek" Snyder for making racially insensitive remarks during an impromptu television interview in a Washington, D.C. restaurant. Asked by the reporter to comment on the differences between black and white athletes, Snyder commented that black athletes could trace their athletic skills back to the Civil War, where "slave owners would breed big black men with black women to produce big black kids." The network originally defended Snyder, but the timing of the story — coming just a few days before the newly established Martin Luther King Jr. holiday — could not have been worse. After several days of controversy, the network dismissed Snyder.

The Cosell and Snyder incidents were eventually forgotten (except for their obituaries and online biographies), but a more long-lasting controversy, this one involving comedian Jerry Lewis, began in 1992. Lewis, who for 26 years had hosted a televised fund-raising program to support the Muscular Dystrophy Association, made several offensive remarks in media interviews, mostly showing condescension toward both adults and children with the disease.

Prior to Lewis' comments, many organizations serving the disabled and individuals with serious illnesses developed "style guidelines" to help media organizations choose the correct words and avoid offending readers. The suggestions included replacing "suffers from X disease" with "a person with X disease," "wheelchair bound" with "wheelchair user," and "cancer patient" with "cancer survivor."

Not only did media organizations agree to use the more sensitive terms, they also revised their style manuals to avoid negative or offensive phrasing in other areas. Examples include adjectives used to describe professionals, such as "black lawyer" and "Hispanic doctor." To use adjectives in that way may imply to readers that it is unusual for minorities to achieve those professional positions, and therefore style manuals recommend they be used only when pertinent to the story, such as, "the suspect insisted on having a black lawyer" or "Martinez is the first Hispanic doctor to receive the grant."

Media stylebooks also discourage journalists from using stereotypical labels such as *welfare mother, slumlord, grumpy old man, social butterfly,* or *town drunk.*

The modern era of political and racial insensitivity began in 1997, when professional golfer Fuzzy Zoeller was attempting to be funny in a television interview on the final day of the Masters' Golf Tournament. Alluding to the tournament's tradition of having the winner select the menu for the pre-tournament players' dinner the following year, Zoeller commented that he hoped that African American winner Tiger Woods didn't plan on serving "fried chicken, collard greens, or whatever the hell those people eat." Zoeller and his defenders insisted it was an attempt at humor, but the incident created negative media publicity far outside of golf circles. Despite numerous public apologies, Zoeller lost two of his corporate sponsors and was the target of criticism for years after the incident.

In 2000, Atlanta Braves relief pitcher John Rocker was suspended for part of the season after making comments in a *Sports Illustrated* article that many considered racist, sexist, and homophobic. Commenting on why he would not want to play for the New York Mets or New York Yankees, Rocker described people he saw on the New York subway system as "kids with purple hair, queers with AIDS, a 20-year-old mom with four kids, and too many foreigners who don't speak English." Rocker later apologized, but qualified it by explaining that he was "only saying what a lot of other people thought."

In 2001, media critic David Horowitz angered many university officials around the country by attempting to place an ad in college newspapers across the country — the content of which many of the papers found objectionable but published nonetheless. The ad, titled "Ten Reasons Why Reparations for Blacks is a Bad Idea for Blacks — And Racist Too," outlined his view of the public debate over slavery reparations. Of the newspapers that received the ad, many rejected it outright. Other newspapers published the ad but elsewhere in the same issue denounced its message while explaining their First Amendment right to publish it. Other papers published the ad without explanation and later apologized to their readers.

In December 2002, Senate Minority Leader Trent Lott created a controversy when speaking at a birthday party for South Carolina Senator Strom Thurmond. Referring to Thurmond's 1948 unsuccessful campaign for the presidency, Lott commented that "the country would certainly be better off today" if Thurmond had won. Although Lott later insisted that his comments referred to Thurmond's long years of public service rather than specific campaign issues, critics assumed he was referring to the segregationist beliefs that Thurmond expressed earlier in his life and during the 1948 campaign. The incident caused problems for Lott — not only in his home state of Mississippi, but nationwide — as civil rights leaders chastised him for weeks on television talk shows and in other venues. Under pressure from his colleagues and snowballing media publicity, Lott resigned his position as Senate Minority Leader, but retained his Senate seat until 2007.

In July 2006, actor and director Mel Gibson created controversy when he was arrested for drunk driving. According to police reports, which became the topic of print and broadcast news stories, Gibson responded with a string of racial and ethnic insults that some entertainment journalists believe may have permanently damaged his career.

In April 2007, radio talk show host Don Imus made racially insensitive remarks on his morning radio show that was simulcast on the cable network MSNBC (see Case Study 3-D). At first, the controversy generated by Imus' remarks focused on the offense taken by the African American community. But as the controversy continued to grow, it also stirred debates over issues of prejudice, racial stereotypes, hypocrisy, and the roles played by talk radio and rap music in popular culture. The Imus incident came after a decade of entertainers, athletes, and politicians creating controversy through careless remarks that were intended to be complimentary or humorous, but were taken as insults by the audience.

In early 2007, actor Isaiah Washington created controversy when he reportedly directed anti-gay slurs at fellow cast members of the ABC television series, *Grey's Anatomy*. Even after promising to seek counseling and apologizing both publicly and privately, Washington was fired from the show. That same year, comedian Michael Richards responded to heckling during his nightclub act with a profanity-laden tirade during which he called the offenders "niggers" and made other inflammatory remarks. Video of the tirade quickly appeared on the Internet service YouTube, beginning weeks of negative news stories and a series of apologies from Richards. Much like the Imus story, the Richards story also sparked a national dialogue over the apparent double-standard applied when racial slurs are used by white and black speakers.

As candidates began positioning themselves for the 2008 campaign, Delaware Senator and democratic candidate Joe Biden was asked to comment on the candidacy of Illinois Senator Barack Obama, who was already one of the front-runners for his party's nomination. Biden thought he was complimenting his Senate colleague when he described Obama as the first African American presidential candidate who was "mainstream" and that he was "articulate and clean cut . . . a really nice-looking guy." Instead of being taken as a compliment, Biden's remarks were considered a slap at previous black presidential candidates and African Americans in general.

In 2009, the Little People of America, an advocacy group, asked the FCC to ban television networks from using the word "midget" to refer to little people. The incident that prompted the request occurred on the NBC program *Celebrity Apprentice*, in which contestants created a detergent ad titled "Jesse James and the Midgets." The contestants, including comedienne Joan Rivers, suggested bathing little people in the detergent and hanging them out to dry. The advocacy group claimed the word "midget" is as offensive to little people as "nigger" is to African Americans.

Some examples of political correctness do not involve people and their comments, but how otherwise non-controversial words became controversial when used in certain contexts. In the early 1990s, for example, Mothers Against Drunk Driving (MADD) began a campaign to persuade law enforcement personnel and the media to refer to vehicle collisions involving intoxicated drivers as "crashes" rather than "accidents" — based on the belief that "accident" implies no one was at fault. Early in the 2000s, the National Collegiate Athletic Association began discouraging the media from referring to the annual football game between the universities of Florida and Georgia as "the world's largest outdoor cocktail party." The game, held each year at the neutral site in Jacksonville, Florida, often results in more tailgating than seen at most other sporting events, and as a result, post-game drunk driving arrests are also proportionately higher.

Today, the conflict between freedom of speech and political correctness is a popular topic in college classes and on newspaper editorial pages.

At many universities, administrators have established "speech codes" that punish students (and sometimes faculty members) for making comments offensive to minorities. Defenders of such policies claim they are necessary to maintain a "comfortable learning environment," but critics claim that while eliminating offensive speech, they are also broad enough to also prohibit other forms of speech theoretically protected by the First Amendment. In 2005, for example, Harvard University President Lee Summers lost his job partly due to his public comments that gender differences explained the lack of women in professions related to science, math, and engineering.

More recently, the idea of speech codes has trickled down to elementary schools. In 2007, for example, an elementary school principal in Fresno, California sent a letter to parents asking them to talk to their children about inappropriate use of the word "gay." Attempting to stop students from making comments such as "that's so gay," or other references that might be considered offensive, the school threatened to punish those students with detention or suspension. While many parents complained that the rule was silly and a possible violation of free speech, no law suits have yet resulted from the rule.

In 2010, National Public Radio fired commentator Juan Williams after he said on Fox News — his other employer — that when he boards an airplane and sees other passengers wearing Muslim clothing, he fears they might be terrorists. After NPR let him go, critics claimed that the move increased public perception that the network was liberally biased and overly concerned with political correctness. A *USA Today* editorial critical of the firing claimed that while Williams' comments were "clumsy and illogical" (based on the assumption that real terrorists would rather blend in than dress in Muslim clothing), those comments "fell short of a firing offense." Within a few days, Williams was hired by Fox News full-time.

In 2010, two elected government officials in Escambia County, Florida had to apologize to their constituents after making crude comments about the county's indigent population during a public meeting. Discussing why the cremation costs were higher for obese persons than for those of normal size, one commissioner said that he couldn't understand how poor people could become obese and quipped that he didn't see "how the indigents can afford that many groceries." The second commissioner added that the county should "put them on a weight loss program before they died." A third commissioner did not make a comment about the issue, but apologized nevertheless because he was caught on video laughing about the other two comments.

Apart from university campuses, the political correctness phenomenon is often manifested in government documents and company personnel policies. Critics of the PC movement claim that such policies are examples of governments and companies attempting to "legislate politeness."

Conservative columnist Kathleen Parker is one of a number of voices speaking out about the issue. In a 2007 newspaper column, Parker called political correctness on university campuses and the halls of government "the new McCarthyism," analogizing the problem to the communist "witch hunt" of the 1950s. "To be called a racist, sexist, or homophobe today is tantamount to being called a communist sympathizer 50 to 60 years ago," she wrote.

In other circles, political correctness has been described as "the greatest threat to the First Amendment in our history" (Rush Limbaugh), the equivalent of the Nazi brownshirt thought control movement" (economist Walter Williams), and "an ideological virus as deadly as AIDS" (David Horowitz).

Are Television and Movies Obligated to Be Realistic?

In the early 2000s, real-world forensic scientists and other law enforcement professionals began complaining about how their work is inaccurately portrayed in television crime dramas such as *CSI, Law & Order,* and *Crossing Jordan.* Labeling it the "CSI Effect," they claimed that those television programs include technical inaccuracies, and present complex scientific concepts in a simplistic manner that misleads the public and affects the way that jurors decide cases (see Case Study 3-E).

In 2003, CBS bowed to pressure from the Republican National Committee and other conservative groups and cancelled plans to air *The Reagans*, a "docudrama" concerning the lives of President Ronald Reagan and his wife, Nancy. An RNC spokesperson claimed the film's fictional dialogue showed the couple in a negative light. Other critics claimed the program exaggerated the president's tendency toward forgetfulness and portrayed him as being insensitive to the AIDS epidemic, while portraying Nancy Reagan as an over-controlling First Lady who abused the White House staff and sought advice on policy matters from astrologers.

That same year, the National Football League Players Association complained about the ESPN television series *Playmakers*, because of its portrayal of players for a fictional professional football team as drug addicts and spouse abusers. Officials at ESPN claimed the program was clearly labeled as "fiction" rather than "documentary," but the NFLPA claimed that most audiences would not draw such a distinction. "They pile on all this exaggerated negative stereotyping in every character, and that is not real life in the National Football League," a NFLPA spokesperson told the media. "ESPN is perpetuating a fraud on the consumer." Many individual players from real NFL teams complained that the program presented only the negative behavior of a small number of players, while not showing any of the players' charitable work or other positive behaviors.

In 2005, adoption agencies across the country protested the airing of *Who's Your Daddy*, a FOX Network reality special in which a young woman attempted to identify her biological father from a group of eight men. Claiming that the program trivialized the serious nature of the adoption process, the groups urged FOX affiliates not to air it. Only one of 182 affiliates — WRAZ in Raleigh, North Carolina — agreed not to air it and instead aired a serious documentary about the adoption process. "We just don't think adoption should be turned into a game show," said a spokesperson for the station. Added a spokesperson for the National Council on Adoption: "The program exploits the sensitive emotions of adoption . . . adoption is a very personal, meaningful experience, and it should not be commercialized like this."

While the majority of such criticisms are launched at television programs, similar criticisms are also made about theatrical films. Film producer Oliver Stone, for example, was criticized for an alleged overly negative portrayal of President Richard Nixon in his 1995 film, *Nixon,* and an overly romantic and glamorized portrayal of President John F. Kennedy in his 1991 film, *JFK.* Some critics believe the latter film is at least partially responsible for keeping alive conspiracy theories regarding the 1963 assassination. According to critics, Stone took liberties with known historical facts, created one character's emotional courtroom speeches based not on court records but on his own imagination, and took other shortcuts that Stone described in interviews as products of his "literary license."

While the 1994 film *Forrest Gump* was never criticized for any negative portrayals of real historical characters, many moviegoers were confused about how much of the film was true and how much was fiction. The film told the story of a mildly retarded man who played college football at the University of Alabama in the 1960s and had subsequent adventures set against the backdrop of historical events of that decade.

Nearly all of the story was fictional, but that didn't stop football fans from scouring NCAA record books to learn more about Gump. When they were unable to find references to him, some fans called newspaper sports departments to ask what year Gump played for Alabama.

In 2005, labor unions representing airline flight attendants called for a boycott of the motion picture *Flight Plan* due to the negative portrayal of flight attendants. The story line portrayed one flight attendant as being part of a criminal conspiracy and several others as treating passengers rudely. "Should there be another 9/11, it would be critical for cabin crews to have the support of the passengers, not the distrust that this movie may engender," said a spokesperson for one of the unions. "Our fellow crew members who perished in the line of duty (on September 11) deserve more respect." Disney Films, the movie's producer, responded that, "We are confident that the public will be able to discern the difference between fiction and the incredible job that real-life flight attendants perform on a daily basis."

That same year, officials of the Catholic Church complained about the many inaccuracies and the negative portrayal of the church in the feature film, *The Da Vinci Code*.

The Debate Over Video News Releases

As the term indicates, video news releases are electronic versions of the more commonly used news releases issued (on paper) by individuals and organizations as part of the public relations process. The idea was born in the mid-1980s, when advances in technology allowed public relations professionals to produce video products quickly and inexpensively. Today, video news releases can either be provided on digital video disks or through the organization's website or other digital delivery method. The most common applications of video news releases are to introduce new products, respond to crises, or address other news stories that have a substantial need for video content.

Most public relations professionals who produce VNRs, as well as the reporters who accept them, see the issue as one of convenience. Television news directors and other policy makers, however, object to the use of VNRs because they consider it a shortcut to accept any materials directly from the source. Many news directors believe that "if it's important enough for us to do a news story on the topic, it's important enough for us to shoot our own video." Some news directors are also concerned over the authenticity of the video. In an age of video manipulation and computer-generated images, some news executives worry that accepting video from outside sources leaves them vulnerable to hoaxes. Still other news directors see them as superficial attempts at free publicity presented in the form of what many respondents to a *TV Guide* survey referred to as "fake news."

The Radio Television Digital News Association includes in its code of ethics a set of guidelines that broadcasters should use in determining the appropriateness of using video provided by pubic relations representatives or any other party. Referring to such materials as "non-editorial video and audio," the guidelines suggest that such material is acceptable if (1) similar material cannot be recorded by the station's own reporters and is not available from other sources, (2) the source of the material is disclosed to the audience, (3) news directors have evaluated the motives of the organization providing the material, and (4) news directors have made sure that the producers of the material adhered to standard journalistic principles, such as those regarding truth, objectivity, and conflicts of interest.

Labeling VNRs with a simple subtitle reading "video courtesy of X" or "video provided by Y" is usually enough to prevent readers from confusing VNR content with station-produced or network-produced video. That step was missed in one incident in 2004, when television stations around the country aired a 90-second VNR, produced by the federal government, promoting its new prescription drug benefit for Medicare recipients. The segment showed an elderly couple discussing the plan with their pharmacist, and all three agreed that it is a good idea. At the end of the segment, a voice-over artist is heard saying, "In Washington, this is Karen Ryan reporting." Failing to delete that portion of the audio led audiences to believe the segment was part of an objective news story rather than a partisan promotional video.

(Alleged) Over-Dependence on News Releases

Depending on which survey is being considered, somewhere between 25 and 75 percent of the content found in "traditional" news source (newspapers, radio, and television) has its origins in public relations materials. In extreme cases, a newspaper employee will either re-type the content of a hard-copy news release or copy-and-paste it from an incoming email and submit it for publication under his or her own byline.

There is little criticism when the content of the news release involves the straight-forward, non-controversial items such as announcements regarding upcoming events that are typically found on the business or social calendar of the newspaper. A more serious problem occurs when the content of more detailed news releases is published with little or no additional reporting, editing, or scrutiny. Daily newspapers would never allow their reporters to generate news stories in this manner, but weekly newspapers with limited reporting staffs often resort to that shortcut.

Critics of the public relations profession often point to such as examples to support their opinion that the public relations industry has too much influence over what audiences receive as news. That criticism is often pointed directly at the public relations business, even in cases when the root cause is the laziness of newspaper reporters.

In the late 1990s, editors at the *Los Angeles Times* detected (almost by accident) that entry-level reporters writing for the newspaper's real estate section were taking material from news releases, placing their own bylines on them and publishing them with little or no revision. When the editors noticed a competing newspaper was publishing stories in its real estate section that were nearly identical to those published in the *Times*, at first they believed the other newspaper was guilty of plagiarism. But an internal investigation revealed that the other paper was not guilty of plagiarism; the reason behind the nearly identical verbiage was that reporters for the other publication had received the same news releases and were also publishing them with little or no revision.

The Debate Over Television Indecency

The terms obscenity and indecency are often confused, but the concepts are quite different in the eyes of the Federal Communications Commission, watchdog groups, and the courts. **Obscenity** (from the Greek for "filth") is a legal term used to describe sexually explicit material that is so offensive that it does not deserve First Amendment protection. **Indecency** (from the Latin for "the opposite of something that is fitting") is a much broader term used mainly to refer to broadcasting and musical performances.

While most indecency has sexual connotations, this category also includes profanity and references to bodily functions. Material labeled "indecent" may be offensive to many audiences, but is not offensive enough to qualify for the "obscenity" label as determined by state and federal laws.

A 1927 law gave the Federal Radio Commission — later to become the Federal Communications Commission (FCC) — the authority to regulate indecent language on the radio. The first case of a broadcaster being criticized for indecent content was believed to have taken place in 1937 when the National Broadcasting Company (NBC) aired a radio program featuring actress Mae West and ventriloquist Edgar Bergen. West and Charlie McCarthy, Bergen's famous wooden dummy, engaged in a conversation loaded with vague sexual references and double-entendres that would be considered harmless by today's standards. But NBC and other networks were so concerned by the audience reaction that they banned West from performing on the radio and wrote formal guidelines for any future programs that included sexual references.

In 1948, Congress passed a law that banned indecent programming on both television and radio, and put the FCC in charge of enforcing it. It was not until the 1970s, however, that the FCC attempted to enforce the rule to any great degree. The most noteworthy case involved a 12-minute skit by comedian George Carlin titled, "Filthy Words." Although the station provided a warning prior to the beginning of the skit, a listener complained to the FCC, prompting the investigation. Instead of fining the station, the FCC simply documented the incident and withheld judgment while it waited to see if other complaints would follow. No other complaints were received, but the FCC nonetheless decided to take action.

It established a rule that radio stations could air indecent material only between the hours of 10 p.m. and 6 a.m., a time of day that would later become known as the "safe harbor time." The FCC (and later the Supreme Court) justified the rule by claiming that the radio audience is much different from one that might attend a live performance by Carlin or other performer, or purchase a recording with similar content. The radio listener might be unprepared for the coarse language, the FCC determined, while someone attending the performance or purchasing the recording is doing so voluntarily.

For both television and radio stations, prosecutions under the new rules were rare until the late 1980s. One example was a Kansas City television station that that was fined for airing the soft-core pornographic movie *Private Lessons* during prime time. A Detroit radio station was fined $2,000 for airing "Walk With an Erection," a parody of the Bangles hit, "Walk Like an Egyptian."

In the decade that followed, the era of "shock jocks" such as Howard Stern created a new culture of crude and offensive material on the radio airwaves, and more public pressure on the FCC to limit or punish the broadcasters. The FCC fined several national radio conglomerates for allowing indecent speech by their on-air personalities, but the minimal amounts of the fines (considering the profits produced by the programs) made the fine system ineffective.

Congress eventually authorized the FCC to dramatically increase the financial penalties for indecency. Under this new threat, Stern moved his program to a satellite radio company, where it would be out of reach of FCC regulators.

The issue of television indecency surfaced again following the halftime show of Super Bowl XXXVIII in January 2004. The game was broadcast by CBS, which also planned the halftime show. The main performers were pop stars Janet Jackson and Justin Timberlake, and at one point in the performance, Timberlake pulled away part of Jackson's costume, briefly revealing one of her breasts. He later described it as a "wardrobe malfunction" and claimed there was supposed to be another garment underneath. The

FCC received numerous complaints about the incident, and in September of that year it fined Viacom, the network's parent company, $550,000.

The size of the fine created a "chilling effect" that prompted networks and local stations from airing controversial programming. Two months after the FCC announced the fine, for example, numerous ABC affiliates declined to air the movie *Saving Private Ryan* for fear that its graphic violence and course language might result in similar fines.

Following the Super Bowl incident, a number of awards programs were criticized when hosts and award winners sprinkled their comments with profanity. When the networks carrying the programs were fined by the FCC, they appealed through the courts system. Lower courts ruled in favor of the networks, claiming that the FCC's ban on "fleeting expletives" was too arbitrary. The Supreme Court, however, reversed those rulings in 2009, determining that the FCC had the authority to penalize the networks for not taking necessary precautions to prevent airing the profanity, such as arranging for the programs to broadcast on a 7-second delay.

Since the 1950s, the major television networks (and since the 1980s, cable networks) have internal departments called "standards and practices" that periodically update their policies regarding acceptable content for both programming and advertising. Those policies vary greatly by the genre of the program and the time of day or evening; language and images that are acceptable in a prime-time police drama might not be acceptable in a Saturday morning cartoon. Likewise, content that might be acceptable for a prime-time situation comedy aimed at an adult audience might not be acceptable for a nightly news broadcast, when children might be watching.

In 1996, the National Association of Broadcasters and the National Cable Television Association established a set of television program ratings patterned after those established for motion pictures in the 1960s. The ratings are displayed on television screen for the first 15 seconds at the beginning of each program and are repeated every hour for programs that last more than an hour. No genres of program — even live sporting events — are exempt. The four ratings are:

TV-G (general audience): Suitable for audiences of all ages. The rating guide indicates this rating does not automatically mean a program is designed specifically for children, but that most parents may let younger children watch this program unattended. These programs contain no objectionable language and little or no violence or sexual dialogue or situations.

TV-PG (parental guidance): These programs contain material that some parents may find unsuitable for younger children, and parents are advised to watch it with their younger children. The TV-PG label is sometimes accompanied by additional letter codes such as V (moderate violence), S (sexual situations) L (coarse language or mild profanity), and D (suggestive dialogue).

TV-14 (parents strongly cautioned): These programs contain some material that many parents would find unsuitable for children under the age of 14. Parents are urged to exercise greater care in monitoring these programs and are cautioned against allowing children under the age of 14 to watch unattended. The label is often accompanied by one or more letter codes such as V (intense violence), S (intense sexual situations), L (strong coarse language or profanity), and D (intensely suggestive dialogue).

TV-MA (mature audiences only): These programs are intended for adults and therefore may be unsuitable for children under the age of 17. This label is always accompanied by one or more the following labels: V (graphic violence), S (sexual activity), or L (strong and crude language or profanity).

In addition to the ratings systems and the standards and practices departments, there are a number of watchdog groups that deal with potentially objectionable material on television. The most active of these is the Parents Television Council, which was founded in 1995 to reduce the level of objectionable material on both network and cable television. For four hours every night, volunteers videotape prime-time television programs, including dramas, situational comedies, movies, news magazines, and other programming. They even record sporting events — not for the competition itself, but for the commercials. They are looking for violence, profanity, partial nudity, drug use, or references to sexual behavior or any other content that some might consider objectionable. The newest category on the PTC list of problematic content is "disrespect for authority," meaning that every instance of a child talking back to a teacher or an adult not complying with the directives of a police officer is recorded and scrutinized.

Despite its lobbying efforts, the PTC claims that parents bear the primary responsibility for monitoring the viewing habits of their children. However, the organization also challenges actors, writers, producers, musicians, game-makers, and advertisers to be aware of the role they play in shaping American culture.

The Debate Over Citizen Journalism

One of the fastest-growing trends on the Internet is that of **citizen journalism** or **open-source journalism.** It take two forms: (1) the contribution of photographs or video to traditional media outlets and (2) the distribution of that material through personal Web pages or Internet services such as Flickr (photographs) or YouTube (videos). Advances in technology such as small, hand-held cameras and video recorders (many of them built into cellular telephones) caused both forms of citizen journalism to expand exponentially in the early 2000s.

The first form of citizen journalism, however, can be traced back to the latter half of the previous century. From the 1960s through the 1990s, individuals who were at the "right place at the right time" could take their photographs or video to the nearest newspaper or television station and negotiate a price. The most famous example is that of Abraham Zapruder, a Dallas clothing manufacturer who recorded the 1963 assassination of President John F. Kennedy using a hand-held 8mm movie camera. He later turned the camera over to the U.S. Secret Service so the film could be processed, after which agents returned the camera along with a copy of the film. While the original became part of the law enforcement investigative materials, Zapruder sold his copy to *Life* magazine for $150,000, a portion of which he donated to the widow of a Dallas police officer who was killed attempting to question the assassin the day of the crime.

In 1991, amateur videographer George Holliday captured the beating of Rodney King by Los Angeles police officers. He gave (not sold) the 8-minute tape to local television station, KTLA. The tape was later part of the key evidence in the police officers' trial and became part of world-wide television coverage of the case.

Today, television networks and local stations occasionally accept such videos, but most are not as dramatic as the Zapruder film or King video, and networks and stations seldom pay for them. The most common examples are videos showing a tornado moving through a neighborhood or the results of a plane crash or other accident. The idea is more popular on cable television, as Cable News Network (CNN) and Fox News both actively encourage viewers to submit video clips through their Web sites, referring to them as iReports and uReports, respectively. While newspapers employ freelance contributors who are paid and agree to follow accepted principles of journalism, most citizen journalists have no training and are not compensated for their contributions — they offer their photographs or video simply believing they are performing a public service or for the notoriety of seeing their names on television. Individuals not wishing to work through television stations or networks (or having their contributions rejected) can post their work products directly on the Internet.

Some of the more popular or dramatic videos will end up on television anyway. The original contributors are not compensated or even identified; in most cases the only credit line reads "from YouTube" or something similar. Law enforcement agencies often scan sites such as YouTube for evidence of possible criminal activity, but before they begin an investigation, they confirm that the photographs or videos have not been altered.

For Discussion

Case Study 3-A   **The Lesser of Two Evils**

In the 1991 race for governor of Louisiana, both the voters and the media were forced to choose the "lesser of two evils," as both of the candidates entered the campaign with far more negative qualities than positive. The favorite was Edwin Edwards, who had already served three non-consecutive terms that had him in office for 12 of the preceding 20 years. Despite having already stood trial and acquitted on federal charges of bribery and obstruction of justice, Edwards was intent on a fourth term. The only factor that made his campaign palatable for voters and the media was that his opponent was David Duke, the grand wizard of the Knights of the Ku Klux Klan, a white supremacist group with a large following in the South. Two years earlier, Duke had won a seat in Louisiana House of Representatives as a republican, but once his racist views became more widely known, the Republican Party refused to back him in his 1990 U.S. Senate race. Based on Louisiana law, the governor's race was non-partisan, meaning Duke did not need party support to seek that office the following year.

In his bid for governor, Duke distanced himself somewhat from his KKK background, and instead claimed to be running on a platform that emphasized "white rights." Early in the campaign, both statewide and national media treated Duke's candidacy as a comedy act. He appeared on national interview shows such as *Good Morning America, The Today Show, Nightline,* and *Larry King Live.* Some political observers said that Duke made such a fool of himself by expressing his racist, sexist, and homophobic views on statewide and national television that few voters would take him seriously.

But when polls in Louisiana continued to show him running dead even with Edwards as the campaign moved into the fall, the state's media decided to expand their involvement in the campaign — not to support Edwards, but to oppose Duke. Most prominent among those media was the *Times-Picayune,* the New Orleans-based daily newspaper that was one of the most influential media outlets in the state. Edwards' legal problems and overt dislike for the media was troublesome for many journalism traditionalists at the newspaper, but with Duke as the alternative, the editorial board reluctantly endorsed Edwards.

Endorsing Edwards on the editorial page — where media ethicists would insist the newspaper's involvement stop — was just the beginning. The company-wide support for Edwards spread to the newspaper's political columnists, editorial cartoonists, and the employees whose job descriptions theoretically called for objectivity — reporters and photographers. Many of the state's other daily newspapers, as well as television and radio stations, followed the lead of the *Times-Picayune.*

Edwards won the race, most likely because of the media's expanded involvement in the campaign. In hindsight, the management of the *Times-Picayune* admitted to having "unclean hands" and "failing in the traditional standards of journalism" in its overt support for Edwards, but claimed in a post-election editorial that in pursuing the objective of preventing Duke from becoming governor, such transgressions were "a small price to pay."

Editor Jim Amoss defended the newspaper's tactics. "Newsrooms pride themselves on being at the epicenter of momentous events, monitoring tremors, privy to the excitement, yet always at a dispassionate distance," Amoss wrote in an op-ed piece published in an industry newsletter. "For Louisiana journalists, our recent governor's race broke that mold. Our state was shaken to the core. And the newsroom of the *Times-Picayune* quaked with it, knowing that our future was at stake. It was a battle for the soul of the electorate, and we found ourselves in the thick of it."

- Do you agree with the newspaper's claim that it endorsed Edwards because he was objectionable, but not as objectionable as his opponent?

- Journalism historians have documented numerous cases in which the endorsement by a major newspaper was the deciding factor in a close race for political office. But more recently, newspaper endorsements of candidates have considerably less impact of a race because of decreasing market share (compared to television, the Internet, and social media) and that the whole idea of newspapers endorsing political candidates is outdated. Agree or disagree?

- In many communities, daily newspapers have a track record of endorsing a mix of liberal democrats and conservative republicans, and in some cases endorse more republicans than democrats. Does this affect your view of the alleged "liberal bias of the press"?

Case Study 3-B   **Amtrak Tries to Detail Leno**

In the early 1990s, executives at Amtrak complained to NBC about the late-night host Jay Leno's repeated jokes about the safety record of Amtrak, the government-subsidized train service serving mostly routes in the Southeast and Northeast. In a series of accidents — some of them blamed on Amtrak, others on bad weather or faulty tracks and bridges — dozens of passengers were killed and hundreds injured.

In one monologue, Leno ridiculed an Amtrak television ad showing a traveling couple falling asleep in each other's arms. "Of course," Leno said, "a near-death experience always bring you closer together." After the company announced plans to lay off more than 600 managers, Leno speculated that it "wouldn't fire them, it would just put them on one of its trains."

Few viewers complained about the jokes, but the company didn't think the jabs were that funny. It announced plans to cancel $2 million in advertising on NBC, a threat it eventually carried out. It announced that it would spend more money in other forms of advertising in order to compensate for the negative image of the company that it claimed Leno perpetuated. In a letter to NBC President Robert C. Wright, Amtrak Chairman Thomas M. Downs wrote that "NBC can write Amtrak jokes faster than we can spend advertising dollars on your network, so I am directing our advertising agency to withdraw all of our ads from NBC as soon as possible."

In his response to Downs, Wright responded that he would "bring the issue to Jay's attention," but stopped short of indicating that any change on monologue content would result. He also indicated that the network would have preferred to have learned about Amtrak's concerns without the accompanying threat.

In a later letter to NBC, Downs indicated that his decision to cancel advertising was not a "threat," but rather a recognition of NBC's relationship with its talent. "We are sensitive to any appearance of an attempt to infringe upon a First Amendment right," Downs wrote. "As an advertiser, we have no right to expect any ability to control what is said on your network."

- Late-night comedians such as Jay Leno, David Letterman, Stephen Colbert, and Jon Stewart often claim they have a First Amendment right to ridicule political candidates and other public figures. But what about companies such as Amtrak? (keep in mind that in libel law, large companies are considered the equivalent of public figures).

- Because some passengers died in those accidents, does that make the subject off-limits for ridicule?

- Do you agree with Amtrak's strategy of cancelling its advertising on NBC? Would it have been more appropriate to first ask the network to stop making such jokes and use its advertising contract as leverage? (before deciding, read the section on "advertising boycotts" in Chapter 6).

Case Study 3-C   **Tragedy at Virginia Tech**

On the morning of April 16, 2007, a mentally disturbed 23-year-old student at Virginia Polytechnic Institute killed two students in a campus dorm. Less than an hour later, he entered a building on the opposite side of campus, where he killed 29 other students and faculty members and eventually himself. In the first few days following the tragedy, the national news media were praised for their tasteful and restrained coverage. Univer-sity officials, law enforcement personnel, and media critics commended the print and broadcast journalists and their employers for respecting the privacy of the families affected. Many critics commented that the media appeared to have learned from the mistakes they made in covering previous tragedies.

Two days after the massacre, the offices of NBC News in New York received a package that investigators believed the gunman mailed during the time that elapsed between the dormitory murders and the classroom killings. The package contained what investigators called a "multi-media manifesto" — a lengthy, rambling video in which the killer criticized the university and his classmates. Before turning over the package to law enforcement agencies, NBC made a copy that it aired in its entirety on the evening news. Other networks copied it from NBC's broadcast and aired either parts or all of it on their own news programs.

NBC was heavily criticized by many of the same individuals and organizations that had praised it a few days earlier. Viewers wrote letters, called the network switchboard, and used the company's interactive World Wide Web site to register complaints. Media critics also blasted the network for its "reckless and irresponsible" decision to air the tapes, and family members of those killed protested by canceling scheduled appearances on NBC's *Today Show*. Other television networks, as well as national newspapers, were criticized for showing the video photographs taken from the video that showed the suspect in various threatening poses. The criticism was based on their belief that such photos glorified the perpetrator. In contrast, national magazines such as *Time* and *Newsweek* chose their cover illustrations and inside text more tastefully — emphasizing the suffering by the victims' families and alleged failures of the mental heath care system.

The university was closed for a week following the tragedy, and when students returned, the media became more aggressive in attempting to interview students who would have preferred to put the matter behind them and concentrate on resuming their education. A few days after their return to campus, many students posted signs on campus that read "media go away."

- Do you agree or disagree with NBC's decision to air the video? Does the newsworthiness of the video outweigh the family member's privacy concerns? Should the network have also considered the possibility that airing of the video might inspire copycat crimes at other universities?

- In cases such as this, is it practical to have a pre-determined policy about the airing of controversial videos such as the one involved in this case? Or is each incident so unique that a fixed policy would be ineffective? Is it more practical to make such decisions based on the merits and circumstances of each case?

- Are there any provisions of the Hutchins Commission findings that are applicable to this issue? What about professional codes of ethics? Which philosophers or philosophies (from Chapter 2) are applicable here?

Case Study 3-D   **The World According to Don Imus**

On April 4, 2007, radio talk show personality Don Imus was reviewing current events on his early morning program when the subject turned to the NCAA Women's Basketball Championship tournament that had just concluded. Showing video clips of the final game as his show was simulcast on cable network MSNBC, Imus commented on the appearance of the players representing Rutgers University, a team that was largely African American. "Those are some rough-looking women," Imus said. "Those are some nappy-headed hos."

For the remainder of the show and later that day, nothing else was said about the matter. But the following day, an excerpt of the MSNBC show that included Imus' remark found new life on the Internet service YouTube. Several weeks of controversy followed, and Imus responded with a series of apologies — at a news conference, on the radio show of civil rights leader Al Sharpton, and even in a face-to-face meeting with the Rutgers team and its coach. The apologies weren't enough, however. At first, Imus was suspended by the CBS Radio Network for two weeks, and MSNBC permanently dropped the simulcast of his show. But under continued pressure from civil rights leaders, CBS radio eventually fired Imus.

While Imus did not defend his comments, preferring instead to simply apologize, his fans and other observers pointed out the double-standards applied to white and black speakers making racially insensitive and stereotypical remarks. Many observers believe it was inappropriate for black leaders to criticize Imus while not criticizing rap music for using similar words. *Kansas City Star* sports columnist Jason Whitlock said that even the players themselves likely listened to rap music that included similar expressions.

- Is the Imus case an example of free speech, or political correctness gone too far? Is there any merit to the position of Imus' defenders that he was the victim of a double-standard, based on the inclusion of similar language found in rap music performed by African American artists?

- Are there any provisions of the Hutchins Commission findings that are applicable to this issue? What about professional codes of ethics? Which philosophers or philosophies (from Chapter 2) are applicable here?

Case Study 3-E   **The CSI Effect**

During the 2000 television season, one of the most popular new programs was *CSI* (short for "crime scene investigation"), a hour-long drama based on the work of forensic scientists who solved crimes based on their examination of microscopic evidence in the form of blood, semen, hair, and clothing fibers. The first-year success of *CSI* gave birth to spin-offs *CSI Miami* and *CSI New York*, giving its network, CBS, three solid hits with a collective audience of more than 60 million viewers.

Since the initial success of those three series, competing networks attempted copycat programs, but so far most have come up short. But other series, such as NBC's *Law & Order* and *Crossing Jordan*, began to incorporate more forensic science into their story lines.

A television critic for *U.S. News & World Report* wrote in 2005 that in the three *CSI* series, "the forensic science is sexy, fast, and remarkably certain, a combination that has propelled the three-show franchise to the top of the ratings." But, the critic added, the fact that the shows are popular is not necessarily because they are realistic.

Real-world forensic scientists who have watched the programs point out that while there are few inaccuracies in the program, much of the dialogue and action is misleading. To begin with, they claim, the shows imply that forensic evidence is a major part in every criminal investigation, while in the real world it plays only a minor part in most cases and no part at all in many others. They also complain that the programs portray the process as taking place within hours, while in the real world the work takes days or weeks. On television, every police department has its own laboratory and the most modern equipment, while in the real world, police departments often share laboratories, adding to the delay.

While producers of the program claim that nearly every television drama takes "literary license" in order to produce effective drama, critics point out the stakes in this case are much higher. Across the country, prosecutors claim that juries enter the courtroom expecting to be shown forensic evidence like they see on television, and when they don't see it, they are more inclined to acquit suspects without regard to other evidence.

"Jurors now expect us to have a DNA test for just about every case," says Josh Marquis, the district attorney in Astoria, Oregon. "They expect us to have the most advanced technology possible, and they expect it to look like it does on television." As a result, Marquis says, he and other prosecutors usually ask about prospective jurors' television viewing habits during jury screening. Former prosecutor Wendy Murphy, now a spokesperson for the National District Attorneys Association and a consultant for CBS News, says that jurors will make comments and ask questions during and after the course of a trial that indicate they've been heavily influenced by programs such as *CSI*, and should therefore have been disqualified.

False impressions and expectations do not affect only jurors. Many crime scene investigators report that victims of residential burglaries often watch and scrutinize their work. One investigator for the Los Angeles County Sheriff's Office reports that many times victims will watch her dust for fingerprints and comment that, "That's not the way they do it on television."

Tammy Klein, another investigator for the LACSO, believes the "CSI Effect" presents a much bigger problem by changing the ways in which crimes are committed. She believes that many criminals have learned from the program new techniques for destroying evidence or otherwise covering up their crimes.

- Considering the case of *CSI*, as well as those examples provided earlier in this chapter, should the producers of movies and television programs be obligated to present a realistic picture of their subject matter? Or should they continue to enjoy the "literary license" that allows them to exaggerate in order to create more interesting entertainment material?

- Are there any provisions of the Hutchins Commission findings that are applicable to this issue? What about professional codes of ethics?

- Which philosophers or philosophies (from Chapter 2) are applicable here?

Discussion Problem 3-A   **Ghost Walk**

You're the editor of the features section for a mid-size newspaper in New England. A few days ago, you assigned one of your best feature writers to develop a story about a small company that offers narrated walking tours of the downtown area. While the traditional walking tours of the city's historical sites are offered during the day, the most popular tours are those offered after dark, as they include several abandoned homes, hotels, and movie theaters reputed to be haunted. The so-called "Ghost Walk" tours have been the subject of light feature stories in regional and national tourism publications for years, but have not been the subject of any stories in your newspaper.

After interviewing the proprietor of the tour company, the reporter comes to you with a dilemma. At the invitation of the company, he took one of the tours himself and took several pages of notes that included the names, dates, and other historical details provided by the tour guide. But after conducting additional research in both newspaper clip files and library books dealing with the history of the town, he was unable to verify many of those details. When he questioned the owner of the company about the discrepancies, she replied, "Well, don't put this in your story, but most of that stuff we just made up."

The reporter says he is uncomfortable with the idea of including information in the story that he knows to be false, yet he knows the story will not be complete without some of the colorful tales that the tour guides have been telling for years. But he also does not want to "blow the whistle" on the company, despite the fact that it receives money from the city government's tourism development fund and is therefore analogous to an agency of local government.

As editor, which of the following actions would you take?

a.   Suggest that the reporter continue writing the story, fictional details and all, under the rationale that most people familiar with the tours know that most or all of the narration is fictional anyway.

b.   Suggest that the reporter write a story that "blows the whistle" on the company under the rationale that as a recipient of government funds, the tour company is subject to the same media scrutiny as government agencies.

c.   Suggest that the reporter write the story doing the best job he can, but without including any fictional details and without revealing the deception.

d.   Cancel the story altogether.

Are there other alternatives?

Are there any provisions of the Hutchins Commission findings that are applicable to this issue? What about professional codes of ethics? Which philosophers or philosophies (from Chapter 2) are applicable here?

Discussion Problem 3-B   **Tell Me More**

You've recently moved to a new town and subscribed to the local daily newspaper. The first week in town, two stories caught your eye. One was a story about a local family that lost its home in a fire. No one was hurt, but the house was destroyed, and the family's insurance was insufficient to rebuild it. The other story was about a local charity that was in financial trouble and was in danger of closing if it could not pay its office rent and utility bills that were past due.

The newspaper is conducting an experiment called "Tell Me More." At the bottom of each story is a Web address and a note reading, "For more information on this story, visit our website at . . . " In the on-line edition, there is a link at the bottom of each story that reads, "Tell Me More."

You click on a few of the links, but before you can find out more, the site requires that you register as a "member." It does not cost anything, but you did have to provide your name and email address. In addition to reading a more detailed version of each story, the site offers you the option of signing up for email alerts providing future updates for stories you select.

A few weeks later, you begin getting email updates that provide new information about the family that lost its home and then asks, "Would you like to help the family?" It offers you the opportunity to make a donation by entering your credit card information. The next day, you get an email update on the story about the charity about to lose its lease. At the bottom of the item, it asks, "Would you like to make a donation to the charity?" Again, it asks you to donate money by entering your credit card information.

a. Are these two scenarios examples of an "innovative role" for a daily newspaper (as the newspaper management claims), or an example of public service journalism gone too far?

b. If the link had read, "Here's How You Can Help" instead of "Tell Me More," would you be more accepting of the newspaper's project?

c. Are there any provisions of the Hutchins Commission findings that are applicable to this issue? What about professional codes of ethics? Which philosophers or philosophies (from Chapter 2) are applicable here?

Discussion Problem 3-C   **Big Problems in Brookwood**

You're the city-hall reporter covering the town of Brookwood, a mid-size community in the southeastern United States. The town is named after John Brookwood, a patriarchal figure who was one of the state's leading agricultural pioneers. He founded the town in 1848.

The city's public information officer has sent you a news release and other publicity materials regarding a public event to be held in conjunction with a larger annual celebration of the town's anniversary on October 10. The purpose of the event is to name a new street and public park in honor of Mr. Brookwood.

Among the invited guests for the events will be members of the Brookwood family and several descendents of the slaves who worked on Brookwood's farms and in his home in the 1840s and 1850s. The public information officer relays to you the mayor's request that local media refer to these individuals in news stories as descendents of Brookwood's "personal staff" instead of "slaves." Before making a decision as to which term to use, you interview a local historian who tells you that even though Mr. Brookwood was a slave owner, he was not a tyrant such as those portrayed in television documentaries about the period; he was respected and beloved.

a. Do you refer to the guests in question as "descendents of slaves" (the more accurate description) or "descendents of Mr. Brookwood's personal staff" (the mayor's preference)?

b. Can you avoid the issue by leaving them out of your news stories altogether?

c. To what extent should you explain the historian's point of view about Mr. Brookwood being loved and respected?

d. Suppose you use the term "descendents of his personal staff" in the first draft of your story and the editor working on your story asks, *Does that mean they were his slaves?* How do you answer that question?

Discussion Questions

301. If you were asked to select five current television programs to be compiled onto a DVD and included in a time capsule to be buried and then uncovered and opened in 100 years, what five programs would you choose? If a cultural anthropologist working 100 years from now viewed those programs, what conclusions (positive or negative) about American culture might they draw from watching them?

302. Re-read the excerpts from professional codes of ethics provided earlier in this chapter. In your opinion, do today's journalists and the media organizations they work for do a good job or poor job of living up to these ideals?

303. Consider the role of YouTube and similar Internet programs in incidents such as those involving Don Imus and Michael Richards. Do you believe (a) the dissemination of such video on the Internet serves a valid purpose by exposing inflammatory comments and behavior, thus generating constructive debate; or that (b) such dissemination is harmful because it generates news stories that inflame passions based on incidents that otherwise would be quickly forgotten.

304. Between now and the next class, watch at least one national television newscast (NBC, CBS, ABC, CNN, Fox or MSNBC) or listen to either the morning or evening news on National Public Radio. Make mental (or written) notes concerning your perceptions of the news being slanted to reflect either a "liberal" or "conservative" viewpoint and be prepared to discuss your opinion with the class.

305. Were local radio stations justified in ridiculing the sports director arrested for drunk driving and the news anchor caught soliciting a 15-year-old prostitute (p. 58)? Libel law says that public figures must accept a certain level of public criticism and ridicule as part of their roles, but did the disk-jockeys mentioned cross the line?

Notes

51   **"march in the parade at the same time":** *Headlines & Soundbites: Is That The Way it Is?* Cronkite-Ward Videos, 1995.

53   **"and avoid the use of stereotypes":** Michael J. Bugeja, *Living Ethics: Developing Values in Mass Communication.* Boston: Allyn & Bacon, 1996, p. 196.

54   **"for which our troops are fighting":** David Shaw, "Skepticism's Not Unpatriotic." Syndicated newspaper column, date unknown.

55   **"but hopelessly out of date":** Bernard Goldberg, *Arrogance: Rescuing America from the Media Elite.* New York: Warner Books, 2003. p. 1.

55   **"leave their own political slant out of their stories":** Pat Rice, "The Internet is Making Newspapers Better." *The Northwest Florida Daily News,* June 10, 2007, p. 8-F.

57   **"because it dealt with a legal product":** Bugeja, p. 261.

59   **"but so is the environment our brave troops are working in":** "Editorial Cartoon Draws Political Ire." Associated Press report, December 11, 2004.

61   **"black women to produce big black kids":** Bugeja, p. 202.

64   **"fell short of a firing offense":** "Lines Blur as Journalism Heads Back to the Future." *USA Today,* November 10, 2010, p. 8-A.

64   **"weight loss program before they die":** Jamie Page, "No Laughing Matter: Officials Apologize." *Pensacola News Journal,* October 22, 2010, p. 1-A.

64   **"a communist sympathizer 50 or 60 years ago":** Kathleen Parker, "Today's Diversity Requires Sameness of Thought." Syndicated newspaper column, September 27, 2007.

65   **"and it should not be commercialized like this":** David Bauder, "N.C. Station Pulls Reality Show." Associated Press report, January 4, 2005.

66   **"that real-life flight attendants perform on a daily basis":** "Flight Attendants Urge Boycott of Film." Associated Press report, September 30, 2005.

67   **rather than a partisan promotional video:** Gene Foreman, *The Ethical Journalist.* Malden, MA: Wiley-Blackwell Publishing, 2011, p. 170.

72   **"a small price to pay":** Kerwin Swint, *Mudslingers: The Twenty-Five Dirtiest Political Campaigns of All Time.* New York: Union Square Press, 2008, p. 61.

72   **"we found ourselves in the thick of it":** Ibid.

73   **"put them on one of its trains":** Paul Farhi, "Amtrak Derails NBC Over Leno's Jokes." *Washington Post,* October 14, 1994.

73   **"from NBC as soon as possible"** and **"what is said on your network":** These comments were taken from correspondence provided by the Amtrak media relations office.

76   **"to the top of the ratings":** Kit Roane, "The CSI Effect." *U.S. News and World Report,* April 25, 2005.

76   **"expect it to look like it does on television":** "Prosecutors Feel the CSI Effect." CBSNews.com. February 10, 2005.

76   **"not the way they do it on television":** Stefan Lovgren, "CSI Effect is Mixed Blessing for Real Crime Labs." *National Geographic News,* September 23, 2004.

CHAPTER 4

Journalism, Broadcasting, and Entertainment: Personnel Issues

Background

- Responding to criticism by minority groups, a television network adds Asian, Hispanic, and African American characters to the cast of a popular television program, even though their roles are not necessary to support the story line.

- A restaurant critic and her husband visit an upscale restaurant to celebrate their wedding anniversary, not to write a review. The service is far below the establishment's customary standard. Annoyed with the perceived rudeness of the server, the critic asks to speak to the manager. The manager, not aware of who the woman is, is also discourteous. "How dare you speak to me like that," the critic says. "Don't you know who I am?"

- A business reporter for a daily newspaper writes a negative story about a local business, causing its stock price to drop dramatically. He then calls his stockbroker and buys 1,000 shares. The following week, he writes a positive story about the same company, causing its stock to rebound. He sells his own shares and makes a sizable profit.

- At the suggestion of his agent, a national news anchor accepts an invitation to be the keynote speaker at the annual meeting of a national nonprofit organization. The agent negotiates a speaker fee of $2,000. A few weeks later, several employees of the organization are charged with stealing money from its treasury. Because the network's reporter who customarily covers the organization is on medical leave, the network asks the anchor to report the story.

- A popular newspaper advice columnist decides that for the last several months, the letters she has received have been dull, uninteresting, and focused mostly on trivial issues. In order to keep her column interesting and relevant, she goes through her files and recycles letters and responses that were published 10 to 15 years in the past — certain that no one will notice — and in most cases makes slight changes in the wording of both the letter and her response. After a few weeks, she runs out of good recycled letters, so she simply begins making up letters and problems.

- The publisher of the local daily newspaper accepts an "honorary" membership at a local country club. While he plays golf only a few times a year, he uses the fitness center at least once a week. He also uses the dining facilities to entertain friends, family, and business acquaintances. He does not pay the club's standard initiation fees nor the monthly dues. While he pays full price for meals and beverages, he does not pay for rounds of golf or use of the fitness center.

- A reporter is working on a series of stories about the lifestyle of prostitutes working in the downtown area of the city. One of the prostitutes interviewed says she wants out of the business and asks the reporter for transportation to a homeless shelter sponsored by a nonprofit organization running a program to help prostitutes make the transition to a better life. When the reporter and prostitute arrive at the shelter, they find that it has been closed for renovations and there is no one there to direct them to an alternative shelter. The woman is afraid that if she is goes back to her street corner, her pimp may hurt or kill her, so the reporter allows the prostitute to stay in the her home overnight.

The Society of Professional Journalists Code of Ethics, in its section titled, "Act Independently," requires journalists to:

- avoid conflicts of interest, real or perceived;

- remain free of associations and activities that may compromise integrity or damage credibility;

- refuse gifts, favors, fees, free travel and special treatment, and shun secondary employment, political involvement, public office, and service in community organizations if they compromise journalistic integrity.

The American Society of Newspaper Editors Statement of Principles states that journalists "who abuse the power of their professional roles for selfish motives or unworthy purposes are faithless to the public trust."

The Radio Television Digital News Association Code of Broadcast News Ethics requires that broadcasters "strive to conduct themselves in a manner that protects them from conflicts of interest, real or perceived."

Current Issues and Controversies

Conflicts of Interest

Much like governmental officials, journalists hold positions of trust in American society. Even though they have not been elected by the people they serve, they are still accountable to the public and must avoid situations in which that trust is compromised — or appears to be. Commenting on the problem of conflicts of interest in the journalism business, media critic Howard Kurtz admonishes print and broadcast journalists for employing a double-standard in reporting on the ethical shortcomings of other people while failing to recognize them in their own work. "It's striking how often we in the news business fail to live up to the high-minded standards that we prescribe for everyone else," Kurtz wrote in his 1994 book, *The Media Circus*.

Most professional codes of ethics use terms such as "conflicts of interest, real or perceived" to emphasize that journalists should avoid not only those situations that present an *overt* conflict, but also those that may create the *appearance* of impropriety.

Here are some common problem areas related to conflicts of interest, both real and potential:

Personal friendships, family relationships, and romantic relationships. Journalists should never be in a position in which they are reporting a story that involves a friend or family member, or one in which a friend or family member will be affected by the outcome. If that is not possible, at minimum the journalist should disclose the potential conflict to an editor before beginning work on that story. In short-term situations, the editor will likely re-assign that story to a different reporter. In long-term situations, some editors may assign a different reporter to cover those stories, while others may allow the reporter to continue on that beat, but will monitor his or her stories to check for signs of possible bias.

In the 1970s, the *Philadelphia Inquirer* was unaware of a romance between political reporter Laura Foreman and State Senator Henry Cianfrani, who she often wrote about. When editors confronted her with their suspicions about a possible relationship, Foreman claimed that the rumors were the result of office gossip and professional jealousy, and she was allowed to continue covering the senator's work and re-election campaigns. But after she had moved on to the *New York Times*, she was questioned by the Federal Bureau of Investigation as part of its probe into misconduct by the senator, which eventually led to him going to prison for income tax evasion. That probe revealed the nature of the relationship and gifts that Cianfrani gave Foreman while she was still working for the *Inquirer*, including fur coats, jewelry, and a sports car. When the *Times* learned about the results of the investigation, they requested and received her resignation. Foreman and Cianfrani were married after he completed his prison sentence.

Later that decade, advice columnist Ann Landers was criticized by the *Columbia Journalism Review* for writing a column defending the funeral home industry against what she called "unfair criticism" without revealing that her son-in-law was a funeral director.

While *Harvard Business Review* editor Suzy Wetlaufer conducted a series of interviews with General Electric Chairman Jack Welch for an in-depth profile, the two developed a romantic relationship, even though Welch was married at the time. Wetlaufer disclosed the relationship to her superiors and asked that the profile be re-assigned to someone else. It was, but Wetlaufer was still fired. Wetlaufer and Welch eventually married, and today they co-author a syndicated newspaper column about ethical issues in the workplace.

In 1989, television news anchor Donna Hanover Giuliani was allowed to remain on the air as her husband, U.S. Attorney Rudy Giuliani, ran for mayor of New York City. She occasionally did field reporting in addition to her anchor job, but she was not allowed to participate in any stories in which her husband was mentioned. In her anchor role, she was not allowed to write or narrate segues in or out of other reporters' stories that mentioned her husband. She was also required to disclose to viewers that she was married to the mayoral candidate.

In the early 1990s, an art critic for the *New York Times* wrote a review of an art museum in Sarasota, Florida that was so positive that it caused his co-workers and editors to be skeptical about his objectivity. Upon further investigation, they learned that the critic's wife, a noted art historian, accompanied him on the visit and was paid $8,000 for presenting a brief lecture to museum patrons. Although the critic denied the financial compensation influenced his review, the fact that the museum had no history of paying other guest speakers cast doubt over the couple's claim that the husband's positive review and the wife's acceptance of the speaking fee was an "unfortunate coincidence."

Business relationships and organizational memberships. One example of a conflict of interest is when a print or broadcast journalist is assigned to cover a story involving an organization of which he or she is a member, or a person with whom he has a business or personal relationship. Memberships in political organizations or other groups involved in controversial public issues have the potential to reflect poorly on the credibility of both journalists and their employers. Even memberships in non-controversial organizations such the Rotary Club, chamber of commerce, or Parent-Teachers Association may be problematic.

While all media organizations address such potential conflicts in their personnel policies, they vary greatly in the degree to which those relationships are scrutinized. The most lenient policy would not forbid journalists from joining community organizations, but might caution them to avoid accepting reporting assignments on the organization itself or any issue in which the organization is involved. On the opposite extreme are those policies that prohibit all organizational memberships, regardless of how non-controversial they may be and how far removed their work might be from the reporter's area of expertise.

Some other media employers might allow reporters to belong to organizations, but would prohibit them from serving in leadership positions in which their public statements might be the subject of media coverage.

To avoid such conflicts, many media organizations require more detailed information (compared to other types of employers) on employment applications regarding past and current organizational memberships and places of employment. Employers may also inquire about the organizational memberships and places of employment of a reporter's parents and spouse. A reporter whose parent or spouse is a member of the school board or other governmental body, for example, would obviously not be allowed to report on the activities of that body.

Journalists need not join nonprofit organizations to create potential conflicts of interest. Many television stations, for example, have policies that limit the public appearances of their news anchors, who are often invited to serve as masters of ceremonies for beauty pageants, parades, and other community events.

Some media organizations go so far as to prohibit their employees from signing petitions related to political causes, as such documents are public records and may indirectly associate employees with potentially controversial issues.

Political involvement. Journalism history is full of examples of journalists becoming public officials and attempting to serve in both roles. For months after being inaugurated as president in 1921, Warren G. Harding still held the title of publisher of the *Marion Star* in his hometown in Ohio. Ironically, Harding had won the 1920 election over James Cox, who served three terms as governor of Ohio while still publisher of another newspaper in the state. In the early 1970s, William P. Hobby Jr. served as lieutenant governor of Texas while still the president of the *Houston Post* newspaper chain.

Today, nearly every media organization has a conflict-of-interest policy that prohibits its employees from seeking or holding public office. Running for office would be especially problematic for those working in television news because of their advantage in name recognition. In the 1980s, for example, a television reporter in Kansas City, Missouri refused to resign prior to running for the city council, and after being suspended by the station, he unsuccessfully sued. In 1999, television news anchor Bob Young resigned his position at a station in Augusta, Georgia, in order to run for mayor of the city, an election he won easily.

In addition to employer rules, the majority of states have election laws that require television stations to provide equal time to all candidates running for office, meaning that television anchors and reporters who remained on the job would create substantial legal problems for their employers. Most voluntarily agree to take unpaid leaves of absence.

In 2000, controversial television journalist Geraldo Rivera briefly considered running for mayor of New York City, and in 2008, radio talk show host Michael Savage told listeners he might seek the republican nomination for president. In both cases, employers informed them they would have to take unpaid leaves of absence prior to officially entering the races. After examining the financial realities of having no income for six months, both decided that their political ambitions could wait until later in the careers.

Some journalists have claimed that because of the value that society places on public service, to not allow them to seek public office is a violation of their basic rights as citizens. Their employers and the courts disagree, however, and respond with a simple policy: "You have the right to run for public office. You have the right to work as a journalist. But you don't have the right to do both at the same time."

During the 2000 presidential election campaign, CBS anchor Dan Rather embarrassed his network after making a paid appearance at a Democratic Party fund-raiser in his home state of Texas. Rather later apologized to his CBS colleagues and viewers, calling his decision a "serious lapse in ethical judgment."

In 2002, the *Boston Globe* reported that several Boston-area journalists — including many working at the *Globe* — had contributed to the gubernatorial campaign fund of Robert Reich. Their combined donations of $2,500 were insignificant considering that the overall campaign cost the candidate more than $1 million, but editors and media critics claimed that the issue was not the size of the donations, but that the donations were made in the first place. In addition to the *Globe* reporters, others caught in the mini-scandal included reporters from WGBH, a public television station, and the *Newton Tab*, a weekly paper owned by one of the *Globe's* competitors. The *Newton Tab* reporter turned out to be the central figure in the incident, as he wrote a glowing article about Reich shortly after making a donation to the campaign.

Public Broadcasting Service anchor Gwen Ifill was criticized for accepting the role as moderator for the 2008 vice-presidential debate between democrat Joe Biden and republican Sarah Palin. Ifill was known to be working on a book about the election campaign scheduled for release on January 21, 2009 — the day after Election Day — regardless of which candidate won. Although described as a book about the campaign itself that would not focus on either candidate to the exclusion of the other, its title, *Breakthrough: Politics and Race in the Age of Obama*, prompted conservatives to challenge Ifill's ability to be objective in her role as moderator. "She is so far in the tank for the democratic presidential candidate that her oxygen delivery line is running out," wrote conservative commentator Michelle Malkin in her *New York Post* column.

In defending her refusal to turn down the role, Ifill said in media interviews that "the proof will be in the pudding . . . anyone who is concerned (about bias) can watch the debate and make their own decisions." Republican presidential candidate John McCain dismissed the concerns, saying in a television interview that "Gwen Ifill is professional who is capable of doing a completely objective job because she is a highly respected professional."

After the debate, Ifill was widely praised for her performance. The *Boston Globe* reported that she "should receive high marks for her equal treatment of both candidates," and *Washington Post* media critic Howard Kurtz wrote that she "acquitted herself well." In a poll taken the day after the debate, 95 percent of those surveyed said they were pleased with her objectivity, while only 4 percent were not.

Following the 2010 mid-term elections, MSNBC commentator Keith Olbermann was suspended for two days after network executives learned that he contributed money to several democratic candidates, which violated the policy of the network's parent company, NBC Universal. That policy, which is similar to that of other print and broadcast news organizations, prohibits journalists from "doing anything that might call into question their impartiality, such as putting up a candidate's yard sign, making a political donation, or marching at a rally."

In a *USA Today* editorial, the national newspaper admonished the network for being "too soft" on Olbermann, suggesting that such blatant disregard for company policy, combined with Olbermann's influence as a political commentator, called for a stronger punishment — perhaps even firing. The newspaper drew a distinction between the MSNBC decision and a decision that its own management made in 2004. In that case, three journalists received nothing more than written reprimands for donating money to political candidates. The paper claimed that the light punishment was based on the fact that the reporters in question did not cover politics. After weeks of criticism, Olbermann left the network in January 2011, but it was never announced whether he was fired or resigned voluntarily.

In 2015, ABC News anchor George Stephanopoulos was criticized — but allowed to stay on the air — after it was learned that he donated $75,000 to the Clinton Global Initiative, an international foundation headed by former President Bill Clinton, for whom Stephanopoulos worked as a White House aide in the 1990s. Stephanopoulos defended the donation by emphasizing it was to the foundation and not to the 2016 presidential campaign of former First Lady Hillary Clinton, but critics said the close relationship between the foundation and presidential campaign made that point of little significance.

Stock market considerations. Business journalists, especially those who write stories that may affect a company's stock prices, are prohibited from investing in the stock market. Not only would writing stories that affect the stocks they owned present an obvious conflict of interest, but doing so might also result in charges of insider trading, a violation of a federal law called the Securities and Exchange Act of 1934.

Speaking and consulting fees. One of the most recent issues in the conflict-of-interest arena also involves the journalists' financial matters. In the 1990s and early 2000s, a series of well-publicized cases surfaced in which television commentators and nationally known newspaper columnists accepted large fees for speaking to national organizations such as political think tanks and industry associations they also covered in their role as journalists. Employers, as well as media critics, took notice of the trend and criticized it as one that compromises the integrity of the journalism profession and caused perceptual problems for a profession already in trouble. While most critics claimed they were confident that accepting speaking fees would not influence the reporters' news judgment, they were more concerned about public perception that journalists were for sale. In essence, the critics said, the issue was not what the situation was, but what it might look like.

ABC News reporter and weekend anchor Cokie Roberts was criticized in 1995 for accepting a $30,000 speaker fee from the Junior League of Greater Fort Lauderdale — an arrangement that was approved by network executives because it involved speaking to a nonprofit organization whose work was unlikely to be the subject of any future ABC News reports. What the executives did not know at the time was that the fee was actually paid by a private company responsible for the distribution of Toyota automobiles in the United States. That same year, the network was criticized for not scrutinizing the work of Sam Donaldson, who was allowed to research and produce stories about waste and fraud in the government's system of agricultural subsidies without disclosing the fact that he owned a sheep farm in New Mexico and received subsidies under that system.

A similar conflict occurs when journalists are paid for advising business owners on the operation of their businesses. One common example involves restaurant critics who receive consulting fees from restaurant owners seeking advice on the operation of their businesses, a practice that would be prohibited by most daily newspapers.

Likewise, reporters who appear on television and radio talk shows are not allowed to accept compensation for their appearances, although in most cases they may accept reimbursement for expenses related to travel to and from the studios. They are also cautioned not to reveal any information on the shows that may compromise ongoing investigations that the newspaper or television station is pursuing.

Abuse of position or name recognition. One form of conflict of interest that is seldom addressed in policy manuals is the problem of journalists who exploit their positions at the newspaper or television station or the name recognition of their employers. Although documented cases are rare, they are not unheard of; especially with younger, less experienced reporters who believe they are justified in using their positions for personal gain. They may not realize, however, that such conduct reflects poorly on them and their employers. Examples include food critics who visit restaurants without intending to write reviews, but identifying themselves in order to secure a preferred table, free meal, or other considerations; sportswriters who use their positions to secure free or discounted memberships at athletic clubs by implying they may write articles about the facilities; or consumer affairs reporters who visit retail stores and use their name recognition to solicit discounts or a higher level of customer service not available to other shoppers.

Moonlighting and double-dipping. Few newspapers and magazines allow their reporters to write articles for other publications. Editors may grant their reporters permission to do so, however, in cases in which the second publication is not a competitor and the author is identified as a staff writer for the first publication.

Examples include a sportswriter who is invited to write a "season preview" article for a college or professional sports team's media guide, or a travel writer invited to submit an article for the chamber of commerce's visitor guide. In both cases, the publications are not in direct competition with the writers' primary employers, and having the authors identified by their primary jobs is an opportunity to promote those publications. In some cases, articles that previously appeared in a daily newspaper may be reprinted in non-competing publications. If compensation is offered, however, it would go to the newspaper and not the individual journalists or photographers because they have already been paid for producing the articles or photos. Reporters and photographers would not be allowed to accept direct compensation, because in doing so they would be compensated twice for the same work, a practice known as **double-dipping.**

Moonlighting may be problematic even in cases in which journalists are not paid for their secondary roles. In 2002, a reporter for the *St. Petersburg Times* served as a volunteer "media relations consultant" for one of the community's largest Catholic churches. At first, the job consisted mostly of publicizing the church's non-controversial activities and fund-raisers. But when several female members of the church accused one of the priests of making sexual advances, the story became front-page news, and the reporter found herself with competing loyalties. As a consultant for the church, her duties included writing news releases about the case and preparing church officials for media interviews. In her role as a journalist, she did not cover the investigation itself, but worked near the reporters who did, and her editors became uncomfortable when the reporter found herself shifting back and forth between the two roles while "on company time." In hindsight, they determined that what she did had not violated the newspaper's conflict-of-interest policy, but she was admonished for not disclosing the potential conflict earlier, as well as for listing her work phone number at the *Times* as the "media contact" number for the church.

Cases in which journalists use their employers' resources may also be problematic. In 1996, for example, a daily newspaper in New Jersey fired one of its reporters after learning that he was using the newspaper's access to motor vehicle records to track down individuals as part of his side job as a private detective.

Getting too close to a story, or becoming part of it. Yet another conflict-of-interest issue is that of journalists who either intentionally or unintentionally get involved in news stories they are covering.

In 1989, more than 300,000 activists representing both sides of the abortion debate gathered in Washington, D.C. to await the U.S. Supreme Court's ruling in an abortion rights case. Among them was Linda Greenhouse, who covered the case and the abortion issue as a reporter for the *New York Times*. She wasn't the only journalist in the crowd. Dozens of others later admitted they had also taken part — some claiming to be acting as journalists simply seeking to cover the events close-up and others claiming to be acting as private citizens with no intent of writing about their experiences. But Greenhouse insisted she was capable of doing both at the same time, a claim that her editors at the *Times* found troubling. One of those editors was Max Frankel, who said that while *Times* reporters were not expected to be completely without political leanings or opinions, they "were not allowed to cover the White House while wearing a campaign button."

Greenhouse got off with only a reprimand and was allowed to continue covering the abortion issue and other cases reaching the Supreme Court. Her editors said the matter was closed, but that didn't spare Greenhouse from criticism by her peers. Her counterpart at the *Boston Globe*, who also covered the abortion issue but did so from a distance, wrote that Greenhouse made a "big mistake" by taking part in the public gathering and that the *Times* had made a "bigger mistake" by allowing her to continue on the Supreme Court beat.

A similar example was a 2004 case of two female reporters who had written a series of stories on gay issues for the *San Francisco Chronicle*. When the reporters announced their plans to legalize their relationship under California's new domestic partnership law, the newspaper's management prohibited them from covering gay issues in the future.

The don't-get-involved-in-the-story rule would not apply in cases in which reporters witnessed crimes being committed or encountered persons in dangerous situations. In those cases, reporters often close their notebooks and turn off their television cameras and take steps to report the crime or save people from tragedy. When serious crimes or a possible loss of human life is involved, even the strictest media ethicists agree that an individual's obligations as a human being outweigh his or her obligations to the journalism profession.

In 1998, for example, two reporters for a major daily newspaper prepared a multi-part series of stories about families living in poverty, emphasizing the effect the conditions had on children. The reporters observed bruises and other injuries on several children that led them to believe they were being abused by their parents or other family members. The reporters consulted their editor, who at first forbade them to report their suspicions to government agencies that investigated allegations of child abuse, saying their job was to "hold up a reflective mirror to society, not to function as social workers." When a local child welfare agency learned about the reporters' suspicions, she rejected the "reflective mirror" rationale and said the reporters were responsible for whatever harm came to the children in the future. The editor eventually changed his mind and allowed the journalists to report their suspicions.

In other cases, journalists get involved in news stories that do not involve life-and-death situations, and as a result, they create awkward situations and questions about the proper role of journalists. The philosophy of most newspaper publishers is that, "It is our job to witness and publish the news, not to participate in it." One example of a reporter becoming part of the story is the case of *Sports Illustrated* writer Michael Bamberger, which is detailed in Case Study 4-B.

On a related issue, many media organizations prohibit their employees from becoming involved in matters that have the potential to influence the news, regardless of how indirect that effect might be. In 2004, for example, the Associated Press announced that it would no longer allow the results of its college football polls to be used in computing rankings for the Bowl Championship Series (BCS), a system developed to determine which college football teams played for the national championship. The AP generates the poll based on the votes of sportswriters and sports broadcasters affiliated with the wire service. In announcing its decision, AP claimed that individual journalists should not be associated with decisions that were potentially controversial, and that separating itself from the BCS was necessary in order to protect its reputation and integrity. In addition, the AP claimed, many football fans might transfer their animosity for the BCS system to the AP.

Diversity as a Personnel Issue

The value of diversity in the American workplace is an important issue for American businesses in the 21st century. While just about any business would benefit to some degree by having a workforce that is diverse in terms of age, gender, race, and national origin, the idea is especially important for media organizations. If a newspaper, magazine, online news service, or television or radio station seeks to properly serve a wide variety of audiences, it should employ reporters and editors who can identify with those audiences and can be identified by them.

For example, media organizations with African American, Hispanic, or Asian reporters can do a better job of reporting on issues important to those groups than organizations staffed with reporters and editors who are mostly white. Employing female reporters and those older than the norm represent similar opportunities. While valuable for the print media, it is even more important in television, as audience members like to get their news from reporters and anchors "who look like them."

Although most journalists and members of their audiences believe that "diversity" is a new concept, it is not. As far back as the 1940s, the Hutchins Commission (see Chapter 3) listed as one of the ideals the media should aspire to the need to "provide a representative picture of the constituent groups in society." Although the terms "diversity" and "multiculturalism" were not applied to this concept until a half century later, it was the Hutchins Commission that first suggested the idea.

In 1968, a government-sponsored investigation called the Kerner Commission was charged with determining the root causes for racial strife in the U.S. Although it concluded that the racial divide in the country was too complex to be blamed on one factor, the commission did assign part of the responsibility to the news media, which it accused of over-covering negative stories about racial minorities and under-reporting positive stories. The study also found that the journalism business was running way behind other professional fields in recruiting, hiring, training, and promoting minority employees.

Beyond simply hiring more minority journalists, media organizations also need to do a better job of retaining them. A 2008 survey by the National Association of Black Journalists found that 68 percent of African American journalists become disillusioned early in their careers and begin to consider other employment fields. The most common reason given for that opinion was the lack of advancement opportunities with their current employers. *Newsday* reporter Herbert Lowe, commenting on the findings of the survey, wrote that "every day, black journalists are leaving the industry because they feel disrespected, unappreciated, undercompensated, underdeveloped, and uninspired."

Media critics believe the downturn in the national economy and declining market share for traditional forms of media have made the problem worse. According to a 2010 study, the number of African American journalists employed full-time had dropped 32 percent since 2001, while the number of white journalists has dropped only 21 percent.

Despite the obvious benefits of a diverse workforce to media organizations, the idea is not totally without resistance. Some television station managers object to affirmative action and other diversity programs, claiming that reporters and editors should be hired based on their job skills rather than demographic factors, and placing too much emphasis on the latter results in having to work with employees with marginal skills. To address those concerns, many journalism schools and national media organizations are developing college scholarships and other programs aimed at interesting more high school and college students from diverse backgrounds in pursuing careers in journalism and broadcasting.

While major daily newspapers and television stations and networks have made some progress in the area of newsroom diversity, the same cannot be said about their online counterparts.

In a 2011 column in *USA Today*, attorney and media critic Yolanda Young pointed out that much like traditional journalists of previous generations, today's online journalists and their editors tend to be largely white and male. She also reported that when the American Society of Newspaper Editors (ASNE) conducts its annual study of newsroom diversity, many online news operations decline to participate, meaning that the picture might be even worse than it appears.

While the majority of the diversity discussion concerns the people who gather and report the news, there is also concern about how minority groups are represented in entertainment programming. The National Association for the Advancement of Colored People (NAACP) has been at the forefront of the campaign for nearly a decade.

In many cases, an organization's attempts to show a diverse workforce are misleading and deceptive. In his 2003 book, *When the Game is on the Line*, sports attorney Rick Horrow recalls his experience as a consultant to a multi-national company specializing in golf course real estate and other sports-related ventures. He was asked to produce a client-recruitment brochure but told company officials the photographs should reflect the company's diverse workforce, unaware that all of the employees in upper management were middle-aged white men. When he told company leaders that such photographs would be ineffective in recruiting African American clients, they responded by finding a black man to put on a suit and tie and pose for the photograph. "His only connection to the company," Horrow wrote in disappointment, "was that he came by once a month to wash the windows."

The Problems of Plagiarism and Unlabeled Fiction

The phenomena of journalists stealing news stories from other sources — or creating fictional stories and presenting them as fact — was widespread in the early days of print journalism. In 1984, for example, journalist Alastair Reed admitted to a *Wall Street Journal* reporter that while working for *The New Yorker* earlier in his career, he often used composite characters and made up fictional settings and invented quotes in what were presented as nonfiction articles.

Such cases are rare in the modern era — at least that's what editors, publishers, and readers hope.

One such case took place in 1981, when the *New York Times* published a series of stories by Christopher Jones, a 24-year-old freelance writer who claimed he had spent several days visiting the training camps of the Khmer Rouge, a violent band of terrorists creating post-war havoc in Thailand, Cambodia, and Vietnam. His deception was eventually uncovered when government officials in those countries reported to *Times* editors that Jones was describing places that did not exist and was quoting government officials whom no one could remember. It was later discovered that Jones had never been to Southeast Asia and that much of the material for the stories was taken from a little-known novel published in 1930.

That same year, *Washington Post* reporter Janet Cooke won a Pulitzer Prize for her emotionally gripping story about Jimmy, an 8-year-old heroin addict growing up in an economically depressed neighborhood near downtown Washington, D.C. Cooke's story shocked many of the newspaper's readers, while city officials were angered. The mayor ordered police officers to canvass the city in order to locate the child, and when that failed, the police chief threatened to have Cooke and her editors subpoenaed if they did not help locate him.

The *Post* refused to cooperate, but eventually the editors became suspicious themselves and began their own investigation. Cooke simply blamed the inability to locate Jimmy on the likelihood that he and his mother had moved.

Despite their concern for the validity of the story, editors allowed it to be entered in the annual Pulitzer Prize competition, in which it won first place for investigative journalism. That turned out to be Cooke's undoing, as the biographical sketch that accompanied the entry also turned out to be largely fictional. Based on information taken from Cooke's own employment application, the sketch claimed that Cooke had a degree from Vassar (when she had actually attended a less prestigious university), had won six journalism awards at her previous newspaper (false), and was fluent in several foreign languages (she wasn't). When the exaggerations in the sketch were exposed, Cooke also admitted the "creativity" she used in the "Jimmy" story, but insisted he was a composite character of several children she had met and that her descriptions of his life were common for children living in that setting. Unconvinced, the *Post* fired Cooke, returned the Pulitzer, and apologized to its readers.

In 1998, *The New Republic* fired associate editor Stephen Glass after an internal investigation revealed he had fabricated all or parts of 27 stories he had written for the magazine over a three-year period.

Shortly after Glass was fired from the *New Republic*, the *Boston Globe* fired columnists Patricia Smith and Mike Barnacle after they admitted making up people, quotes, and events in their columns.

The Associated Press fired a reporter who fictionalized a story about drag-racers in California who reached speeds up to 200 mph on the state's freeway system. The reporter claimed first-hand knowledge of the practice because the dragsters allowed her to ride along with them. The stories quoted California Highway Patrol officers who said they had given up on trying to stop the dragsters because their vehicles could not keep up with them, but those officers later denied having spoken to her. The reporter was fired after her editors discovered that not only had she not been directly involved in the races, she did not have direct knowledge of them and had not interviewed anyone who did — she merely lifted the details from a local tourism magazine.

In 2003, the *New York Times* fired reporter Jayson Blair for similar practices, but the firings did not end there. The newspaper's parent company also fired two senior editors who supervised Blair for not being more suspicious of his work even after several of his stories raised suspicions. In its public apology, the *Times* called the Blair scandal "a low point in the 152-year history of the newspaper."

In 2006, American author Greg Mortenson published *Three Cups of Tea*, a book chronicling his work in building schools and engaging in other philanthropic activities in Pakistan and Afghanistan. Claiming to donate all of the proceeds from the book to charities in those countries, Mortenson saw his book become a best-seller within weeks of its release, with sales exceeding 3 million copies.

The following year, news reports indicated that one of the primary beneficiaries of the book, a charity called the Central Asia Institute, was accused of mismanaging its funds, including those generated by the book. Further investigation revealed that CAI funneled much of its donations into supporting Mortenson's book tours. Mortenson, in turn, greatly exaggerated the number of schools that he and the CAI claimed to have built and fabricated a story about being held prisoner by the Taliban during the late 1990s.

The deception came to the attention of American audiences on an April 2011 episode of the CBS newsmagazine, *60 Minutes*. Within weeks, two members of Congress launched an investigation into Mortenson's financial affairs and indicated they might organize a class-action lawsuit aimed at recovering some of Americans' donations to the CAI that were prompted by Mortenson's book.

The Debate Over Immersion Journalism

As the term indicates, **immersion journalism** is a form of newsgathering in which the researcher operates within an organization or among the individuals being researched; much like an undercover law enforcement officer would do to investigate possible crime. This goes beyond the simple "sting operations" that journalists occasionally conduct to investigate alleged misconduct by shady businesses or corrupt politicians. The two significant differences are that in immersion journalism, the research often takes place over the course of weeks or months, whereas sting operations are typically short-term operations (the ethical considerations of misrepresentation are discussed in Chapter 5). The end products of immersion journalism are often books rather than articles. The other significant difference is that while sting operations are typically aimed at uncovering illegal or unethical behavior, a journalist practicing the immersion method begins with an open mind, not knowing what he or she will learn, and often produces a work that is positive or neutral in its tone.

Advocates of immersion journalism claim this research methodology allows authors to present a realistic picture of an organization or group without being limited by the traditional need for "objectivity" and without their work being compromised by what social science researchers call the **Hawthorne Effect** — the tendency of research subjects to act differently if they know their behavior is being observed and/or recorded. Critics of the technique, who sometimes call it "stunt journalism," contend that by using such methods, researchers are just "playing tourist" in the lives (and sometimes tragedies) of other people.

The technique of immersion journalism can be traced back to Upton Sinclair, who in 1904 spent seven weeks working in a meat-packing plant to research his expose of the industry's labor practices. His award-winning book, *The Jungle,* was published in 1906 and resulted in massive changes to federal labor laws and food safety rules.

In 1963, sportswriter George Plimpton pretended to be a professional quarterback and participated in summer training camp and part of the regular season with the Detroit Lions in order to research his book, *Paper Lion,* which focused on the behind-the-scenes lives of professional football players. The book was made into a 1968 movie of the same title, with Alan Alda portraying Plimpton. Later in his career, Plimpton played goalie for the Boston Bruins while researching a book about professional hockey and spent several weeks attempting to play professional golf while researching a book about that sport.

A more recent example of immersion journalism is the work of Thomas French, a police-beat reporter for the *St. Petersburg Times* and author of several true crime books. Today, he is retired from full-time reporting and teaches journalism at Indiana University while still writing occasional newspaper columns and features. He is best known for his book, *South of Heaven: High School at the End of the Twentieth Century*. His research began in the late 1980s when he obtained permission of school administrators and spent a year blending in with a class of high school seniors. While not pretending to be one of them, he gained their confidence and was able to attend classes, club meetings, sporting events, and social activities. While writing a series of weekly columns based on his experiences, he changed or omitted names and created composite characters while documenting issues such as teenage sex, drug and alcohol abuse, peer pressure, violence, and suicide. When the school year was complete, his newspaper gave him additional time off to expand his newspaper stories into the book, which was published in 1993.

Other recent practitioners of immersion journalism include H.G. Bissinger, author of *Friday Night Lights*, a story of high school football in Texas; and Barbara Ehrenreich, author of *Nickel and Dimed* and *Bait and Switch.*

To research his 1990 book, *Friday Night Lights*, Bissinger, at the time a sportswriter for the *Philadelphia Inquirer*, spent the entire 1988 high school football season traveling with and observing the practices and private lives of the Permian High School team in Odessa, Texas. In 2002, the book was named the fourth-best nonfiction sports book of all time by *Sports Illustrated*. In 2004, it served as the basis for a movie of the same title, and from 2006 to 2011, it was the basis for a popular NBC television series.

To research *Nickel and Dimed*, Ehrenreich spent three months working in a number of low-wage jobs in the retail and food-service businesses to document the long hours, low pay, and lack of respect that she and her peers received from supervisors and customers. Some observers considered the book, published in 2001, a thinly disguised criticism of the economic policies of new President George W. Bush and other conservative politicians. Many literary critics disagreed, praising her work and referring to her as a "modern-day Nellie Bly."* To research *Bait and Switch*, Ehrenreich moved up a few notches on the economic ladder and spent almost a year pretending to be an out-of-work female executive and touring the country meeting with employment counselors and attending job fairs and other networking events. Her point was to not only document the frustrations that the unemployed face during an economic downturn, but also the issue of employment discrimination affecting older women. The book was published in 2005.

Perhaps the most unusual example of immersion journalism is Norah Vincent, a lesbian journalist who spent 18 months disguised as a man. She wore men's clothes, cropped her hair short, and each day applied make-up to her face intended to create the appearance of razor stubble. She even wore a tight-fitting bra to flatten her chest and a jock strap with what she called a "generous amount of padding." She also underwent months of training with a professional voice coach in order to change the pitch of her voice.

Calling herself "Ned Vincent," she worked in a number of occupations customarily male-dominated, such as construction and home repair. She joined her male co-workers in after-work socializing at bars and strip clubs, and even joined an all-male bowling league. "Many of the guys thought I was gay, but none of them suspected I was a woman," she said in media interviews. Her goal, as she explained in her 2006 book, *Self-Made Man*, was not to undercover any discriminatory behavior or other wrongdoing, but just "to see what life was like on the other side of the gender divide."

After finishing that work, Vincent spent almost a year recreating Bly's mental health project, pretending to be a mental patient being bounced around among agencies and clinics, and for part of the time being confined to a mental hospital. She documented her experiences in her 2009 book, *Voluntary Madness: My Year Lost and Found in the Loony Bin*.

---

*The story of reporter Nellie Bly is discussed in more detail in Chapter 5.

For Discussion

Case Study 4-A   **A Case of Drunk Driving**

In 2003, Chris Thomas, a popular and easily recognized sports director at WFLA-TV in Tampa, Florida, was arrested for drunk driving. Even before his courtroom appearance, he admitted to station management that he was guilty and apologized on the air for embarrassing the station and "letting down his fans." Letters and phone calls supporting Thomas poured into the station, yet a few days later an executive with the station's parent company in Richmond, Virginia ordered that Thomas be fired. The company claimed that as a representative of the station and as a public figure and "opinion leader" in the community, Thomas had an obligation to conduct himself in an appropriate manner and not engage in such risky behavior. Local radio stations jumped on the story and ridiculed Thomas, not only because of the seriousness of the drunk driving charge, but because the incident took place in a part of town known for drug-dealing and prostitution. "Everyone knows that if you go into that part of town late at night, you're looking for one of two things," one early morning disc jockey said.

- Do you agree with the company's decision and how it justified firing Thomas? Is a television personality entitled to make mistakes and learn from them like everyone else?

- Does that fact that it was Thomas' first offense (as opposed to being a habitual drunk driver) change your opinion?

- Were local radio stations justified in ridiculing Thomas? According to libel law, public figures must accept a certain level of public criticism and ridicule as an aspect of their fame, but did the disc jockey cross the line with the comments above?

Case Study 4-B   Bamberger Blows the Whistle

The issue of journalists affecting the outcome of events they were assigned to cover was raised in October 2005 when *Sports Illustrated* reporter Michael Bamberger was covering a women's professional golf tournament in Palm Desert, California. The star attraction at the tournament was Michelle Wie, a talented 16-year-old playing in her first professional event after an impressive amateur career. Bamberger was on the course and following Wie's group during Saturday's third round when he witnessed what he thought was a rules violation. During Wie's post-round news conference, Bamberger asked her about the incident, but she provided what reporters described as a "vague" answer.

On Sunday afternoon — the final day of the tournament — Bamberger approached a tournament administrator and described the incident. A rules official then questioned Wie and took her and her caddie back to the place on the course where the incident had taken place the day before. After watching a videotape of the incident, the official ruled that Wie had indeed violated the rules and disqualified her from the tournament, which cost her a fourth-place check for $53,126.

For decades, golf has been heralded as a "game of honor" in which the players police themselves. At the professional level, one of the guiding principles is that golfers, who typically play in groups of two or three, are responsible for monitoring each other and ensuring a fair competition for the entire field. There are rules officials at every event, but not enough to assign one to each group, so golfers often consult with other players in their group if there is a rules question.

In the 1990s, however, advances in technology allowed television coverage of professional tournaments to become more "close up," and fans watching a telecast from home would often call the tournament office to report alleged violations. In several cases, players were either penalized or disqualified from tournaments as a result of fans reporting rules violations, raising the issue of the role of the television networks and fans in the administration of a competition.

In the Bamberger case, many sports journalists, media ethicists, and golf fans complained that a reporter covering the event should be limited to just that — covering the event — and should not become involved in the administration of the rules. Tournament officials and fans defending Bamberger contended "rules are rules" and that anyone — fan, journalist, or other individual — who witnessed a possible violation should bring it to the attention of tournament officials. Others questioned why Bamberger waited for more than more than 24 hours after witnessing the incident to report it to tournament officials. Still others questioned his motives and accused him of reporting the incident simply to earn notoriety as the person who cost Wie her first professional paycheck.

As a result of the incident, Internet bulletin boards and sports talk shows on television and radio featured lengthy discussions of the topic, with commentator and audience opinions equally divided. While many fans were supportive of Bamberger — a respected golf journalist and author of several books on the sport — many others wrote letters of complaint to *Sports Illustrated,* with some readers even canceling their subscriptions.

- As an abstract concept, do you agree with the general ethical principle that says that journalists should cover the story and not become part of the story (i.e., covering the parade, not marching in the parade)?

- Regarding the specifics of this case, which side do you take on the incident above — that Bamberger did the right thing by reporting the incident, or that his actions were too much a departure from his assigned role?

- When a journalist puts away his or her notebook or television camera in order to help a person in danger — such as cases in which reporters rescue people from a burning building, prevent them from drowning in a river, or talk a person out of suicide — even the strictest journalism ethicists would agree they are acting properly. But the Bamberger-Wie scenario is on the opposite extreme, as no lives were in danger. How does that affect your interpretation of the "don't-get-involved-in-the-story" rule?

- If you were responsible for drafting a formal policy on such matters for the employees of your newspaper or television station, where would your policy draw the line?

Case Study 4-C   **The Unlikely Disciple**

Early in 2007, a Brown University English major and student journalist employed the immersion technique as he spent spring semester as a transfer student at Liberty University, a Christian institution founded by evangelist Jerry Falwell. Kevin Roose first encountered the university while visiting the campus as part of his job as a research assistant for a more established author. Roose had never written anything longer than a traditional college term paper or his weekly column in Brown's student newspaper, but his semester at Liberty gave him enough material for a 324-page book that took nearly two years to write.

Titled *The Unlikely Disciple: A Sinner's Semester at America's Holiest University*, the 2009 work chronicles Roose's attempt to "blend in" at the ultra-conservative university, despite his own upbringing in a liberal, non-religious family. Roose's experience at Liberty included taking classes, attending church, singing in the school choir, and living in an on-campus dormitory with Christian roommates who never questioned why he was there and never suspected that he was working undercover. But his hardest adjustment was adherence to the university's 46-page code of student conduct, which barred alcohol, tobacco, dancing, cursing, R-rated movies, and hugging another student for more than three seconds. Ironically, Roose pointed out, it was his God-fearing roommates who broke the rules far more often than he did.

From the beginning, Roose decided that he would be as honest as possible. "I wasn't eager to sneak around like a spy, and I didn't want the mental burden of juggling a double identity, so I decided to stick with my guns: regular old Kevin Roose . . . no alias, no faked documents, no lies about my past," he wrote. "If people asked, I'd tell them that I came to Liberty from Brown, and if they asked why, I'd say, 'I wanted to see what a Christian college was like.' " Roose added that his second decision was to take no cheap shots. "If I went to Liberty, I would go with an open mind, not to mock Liberty students or the evangelical world in toto."

In order to prepare for the semester, Roose spent three days with a childhood friend who had since moved to another state but agreed to "coach" him on the Christian life, including a crash course in biblical characters and important verses from scripture. "My goal was to see the real, unfiltered picture of life at Liberty University," Roose said in a National Public Radio interview, admitting that he bent some rules of journalism ethics by misrepresenting himself. "It (the deception) did allow me to get a more accurate — and actually a fairer picture of — what life at Liberty was like."

He admits that he may have taken the acting job a bit too far, walking around campus his first week saying "Glory be" and "Mercy" whenever he had the opportunity. "I found out that Liberty students don't talk like that," he said in the radio interview.

- Did Roose violate any important journalistic principles in carrying out his deception?

- Did the fact that Roose was a student journalist affect how you evaluated this case? Or the fact that he was writing a book instead of a newspaper or magazine article?

- How do you evaluate Roose's deception in light of the three-part test described in Chapter 5 (p. 144)?

- If you had been Roose's roommate that semester, how would you react to his deception after you learned about it?

Discussion Problem 4-A   **Plugging the Zoo**

You've watched the same television news program for several years, and for most of that time the station has employed the same meteorologist. During almost every weather segment, he makes comments such as "tomorrow will be a nice day to visit the Willoughby Zoo" or "tomorrow afternoon it looks like rain, so if you were planning to go to the Willoughby Zoo, you should plan to go in the morning."

You send an email to the station manager to indicate your annoyance at the constant references to the zoo. The station manager responds by explaining that the meteorologist sits on the board of trustees at the zoo and is simply trying to help out.

1. Because the zoo is a nonprofit organization and the meteorologist does not profit from its success or failure, is there a conflict of interest in this matter?

2. Should the meteorologist be obligated to disclose his relationship with the zoo in order to continue to make such comments?

3. Are there any provisions in organizational codes of ethics that apply here?

Discussion Problem 4-B   **The Award-Winning
                                               Environmental Reporter**

You're editor of a mid-size daily newspaper, and your star environmental reporter covers a number of local and national environmental issues, including the work of local advocacy groups. Recently, without your knowledge, the reporter attended the annual awards banquet of one of the groups and was presented an award for his "outstanding reporting on environmental issues." The award included a plaque and check for $1,000.

As a life-long hard news journalist, you're not comfortable with the situation. You check the newspaper's policy manual and find nothing regarding such conflicts. So you check with your boss, the newspaper's publisher, who is also not comfortable with the situation but leaves it up to you to decide how to handle it.

1. Which of the following actions do you take?

   a. Allow the reporter to keep both the plaque and cash award and continue reporting on the work of that organization.

   b. Require him to return both the plaque and the cash award.

   c. Require him to return the cash prize but allow him to keep the plaque.

   d. Require that he no longer cover the group's activities as part of his work.

   e. Some combination of b, c, and d.

2. To prevent such dilemmas in the future, the publisher asks you to draft a policy regarding such dilemmas. Do so in two or three sentences.

Discussion Questions

401. After reading the highlights of the SPJ, ASNE, and RTDNA Codes of Ethics at the beginning of this chapter, find provisions within those codes could easily be applied, and find at least one provision of the codes that you believe would be difficult to apply.

402. Re-read the section titled "Conflicts of Interest" under "Current Issues and Controversies." Considering the examples provided (such as personal or business relationships, organizational memberships, and running for public office), do you think it is unfair to expect journalists to forgo some of the same social and business opportunities enjoyed by individuals not working in the media? Or do you believe that journalists should be held to a higher standard and should therefore accept such limitations as "part of the job"?

Notes

85   **"It's striking how often":** Howard Kurtz, *The Media Circus: The Trouble With America's Newspapers.* New York: Random House, 1994, p. 126.

86   **"speaking fee was an unfortunate coincidence":** Kurtz, p. 127.

87   **"a serious lapse in judgment":** Ron Smith, *Groping for Ethics in Journalism.* Ames, IA: Wiley-Blackwell, 2003, p. 371.

88   **"She is so far in the tank," "Gwen Ifill is a highly respected professional,"** and **"acquitted herself well":** "Questions Raised About Moderator's Impartiality." Associated Press report, October 1, 2008.

88   **"or marching at a rally":** "Lines Blur as Journalism Heads Back to the Future." *USA Today,* November 10, 2010, p. 8-A.

88   **made that point of little significance:** Roger Yu, "Anchor Blasted for Clinton Donation." *USA Today,* May 15, 2015, p. 2-B.

90   **"while wearing a campaign button"** and **to continue on the Supreme Court beat:** Smith, p. 366.

92   **"undercompensated, underdeveloped, and uninspired":** Smith, p. 110.

93   **"to wash the windows":** Rick Horrow, *When the Game is on the Line.* Cambridge, MA: Perseus Publishing, 2003, p. 77.

93   **presented as nonfiction articles:** Jeffrey Olen, *Ethics in Journalism.* Englewood Cliffs, NJ: Prentice Hall, 1988, p. 82.

94   **"a low point in the 152-year history of the newspaper":** Bernard Goldberg, *Arrogance: Rescuing American from the Media Elite.* New York: Grand Central Publishing, p. 54.

96   **"Many of the guys thought I was gay"** and **"the other side of the gender divide":** "Self-Made Man." ABCNews.com, January 20, 2006.

100   **"I wanted to see what a Christian college was like"** and **"Liberty students or the evangelical world in toto":** Kevin Roose, *The Unlikely Disciple: A Sinner's Semester at America's Holiest University.* New York: Grand Central Publishing, 2009, p. 11.

100   **"what life at Liberty was like"** and **"Liberty students don't talk like that":** "Undercover at an Evangelical University." NPR.org, accessed May 30, 2009.

CHAPTER 5

Journalism, Broadcasting, and Entertainment: Policy Issues

Background

- A newspaper sends a reporter to a local health clinic with a reputation for over-prescribing dangerous drugs and being sloppy with diagnoses in order to move patients through the clinic as quickly as possible. The reporter claims to be a newcomer to the community with an expired prescription for pain-killers. Not disclosing that she is a reporter, the woman asks the doctor to write a new prescription, without a complete examination, to learn if the clinic's reputation as a "pill mill" is accurate.

- A photographer is assigned to cover a construction accident at a downtown office building. After being denied access to the site by law enforcement officials, the photographer goes to an office building across the street, takes the elevator to the ninth floor, and finds a conference room with a window overlooking the construction site and takes his photographs from there.

- While searching through real estate records at the county courthouse, a reporter stumbles across the divorce filing involving the mayor and his wife. He passes the information along to another reporter who covers the mayor's office so she can develop a story on the couple's pending divorce.

- A weekly entertainment magazine publishes an ad announcing that it has just hired two new restaurant reviewers. The ad encourages restaurants in town to send sandwich platters to the magazine's offices at lunchtime and to host the staff's dinner meetings — all at no charge to the magazine. In return, the magazine promises to write positive reviews of those restaurants.

- A state university hires a new football coach, who moves to town with his wife and children. The couple buys a multi-million dollar home in an upscale community. Using real estate records open to the public, the local newspaper publishes a story that lists the address of the new home, the number of bedrooms and bathrooms, the size of the backyard swimming pool, the square footage of the home, and the purchase price. It also lists the name of the previous owner and how much he paid for the house five years earlier.

The Society of Professional Journalists Code of Ethics addresses a number of issues related to policy. In the section titled "Seek Truth and Report It," the code requires that journalists "distinguish between advocacy and news reporting; analysis and commentary should be labeled and not misrepresent fact or context."

In the section titled "Minimize Harm," the code requires that journalists:

- show compassion for those who may be affected adversely by news coverage and use special sensitivity when dealing with children and inexperienced sources or subjects;

- be sensitive when seeking or using interviews or photographs of those affected by tragedy or grief;

- recognize that gathering and reporting information may cause harm or discomfort; pursuit of the news is not a license for arrogance;

- show good taste; avoid pandering to lurid curiosity;

- be cautious about identifying juvenile suspects or victims of sex crimes.

In the section titled "Be Accountable," the code requires journalists to:

- clarify and explain news coverage and invite dialogue with the public over journalistic conduct;

- encourage the public to voice grievances against the news media;

- admit mistakes and correct them promptly;

- expose unethical practices of journalists and news organizations;

- abide by the same high standards to which they hold others.

The American Society of Newspaper Editors Statement of Principles explains that "good faith with the reader is the foundation of good journalism" and that "every effort must be made to assure that the news content is accurate, free from bias and in context, and that all sides are presented fairly."

The ASNE statement provides that journalists "must be vigilant against all who would exploit the press for selfish purposes." The statement also requires that journalists provide the publicly accused the earliest opportunity to respond, exercise caution when promising confidentiality to any source, and use confidential sources only in the rarest circumstances.

The Radio Television Digital News Association Code of Broadcast News Ethics requires that broadcasters:

- guard against using audio or video material in a way that deceives the audience;

- identify people by race, creed, nationality, or prior status only when it is relevant;

- promptly acknowledge and correct errors;

- respect the dignity, privacy, and well-being of people with whom they deal;

- recognize the need to protect confidential sources and promise confidentiality only with the intention of keeping that promise;

- strive to conduct themselves in a manner that protects them from conflicts of interest, real or perceived, and decline gifts or favors which would influence or appear to influence their judgments.

The SPJ Code of Ethics and ASNE Statement of Principles are provided in their entirety in Appendix A. The RTDNA code is currently under revision and was not available at the time this book was published. It is expected to be on the organization's website in late fall 2015 (www.rtdna.org).

Current Issues and Controversies

The Private Lives of Public People

The tension between the media's newsgathering function and the desire of government agencies, businesses, nonprofit organizations, and individuals to keep secrets has created a number of ethical challenges for the print and broadcast media. But the erosion of privacy is a fact of life in modern America, where the media are becoming increasingly more aggressive in their pursuit of news. Government agencies cannot keep secrets as long as they would like, businesses and nonprofit organizations have their activities scrutinized, and individuals find their own privacy eroding. Privacy is becoming more difficult to maintain in all areas of American life, and a more aggressive media and advances in technology share the blame.

Since the early days of the profession, journalists and editors have faced the challenge of balancing the privacy rights of people in the news with the public's right to know what is happening in their communities and around the nation. One newspaper publisher, in speaking to a group of journalism students, told them, "I know how to put out a good newspaper. I also know how to avoid hurting people. But I don't know how to do both at the same time, and neither do any of the editors or reporters who work for me."

The first factor that media organizations consider is whether the person in question is a public official, public figure, or private figure. In legal matters, the courts typically apply the label of "public official" to those individuals who are elected or appointed to a position in federal, state, or local government. A broader category called "public figure" includes not only public officials, but also show business personalities and well-known professional and amateur athletes. Some individuals become "limited public figures" as a result of being in the public spotlight on a short-term or limited basis. The label of "private person" is applied to everyone else. While these labels are used mainly in legal cases such as those involving libel and invasions of privacy, journalists often use those same categories in making ethical decisions about what aspects of a person's life should and should not be part of news stories.

The same issues are involved with photographs and video, which can have a significant impact on newspaper readers and television viewers. The lines dividing good and bad taste are not always easy to determine, and the size and diversity of the audience results in a variety of opinions and reactions — what one person considers a dramatic presentation of the news may be seen by another as unnecessary sensationalism. Photographers and videographers, as well as the editors they report to, must balance the privacy of individuals in the news with the journalistic need to provide the audience with images that illustrate news stories in a meaningful way.

Public officials and other public figures are often the subject of discussion when it comes to both their family lives and marital indiscretions — sometimes based on facts, sometimes merely on rumor and speculation. But whether such matters should be subject of news stories is a popular topic for debate within the journalism profession and society in general.

Recent revelations have found, for example, that the issue of American presidents having extramarital affairs is nearly as old the country itself. But until the late 20th century, the media seldom learned about such behavior, and when they did, they did not report it. Their decision not to report was based on (1) their belief that the public did not care, (2) their belief that a president's personal conduct did not affect his performance in office, or (3) their reluctance to alienate the president and members of his administration and thereby lose access in the future.

President John F. Kennedy was the last president to be spared such media scrutiny. During Kennedy's 34 months in office, rumors of his extramarital affairs circulated throughout Washington social circles, but reporters either dismissed them as politically motivated or simply unsubstantiated gossip. Years after Kennedy's death, however, many of those rumors were found to be based largely on truth.

Two decades later, democratic presidential candidate Gary Hart was rumored to be having multiple extramarital affairs while serving as a U.S. senator representing Colorado and continuing such behavior during his 1988 campaign for the White House. He responded to the rumors by challenging reporters and photographers to follow him 24 hours a day, including time spent between campaign events. Journalists did just that, and unfortunately for Hart, they captured photographs of him and girlfriend Donna Rice on a rented yacht appropriately named *Monkey Business*. Hart eventually dropped out of the presidential race.

Then came Bill Clinton. The press began by investigating rumors that Clinton had numerous affairs while serving as governor of Arkansas prior to running for president. Those news stories began during the 1992 presidential campaign and continued through Clinton's first term in the White House. During his second term, as federal prosecutors looked into a failed real estate venture in which Clinton was involved a decade earlier, more news came to light about Clinton's fling with White House intern Monica Lewinsky — an affair that eventually led to the president's impeachment and acquittal by the U.S. Senate.

When these cases are discussed in journalistic circles, the central questions that often emerge are (1) To what extent does the personal conduct of a president (or any other elected official) affect his or her job? (2) If it does not affect the individual's job, is it any of the public's business?

In response to those questions, many observers contend that a public official's private life has no effect on his or her performance in office. But critics suggest that in the case of presidents, their reckless sexual behavior makes them vulnerable to blackmail by political opponents and foreign governments. If nothing else, they believe, such behavior does reveal information about the individual's judgment and values — something that voters have a right to know about.

While it is common to debate the privacy rights of public figures, it is also common to debate the rights of their children. One factor that is often part of the debate is the age of the children who become central figures in a news story; another is the degree to which the children are part of their parents' public lives or political campaigns.

In 2001, the adult son of the mayor of Wilmington, Delaware was arrested and charged with sexual assault. Editors decided to treat the story the same as it would any other — by identifying the suspect by name. The story did not reveal that his father was the mayor, based on the precedent of not identifying the parents of any other criminal suspects unless it was germane to the story. It is not known if the editors based their decision on the veil of ignorance — making decisions without regard of the identity of those involved (see p. 37) — but the result was the same.

While few media outlets would decline to publish or broadcast a crime story because of the suspect's family connections, some might give the family relationship more emphasis, especially in cases in which irony or hypocrisy was involved. In the early 1980s, for example, the son of an assistant coach with a National Football League team was arrested and charged with drunk driving. The young man was driving west in the eastbound lane of an interstate highway, and the crash killed two passengers in the other car. Local and national media emphasized the identity of the father because he frequently visited high schools to speak to students about the dangers of alcohol and drug abuse.

In 2002, the daughter of Florida Governor Jeb Bush (and niece of President George W. Bush) was arrested and charged with prescription fraud after attempting to help a friend obtain Xanax, a powerful anti-anxiety medication that is highly addictive and often abused. Noelle Bush had previously spent time in an Atlanta drug rehabilitation center, a fact that many Florida journalists were aware of but did not report out of respect for her privacy and because she, unlike her father and uncle, had not become a public figure voluntarily.

After her arrest, however, the media changed its attitude toward the privacy aspect and decided to cover her arrest and prosecution because of the hypocrisy involved. She had pleaded guilty to the charges, but under Florida law was allowed to enter yet another rehabilitation program in order to avoid prison time. The media pointed out that as a candidate for governor and after taking office, Jeb Bush had spoken out against spending government money for drug treatment programs and suggested that tougher criminal penalties were the answer for the state's drug problem. The irony, of course, was that the daughter was benefiting from one of the programs that the father had opposed.

During the 2008 presidential election campaign, journalists covering the republican ticket of Senator John McCain and Alaska Governor Sarah Palin were faced with a similar predicament when it was revealed that Palin's unmarried teenage daughter was pregnant. The McCain-Palin campaign announced the pregnancy shortly before the media was expected to report it. Media critics pointed out that it was appropriate to emphasize the daughter's unmarried and pregnant condition because as governor, her mother had advocated abstinence as a solution to the problem of teenage pregnancy in her home state. One observer quick to point out the hypocrisy was radio talk show host Roland Martin, who quipped that as governor, Sarah Palin had supported abstinence-only while opposing sex education in schools, even though "abstinence-only did not work in her own household."

In his 1994 book, *The Media Circus*, media critic Howard Kurtz wrote that "People who run for office give up their expectation of privacy. If they don't want their dirty laundry aired, they should probably choose a different profession. Besides, readers are more sophisticated than some editors believe. Most people can judge for themselves whether salacious allegations are germane or garbage."

The Private Lives of Private People

Privacy issues are not limited to public figures. In dealing with private figures, media organizations apply a different set of standards and are generally reluctant to reveal private information unless it is germane to the story. Section 5 of the SPJ code, titled "Fair Play," suggests that "journalists at all times will show respect for the dignity, privacy rights, and well-being of people encountered in the course of gathering and presenting the news."

Many states have media privacy laws that provide private individuals with legal recourse if they believe their privacy has been compromised by print or broadcast journalists. Although state laws vary in both thoroughness and terminology, most provide protection in four areas:

False light. The presentation of a person in a news story or other medium in a manner that may not be inaccurate per se, but is exaggerated or misleading. It is different from libel because instead of claiming financial loss or serious damage to reputation, plaintiffs base their claims on embarrassment or humiliation — damage that is less tangible, yet in the eyes of plaintiffs, easier to claim.

Examples of false light include the exaggeration of a person's financial condition or their inclusion in a photograph that is published in a context different from that in which it was taken.

Private facts. These cases deal with the disclosure of truthful information that is embarrassing to the individual involved and not considered to be a matter of public interest. Examples including details of a person's mental or physical health, family relationships, sexual behavior or orientation, victimization of a violent or sexual crime, financial matters, or academic records. When they are the target of a private facts lawsuit, media organizations defend themselves by claiming the information was newsworthy (necessary for audience understanding of the story), the person revealed the information voluntarily, or the information was already publicly known.

Appropriation. The use of a person's photograph, likeness, or voice for advertising or promotional purposes without permission. This is more of a problem for advertising and public relations professionals than journalists.

Intrusion. The invasion of an individual's privacy by physical means (trespassing) or through unlawful video or audio recording. Examples are included in the section titled "Hidden Cameras, Deception, and Misrepresentation."

While the terms above are legal concepts, they are important in an ethical context as well. In many cases, individuals may have ethical claims against media organizations long before they have legal claims, and those ethical claims fall into the same four categories.

The decision on whether or not to publish photographs showing private people at times of stress — usually when they or family members have been victims of a crime or other tragedy — is among the most difficult decisions media managers must make. Here's a typical scenario: A young child is playing in the basement of his home when he finds an abandoned refrigerator. Attempting to hide from his playmates, he crawls inside, and unable to force the door open from the inside, he suffocates. When the boy's lifeless body is discovered, his mother calls paramedics, who place the body on a stretcher and take it out the front door. The mother is standing on her front porch screaming as a newspaper photographer captures the images from the street.

That night at the newspaper office, editors face a dilemma. Do they (a) publish the photographs showing the distraught mother, (b) publish less dramatic photos that preserve the woman's privacy (such as one showing only the ambulance and front of the home, but not the mother or the stretcher), or (c) publish no photos at all?

An editor aiming for maximum impact would choose "a," perhaps based on the desire to illustrate the drama of the story. An editor choosing to respect the privacy of the family would likely choose "c," even if it meant a less dramatic presentation of the story. An editor following Aristotle's Golden Mean — the search for the mid-point between the two extremes — would likely choose "b."

When this hypothetical scenario is presented to reporters and editors at journalism conferences, those working in smaller communities tend to choose "c" because of the sensitivity of their readers. Applying a process-oriented way of decision-making, they believe the need to protect the family's privacy takes priority over the news value involved.

Most serving larger communities tend to choose "a" based on their belief that publishing the most dramatic photographs would best illustrate the tragedy of the situation and perhaps save lives by alerting parents to the dangers of leaving abandoned refrigerators where children may find them. Applying a results-oriented way of thinking in this case — the "ends-justify-the-means" — the editors are claiming that the impact of the story might not have been as strong without the image of the distraught mother.

Dealing with Sexual Assault Victims

One of the most common applications of privacy theory to private individuals occurs when the individual has been the victim or alleged victim of a crime. Prior to 1975, most states had laws prohibiting the media from publishing or broadcasting the names of sexual assault victims, and in some cases, victims of all crimes. Because of a 1975 Supreme Court ruling, however, those laws were declared unconstitutional on the grounds that it was not appropriate to punish media organizations for reporting truthful information. Many of those state laws prohibiting the identification of sexual assault victims remain on the books, but are rarely enforced because of the Supreme Court ruling. The ruling established a three-part test that became known as the **Cox Doctrine**; it allows the media to report names of sexual assault victims provided the information was truthful, part of a public record, and legally obtained.

Despite the Cox Doctrine, most media organizations have voluntarily adopted ethical policies prohibiting the identification of victims of sexual assault. Some also apply that policy to victims of domestic violence. Those situations are complicated, however, by the fact that alleged perpetrators are identified. Critics point out that a policy of not naming victims of domestic violence or family sexual abuse is pointless, because by identifying the alleged perpetrator, the media outlet has indirectly identified the likely victim.

Media critics and most mental health experts advocate maintaining the current policy of not identifying rape victims, however. They believe that rape is different from other crimes in that it's more personal and traumatic than car-jacking or purse-snatching, and that the media should recognize it as such. Some observers say that rape victims would be traumatized twice — the first time by the crime, and the second time by the shame of being publicly identified. They also believe that publishing and broadcasting the names of victims would discourage other victims from reporting similar crimes. They further claim that withholding the name of the victim does not detract from the newsworthiness of the story. If one of the objectives of a news story is to warn the audience of a trend in crimes in a certain part of town, they say, identifying a victim as "a 29-year-old woman walking alone downtown" is sufficient for readers to get the message; they don't need to know the victim's name.

Two prominent individuals who advocate maintaining the current policy are former *New York Post* editor Jerry Nachman and feminist scholar Katha Pollitt.

Nachman contended that if their names are published or broadcast, rape victims would be traumatized twice — the first time by the crime itself, and the second time by being publicly identified. He described his theory as the "Bloomingdale's Scenario" and illustrates it with the example of the victim in a well-publicized rape case receiving unwanted attention several years later when store clerks recognize her name on her credit card.

Pollitt adds that rape is different from other crimes in that the victim is often considered to be partly responsible. "There are no other crimes in which the character, behavior, and past of the complainant are seen as central elements in determining whether a crime has occurred," she wrote in a 1991 op-ed piece in *The Nation*. "When my father was burglarized after forgetting to lock the cellar door, the police did not tell him that he was asking for it."

There are some media practitioners and critics who believe that rape victims should be identified, but they are in the minority. Some believe that because media organizations publish and broadcast the names of victims of other crimes, they create a double-standard when they do not identify rape victims. They contend that if media organizations identify victims of robberies, muggings, car-jackings, and purse-snatchings, they should also do so in cases of sexual assault. They also believe that publishing and broadcasting the names of victims will prevent individuals from making false accusations of rape, and because the defendants in rape cases are typically named, their accusers should also be named. Others contend that withholding the names of rape victims perpetuates misconceptions about rape, including the perception that victims are partly to blame.

Michael Gartner, former president of NBC News, believes that journalists are in the business of "disseminating news, not suppressing it." He supports the position of identifying rape victims because "names add credibility, round out the story, and give the viewer or reader the information he or she needs to understand the issues and make up his or her own mind about what's going on." Gartner also opposes media policies that state the victim's name will be used only with his or her permission. "In no other category of news do we give the newsmaker the option of being named," Gartner wrote in a 1991 column in *Columbia Journalism Review*.

Rape cases are customarily covered only by local media, and in most cases both print and broadcast journalists respect the privacy of the victims and do not identify them by name. When the suspect is a public figure, however, the cases draw national media attention and it becomes more difficult to protect the victims' identity. Two such examples were the 1991 rape trial of William Kennedy Smith — a member of the extended family of U.S. Senator Edward Kennedy — and the 2004 trial of professional basketball player Kobe Bryant. In both cases, law enforcement personnel, court officials, and journalists did a good job of protecting the victims' privacy in the early stages of those trials, but as national media interest intensified, the names became public as a result of sloppy reporting on the part of individual journalists. Once the names became public, other media felt that continuing to conceal their names was no longer necessary. Some media defended their decision to name the victims based on their "cat's-out-of-the-bag" rationale.

Harassment and the Paparazzi

The harassment of public figures — especially Hollywood celebrities and professional athletes — has been a problem ever since the media began reporting on those individuals' private lives in the late 20th century. Some celebrities seem to enjoy the spotlight while others don't. But most simply accept the fact that such attention, including the invasions of their privacy by tabloid photographers, is an unavoidable part of the celebrity lifestyle. In rare cases that celebrities attempt to stop the harassment, the court system has little sympathy, as the celebrities chose their careers voluntarily and therefore must accept the negatives that go with it.

One of the most famous exceptions to that general rule was the case involving former First Lady Jackie Kennedy-Onassis and freelance photographer Ron Galella. Galella had followed and photographed Onassis and her children for much of the late 1960s and early 1970s. Onassis eventually sued Galella for intrusion and in 1972 won a restraining order that required Galella to stay at least 25 feet away from her and 30 feet from her children. But in the four decades that have passed since that case, political wives, Hollywood and television celebrities, and professional athletes have had little success in keeping tabloid reporters and photographers at a distance.

In 1997, a car carrying Princess Diana and a friend was being chased at high speeds by tabloid photographers through the streets of downtown Paris. The car crashed in a tunnel, killing Diana and seriously injuring her friend and the driver. Following the tragedy, worldwide attention focused on the conflict between journalists' right to photograph newsworthy celebrities in public and those celebrities' claims that even when in public, they deserve a certain level of privacy. Congressman Sonny Bono of California — himself a celebrity often pursued by tabloid photographers — introduced in Congress a bill that would have made harassment by news photographers a federal crime. Bono's proposal, as well as similar bills introduced by other national lawmakers, was never passed.

In 1999, however, California became the first state to incorporate an "anti-paparazzi" clause into its privacy law. The legislature revised the law in 2005 and 2009, but as of 2014, the law had not yet been tested in court.

Helping shield celebrities from tabloid photographers is seldom a priority for local law enforcement, and celebrities who hire private bodyguards often find confrontations between them and tabloid photographers often lead to larger publicity problems.

The term *paparazzi* has been around for several decades, but it was not widely used before the death of Princess Diana. While some believe the term to be an Italian word for "freelance photographer" or "photographic stalker," the term was actually derived from Paparazzo, a character in the 1960 film *La Dolce Vita*, which reminded director Federico Fellini of "a buzzing insect, hovering, darting, stinging."

Dealing with Suicide

More than 30,000 Americans commit suicide each year, making it the eleventh leading cause of death, according to the American Foundation for Suicide Prevention. The AFSP reports the major causes are mental illness, drug and alcohol addiction, financial distress, and domestic conflict.

How to deal with the issue has been a subject of reflection and debate within the journalism profession and the entertainment media for several decades. Questions include:

(1) How much detail, if any, should the media provide the public when a person has taken his or her own life?

(2) If a person commits suicide in public, and there are photographs or video available, should the images be published or broadcast?

(3) What responsibility do the media have to cover the issue in a way that does not glamorize suicide nor present it as an appropriate way out of one's problems?

(4) How much responsibility does a newspaper or television station bear when a person that is the subject of a news story commits suicide, or threatens to?

Should we report this at all? Many newspapers have policies of not reporting suicides unless one or more of the following conditions exist: (a) the deceased is a well-known person, (b) the death takes place in public, or (c) there is some doubt as to whether the death was the result of suicide, homicide, or an accident.

In January 1991, Tampa marketing executive Dave Jovanovic killed his wife and then himself. The couple was more than $100,000 in debt. Because the couple was well-known in business and social circles, media in the Tampa area believed were justified in covering the deaths as a news story, but out of consideration for family members on both sides, they did so tastefully. Ten months later, however, the *Tampa Tribune* published a lengthy article about the couple, focusing on how their financial problems spiraled out of control in the year prior to their deaths. The article was illustrated with excerpts from Jovanovic's suicide note and police photographs showing the blood-spattered walls and floor of the home, but not the bodies. The couple's families and friends were outraged, but the *Tribune* defended the article as "tastefully presented" and pointed to the fact that it did not glamorize suicide, but instead suggested that other people in similar circumstances need not resort to such drastic measures. The article even posed the question, "Why didn't the Jovanovics do what millions of other Americans do . . . declare bankruptcy or seek financial counseling?"

What about video and photographs? Whether or not to show photographs or video of individuals committing suicide is a topic of ongoing discussion.

In 1987, Pennsylvania State Treasurer R. Budd Dwyer had been convicted of mail fraud and conspiracy and was facing a lengthy prison sentence. He invited reporters to a news conference in his office at which he was expected to resign. Instead, he delivered a long, rambling speech in which he blamed his legal problems on his political opponents and the news media, then pulled a gun from a large envelope and shot himself. The event was captured in graphic detail by still and video cameras, presenting the media with a dilemma: Should they use the photos and video in their entirety in order to capture the drama of the event; use only some of the photos and video, leaving out the graphic parts;

or tell with story with no photos or video at all? Local and national media were evenly divided.

On the noon news that day, only one Pennsylvania news station showed the graphic video. Others showed the events leading up to the suicide, but cut away just before Dwyer pulled the trigger, then showed a less-graphic scene of Dwyer's body lying on the floor.

While no media were criticized for *not* using the photographs or video, the TV stations that did use it were strongly criticized by parents who complained that their children were watching. Even though many television stations and networks warned viewers in advance, they nevertheless continued to receive complaints for several weeks.

Dwyer's widow said she did not know of her husband's plans in advance, but assumed he chose to die publicly in order to call attention to what he believed was a conspiracy between his political opponents and the media to ruin him.

In Alexandria, Louisiana in 1994, Deputy Sheriff Paul Broussard murdered his wife and then walked calmly down the street and sat on a park bench. He sat there for more than two hours, talking with a priest, while television news crews waited to capture what they thought would be Broussard's dramatic surrender. Instead, he pointed the gun at his head and pulled the trigger, and the scene was broadcast live on local television. The television station's news director said later that he had no idea the story would end so violently, yet he defended his decision to show the scene live.

One day in 1998, a man led law enforcement vehicles on a high-speed chase on a Los Angeles freeway. For much of the previous decade, such chases had been common occurrences in southern California, and local television news stations often used their helicopters and interrupted afternoon television programming to cover them live. Aware of that phenomenon, the man waited until he was sure the helicopters were place, then stopped his truck and spread a banner across the ground that carried a message critical of the health care system. He then set his truck on fire and killed himself with a shotgun. It was later determined that the man was HIV positive and staged his public suicide to protest the lack of health care for AIDS patients. Television executives defended their decision to show the conflict live by claiming that they had no way of knowing in advance how it would end, yet parents complained to the stations because they had cut into children's afternoon programming to show the incident.

Framing the issue. Newspapers and television stations and networks that deal with suicide-related stories insist that they do so in good taste and are careful not to glamorize it nor present it as an appropriate way to deal with personal problems. That concern goes back to the 1962 suicide of actress Marilyn Monroe. In the month that followed, suicides jumped 12 percent nationwide, with an even larger increase seen in women in their 20s and 30s. Following the 1977 suicide of comedian Freddie Prinze Sr. and the 1994 suicide of rock musician Kurt Cobain, suicides among young men also increased dramatically.

Following the 2014 suicide of comedian Robin Williams, a different trend was observed. Crisis hotlines across the country reported that the number of calls they received doubled, and for months afterward remained "well above average." Suicide researchers believed that such publicity, when coupled with proper framing of the issue and the publication of suicide hotline numbers and reminders about other resources available, are more likely to save lives than cause copycats.

Child psychologists and other experts worry that media coverage of suicides may have an adverse effect on teenagers, for which suicide is the third-leading cause of death. According to the National Center for Health Statistics, the suicide rate among American teenagers more than tripled in the five decades between 1960 and 2010. Experts suggest that when explaining the cause of an individual's death, reporters should be careful not to over-generalize or draw conclusions in a way that gives readers an incomplete or mis-leading picture of the persons' reasons for taking their own lives. Mental health coun-selors contend that suicide is rarely based on one event or cause, but more often is due to a combination of factors, with one factor being underlying mental health issues. The media, they warn, should not publish or broadcast stories indicating that a teenager or young adult committed suicide simply over bad grades or the end of a romantic relation-ship.

Many media organizations go as far as consulting with local mental health agencies when doing stories on teenage suicides in order to prevent "copycats." When publishing or broadcasting stories in communities in which several teenagers have taken their own lives, media organizations typically include warning signs that parents should look for in their own children, as well as the phone numbers of suicide hotlines that teenagers (or ad-ults) can call in times of crisis. While many critics believe the media should stay out of the business of reporting teenage suicides altogether, mental health experts agree that the value of providing the warning signs and hotline numbers outweighs the risk involved in suicide copycats.

Concerns about suicide copycats are not limited to news media. Movies and televi-sion programs in which suicide is a major theme result in mixed opinions on the part of mental health experts. Two examples were *The Deer Hunter*, a 1978 film that dealt in part with the epidemic of suicides involving Vietnam veterans struggling to re-adjust to civilian life, and *A Reason to Live,* a 1985 film about a soon-to-be-divorced father strug-gling with suicidal tendencies. While some experts fear such films might put suicidal thoughts into the minds of troubled people, others cited an increase in phone calls to sui-cide and crisis help lines as evidence that the films did more good than harm.

Responding to suicide threats. What media organizations should do when a person threatens suicide is a more difficult issue. Newspaper editors and television news directors report that the phenomenon of news subjects threatening to commit suicide in an attempt to dissuade them from publishing embarrassing stories happens more often than the public is aware of. While the majority of those are seen as empty threats, there are reported cases in which the subjects of news stories carry them out, leaving family members angry and media decision-makers plagued with guilt.

In 1976, a Dallas-based oil company executive whose job required him to travel back and forth to the Soviet Union was found to be a spy and double agent, selling American secrets to the Russian government and Russian secrets to the American government. When he learned that the *Dallas Times-Herald* was about expose his secret, he threatened to commit suicide. The newspaper ignored his threat and published the story, prompting the man to kill himself the same day.

In other cases, subjects of news stories take their own lives without making threats or even dropping hints. In 1996, Navy Admiral Jeremy Boorda, a high-ranking official at the Pentagon, committed suicide after learning that *Newsweek* was researching a story criticizing him for wearing medals on his uniform that he was not entitled to wear. Boor-da's family and friends, as well as the staff of the magazine, were puzzled as to why Boorda would take such a drastic step instead of simply removing the medals in question and apologizing to those offended. Navy officials responded that it was a matter of pride and protocol that "civilians would not understand," while others speculated that Boorda may have had some undiagnosed psychological problems as well.

Ten years later, another well-publicized suicide put the issue of media sensitivity in the spotlight again. During the investigation into the disappearance of her 2-year-old son, 21-year-old Melinda Duckett committed suicide the day after a pre-recorded television segment during which an interviewer questioned her in an overly aggressive manner (this case is discussed in more detail in Case Study 5-C).

The Debate over Confidential Sources

Most reporters and editors use the term "anonymous sources," but the more correct term is "confidential sources."*

When deciding whether to use confidential sources, reporters and editors typically consider five factors:

How significant is the story? Nearly every discussion about confidential sources includes the example of Bob Woodward and Carl Bernstein of the *Washington Post*. In the early 1970s, the two young reporters used confidential sources in breaking their story about Watergate, a political scandal that resulted in the resignation of President Richard Nixon and changed the nature of investigative journalism for decades. Without such sources, the reporters and their editors claim, their stories would not have been as complete, and the misconduct of the Nixon administration might not have been exposed.

The motives of the source. Why is the source coming forward? Is he or she performing a public service, seeking revenge against a political enemy or former employer, or simply attempting to advance his or her own interests?

While reporters and editors often consider an individual's motives in such cases, the finding of a negative motive does not disqualify the person as a source — but it should signal the need for additional scrutiny in order to verify the accuracy of the information. In some cases, it may be true that a "disgruntled former employee" is simply trying to strike back at his or her former employer, but reporters and editors may conclude that the significance of the story (along with additional verification) outweighs any concerns about the individual's motives.

The reason for his or her request for anonymity. Why is the promise of confidentiality important to the source? Does he or she have a legitimate reason to be concerned about his or her safety or that of his or her family? Or is he or she simply trying to accomplish one of the motives listed above while enjoying the cloak of confidentiality?

Track records of the source and reporter. Has the source provided reliable information in the past? Has the reporter made good decisions about his or her use of confidential sources in the past?

---

*In social science research, "anonymous" means that no one (not even the researcher) knows the identity of research participants, while "confidential" means the researcher knows the participants' identity but is ethically prohibited from revealing it. Applying these definitions to journalism, nearly all unidentified sources are "confidential" rather than "anonymous" because no serious journalist would use sources without knowing their identity.

Alternative sources. Is the same information available from other (on-the-record) sources? Because of the increased level of confidence and credibility involved when sources agree to be identified, most editors will encourage reporters to exhaust all other possible sources for the same information before condoning a reporter's promise of confidentiality.

At the height of the investigative journalism era of the 1970s and 1980s, some editors of major daily newspapers estimated that up to one-third of the stories they published included information from at least one confidential source. Since that era, however, a dramatic increase in the number of libel cases and the size of damage awards has prompted media organizations to limit their use of such sources. Multiple studies have indicated that the use of confidential sources has dropped significantly over the last 20 years, with many editors banning them altogether.

One example of the appropriate use of confidential sources is the case of "whistle-blowers" who provide information on government waste and corruption or illegal activities of businesses. In these cases, sources ask not to be identified because they fear losing their jobs or placing in danger their lives or the lives of their families.

Editors who oppose the use of confidential sources cite two reasons to support their positions.

The first consideration is the relative credibility of named and unnamed sources. Sources who agree to be quoted by name in a newspaper story or have their names and faces shown during television interviews are automatically considered more credible (by both journalists and their audiences) than those who do not. Information from sources who insist on not being identified by name in a newspaper story or not appearing on camera in a television story is treated with some degree of suspicion.

The second factor is the potential for individuals to use the media to advance personal grudges against former employers or damage the campaigns of political opponents.

Most media organizations have policies that prohibit reporters from making promises of confidentiality to sources without the permission of an editor or news director. Most editors and news directors will support such a promise only if there is a significant danger that a source will face physical or financial harm if his or her name is revealed.

In those rare cases that use of a confidential source is approved, journalists should be careful when using labels such as "a source close to the investigation" and "a person in the governor's office," as too specific a label might result in other persons being able to guess the person's identity.

In politics, members of a public official's staff may "leak" information to journalists while asking not to be identified. The most common example is the "trial balloon" — information about a preliminary idea that is leaked to the media and described in a way that makes it sound like it is being considered more seriously than it actually is. The staff will then monitor how the media covers it and how the public reacts. If the reaction is positive, the proposal is implemented; if the reaction is negative, the politician discards the proposal and claims it was never a serious idea to begin with. Reporters and editors don't like being used in this way, but many admit that it is part of the give-and-take of covering politics. If they don't play along, they claim, the trial balloons will be floated somewhere else, and they will miss out on valid stories.

Closely related to the debate over confidential sources are the concepts of "off the record," "not for attribution," "on background," and "on deep background."

Some reporters and editors have a strict policy of never taking part in any interview which the source labels as *off the record*, believing that any interview taking place under that condition is immediately suspect. Others, however, accept such conditions because those interviews might lead to other sources willing to talk on the record, and in other cases may prevent the reporter from making serious mistakes.

Not for attribution means the source's words appear within quote marks, but the attribution reads "said a source familiar with the negotiations" or "said an individual requesting his name be withheld." Most newspapers have policies of using "not for attribution" sparingly, worried that excessive use of those phrases causes readers to be suspicious of the information.

Sometimes the phrases used to describe "not for attribution" sources are so detailed that they give away the person's identity, sometimes intentionally. In the early 1970s, for example, Secretary of State Henry Kissinger was famous for giving media interviews during which he asked journalists to identify him as a "high-ranking State Department official traveling on the Secretary of State's airplane."

On background means the sources are providing information that will not be quoted and is not directly related to the story. For example, an employee of a chemical or technology company might provide a journalist with a "crash course" in a particular scientific or technical topic in order to help the journalist understand what he or she is reporting about.

On deep background means the source does not volunteer any information, but simply agrees to review information the reporter already has and tell him or her whether or not it is correct.

Issues in Interviewing

Interviewing news sources is an ethical minefield for journalists. Here are some of the most common issues with which journalists who are new to the field may struggle.

Promising confidentiality. Reporters sometimes promise their sources that they can remain confidential, but once the story is complete, the reporter no longer has control over it. An editor who knows the identity of a source may decide to insert the source's name without telling the reporter, which leads the source to believe the journalist was at fault.

In a 1982 case in Minnesota, for example, a newspaper reporter promised a source with inside knowledge of a local political scandal that he could remain anonymous. The editors over-ruled the reporter and inserted the name. The source sued the newspaper for breach of confidentiality and was awarded a sizeable financial settlement because he had been fired from his job as a result of being identified in the story.

Promising confidentiality to sources without first getting permission from an editor is discouraged. Reporters should also warn sources that the promise of confidentiality could be over-ruled by an editor.

Promising to provide a copy of story before it is published. This is very seldom done. Sometimes an individual with little or no experience being interviewed will ask to see a copy of the story in advance, but those with experience dealing with journalists know it is unlikely that the journalist will agree. In some cases it may be helpful because the source will point out errors, but more often the source will deny having made a specific comment, agree that he or she said it but still ask that it be deleted, may want to respond to another source's quotes, or in some cases, may want to argue about semantics.

Therefore, showing a source the story in advance is *permissible but strongly discouraged.* If the source is concerned about possibly being misquoted, a better alternative is to contact the source once the story is complete and discuss over the phone only those quotes, facts, or statistics that are in question.

The practice of **readbacks** allows the source to modify or retract controversial quotes. While most editors allow reporters to make their own decisions regarding readbacks, at some magazines — *Time, National Geographic,* and *The New Yorker* — it is standard procedure.

In order to deal with sources who routinely claim they are misquoted, some reporters either tape record in-person interviews or ask questions by electronic mail so an electronic record of the interview will be created.

Lying to sources. Some journalists may tell Source A that he or she has already interviewed Source B (often a competitor) in order to coax Source A into agreeing to an interview, even though no such Source B interview has taken place. *Never acceptable under any circumstances.*

Threats and ultimatums. A reporter frustrated with a source's refusal to be interviewed might say to that individual, "If you don't speak to me, I will get the information from somewhere else, publish the story anyway, and it will make you look bad." Or worse: "If you don't speak to me, I will publish the story anyway and if anything in the story is inaccurate, it will be your fault." *Both of these tactics are never acceptable.* A better alternative: "Everyone else involved in this situation has agreed to talk with me, and if you don't, you will lose your chance to tell your side of the story."

The ambush interview. Another sign of a reporter's frustration is showing up unannounced at the potential source's home or place of business. Television journalists often do this, usually claiming it is either because of a tight deadline or a source's refusal to return phone calls; more often they do it for dramatic effect. Print journalists, however, should give the potential source adequate opportunity to return phone calls or otherwise agree to the interview.

Bait and switch. An inexperienced reporter might tell a potential source that the story being researched is about one topic, when it's really about another. *Never acceptable under any circumstances.*

The interview re-edit. An interviewee is asked questions by a reporter who is never shown because only one camera is available. After the interviewee has left the room, the camera is then used to record the interviewer asking the questions; the two tapes are then edited together to make it appear as if it was a two-camera interview. In some cases, the person appearing to do the interview was not even in the room at the time; the source answered questions read by someone else, and a different interviewer is taped asking the same questions later. If well-edited, most viewers could not tell how the interview was actually conducted.

Although most television stations deny using either of the above tactics, many do. In most cases, it is because the news crew has only one camera and it would be awkward to swing it back and forth between the interviewer and the interviewee. In other cases, it is done for dramatic effect. The latter example was seen in the 1986 movie *Broadcast News* when a male television reporter interviewed a female crime victim with the camera focused on her the entire time; after the interview was over and the woman left the room, the camera operator recorded the interviewer asking the same questions again, but this time using facial expressions that artificially showed empathy for the woman's ordeal. *Acceptable only when correcting the interviewer's stumble over words; not acceptable for dramatic effect.*

Tabloid television programs are often accused of worse conduct: Re-editing the interview to make a source appear to answer questions different from those actually asked in order to make him or her look foolish. *Never acceptable.*

Condensing, paraphrasing, and altering quotes. Another issue associated with quotations is how much "literary license" a print journalist should have altering the wording of quotes.

Sometimes a source may provide a valid answer to a question but take way too long to get to the point. Should the journalist condense what the individual said? Or what if a scientist interviewed for a story can only speak in technical jargon? Should the journalist paraphrase what the scientist said so that the readers will understand it? What if the source provides a quote that includes slang terms or profanity not acceptable in the newspaper? Should the journalist change the words to ones that are less offensive? What if the source uses incorrect grammar? Should the journalist change "the company is proud of their employees" to "the company is proud of its employees" in order to be grammatically correct? What about changing "between the three labor unions" to "among the three labor unions"?

Most newspapers have policies that allow such alterations only in cases of paraphrasing. "If the words are surrounded by quote marks, we're telling the readers that those are the speaker's exact words," says one newspaper policy manual. No one expects reporters to be as accurate as professional stenographers or court reporters who are capable of producing verbatim transcripts, but the closer they can get to that ideal, the more accurate the reporting will be.

The *Associated Press Stylebook* states that reporters should "never alter quotations, even to correct minor grammatical errors or word usage." Individual reporters and editors, however, prefer to clean up quotes in order to avoid embarrassing an individual or portraying him or her as uneducated or inarticulate. In these cases, it would be a good idea for the reporter to call the source once the preliminary draft of the story is completed and read what the altered version of the quote says.

Profanity has long been prohibited by publishers of most daily newspapers. In some cases, however, editors may allow journalists to use slang terms or profanity in stories if they decide that only a verbatim quotation can properly illustrate a person's character or attitude. In those cases, the newspaper may put a warning at the top of the story that it "includes language that some readers may find offensive."

In an interview with a colorful southern business owner, a reporter quoted him about how he viewed his competition. "If we're going to run with the big dogs, we have to know how to piss in the tall grass," the man said. The reporter checked the newspaper's style manual and found that "piss" was listed as a substandard term for "urinate." After convincing his editor that "urinate in the tall grass" did not have the same impact, the quote was allowed to run in its original form.

When the *Los Angeles Times* published a story in which it quoted police officers making offensive comments about women, editors instructed reporters to use paraphrasing instead of verbatim quotes, describing the term they deleted as a "four-letter term used to refer to a woman's vagina." The reporters later complained that the original language should have been used because it better illustrated the officers' demeaning attitudes toward women.

In other cases, the concern of editors over the sensibilities of readers causes more problems than it solves. In reviewing a story that quoted President Jimmy Carter, *New York Times* editors decided that a quotation in which Carter used the term "screw" might be too offensive for the conservative era of the 1970s. They instructed the reporter to paraphrase Carter's comments and indicate that he used "a vulgarism for sexual relations." Once the story was published, they realized that some readers might assume Carter used the word "fuck," so they ran a clarification the next day indicating Carter had used "a common but mild vulgarism for sexual relations." Media critic David Shaw pointed out the absurdity of the incident by writing that the *Times* had "used eight words to clear up the confusion caused by having used five words to replace one word."

Deception, Misrepresentation, and Hidden Recording Devices

Many journalism historians believe that the undercover technique can be traced back to the work of Nellie Bly, 19th century journalist whose real name was Elizabeth Jane Cochrane. Working for the *New York World* at the age of 21, she developed the idea of researching the inner workings of a mental hospital by pretending to be a mental patient.

Adopting the persona of a mentally disturbed woman, she exhibited enough bizarre behavior in public to convince a court to send her to a noted women's mental hospital in New York, where she stayed for 10 days. In her subsequent newspaper article, "Ten Days in a Mad House," she described the unsanitary conditions and patient neglect she observed, as well as the physical, psychological, and sexual abuse she experienced or witnessed. Her article was later incorporated into a book, *The Complete Works of Nellie Bly.* Today, leaders in the mental health business say that her work laid the groundwork for decades of reforms, and her legacy is celebrated in her hometown of Cochran's Mills, Pennsylvania.

In 1965, a reporter for the *Cleveland Plain Dealer* attempted to replicate Bly's work, but this time as an attendant, rather than a patient, at a state mental hospital. He did so for seven weeks. He applied for the job using his real social security number and his middle name as his first name, but his work history was falsified. After his stories were published, the governor of Ohio ordered a series of reforms that improved conditions at that facility as well as others in the state.

In the 20th century, one of the most notable examples of misrepresentation was Ben Bagdikian's 1971 series of articles published in the *Washington Post* that described problems within a state prison in Pennsylvania. In cooperation with the state attorney general's office, Bagdikian researched the article by posing as an inmate. After the series was published and the ruse admitted, the response to Bagdikian's tactics was mixed. Many observers of the journalism profession praised his initiative and courage in taking on such a risky assignment, while others, including *Washington Post* editor Ben Bradlee, were not comfortable with the tactic. Even though he had originally approved Bagdikian's approach, Bradlee later admitted to having second thoughts, contending that if journalists were to do an effective job of exposing government officials who lied and tricked other people, they must not lie and trick people in their own work. A few years later, however, Bradlee approved the use of deception and anonymous sources in the newspaper's coverage of the Watergate scandal — work that led to the toppling of the Nixon administration and is now heralded as a landmark case in investigative journalism.

Veteran *Chicago Tribune* journalist Mike Royko admitted having used dozens of false identities during his lengthy career. Royko claimed that a fake police badge gave him access to crime scenes that his media credentials would not have, and that his ability to disguise his voice in phone conversations allowed him to impersonate a county coroner, a female high school principal, and other officials.

A famous case of misrepresentation began in 1992 when reporters for ABC's *Prime Time Live* posed as employees and used hidden cameras to document unsanitary conditions in Food Lion grocery stores. After the story aired, Food Lion sued ABC for trespassing and fraud, and a North Carolina jury awarded Food Lion $5.5 million. ABC claimed that at least part of the loss was because of the jury's anti-media bias.

ABC appealed the judgment, and while the decision was not reversed at first, the network was successful in having the damages reduced to $2.

In early 2011, online journalist Ian Murphy misrepresented himself as a wealthy political contributor in a phone call to Wisconsin Governor Scott Walker. Murphy said he was angry that the governor seemed unsympathetic to the plight of the state's public employees in their attempt to save their union from decertification, and while the governor returned phone calls to republican lawmakers and political allies, he refused to return phone calls from democratic legislators or journalists.

Knowing the name and some basic facts about one of Walker's big donors, Murphy engaged the governor in a recorded phone call and lured him into a conversation in which he joked about "hitting democrats over their heads with baseball bats" and admitted that he considered planting "troublemakers" among the union members in order to disrupt their protests.

When transcripts of the conversation appeared on Murphy's website, The Beast, media ethicists were stunned. "The tactic and deception used to gain this information violate the highest levels of journalism ethics," said Kevin Smith, chairman of the Society of Professional Journalist's Ethics Committee. "To lie to a source about your identity and then to bait that source into making comments that are inflammatory is inexcusable and has no place in journalism."

One journalist defended Murphy's tactics by claiming that "a journalist not only has the right to misrepresent himself, but sometimes, as Murphy demonstrated, it is a journalist's only option."

In a 1975 article in *Washington Monthly*, Timothy Ingram discussed the issuing of journalists misrepresenting themselves during the newsgathering process. According to Ingram, a journalist might call the telephone company and pretend to be a person questioning long-distance calls on a bill or call a finance company and pretend to be a person calling to check on the status of a loan application. In the four decades since Ingram's article, both government regulations and company policies have greatly restricted the journalists' ability to conduct such undercover work. Nevertheless, unsubstantiated stories of similar behavior still persist in journalism circles.

Today, nearly every media organization has one or more policies dealing with deception, misrepresentation, and hidden recording devices such as cameras and microphones. Common examples of misrepresentation include a print or broadcast journalist pretending to be a job applicant in order to expose a business's alleged discriminatory employment practices or pretending to be a potential apartment renter in order to expose a landlord's exclusion of minority tenants.

In most cases, such policies (which also apply to cases of hidden cameras and microphones) include a three-part test:

1. The news story being pursued must be a substantial one for which the reporter has determined the need for further investigation (the search for the so-called "smoking gun"). The policy does not allow for "fishing expeditions."

2. The journalist must have exhausted all other possible reporting methods to obtain the desired information before resorting to hidden cameras and/or misrepresentation.

3. The journalist must have approval in advance from either an editor (in the case of a newspaper or magazine) or news director (in the case of television or radio).

In cases in which the main issue is deception or misrepresentation, some media outlets have codes of ethics that include one or both of two other conditions.

The first additional condition is that the deception must not place the reporter or innocent people in danger. A journalist posing as a law enforcement officer, firefighter, or paramedic would fail that part of the test because his or her lack of training would likely present a danger for co-workers as well as civilians depending on emergency services.

The second additional condition is that before a story based on such deception is published or broadcast, the reporter must contact the subject of the story, admit to the deception, and offer him or her opportunity to tell his or her side of the story.

Closely related to the issue of hidden cameras is the matter of recording telephone conversations with news sources without their knowledge. The main value of an audiotape or videotape is that it can be used later to contradict the claims of an individual that he or she was misquoted.

In addition to applying the ethical policy explained above, journalists should also be aware of state laws regarding telephone privacy. Some state laws allow telephone conversations to be recorded as long as one party is aware of it, but some state laws require that both parties (or all parties) consent to the recording.

One of the concerns involved in misrepresentation is the potential for **entrapment,** which is actually a legal term that means that law enforcement personnel may not take any steps to induce a person to commit a crime; they must wait for the suspect to initiate the illegal behavior.

One recent example of tactics that critics say bordered on entrapment was NBC's popular "To Catch a Predator" series that it incorporated into its news program, *Dateline*. Working with law enforcement agencies and a nonprofit organization called Perverted Justice, the project involved a house wired with hidden cameras and recording equipment. Volunteer "decoys" — many of them actresses in their 20s pretending to be teenage girls — communicated via the Internet with potential sexual predators and many times agreed to have the suspects visit them at the house for sexual encounters. After arriving at the house, suspects were videotaped as they were interviewed by host Chris Hanson and were then arrested as they attempted to leave.

Attorneys for the network and law enforcement agencies were careful not to cross the line into entrapment, having lawyers coach the decoys on what they could and could not say and making sure the suspects initiated the contact.

The show spawned a number of similar programs produced by local television stations around the country. Nationally, as the popularity of the show grew, it generated a number of spin-offs, including *To Catch a Car Thief, To Catch an Identity Thief,* and *To Catch a Baby Broker*, but none of them were as popular as the original.

Although the original program is still seen in re-runs on NBC's sister network, MSNBC, there are no original episodes of the series being produced. Partly because of declining ratings and partly because of a $100 million lawsuit filed by the family of one of the men caught in the sting, the show was cancelled in 2007.

The beginning of the end for the series happened on November 5, 2006, when the crew executed a sting in the small town of Murphy, Texas, in which the target was a 56-year-old district attorney thought to be an upstanding member of the community. He did not show up at the house, but local police believed they had enough evidence against him (based on the transcripts from his online chats with an actress he believed to be a teenage girl) to execute a search of his home.

As a team of police officers entered the home with the television crew waiting outside, the man shot and killed himself. His sister filed a lawsuit against NBC and the police department involved, claiming they failed to take reasonable precautions to prevent the suicide and caused her emotional distress. The case was eventually settled out of court.

Some media ethicists suggest that the use of deception and misrepresentation would be acceptable only if possible targets of the investigations are given fair warning that such tactics may be used in the near future. For example, a newspaper or television station would send letters to all grocery stores in the community with a non-specific warning that it may soon conduct a hidden-camera investigation into allegations of unsanitary conditions in the stores. Or, it might notify local car dealers that because of complaints that some dealers offer higher financing rates to African American customers than white customers, it might send reporters of different races to visit to dealerships (pretending to be potential customers) in order to prove or disprove the allegations.

The cynical view of this suggestion is that it would tip off the subject of the potential story about the investigation and reduce the likelihood that any wrongdoing will be found. After all, would a grocery store or car dealership continue such practices after being warned? Common sense says "no," but anecdotal evidence involving police stings says otherwise. Many law enforcement agencies report that they send numerous warnings to convenience stores about ongoing investigations in which they send underage customers into stores to purchase alcohol. Despite the warnings, many stores continue to violate the law.

Media Ride-Alongs

The popularity of "reality" shows on television has drawn attention to a new and controversial method of newsgathering known as the **ride-along**, in which journalists accompany law enforcement officials and emergency medical personnel and record their work.

One of the earliest known cases involving this newsgathering tactic took place in 1979, when a Los Angeles man suffered a heart attack in the bedroom of his home. A film crew from a local television station, developing a story about the quality of emergency medical care in the community, recorded the event and used the highlights on the evening news. The family sued the station for invasion of privacy, and after six years of litigation, settled the matter out of court (see Case Study 5-B).

Numerous times in the 1990s, media ride-alongs prompted charges of trespassing. One case occurred in 1992 when armed Secret Service agents raided the home of a credit-card fraud suspect in Brooklyn, New York. The agents invited a CBS News camera crew to join them and videotape the raid. One of the agents wore a wireless microphone and provided a running commentary of the proceedings. When the agents arrived at the home, they found the suspect was not home, but his wife (clad only in a nightgown) and their 5-year-old son were. Both were visibly shaken by the raid and the presence of the CBS personnel and equipment. During the search, the camera crew videotaped the wife and her son repeatedly, in spite of the wife's objections, and took close-up shots of the proceedings. When the family sued the network and the Secret Service, both were found guilty of violating the family's privacy.

Later in the decade, two similar cases occurred that wound their way through the legal system and eventually resulted in Supreme Court rulings that the media ride-alongs violated the individuals' rights to privacy. Despite those rulings, however, many reality television programs use similar techniques, and while the producers occasionally face lawsuits, most avoid liability by finding loopholes in state privacy laws or by including disclaimers that "suspects are innocent until proven guilty."

Checkbook Journalism

While no respectable newspaper or television station would pay a source for an interview, individuals caught up in news events of the 1990s found tabloid newspaper and television programs willing to open their checkbooks. These individuals included the neighbor of White House intern Monica Lewinsky, witnesses testifying in the trial of Tonya Harding on charges that she conspired to injure rival skater Nancy Kerrigan, friends of the two high school students accused of carrying out the 1999 massacre at Columbine High School, and jurors in the trial of Los Angeles police officers accused of beating motorist Rodney King.

Most media outlets and professional organizations have strict policies prohibiting the payment of sources. One media ethicist claims that journalism should be based on "the voluntary sharing of information, not their willingness to be the highest bidder."

Some media outlets circumvent ethical policies by paying interview sources "consulting fees" for access to otherwise unavailable documentation, compensating them for travel and hotel costs at a rate several times higher than the expenses actually incurred, or paying sources for photos or video, with the understanding that the sellers will also consent to interviews.

Other journalism ethicists advocate policies that prohibit paying sources directly, but are flexible on the idea of paying for photographs or video (as long as it is not done to circumvent the rules, as described above). "Some of the greatest photographs in history were taken by passersby or participants," says Tom Goldstein, former dean of Columbia University's Graduate School of Journalism. "It makes me uneasy that somebody is profiting from the misfortune of others, but that's what a lot of journalism is about."

ABC News denied rumors that it had paid for an interview with the butler of Princess Diana following her 1997 death, but later admitted that it paid him $300,000 for his "video diary."

A man who escaped from the World Trade Center during the terrorist attacks of September 11, 2001, sought to capitalize on his fame for media stories dealing with the one-year anniversary of the tragedy. He announced that he would do media interviews for $500 per hour, or $911 for two hours. Few American journalists agreed to pay him, but some international media outlets did, claiming that such practice was common in their home countries. The *New York Post* wrote a story about his enterprise, quoting him as justifying the charges because "giving interviews takes time away from (his) business." The *Post* emphasized in its story that it did not pay the man for the interview about his policy of charging for interviews.

In subsequent coverage of the war on terror, Cable News Network and CBS News admitted that they paid Afghan soldiers who allowed themselves to be videotaped training to use chemical weapons by practicing on dogs.

One of most recent cases of alleged checkbook journalism involved *New York Times* reporter Kurt Eichenwald. After more than a decade of uncovering corporate scandals as one of the *Times'* chief business reporters, Eichenwald attempted to take on the grim topic of pornography and sexual abuse affecting children and young adults.

For a series of stories that ran in the newspaper in December 2005, Eichenwald interviewed Justin Berry, a young adult and amateur musician who claimed that as a child, he frequently sold pornographic images of himself and other children and had briefly worked as a male escort. Eichenwald's first ethical misstep was to contact Berry and misrepresent himself as a songwriter wishing to collaborate with him. Once Berry began to confide in him, Eichenwald paid him $2,000 in cash to tell his story. *Times* editors learned of the payment after it was revealed in the legal proceedings for a Michigan man linked to a pornography ring mentioned in the series.

Both the misrepresentation and cash payment violated *Times'* ethical standards, but after Berry's family repaid most of the money, Eichenwald received only a written reprimand and moved onto a new job at the newsmagazine, *Portfolio*. Editors at the *Times* later learned that after the initial payment of $2,000, Eichenwald paid Berry an additional $1,100 through the online credit card payment system PayPal. That revelation led to his resignation at *Portfolio*.

Eichenwald never accepted full responsibility for either the misrepresentation or the payments, instead claiming that the medication he took for depression and epilepsy caused him to make "poor judgments."

One variation of the "checkbook journalism" issue involves television talk shows. While networks do not overtly pay guests for appearing on the programs, there is often a trade-off — the guest agrees to be interviewed, either overtly or by implication, in exchange for the opportunity to promote his or her most recent book.

In his first three years after leaving office, for example, former President Bill Clinton rarely agreed to media interviews because he was tired of answering questions about the scandals that plagued the second term of his administration. But shortly after publishing his 2004 autobiography, *My Life*, Clinton's willingness to be interviewed on television talk shows increased.

Similarly, former Central Intelligence Agency Director George Tenet avoided the media spotlight after leaving that post in 2004, but he changed his attitude when he had the opportunity to appear on CBS' *60 Minutes* and CNN's *Larry King Live*. He agreed to the interviews in part for the opportunity to promote his 2007 book, *At the Center of the Storm: My Life at the CIA*.

More recently, former President George W. Bush and former Secretary of Defense Donald Rumsfield became more willing to appear on television talk shows after publishing their memoirs.

Junkets and Freebies

Most media organizations have formal policies that prohibit employees from accepting "freebies" such as gifts and meals from news sources. Most such policies have been in place for only a few decades. Prior to the 1970s, journalists frequently accepted gifts and free meals from sources, prompting one professional baseball team manager to claim that "you can buy a sportswriter with a good steak."

In defining the "gift" category, most policies use terms such as "more than nominal value," meaning that souvenir items such as pens, T-shirts, or coffee mugs would be allowed, while watches, briefcases, or desk accessories would not be.

Even though there may not be any agreement to alter the content of a news story in exchange for the gift (the Latin term is **quid pro quo**), what media organizations seek to avoid is the *appearance* of any impropriety. Allen Parsons, executive editor of the *Wilmington Star News* in Wilmington, North Carolina, has a simple rule about his reporters accepting such gifts. "It is easy to sell your integrity, but impossible to buy it back," he says. The business editor of the same newspaper recalls a previous publisher's rule that accepting food from a news source was permissible provided the quantity was small enough to be consumed in one day. That policy presented a dilemma for the newspaper staff when one news source provided a quart of whiskey.

One example of a strict freebie policy is that of the New York Times Company; the policy applies not only to the flagship paper but also all of the local newspapers the company owns. The policy acknowledges that, while courtesies such as gifts and meals have an important place in American business, the role of the journalist requires a higher standard. "Gifts accepted from or given to anyone with whom the company does business should be promotional in nature and nominal in value," the policy states. "A business courtesy should not be accepted if it does not fall within the guidelines described above or if the donor expects something in return, may be attempting to gain an unfair advantage, may be attempting to influence the employee's judgment, or if acceptance creates the appearance of any of the foregoing. Employees should also avoid a pattern of accepting frequent gifts or business courtesies from the same persons or companies." To define the terms "promotional" and "nominal," the policy states that "a ballpoint pen with a company logo would satisfy the test of being promotional in nature and of nominal value. An inscribed gold wristwatch may be promotional in nature but would unlikely be nominal in value and, therefore, would not be acceptable."

In defending the policy, *New York Times* attempts to differentiate its journalistic products from other publications with lesser standards. Accepting freebies, the policy states, "debases the profession and creates the impression that the entire press is on the take."

Mitchell Stephens, in his broadcast news textbook, wrote, "Reporters shouldn't accept any gifts from the people they may have to write about — no bottles of Scotch, vacations, fountain pens, or dinners. Reporters don't even want to be in a position of having to distinguish between a gift and a bribe. Return them all with a polite thank-you."

Some journalists have compounded their ethical lapses by using on-line auction sites such as eBay to sell promotional items such as advanced copies of books or DVDs of upcoming movies.

Resorts and theme parks are often criticized by competitors, journalism critics, and media watchdog groups for paying for airline tickets and hotel accommodations for travel writers in an attempt to secure favorable stories. Many ethical codes allow some acceptance of free travel and meals, using terms such as "reasonable" and "legitimate news interest." In some cases, however, the differences of opinion result from the degree of excess. The marketing departments at Disneyland in California and Walt Disney World in Florida, for example, are frequent targets for such criticism because the lavish nature of their media gatherings.

Editors of travel magazines and newspaper travel sections who make such policy decisions are evenly divided on the issue. Some believe that if an event or location is important enough to cover, it is important enough for the publication to pay its reporters' expenses. Other editors, especially those working for small magazines or newspapers with meager travel budgets, simply contend they could not publish a quality travel magazine or newspaper travel section without allowing reporters to accept free travel.

Prominent travel magazines such as *Conde Naste Traveler* and *Travel & Leisure* employ experienced full-time staff writers and established freelancers who are not allowed to accept subsidies in any form. Other travel publications may allow their staff writers to accept free travel and purchase stories from freelancers without asking how much of their travel was subsidized. In between the two extremes are those publications that allow staff writers and freelancers to accept free transportation and accommodations, but only under certain conditions, such as accepting only those arrangements that are available to all media representatives attending the same event, and agreements that no promises as to the content or tone of resulting stories are expected or implied.

Editors of newspaper entertainment sections found a solution to this dilemma many years ago. Instead of sending reporters to Hollywood and other locations to attend glamorous events related to the entertainment industry, they cover those events using wire service stories and material generated by publicists. Not only does that eliminate potential ethical conflicts, but it allows reporters to focus instead on local entertainment stories, such as the productions of nonprofit community theater groups and high school and college drama programs.

The Associated Press provides specific guidelines for newspaper sportswriters who travel to cover college and professional sports teams. Those rules include a requirement that newspapers pay all expenses up front for writers' transportation, accommodations, and food; or if that is not practical, that the newspaper reimburse the home team for such expenses after the fact.

Following the British Petroleum (BP) oil spill in the Gulf of Mexico in April 2010, tourist development organizations in Northwest Florida struggled to inform potential visitors from other parts of the country that the damage caused by the spill was not as extensive as the national media portrayed it. By mid-summer, they had received multi-million-dollar grants from the oil company in order to address that challenge.

In addition to using the BP grants to purchase advertising in newspapers and magazines and on television and radio, the agencies also hosted "familiarization tours" or "famtours" during which travel journalists from across the country visited the affected areas and interviewed year-round residents, summer visitors, and hotel and restaurant owners whose businesses depended largely on tourism.

The organizers did not directly pay for the airline fares for the journalists, but did arrange for their hotels, meals, and local transportation costs to be paid for out of the BP grants. In defending the program, tourism officials insisted that in accepting the "freebies," the writers were under no obligation — either stated or implied — to write positive stories or mention the oil spill in a particular way. They also pointed out that all of the journalists taking part in the program represented either monthly or weekly magazines or online news organizations or identified themselves as freelancers. None represented daily newspapers, most likely because that even without a stated or implied obligation, accepting such expenses violated their ethical codes or "freebie" policies.

While most American media organizations have strict policies about such issues, international media (as well as businesses in other countries) do not, which causes problems and misunderstandings for American journalists working overseas, as well as for international journalists working in the U.S.

When a Moscow cellphone company opened a new retail store, for example, it invited Russian journalists as well as visiting journalists from the U.S., and all were offered the company's most expensive product, a model costing the equivalent of $500 in American money. Beth Knobel, a reporter for CBS News, claimed that her staffers were the only ones attending the event that did not accept the phones.

"We probably could have gotten away with it," Knobel explained in a journalism book she co-authored with CBS veteran Mike Wallace. "But it didn't seem worth it to risk our careers over a $500 phone."

To Report or Not Report

Throughout the history of journalism, print and broadcast journalists have struggled with decisions concerning the publication of controversial information. In many cases, newspaper and magazine publishers, television news directors, and network executives must weigh competing interests such as news value and public interest (in favor of reporting the story) with factors such as national security and personal safety (in favor of not reporting).

One of the first such cases occurred in 1961, when reporters at the *New York Times* learned in advance that American forces were planning the Bay of Pigs invasion in an attempt to liberate Cuba from the dictatorship of Fidel Castro. When President John F. Kennedy and Pentagon officials learned of the newspaper's plans, they persuaded the newspaper not to jeopardize the operation by publicizing it in advance.

A decade later, a case went much further — to the U.S. Supreme Court. The case centered on an investigation into the American involvement in Vietnam, commissioned by Secretary of Defense Robert McNamara. The resulting report, known as the "Pentagon Papers," documented the belief of military leaders that the war was "unwinable." Pentagon officials were concerned that if the report was published, it would further undermine morale and public support for the war, which was already low. The *New York Times* obtained a copy of the report and planned to publish the first installment in June, 1971. The Justice Department, headed by Attorney General John Mitchell, obtained a court order to prevent the newspaper from publishing the report.

The newspaper appealed the case to the Supreme Court, which agreed to hear it on an expedited basis. The court ruled 6-3 that the government did not meet its burden of proof (to show how publishing the report would be harmful) and that prohibiting the newspaper from publishing the report would violate its First Amendment rights.

In 1979, the magazine *Progressive* announced its plans to publish an article that detailed the construction of an atomic bomb. The article was the work of a freelance writer who claimed that all of the information used to develop the article was available from public sources. The editors sent a copy of the article to a number of scientists and scholars in order to verify its technical accuracy. Government officials learned about the article and claimed it posed a danger to national security and might encourage some countries to develop their own nuclear devices. In addition, they asserted that publication of the article would violate the Atomic Energy Act of 1954. Before the case could be appealed, another magazine published a similar article, making the *Progressive* case moot because the information was already publicly available.

A more recent case of the media struggling with the report-or-not-report question occurred when Ted Kaczynski, a domestic terrorist nicknamed the Unabomber, submitted a "manifesto" for publication in two national newspapers. Kaczynski was a former mathematics professor who had become a recluse, living in a remote cabin in Montana. For nearly two decades, he mailed package bombs to university professors and airlines, killing three people and injuring more than 20 others. In his 1995 letter to the *New York Times,* he promised to stop the bombing if either the *Times* or the *Washington Post* published his "manifesto" — a rambling, 35,000-word essay about the evils of technology.

The publishers of the two newspapers considered the idea for several days, debating between (1) the news value of publishing the document and (2) the danger of giving Kaczynski publicity and encouraging copycats. Assisting the law enforcement investigation may not have been a factor, but after both papers published the material, Kaczynski's brother and sister-in-law recognized the writing style and tipped off federal investigators as to the location of Kaczynski's hideout, which led to a successful apprehension.

Staging Photographs and Video

Newspaper editors and television station managers seldom approve the artificial staging of photographs and video, but in some cases such material is published or broadcast without their knowledge because of decisions made by reporters. After the fact, those reporters are often reprimanded or fired.

One such case affected the *Indianapolis Star* in 2002. One of the newspaper's photographers visited a county health clinic to take photographs of children getting vaccinations. With no children waiting to be vaccinated and a desire to get the photograph as quickly as possible so he could move onto his next assignment, the photographer recruited a child visiting the clinic for other reasons to get a "pretend" shot from a nurse willing to participate in the photo. When the staging was discovered, the newspaper reprimanded the reporter and apologized to its readers.

That deception might be viewed as trivial, but in other cases staged news events have consequences that extend beyond the original deception.

In 1991, a television station in Denver investigating local dog-fighting rings aired a videotape it claimed to have been submitted by an anonymous source, showing an actual dogfight. It was later determined that two reporters had staged the fight themselves. Both reporters were fired, and one was later convicted of violating the state's animal cruelty laws.

Two years later, a television news crew in Minneapolis was researching a story about underage drinking. Unable to find a legitimate example to record, a reporter bought two cases of beer for six teenagers willing to cooperate in the staged scene. Not only were the reporter and camera operator fired, but they were also charged with violating state liquor laws. After pleading guilty, they were fined $500, sentenced to 10 days in jail, and were required to do community service.

In 1992, NBC's award-winning *Dateline* magazine program broadcast a story about incidents involving certain models of General Motors trucks that caught fire as a result of a design flaw that left gas tanks unprotected in cases of side-impact crashes. The report included several cases of children who died in those crashes.

In order to demonstrate the danger, *Dateline* staged a crash in which a GM truck was struck on its side by a car, and as expected, it burst into flames. What the report left out, however, was that officials of the independent testing agency were afraid that the truck might not explode as expected, and because it would be too expensive to try the demonstration a second time, they rigged the truck with remote-controlled ignition devices. Whether the explosion was caused by the design of the gas tank (without the artificial assist) or by the supplementary ignition devices was never determined. But after the incident became public knowledge, the network retracted the entire story, even though it included numerous cases involving passenger deaths.

Correction Policies

Research into the subject of media errors indicates that between 40 and 60 percent of all published or broadcast stories include at least one error (as claimed by one or more of the individuals or organizations mentioned in the story). That does not mean that 40 to 60 percent of all stories result in complaints made to media organizations, as many subjects fail — for a variety of reasons — to formally complain about the errors. In most studies, the methodology used in these surveys is the telephone interview, and researchers often find that subjects of news stories would describe errors in telephone interviews that they had not brought to the attention of the media organization.

The same studies also indicate that of the stories claimed by the subjects to include factual errors, the average was 2.5 errors per story. Surprisingly, other research indicates that the perception that errors result mainly from competition and deadline pressure is at least partially erroneous, as stories prepared under deadline pressure actually produce fewer errors than those published under less stressful circumstances.

The terms *clarification, correction,* and *retraction* are often used incorrectly or interchangeably to refer to a media organization's admission that it published or broadcast information that was erroneous or misleading. While the general public may occasionally misuse the terms, it is important that professional journalists (and journalism students) do not.

Clarifications. As the term indicates, a **clarification** is a statement in which the media organization does not admit an error, but instead simply explains how information previously published or broadcast may have been misinterpreted.

Many clarifications follow requests by individuals or organizations that are the focus of news stories and often result not from information that was reported, but from what was left out. For example, a story about a criminal suspect might make reference to a previous case in which the individual was charged with a crime, but omitted the fact that the charges were later dropped, or that he or she had been found not guilty at trial. Without that information, some readers or viewers might assume the individual was guilty of the previous accusation. Because the harm to the individual's reputation is usually minimal, a clarification may or may not be accompanied by an apology. Some newspaper editors and television news directors find requests for clarifications annoying, but they issue them to "avoid having debates about semantics."

Corrections. A **correction** is an item published or broadcast in which the media organization admits the falsity of one or more details included in a story, but contends that the overall story is factual. For example, a newspaper story might report that an incident occurred on Oak Tree Lane when it actually occurred on Oak Tree Avenue, or that an individual in a story was a pediatrician when he or she was actually a podiatrist. Regardless of whether such errors caused any harm, most corrections include an apology to the individuals affected.

Three recent incidents illustrate the need to correct errors as quickly as possible, especially in more serious cases.

In January 2011, Congresswoman Gabrielle Giffords was shot in the head at a public event in Tucson, Arizona. Within a few hours, National Public Radio reported on the air, on its website, and by its Twitter account that the congresswoman had died. Other media then reported Gifford's death, based on the NPR report. Although seriously wounded, Giffords was still very much alive, prompting all of the affected media to correct the error and apologize to both their audiences and the Giffords family. Giffords' husband, astronaut Mark Kelly, was on his way from Houston to Tucson by private plane when he was informed of his wife's death and did not learn for several hours that she had survived the shooting.

On December 14, 2012, the national media reported that 24-year-old Ryan Lanza had gone into Sandy Hook Elementary School in Newtown, Connecticut and killed 20 students, six adults, and himself. It turned out that at the time, Ryan Lanza was 76 miles away in Hoboken, New Jersey. The killer was his 20-year-old brother, Adam, who was carrying Ryan's wallet and identification cards. In the aftermath of the misidentification, media critics urged journalists to not report names of suspects unless they came from official sources. In the Sandy Hook case, the erroneous identification came from sources not authorized to disclose such information.

In April 2013, the media made numerous errors in reporting on the bombing that took place near the finish line of the Boston Marathon. Within minutes, the media reported that 12 people had been killed, but later had to correct themselves — the real number was only three. Television networks then aired surveillance camera footage showing preliminary suspects who law enforcement agencies had already cleared of any involvement. The following day, the media erroneously reported that an arrest had been made in the case, but then corrected themselves the next day, prompting media critic Rem Reider to write in *USA Today*: "It's doesn't matter how many sources you have if those sources don't know what they're talking about."

Retractions. A **retraction** is an admission that the entire story (or a substantial majority of the details in the story) is false, and the media organization responsible is admitting that it should have never been published or broadcast. Because most potentially controversial or damaging stories are thoroughly fact-checked and in many cases reviewed by attorneys prior to being published or broadcast, retractions are rare in today's media business. Several exceptions are described in Case Study 5-D.

Defamation laws of the 50 states vary greatly in the degree to which corrections and retractions affect the outcome of any lawsuits that result. In some states, a media organization's good-faith effort to correct or retract a story may prevent the case from even going to court. In other states, such efforts may not prevent the case from going to trial, but will work in favor of media organizations by either resulting in court rulings in their favor or at least reducing the size of the monetary judgment awarded to the plaintiffs.

In a 1985 textbook intended for use by high school journalists, veteran reporter and educator DeWitt C. Reddick offered the following rules to help journalists — both students and professionals — avoid having to publish clarifications, corrections, or retractions:

- Check the spelling of every name, address, and title in a telephone directory or other official source. Not every John and Mary spells their names the traditional way. In some cases they're Jon and Merrie. Regardless of how it is pronounced, the primary thoroughfare in town isn't always Main Street. It might be Maine Street or Mayne Street.

- Be wary of estimating numbers of individuals involved in a protest, meeting, accident, or other newsworthy event. Use only numbers provided by law enforcement, emergency medical personnel, or other official sources. If verification is not possible, lean toward conservative estimates.

- Avoid giving attention to the families of persons arrested and/or convicted of crimes in a way that exposes them to public ridicule.

- Unless you are writing an opinion column, do not speculate on the motives behind anyone's behavior or public comments. If you believe his or her motives are critical to the story, ask the individual what his or her motives were and then quote him or her directly.

Making information from newspaper archives available to the public has generated a new type of request for correction — those based on newspaper stories from years ago. In some cases, individuals will ask a newspaper to correct information in its archives because they are planning a job change (and fear prospective employers may find negative information) or a run for public office (and fear their opponents may find it).

When reviewing requests for corrections, newspaper staffers must often distinguish between actual factual errors and information that is merely embarrassing.

In the days of traditional hard-copy newspaper archives, which were simply clipped articles organized into file folders and arranged alphabetically in file cabinets, clippings showing the correction, clarification, or retraction would be stapled to the original story.

Today, with nearly all newspaper archives being in electronic form, stories containing errors can be corrected more easily. Some newspapers simply correct the electronic version without indicating it has been revised, while others keep the erroneous story intact but explain the error and provide the correct information at the top of the story.

Errors occurring in online editions are a bit more difficult to correct. At minimum, the newspaper is obligated to correct the text of the story so that readers finding it in the future will not see the error. However, some readers may have already made a printout of the original story and may not see the corrected version. In order to increase the likelihood of readers knowing about the correction, many online newspapers include a correction on its electronic front page that remains there for several days (unlike the print version, which would run the correction only one time).

From the mid-1970s through the mid-1980s, an organization called the National News Council sought to foster positive relationships between media organizations and their audiences by investigating complaints of erroneous or biased coverage of individuals and issues.

The NNC functioned much like professional arbitrators do in cases of disputes between companies or between companies and their customers. For example, the organization allowed both sides in a dispute to present their cases without employing attorneys and required both sides to accept its findings and promise not to pursue their cases through the legal system. Unlike a court, the NNC did not have the authority to punish the media if it sided with the complainant, but it could require the media organization to publish or broadcast either a correction or retraction.

The goals of the NNC process included improving the image of the news media by showing the public that they were making a sincere effort to solicit their feedback, formalizing the correction and retraction process (as an alternative to libel litigation), and helping media managers get a better feel for how the results of their work affected their audiences. While the NNC no longer exists, a few states have their own news councils.

Throughout the latter half of the 1900s, many major daily newspapers employed individuals known as **ombudsmen** who were assigned to monitor the content of the paper, play "devil's advocate" by representing the interests of the readers in newsroom discussions of content decisions, and field readers' complaints submitted by mail, email, telephone, and in person. Many found the latter function to be effective in preventing lawsuits for defamation and invasion of privacy because they were able to diffuse situations before they became volatile.

The *Louisville Courier-Journal* is believed to have been the first American newspaper to experiment with the idea of an ombudsman, establishing the position in 1967. Among other newspapers, the idea reached its peak of popularity in the 1980s.

By the late 1900s, however, ombudsmen had largely disappeared from the journalism industry. The concept re-emerged in the early 2000s, but with new titles such as "public editor," "reader representative," or "reader advocate." Much like the ombudsmen of the previous century, employees in these positions serve as liaisons between the management of newspapers and their readers. In addition, many write their own weekly or monthly columns in which they explain the steps their employers are taking to improve accuracy.

While some of these individuals are criticized as performing a superficial or "public relations" function, the majority are recognized as performing an important role as liaisons between media organizations and their audiences. The position is an ideal one for a semi-retired reporter or editor wishing to work part-time and stay in touch with the newspaper business.

While many media outlets have assigned specific staff members to handle audience complaints and requests for clarifications and corrections, few have formal policies dealing with how they approach the process. The wide variety of complaints and requests they receive call for dealing with each case on its own merits. But most agree that complaints from audience members be dealt with quickly, professionally, and courteously. Another common factor seen in clarifications and corrections is that they do not specifically repeat the original error; they simply acknowledge that there was an error and then provide the correct information.

Smaller newspapers, instead of employing a specific person to carry out that responsibility, spread it among all of their reporters and editors by listing their telephone numbers and email addresses either below their bylines or at the bottom of their stories. National Public Radio has both a corrections editor, who deals with specific requests to clarifications and corrections, and an ombudsman, who deals with larger quality control issues such as accusations of bias.

Digital Manipulation of Photographs

One of the more controversial issues in newspaper and magazine journalism today is the availability of computer programs that allow users to manipulate the content of digital photographs. Even though such programs have made such deception easier, the general idea is not new. As far back as 1862, President Abraham Lincoln arranged for one of his official presidential photographs to show his head on the body of another politician with a better physique. Throughout the 1900s, dictators such as Josef Stalin, Mao Tse-Tung, Adolf Hitler, Benito Mussolini, and Fidel Castro routinely employed technicians to airbrush out of photographs the images of other politicians who had fallen out of their favor.

When computer programs replaced air-brushing as the dominant methodology in the 1980s, deception required expensive technology and highly skilled technicians. The most common example was the use of the technology to remove dimples, freckles, or other minor imperfections in photographs of fashion models before those images appeared in magazines or on billboards. For the most part, such deception raised few ethical concerns.

The nature of the issue changed again in the late 1990s, when the Adobe Corporation introduced Photoshop, an inexpensive program that anyone with average computer skills could use. Since that product's introduction, the technology has been applied to a variety of purposes, some controversial and some not. The use of Photoshop software has become so popular that the brand name is often used as a verb to refer to the alteration of any photograph by electronic means, such as when someone suggests that a certain person or object could be "photoshopped" out of an image.

The code of ethics of the American Society of Media Photographers (ASMP) states that it is never appropriate for a photographer, journalist, or editor to "alter the content or meaning of a news photograph" or condone such manipulation by other parties. It does not, however, prohibit the alteration of photographs for the purpose of color balancing, contrast adjustment, and cropping or enlarging elements of a photograph, provided that such alteration does not change or distort the context of the photo. The guidelines also allow for the masking or blurring of photographs or video to conceal the identity of individuals such as military intelligence officers or law enforcement personnel working undercover.

The code specifically prohibits the manipulation of photographs in order to change spatial relationships (moving persons or objects closer together or further apart), adding or removing elements not in the original photograph, or merging two or more photographs to create a composite.

In addition to the concern of media ethicists, those involved in the judicial process are concerned about what impact photomanipulation may have on the integrity of evidence presented in criminal and civil trials. Lawyers and judges are concerned that in the future, altered photographs may either convict the innocent or free the guilty — if they have not already.

Fortunately, the same technology that allows photographs to be altered has also produced methods by which the alteration of photographs can be detected. Engineers and chemists within the photographic products industry are constantly developing new software programs and other methods for detecting fraudulent photographs.

Despite the admonitions of ASMP, photomanipulation is common today, although few publications admit having done it until the alterations are detected. The most common rationales used to defend instances of photomanipulation are (1) improving photographic content, (2) intentional deception, (3) dramatic effect, and (4) showing subjects in a more flattering light.

Improving photographic content. Examples of non-controversial uses include the case of *National Geographic*, which altered a photograph of Egyptian pyramids in order to move the structures closer together and produce a more balanced photograph for the magazine's cover. Another magazine once altered a photo that originally showed a woman standing on a fishing pier with a pelican perched about 10 feet away. The altered photograph simply moved the two subjects in the photograph to be about five feet apart. The magazine defended the alteration by claiming it was simply avoiding "wasting space" in between. Another daily newspaper electronically removed a soda can from a person's desk in a news photo because it distracted from the content of the photo and the editors wanted to avoid giving the manufacturer free publicity.

Intentional deception. For its 2001-02 student recruiting booklet, the University of Wisconsin wanted a cover photograph showing a diverse student body. Unable to find a suitable photograph in the archives, university officials instructed the publication staff to insert the face of a male African American student into the crowd scene at a football game. Ironically, the African American man had served on a committee to promote campus diversity and said he had never attended a football game in his four years at UW. After the deception was detected by the student newspaper, the university recalled the booklets and had them reprinted with an authentic photograph showing a diverse group of students in the student union.

In 2005, the Republican National Committee produced a video showing an American soldier watching a television screen on which democratic congressional leaders were criticizing President Bush's strategies regarding the Iraq war. The purpose of the video was to claim that military morale was suffering because of democrats' opposition to the war, but it was later determined that the soldier in the video was actually watching the movie, *How the Grinch Stole Christmas*.

The most serious cases of photomanipulation involve politicians, who find their own images altered in positive ways by their supporters and negative ways by their opponents. During the 2004 election campaign, for example, opponents of democratic presidential candidate John Kerry combined an old photograph of Kerry speaking at a 1971 anti-Vietnam War rally in New York with an image of political activist Jane Fonda speaking at a 1972 anti-war rally in Miami Beach. While both were opposed to the war, the two had never appeared at the same event. Also in 2004, supporters of New York City mayoral candidate Virginia Fields altered a photograph to include two Asian faces at one of her rallies in order to create the impression of her support coming from a diverse audience.

In 2008, during a heated congressional campaign between republican Chris Myers and democrat John Adler, supporters of Adler produced a direct mail piece that included a photograph showing Myers walking with President George W. Bush. The photograph, intended to tarnish the image of Adler by associating him with the unpopular president, was actually a composite of two photographs, as Myers and Bush had never met.

Dramatic effect. In 1994, Olympic skaters Tonya Harding and Nancy Kerrigan were shown appearing to skate together on the cover of *Newsday*. A few weeks earlier, friends of Harding had allegedly arranged for Kerrigan to be injured prior to the Olympic trials, so the editorial staff believed the composite photograph (which was identified as such in small print) would be more dramatic than showing them skating separately.

In the same week in 1994, the covers of both *Time* and *Newsweek* featured a photograph of accused murderer O.J. Simpson that had been provided by the Los Angeles Police Department. But there was a striking difference between the two magazine covers. *Time* had used its technology to darken Simpson's skin and add facial stubble, while the *Newsweek* cover showed a more natural-looking Simpson. While looking at the covers separately, many readers would not have noticed a difference, but when looking at the magazine covers side-by-side, the difference was obvious. *Time* editors admitted the idea was to make Simpson look "more sinister" and pointed to its labeling of the cover art as a "photo illustration" rather than a "photograph." But few critics accepted that explanation, and many civil rights groups complained that the deception was based on racial stereotypes of black men as dark-skinned and angry.

In March 2007, the image of former President Ronald Reagan appeared on the cover of *Time*, accompanied by the headline, "How the Right Went Wrong." The image was doctored to include a tear on the face of Reagan, who had died three years earlier. The magazine defended the image by calling it a "conceptual cover."

Showing subjects in a more flattering light. In an August 1989 issue of *TV Guide*, the head of talk-show host Oprah Winfrey appeared on the body of a much slimmer Ann Margaret, without permission of either woman. The deception was detected when Margaret's fashion designer recognized the dress in the photograph. In 1997, the photograph of an Iowa mother who made news by delivering quintuplets was doctored to make her teeth look straighter and whiter. Ironically, the photo had been altered for the cover of *Newsweek*, the same publication that publicly admonished its competitor, *Time*, over the Simpson incident.

In 2002, a newspaper in Los Angeles doctored the photo of a man involved in a freeway car crash to avoid showing that he had wet the front of his pants as a result of the head trauma he suffered in the accident. That same year, a daily newspaper altered a photograph taken at a local zoo, fearing that some readers might have been offended by the sight of a male lion's genitals.

In 2006, as CBS News prepared to introduce Katie Couric in her new role as anchor of the evening news, a publicity photograph was altered to give her a trimmer waistline and thinner face.

For Discussion

Case Study 5-A   Arthur Ashe Has AIDS

In early September 1991, *Sports Illustrated* senior editor Roy Johnson received a phone call from a reputable information source familiar with the world of professional tennis. "You know about Arthur Ashe," the source told Johnson. "He has AIDS."

At first, Johnson, who considered himself a friend of Ashe, dismissed it as simply a rumor. Then a similar call from a different source came in November.

Now believing that the information was valid, Johnson was faced with a dilemma. On one hand, he believed that because Ashe had retired from professional tennis many years earlier, he had regained his status as a private person and had the right to keep his illness secret. But on the other hand, Ashe was still one of the most respected African American men in America, as he had become an advocate for health and education issues in the United States and a champion for human rights around the world. As such, he remained a public figure, and if he was seriously ill, perhaps the public had a right to know about it.

Johnson noticed the contrast in decisions made by Ashe and basketball star Ervin "Magic" Johnson. A few weeks earlier, Johnson announced that he had AIDS, and the public was mostly sympathetic, even though he admitted that his infection was due to a promiscuous lifestyle. Ashe, in contrast, had contracted the disease from a blood transfusion following major surgery.

Because of his friendship with Ashe and respect for his privacy, Johnson decided to keep the information secret, not telling any of his colleagues at *Sports Illustrated* nor asking Ashe about it directly, even though the two often saw each other socially.

Then in April 1992, *USA Today* tennis writer Doug Smith learned the same information and made a different decision. He called Ashe directly and confirmed the details, then broke the story.

The management of *USA Today* called Ashe's illness a "significant news story" and claimed it pursued it with the same zeal it would have if the disease had been cancer or other disease without a social stigma. When *USA Today* defended its decision by claiming that it didn't have "a special zone for AIDS," Johnson replied in his own column, "Well, it's time we created one."

Johnson's condemnation of other media for breaking the story was based on his belief that despite being public figures, active and retired professional athletes deserved the same privacy rights as anyone else. That was especially the case with AIDS, which despite being contracted through blood transfusions and accidental needle sticks, still carries a stigma related to promiscuity, homosexuality, and illegal drug use. Johnson contrasted Ashe's decision with that of Magic Johnson, who chose to reveal his illness in part to warn other professional athletes as well as the general public of the dangers of unprotected sex.

In defending the newspaper's decision, *USA Today* Sports Editor Gene Policinski wrote that "one of the greatest athletes of the century has a fatal illness — by any journalist's definition, that's news." In coming to the newspaper's defense, other editors said they would have made the same decision, some of them adding two other justifycations. The first was that Ashe's illness was inconsistent with the common belief that the disease affected mostly drug addicts and homosexual men. The second was the irony of Ashe sitting on the board of directors of a life insurance company involved in the national debate over insurance coverage for AIDS patients.

Johnson was not alone in his criticism of *USA Today* and other media who disregarded Ashe's privacy. "If the man dies one day earlier because of the stress caused by this story, it's not worth it," said one media critic.

Media critic Howard Kurtz admonished journalists for not reporting the Ashe story once they were aware of it. In his own account of the issue, Kurtz wrote that concealing the illness of a public figure simply because that person is a friend "serves to reinforce people's worst suspicions about the press — that we sometimes get too close to the people we cover."

Ten months after the story broke, Ashe died at the age of 49. Today, he is still one of the most admired individuals in the world, not only for his accomplishments in professional tennis, but also for his humanitarian and civil rights work around the world.

- Evaluate the contrasting decisions made by Roy Johnson of *Sports Illustrated* and Doug Smith of *USA Today*. Which one has the stronger case?

- Which philosophers (from Chapter 2) could you cite in supporting or opposing those decisions? Which ethical codes apply?

Case Study 5-B

**No One Asked You to Leave,
But No One Invited You In**

On October 30, 1979, 59-year-old Dave Miller suffered a heart attack in his Los Angeles home. Alerted to the situation by the screams of Miller's wife, Brownie, neighbors came over and immediately called 911. Paramedics arrived within minutes, but so did a KNBC camera crew that was researching a story on the quality of emergency medical care in the community. While Brownie Miller and the neighbors waited downstairs, the camera crew recorded the drama as the paramedics worked desperately but unsuccessfully to save her husband's life.

In the days that followed, Brownie Miller was busy planning her husband's funeral and didn't give much thought to the presence of the camera crew. But when other family members saw numerous replays of the incident on the television news and commercials promoting the station's series on the training and competency of paramedics, they were outraged. They persuaded Brownie Miller to complain to the management of the station, and — when that didn't work — to sue the station for invasion of privacy, based not only on the physical intrusion by the camera crew and equipment, but also on the emotional trauma caused by watching Dave Miller die over and over again on television.

During the protracted legal battle, station management and attorneys offered the following defenses:

(1) Because there had been considerable criticism of emergency medical services provided by local government, the station was functioning in its "watchdog" role and performing a public service by reporting on a matter of public interest.

(2) The film crew made a special effort to not show Dave Miller's face. Miller's daughter and friends disputed that claim, reporting that they recognized Dave and Brownie Miller, as well as the interior of their home, in the news reports. In court testimony, one employee of the station also contradicted that claim by reporting they were mostly concerned with making sure they did not interfere with the paramedics' work.

(3) Because neither the wife nor neighbors objected to the crew's presence, the rule of "implied consent" should be applied. The family and its attorney responded that the issue was not that no one asked the station's employers to leave, but that no one had invited them in.

During the six years of litigation that followed, a lower court ruled in favor of KNBC, and an appeals court reversed and ruled in favor of the family. Before the case could be appealed yet again to the California Supreme Court, the two sides reached an undisclosed out-of-court financial settlement.

- Which interest should take priority in this case — the family's right to privacy, or the media's right to research stories of public interest?

- Who had the strongest argument in this case? The management of the television station, who argued that "no one asked us to leave," or the family members, who argued that "no one invited you in"?

Case Study 5-C

Is Nancy Grace to Blame for Melinda Duckett's Suicide?

In September 2006, television talk show host Nancy Grace was accused of contributing to the suicide of an unstable young mother whose 2-year-old son was missing. When 21-year-old Melinda Duckett agreed to be interviewed by telephone, she knew nothing about Grace's aggressive and confrontational style. Grace asked questions in an accusatory manner that did not suggest Duckett was guilty in the disappearance, only that she was not as forthcoming as she could have been in interviews with the media and police. By the end of the interview, Grace was pounding her desk and demanding, "Where were you? Why aren't you telling us where you were that day?"

The interview was on tape, and less than 24 hours later, shortly before it was scheduled to be aired on Cable News Network (CNN), Duckett drove to her grandparents' home in Leesburg, Florida, and killed herself with her father's shotgun. CNN learned about the woman's death, but decided to go forward with the broadcast, a decision that angered Duckett's friends and family as well as many in the general public. Grace defended her interviewing style and denied that it influenced Duckett to kill herself. "If anything, I would suggest that guilt made her commit suicide," Grace said in an ABC News interview. "To suggest that a 15- or 20-minute interview can cause someone to commit suicide is focusing on the wrong thing."

Duckett's family disputed any suggestion that the woman hurt her son. They said that the strain of her son's disappearance pushed her to the brink, and the media sent her over the edge. "Nancy Grace and the others, they just bashed her to the end," Duckett's grandfather, Bill Eubank, told the Associated Press.

Some media analysts agree, saying Grace's interview simply went too far. "How is that questioning doing anything but making a person in a desperate situation feeling even more desperate?" asked Hub Brown, a professor at Syracuse University's Newhouse School of Communications.

- When individuals in the news commit suicide, how much responsibility should be assigned to the aggressive nature of the media, and how much lies with the person, whose mental instability may not be known?

- Are there any philosophers or concepts from Chapter 2 that could be applied here?

Case Study 5-D To Err is Human, to Correct Divine

As mentioned earlier in this chapter, clarifications and corrections of errors are common in both print and broadcast journalism. In the case of corrections, media organizations are admitting that a minor detail of the story was false but that the overall story was correct. Retractions, in contrast, represent an admission that the entire story (or the majority of it) was false. Complete retractions of stories are rare, but those instances usually make journalism history, damage the organization's reputation for years, and in some cases cost journalists their jobs.

When producers at Cable News Network were ready to unveil their new magazine program titled *Newsstand* in 1998, they wanted a story for the first episode that would create broadcast news history. It did — but not for the right reasons. The initial episode claimed that during the latter stages of the Vietnam War, U.S. aircraft intentionally sprayed nerve gas on deserting American troops in what was known as "Operation Tailwind."

The primary source for the story was an 86-year-old former Pentagon official who was living in an assisted-living facility. Other CNN reporters said later that they had stopped using him as a source several years earlier because of his declining mental fitness. Much of the story turned out to be false, prompting the network to retract it. Although the network never released the results of its inquiry into how the erroneous story made it on air, outside media critics speculated that the network was so intent on "hitting a home run" with the first installment of its new program that it disregarded reporters' concerns about inconsistencies in the story.

As discussed earlier in this chapter, in 1992 NBC was forced to retract a *Dateline* story about General Motors trucks that caught fire because of a design flaw in their gas tanks. The story included the details of numerous tragedies in which trucks had burst into flames as a result of side-impact crashes. Several family members of the victims were also interviewed.

While much of the story was true, the retraction was still necessary because the independent testing agency the network hired to conduct videotaped experiments had rigged one truck with remote-control ignition devices. Several NBC producers were reprimanded as a result of the retraction, and network president Michael Gartner later resigned.

In 2004, CBS News reported on its Wednesday night edition of *60 Minutes* that President George W. Bush had received preferential treatment that helped him avoid going to Vietnam during his service in the Texas Air National Guard in the 1970s. CBS based its reporting on paperwork reportedly discovered in the files of Bush's commanding officer. The documents were later proven to be forgeries, leading CBS News to retract the story and lead anchor Dan Rather to personally apologize to the president. Media critics referred to "Rathergate" as one of the biggest blunders in journalism history, and it resulted in the firing of one CBS producer and resignations of three others. Rather retired from the network the following year.

In 2005, *Newsweek* magazine published a story about the alleged mistreatment of suspected terrorists being held at the American military prison at Guantanamo Bay, Cuba. The story reported that American soldiers desecrated copies of the Koran, the Muslim equivalent of the Bible, including flushing one copy down a prison toilet. Within days, violent anti-American protests broke out in Muslim countries around the world, including one incident in Afghanistan in which 14 people died.

Pentagon officials investigated the charges, but issued a statement indicating they had found nothing to substantiate the allegations in the *Newsweek* article. The incident with the Koran, it turned out, involved one of detainees (not an American soldier) who flushed a few pages (not an entire book) down a toilet to protest conditions at the prison.

Within a week of the Pentagon's report, *Newsweek* retracted the article. In its own investigation of what went wrong, the magazine's editorial staff claimed that the information came from a confidential source that had been reliable in the past. In addition to the loss of life, the erroneous story damaged the reputation of *Newsweek* (and American media in general) and inflamed the tensions that already existed between Islamic and non-Islamic nations.

In 2015, the news-pop culture magazine *Rolling Stone* retracted a story it has published the previous year about an alleged gang rape in a fraternity house at University of Virginia. Based largely on the account of one female student, who it identified only as "Jackie," the story resulted in the fraternity being suspended and a comprehensive investigation launched by campus and off-campus law enforcement agencies. The story quickly fell apart when *The Washington Post* attempted to do a follow-up story and was unable to confirm the details of the original article. The *Post* reporters did learn, however, that the author of the story did not contact members of the fraternity in order to include their side of the story.

After months of criticism, *Rolling Stone* publisher Jann Wenner asked the Columbia School of Journalism to investigate what went wrong and suggest changes to the magazine's editorial process. A senior administrator at the university, charging that the article implied that she did not take the charges seriously, filed a defamation suit against the magazine and the article's author. The fraternity mentioned in the story also indicated plans to pursue legal action.

While retractions such as those are quite serious (but fortunately quite rare), some minor errors requiring only corrections and apologies are actually humorous. *Dallas Morning News* columnist Norma Adams-Wade once mistakenly referred to local citizen Mary Ann Thompson-French as a "socialist." She apologized to the woman in a subsequent column, clarifying that she meant to write "socialite." The daily newspaper *The East Oregonian* published a story about Pat Venditte, an Oakland Athletics pitcher who threw equally well right- and left-handed. The headline on the story identified Venditte as "amphibious," when it should have read, "ambidextrous."

A college newspaper story about Filipinos who immigrated to California in the 1850s indicated that the name of their boat, Nuestra Senora de Buena Esperanza, translated into English as "Big Ass Spanish Boat." In its next edition, the newspaper corrected its mistake and apologized to its readers and Filipino-Americans in the surrounding community who were offended. The name actually translates into "Our Lady of Good Hope." The newspaper staff admitted that it found the erroneous translation on the Internet, and with no Spanish-speaking students on the staff, it had no way of checking it.

Following the May 2011 raid on the Pakistan hideout of terrorist Osama bin Laden by U.S. Navy Seals, journalists at a German television station searched Internet sources for more information on the Seals, and hopefully some artwork. They found what they believed to be the logo of the Navy Seals, but after the station used it as part of its coverage of the assault, many viewers called the station to report that it had mistakenly used a logo from a fictional organization depicted in the *Star Trek: Deep Space Nine* television series. The erroneous logo included phasers, a Klingon skull, and other artifacts that exist only in the fictional world of the 24th century. Station managers apologized for the error but said they had no idea how the mix-up happened.

- Earlier in this chapter was a description of "ombudsmen" and "reader advocates" whose job it is to field complaints and requests for clarifications and corrections. By creating full-time positions to do such work (instead of having newspaper editors and television station managers), what statement are they making? That they are seriously dedicated to addressing audience concerns? Or that they make so many mistakes that it requires a full-time person to deal with the results?

Case Study 5-E   **Naming Names**

In the weeks following the 2004 presidential election, the *Tennessee Tribune*, a weekly newspaper serving a largely African American readership in Nashville, published the names and addresses of registered voters who did not vote. Obviously, which candidates or issues that individuals voted for or against remained secret, but whether or not they went to the polls is public information under Tennessee's open records law.

The newspaper defended itself by claiming it was simply trying to encourage (its critics used the term "shame") citizens into voting in future elections. But many of those named said their privacy had been invaded.

"Sometimes when you embarrass people, they will do the right thing," said the newspaper's publisher in an interview with a local television station. The publisher added that the goal was to increase voter turnout among African Americans, which she claimed was one of the most effective ways to create social and political change in the city, state, and country.

Although some may question the cause-and-effect claim, the newspaper's strategy may have worked. In subsequent elections, voting records showed an increase in turnout far above state and national averages. Because of the costs of printing such a long list, however, the newspaper now publishes the list of non-voters on its website rather than its hard-copy edition.

Despite the positive results, the topic remains a controversial one among the people of Nashville, regardless of whether they found their names on the list or not. "This seems to be to be a stupid tactic to get someone to vote," wrote one reader responding on the paper's website. "It's no one's business who didn't vote and their reasons." Another reader wrote, "I believe that publishing the names of citizens along with their addresses is a punitive, embarrassing, and dangerous practice."

- Do you agree with the newspaper's explanation of its motives, that it is merely attempting to increase voter turnout, or the opinion of the critics, that this is an invasion of privacy?

Case Study 5-F

A Ryder Truck Outside the Federal Building: Déjà Vu All Over Again

On March 31, 1997, reporters at a television station in Tampa, Florida resorted to an unusual reporting method to test the vulnerability of a federal office building to a terrorist attack. Renting a Ryder truck from a local dealer, the reporters left it in front of the federal courthouse in downtown Tampa, then watched and waited inside the truck to see how long it would take for courthouse security or law enforcement personnel to notice it.

Nothing happened while the reporters remained inside the truck, but when one exited and began walking down the sidewalk, he was questioned by building security and the truck was searched. Once the stunt was exposed, law enforcement personnel admonished the reporters but did not file any formal charges. Their complaint was based on concerns that the incident unnecessarily distracted security personnel and law enforcement from their other duties and placed the safety of the reporters and bystanders in jeopardy, as private citizens acting on their own might have attacked the truck or its occupants.

Media ethicists were quick to point out that the journalists violated the second and third parts of the three-part test commonly used in making such decisions regarding misrepresentation and deception (the test is described on p. 123). While the station might base its defense on the significance of the story — the life-and-death nature of terrorist attacks — the reporters involved had not exhausted other reporting methods and did not have the permission of station management.

Even though he claimed to have no advance knowledge of what the reporters were planning, the station's news director defended their actions and claimed that the significance of the story outweighed any ethical concerns. He analogized the incident to a hypothetical case of an individual who pulls a fire alarm (in the absence of an actual fire) to draw attention to the fact that the fire alarm did not work.

The date of the incident was not a coincidence. That morning, in a courthouse in Denver, domestic terrorist Timothy McVeigh was facing the first day of his murder trial. Two years earlier, McVeigh had loaded a Ryder rental truck with homemade explosives and destroyed the Murrah Federal Building in Oklahoma City, killing 168 people.

- Do you agree with viewpoint of law enforcement personnel and media ethicists, who claim there was too much potential for this incident to take a wrong turn?

- Or do you agree with the position of the news director, who claimed that the significance of the story outweighed any ethical concerns over their newsgathering methods?

- To what degree, if any, is your view influenced by the date chosen for the stunt (the first day of the McVeigh trial)?

Discussion Problem 5-A   **The Senator and the Tattoo**

Senator Batson D. Belfry is a decorated war veteran running for president. One of his campaign issues is a proposed constitutional amendment to provide punishment for desecration of the American flag by burning or any other act the courts determined to be disrespectful. At the height of the campaign, the senator's 19-year-old daughter, a student at Enormous State University, is taken to the hospital after complaining of dizziness and nausea. At the hospital she is diagnosed with hepatitis, and the media covering the senator's campaign soon learn the cause of the infection — the tattoo of an American flag on her left buttock.

1. Do the media have the right to report the cause of the daughter's illness?

2. Does the inconsistency between the senator's position on flag desecration and the daughter's choice of body art make the issue more newsworthy?

3. Is the daughter's age a consideration? What if she was 16? What if she was 25?

4. Does the daughter's role (or lack of it) in the campaign affect your answer? If she plays an active role in the campaign, including supporting (or opposing) the flag desecration amendment, does that affect your answer?

5. Which of the philosophers studied in Chapter 2 might help a journalist make this decision? What about the ethical codes?

Discussion Problem 5-B   The Mayor and the Missing Kid

Just one year into his term, the mayor of your city has died unexpectedly. The city's charter stipulates that in the event of the mayor's death or resignation, the city council chooses from among its own members a person to serve the balance of the mayor's term. After several days of debate, the council is hopelessly deadlocked and is unable to choose between the two council members interested in the job. Then one member suggests a compromise candidate: the newest member of the council, who is at first reluctant but eventually agrees to take the job. At 28, he is the youngest member of the council and the least experienced, but he is the only member that all of the other members can agree on to ascend to the mayor's office.

You're the city hall reporter for the local daily newspaper and have the primary responsibility for covering the activities and personalities involved in the city council and the mayor's office. As soon as the council's decision is made public, you decide to write an in-depth profile of the new mayor, who will be the youngest mayor in the country and has become a national news story almost overnight.

In your profile, you want to go beyond his political career and include some personal information, but because of his short period of time on the council, his family life is a mystery. You decide to conduct extensive background research on the man, spending several days gathering information from previously published newspapers and magazine articles, Internet sources, and public records. But you notice an interesting discrepancy regarding the mayor's family: In all of the articles published prior to 2010, the mayor and his wife are said to have three children, and their names and ages are listed. But in all of the articles published in 2010 and since, only the two youngest children are listed. Because the information is consistent among the two categories of news stories, there is no doubt that something must have happened to the oldest child.

1. Would you ask the mayor about the oldest child? If your answer is "yes," explain why you believe that information is of public interest, and how you would attempt to overcome the mayor's objections to having that information released. If your answer is "no," explain how you would deal with the likelihood that other reporters will notice the discrepancy and will want to ask the mayor the same question.

2. What are other possible solutions to this dilemma?

3. Which philosophers discussed in Chapter 2 might help you make this decision? Which ethical codes and provisions might apply?

Discussion Questions

501. Re-read the highlights of the ethical codes provided earlier in this chapter. Which of those provisions do you believe are realistic and easy to enforce, and which do you believe would be unrealistic and difficult to enforce if journalists are to do an effective job of reporting on public affairs and functioning as the "government watchdog"?

502. Assume the position of editor of a daily newspaper or news director of a television station. A reporter comes to you with the idea to dress up as a homeless person and panhandle for money on a downtown street corner with the intention of writing a story about his experiences. A photographer will be concealed nearby to take photographs (or in the case of a television reporter, a videographer will record the conversations on both video and audio). What are your ethical concerns about allowing this? What conditions or ground rules would you give the reporter and photographer (or videographer)? What happens to the money collected?

503. Assume that you approved the newsgathering technique described above and the story is successful. Now the same reporter comes to you with the idea of pretending to be homeless person seeking admission to one of the city's homeless shelters.

In version A of the scenario, there is no suspicion of wrongdoing; the reporter simply wants to use the deception to research a story about homelessness and shelter conditions in the city. What are your ethical concerns? What conditions or ground rules would you give the reporter?

In version B of the scenario, suppose there had already been some accusations that the shelter was unsanitary, served substandard food, and that its employees often verbally abused those seeking services. In giving the reporter permission to carry out the deception, do the ends justify the means?

504. Re-read the three cases involving the son of the football coach, the daughter of the Florida governor, and the daughter of 2008 vice-presidential candidate Sarah Palin (pp. 109-10). Do you agree with the policy that children of public figures are not treated differently than the children of private persons? Do you agree with media's decision to treat these two cases differently because of the inconsistency between the children's behavior and the parents' public comments?

Notes

110   **"abstinence-only did not work in her own household"**: Howard Kurtz, "From the Radio Right Comes an Amen Chorus for Palin." *Washington Post,* September 4, 2008, p. 25-A.

110   **"People who run for public office give up their expectation of privacy"**: Howard Kurtz, *The Media Circus: The Trouble with America's Newspapers.* New York: Random House, 1994, p. 155.

112   **"When my father was burglarized"**: Katha Pollitt, "Naming and Blaming: Media Goes Wilding in Palm Beach." *The Nation,* June 24, 1991, pp. 833-838.

112   **"make up his or her own mind" and "In no other category of news"**: Michael Gartner, "Naming the Victim." *Columbia Journalism Review*, July/August 1991, pp. 54-55.

113   **"a buzzing insect"**: Randy Bobbitt, *Exploring Communication Law*. Boston: Allyn & Bacon, 2008, p. 149.

114   **"Why didn't the Jovanovics"**: Patty Ryan, "Buried Secrets." *The Tampa Tribune*, September 30, 1991, p. 1-D.

115   **more likely to save lives than cause copycats**: Zach Schonfeld, "Two Months After Robin Williams' Death, Suicide Hotlines Still See a Spike in Calls." *Newsweek*, October 12, 2014.

119   **"a high-ranking State Department official"**: Ron Smith, *Groping for Ethics in Journalism.* Ames, IA: Wiley-Blackwell, 2003, p. 181.

121   **"never alter quotations"**: *Associated Press Stylebook*, p. 203.

122   **"used five words to replace one word"**: Smith, p. 143.

123   **"To lie to a source about your identity"**: "Remember Ethics in Wake of Fake Phone Call to Wisconsin Governor." *SPJ News,* February 23, 2011.

123   **"a journalist's only option"**: Paul Smith, "Prank Call to Governor Was Good Journalism." *The Voyager* (University of West Florida), March 2, 2011, p. 3.

126   **"Some of the greatest photographs in history"**: "Critics Say ABC Opened its Checkbook for a News Source." *New York Times*, May 31, 1999, p. 1-C.

126   **"giving interviews takes time away from (his) business"**: Ron Smith, *Groping for Ethics in Journalism.* Ames, IA: Wiley-Blackwell, 2003, p. 185.

127   **"poor judgments"**: Kurt Eichenwald, "A Reporter's Essay: Making a Connection with Justin." *New York Times*, December 19, 2005.

127   **"It is easy to sell your integrity"**: Randy Bobbitt and Ruth Sullivan, *Developing the Public Relations Campaign.* Boston: Allyn & Bacon, 2009, p. 217.

128   **"A business courtesy should not be accepted" and "the entire press is on the take"**: New York Times Company Code of Ethics.

128   **"return them all with a polite thank-you"**: Mitchell Stephens, *Broadcast News.* New York: Holt, Rinehart and Winston, 1986, p. 177.

130   **"but it doesn't seem worth it"**: Mike Wallace and Beth Knobel, *Heat and Light: Advice for the Next Generation of Journalists.* New York: Three Rivers Press, 2010, p. 176.

132   **"It doesn't matter how many sources you have":** Rem Reider, "Race to be First Becomes a Race to be Wrong." *USA Today*, April 19, 2013, p. 2-B.

133   **"Check the spelling of every name":** DeWitt C. Reddick, *The Mass Media and the Student Newspaper*. New York: Wadsworth Publishing, 1985.

138   **"a special zone for AIDS" and "It's time we created one":** Roy Johnson, "None of Our Business." *Sports Illustrated*, April 20, 1992, p. 82.

139   **"by any journalist's definition, that's news":** Gene Foreman, *The Ethical Journalist*. Malden, MA: Wiley-Blackwell Publishing, 2011, p. 245.

139   **"sometimes we get too close to the people we cover":** Kurtz, *The Media Circus: The Trouble with America's Newspapers*. New York: Random House, 1994, p. 154.

140   **"Because there had been considerable criticism**:" Ellen Alderman and Caroline Kennedy, *The Right to Privacy*. New York: Alfred A. Knopf, 1995, pp. 176-88.

141   **"To suggest that a 15- or 20-minute interview," "Nancy Grace and the others," and "How is that questioning":** Bob Jamieson, "Nancy Grace Ripped After Missing Boy's Mom Kills Herself." ABCNews.com, September 14, 2006.

144   **"Sometimes when you embarrass people," "it's no one's business," and "I believe that publishing the names":** "Paper Lists Registered Non-Voters." NewsChannel5.com, October 15, 2008.

CHAPTER 6

Ethical Issues in Advertising

Background

- A local fast-food restaurant chain often receives low sanitation scores based on the health department's random inspections. Those results are published in the daily newspaper and broadcast on television news. Frustrated with the negative coverage, the franchisee sends letters to both the newspaper and television station threatening to cancel the company's advertising if those media outlets continue to publicize the low sanitation scores.

- A local tourism magazine has a policy it calls 4-to-1. For each issue, the advertising sales department promises major hotels and restaurants that for each four column-inches of advertising space purchased, the magazine will publish one inch of "free" publicity in the form of a positive news story about that hotel or restaurant.

- A state lottery agency introduces a new scratch-off ticket game scheduled to begin on Memorial Day and conclude on the Fourth of July. While there are thousands of prizes between $5 and $1,000, there is only one grand-prize ticket worth $1 million. That winning ticket is bought and redeemed on June 2 — the first week of the game. However, the lottery agency continues to run the ads promoting the $1 million grand prize. When the media pursue the story and accuse lottery officials of deceptive advertising, the agency's response is, "We should all remember that lottery proceeds go to support education."

By its nature, advertising is a biased formed of communication. It either advocates a point of view, encourages audience members to take specific actions (often to purchase a product or service), or both. Unlike journalism and public relations, it has never claimed to be a neutral or unbiased source of political or consumer information. As John Crichton, former president of the American Association of Advertising Agencies, once wrote:

"The seller sees a house he owns as it ought to be: 'Brick colonial, 7 rooms, 2 baths, quiet neighborhood, old shade, gardens, brick patio.' It never occurred to him that his ad might read, 'Brick colonial, 7 small rooms, 2 baths of which one needs new tile, old trees but the elm is dying, gardens which require maintenance, brick patio which doesn't drain well, and a roof that will need replacement in two years.' "

There are six major venues for advertising: print, broadcast, direct mail, outdoor, transit, and Internet. Those distinctions are important because those venues are subject to varying degrees of government regulation, and the ethical codes of different professional organizations apply. In addition to those labels, most advertising can be placed in one of three categories: **traditional retail advertising** (that encourages consumers to visit a retail establishment), **direct response advertising** (that encourages consumers to either call a toll-free telephone number or visit a website), and **behavioral advertising**, which matches online users to their interests based on their online activities.

The latter form of advertising is the newest and most controversial. Since the mid-1990s, a program known as "cookies" has allowed marketers to develop individualized profiles of Internet users, based simply on websites they visit, and sell that information to advertisers. A user visiting websites dealing with how to buy a new car would be presumed to be in the market for such a purchase, for example, and would likely be the target of pop-up ads and other unsolicited information from local car dealers. An individual who spends a lot of time reading tennis news and following the results of professional tennis tournaments online would likely begin receiving solicitations from local sporting goods stores highlighting their latest tennis-related products.

Cookies has since been overshadowed by more sophisticated information-gathering techniques. GMail, Google's free email program, targets advertising to computer users based on keywords that appear in outgoing email messages. Social networking sites such as Facebook, Twitter, and Instagram have employed similar techniques, and periodically make changes to their privacy policies in response to consumer complaints and threats of regulatory action by the Federal Trade Commission. Much of the technology is proprietary, and its creators are reluctant to explain how it works; they simply respond to the criticism by claiming that Internet users voluntarily give up part of their privacy when they surf the Web or send an email.

Legal and Ethical Framework

Much like other potential problem areas in mass communications, advertising is subject to both legal restrictions and ethical limitations. The Federal Trade Commission is the primary government agency in charge of regulating the advertising industry, but it prefers that advertisers voluntarily produce work that is tasteful, truthful, and in its correct context. The primary professional organization providing ethical guidance is the American Advertising Federation (AAF).

The AAF Code, perhaps the most concise ethical code among those of the major professional organizations dealing with the mass media, requires that advertising content reflect the truth, avoid misleading consumers, and be in good taste. The code also prohibits bait-and-switch advertising and false comparisons and advises members to be cautious in developing advertisements that involve testimonials, price claims, guarantees, and warranties. The code is provided in its entirety in Appendix A.

The American Association of Advertising Agencies Standards of Practice, also quite concise, simply prohibits five specific actions, all related to the content of advertising: (1) false or misleading statements or exaggerations, (2) testimonials which do not reflect the real opinion of the individual(s) involved, (3) price claims which are misleading, (4) claims insufficiently supported or that distort the true meaning of statements made by a scientific authority, and (5) statements, suggestions, or pictures offensive to public decency or minority members of the community. The list of standards is provided in its entirety in Appendix A.

Government Regulation

The history of commercial advertising in the United States can be divided into three time periods.

Throughout much of 1800s, American merchants promoted their products through newspaper and magazine advertisements and flyers distributed door-to-door and displayed in public gathering places. Advertisers could make exaggerated or purely fictional claims, and with little regulation by government agencies or professional regulatory organizations, consumers who were misled or cheated had little recourse. The Latin term **caveat emptor** ("let the buyer beware") was the guiding principle.

In the early 1900s, however, the pendulum swung to the opposite extreme, as state governments adopted advertising regulations that were collectively known as "printer's ink statutes," named after a suggested model published in *Printer's Ink* magazine in 1911. Most of the state laws involved fines rather than imprisonment, but enforcement was vigorous. The federal law that created the Federal Trade Commission (FTC) was signed into law by President Woodrow Wilson in 1914, but the FTC did not become a major authority in advertising regulation until Congress passed a series of consumer protection laws in the 1960s and 1970s and put the FTC in charge of enforcing them. Many of those laws were introduced by Senators Philip Hart and William Proxmire, who claimed that the legislation was prompted by complaints from their constituents about the distortion and untruthfulness contained in both print and broadcast advertising.

In addition to the FTC, numerous other federal government agencies regulate advertising to a lesser extent. Those agencies and their areas of authority include:

- The Federal Communications Commission regulates television and radio advertising.

- The Federal Elections Commission regulates political advertising.

- The Food and Drug Administration regulates the advertising of food and pharmaceuticals.

- The Department of Housing and Urban Development regulates housing and real estate advertising.

- The Environmental Protection Agency requires car manufacturers to include gas mileage figures in their advertising.

- The Civil Aeronautics Board regulates airline advertising.

- The U.S. Postal Service establishes and enforces regulations on the proportion of advertising-to-news in newspapers, magazines, and newsletters sent through the mail; the higher the percentage of advertising, the higher the mailing cost.

While the FTC and other agencies still attempt to protect consumers from blatantly false and misleading advertising, those agencies, as well as the courts, believe that consumers bear some responsibility for protecting themselves by being skeptical of questionable advertising claims. In addition, court rulings have found that some commercial speech has value far beyond the promotion of products and services; it also provides consumers with important information to assist them in their purchasing decisions. By providing this limited First Amendment protection to advertising, the courts are protecting not only the advertisers' right to disseminate that information, but also the consumers' right to receive it.

Today, in addition to the FTC's regulations on advertising in general, all 50 states have revised their consumer-protection laws (originally passed in the early and mid-1900s) and added new ones that regulate advertising at the state level. At the local level, advertising is regulated in the form of restrictions placed on handbills, illuminated signs, transit advertising, and outdoor advertising such as billboards and benches. The courts generally uphold such regulations after determining that they do not violate the First Amendment.

Current Issues and Controversies

False and Deceptive Advertising

While the Federal Trade Commission has the responsibility for enforcing "truth in advertising" laws on a national level and most states have similar mechanisms in place for regulating advertising, numerous "watchdog" groups also scrutinize the industry and apply many of the same terms as the FTC and state agencies, including "false" and "deceptive."

What is the difference between an advertisement that is "false" and one that is merely "deceptive"? The dividing line is difficult to detect, but here are some examples that may help to clarify the difference: An advertisement is considered "false" if it makes claims that are not true, such as those related to a product's ability to produce a certain result that in reality it cannot. In order to substantiate such a claim of false advertising, however, the FTC, state agency, or watchdog group would have to prove that the advertiser knew the product's true characteristics but published or broadcast the advertisement nevertheless.

Other examples of outright false advertising include the inclusion of fictional endorsements or test results, such as "the American Heart Association recommends eating product X daily" (if no such recommendation was made) or "scientists at University of X tested our product and found that..." (if no such tests were actually conducted).

Conversely, an advertisement is merely "deceptive" if it makes no false statements, yet leaves out important information or is otherwise misleading. One example is the presentation of case studies showing results of product use without mentioning the length of time required; without such information the audience might infer that results are immediate. Another example is found in the advertisement that claims that product A costs less than product B, yet omits the fact that product A is sold in 32-ounce bottles while product B is sold in 48-ounce bottles.

To determine if an advertisement is deceptive, the FTC uses the **reasonable consumer standard,** meaning that each advertisement in question would be evaluated according to the likelihood that a "reasonable consumer" would be deceived. FTC guidelines clarifies that an advertisement would not be deemed to be deceptive if "only a few gullible consumers would be deceived." The FTC admits that a company "cannot be liable for every possible reading of its claims, no matter how far-fetched," and that the law "could not help a consumer who thinks that all french fries are imported from France or that Danish pastry actually comes from Denmark."

One of the first legal cases to deal with deceptive advertising began with the FTC's accusations against the Colgate-Palmolive Co. The company produced a television commercial for a shave cream called Rapid Shave, which included a demonstration in which the product appeared to shave sand off sandpaper. What was really happening, however, was that the producers of the commercial had put loose sand on an ordinary sheet of plastic and made it look as though it was sandpaper.

The FTC ruled that it was a deceptive advertisement and ordered Colgate-Palmolive to take it off the air, but the company challenged the ruling to the Supreme Court, which ruled in favor of the FTC. The ruling set a precedent and reinforced the FTC's authority to charge advertisers suspected of staging dishonest demonstrations and other types of deception.

Another major FTC court victory came against the Beneficial Corporation in 1976. The FTC claimed that the tax accounting firm was engaging in misleading advertising when it claimed that it could provide "instant tax refunds" to clients, when in fact the company was merely loaning the client the money until the refund check was received. The ad also omitted the fact that clients had to complete applications for and be qualified for the loans, thus making the loans not as "instant" as it was leading potential clients to believe.

Today, the most common advertising areas for regulatory scrutiny are food products and nonprescription or "over-the-counter" (OTC) drugs. For example, the FTC forced orange juice processor Tropicana to cancel a 2005 ad that claimed its product was "heart-healthy" because it lowered consumers' cholesterol and blood pressure. The FTC challenged the company to produce scientific evidence to support its claims, which it could not.

On a related issue, an advertisement for a medication cannot claim or even imply that it prevents colds or flu when in actuality it can only treat the symptoms. On more serious issues, the Food and Drug Administration would not allow a food or pharmaceutical company to claim in its advertising that a certain product prevents the onset of cancer, heart disease, or arthritis, without scientific medical studies to document such benefits. The FTC and other government agencies and watchdog groups uses the term "sound scientific basis" to refer to the advertisers' burden of proof in documenting their claims.

The FTC and FDA are also skeptical about promotional phrases used on packaging and in advertising copy such as "new and improved," vitamin-enriched," and "special formula." One of the newest phrases causing regulatory problems for the makers of OTC drugs is "prescription strength." The term implies that the dosage provided is the same as the dosage in the prescription form of the drug, but upon checking, many such OTC drugs claiming to be "prescription strength" actually include less than half the number of milligrams found in the prescription version. In a similar case, one major drug manufacturer was recently ordered by the FDA to stop using the phrase "next generation" to refer to products unless they featured significant improvements over previous versions.

Because regulatory agencies and watchdog groups do not differentiate between advertising and public relations and often apply advertising regulations to public relations materials, professional communicators should apply the same level of scrutiny to news releases that they do to paid advertisements. FDA rules, for example, require that news releases regarding the introduction of new medications show "fair balance" by telling consumers about both the risks and benefits of new drugs and treatments and must also explain their limitations.

Another factor that advertisers must approach with caution is the inclusion of research information derived from government tests or reports. For example, if the Department of Transportation performs crash-test studies to determine which new cars are the safest and mentions that a specific product is either at or near the top, the manufacturer can quote that report in its advertising but must be careful to present the information fairly. The ad can claim that Car X was ranked first in its category or finished in the top 10 for three years in a row (if true). The ad cannot, however, state or imply that the Department of Transportation encourages consumers to buy Car X, because the DOT is a neutral government agency and does not make such endorsements.

In addition to being scrutinized by the FTC, advertisements making questionable claims can also result in legal action being taken by competing companies. Early in 2005, for example, a manufacturer of dental floss filed suit against a company that claimed its mouthwash was as effective as dental floss in reducing plaque and gum disease (see Case Study 6-F).

In 2009, St. Louis University Hospital in Missouri claimed in its advertising that it was the "official" hospital for the St. Louis Rams, the city's National Football League team. Other hospitals in the city contended that was false advertising, as injured players were actually treated at other local hospitals. Officials for the team and SLUH denied the charges and pointed out that nowhere in the ads did the hospital claim a role in treating Rams players or other employees. Instead, they claimed the advertisements represented a "marketing agreement," but the other hospitals contended that most readers would infer that the hospital treated Rams players. The case never went to court. After the controversy, the *St. Louis Post-Dispatch* conducted a survey of all 32 NFL teams, as well as teams from other major professional sports, and found that more than half maintained "marketing agreements" with hospitals in the communities in which they were located. It found no other cases in which the designated "official hospital" was one that did not also treat the team's players.

The Debate Over Product Placements

"Product placement" or "imbedded marketing" is a form of advertising in which a company's product appears in movies and on television programs as a prop or as part of the scenery. Products such as clothing, soft drinks or other food items, and automobiles often have their actual brand names visible because those companies have paid to have those products appear. It is a form of "indirect" or "subliminal" advertising that has become more popular in the last four decades because of home video recorders and other devices that allow viewers to bypass traditional commercials.

The history of product placements can be traced back to Marlon Brando's wardrobe in the 1954 movie, *The Wild Bunch*, even though it was not the result of a formal agreement. In the early 1950s, sales of blue jeans were limited because of the public perception that jeans were appropriate only for work in industrial settings. But after Brando wore jeans in a variety of non-work settings in the movie, that perception changed and blue jean sales increased dramatically.

The modern era of paid product placement began in the 1970s. Prior to that decade, any time a soft drink was used in the movie, it was just a red-and-white can with no visible logo. Today, on both television programs and in the movies, audiences see actual products. More recently, the trend has spread to movies, Broadway plays, and video games.

One of the first television programs to use such a device was the NBC television program *The Rockford Files,* which debuted in 1974. Throughout the series' eight-year run, the principle character, a rugged private investigator portrayed by James Garner, was always seen driving Chevrolet products, even when flying to other cities and renting cars. One of the first comedies to use the technique was NBC's hit, *Cheers.* When the show debuted in 1982, producers collected a substantial fee from Nike in exchanging for having lead character Sam Malone, played by Ted Danson, dressed in the company's clothing with the familiar "swoosh" logo. After the Nike contract expired, competitor Dockers took over as Danson's wardrobe provider. Also in 1982, product placement was a feature of the film *ET: The Extraterrestrial.* Reese's Pieces were the candy of choice for the lovable alien, for which the company paid a substantial fee.

Later in the 1980s, Brown & Williamson Tobacco paid actor Sylvester Stallone $500,000 to smoke the company's cigarettes in his movies. Health-care organizations around the country called for a ban on such product placements, but lawmakers were reluctant to create such legislation because of First Amendment concerns.

When Stallone played a law enforcement officer and Wesley Snipes played his sidekick in *Demolition Man,* a futuristic crime drama produced in 1992 but set in the year 2032, they patrolled their route in an Oldsmobile — a placement for which the company paid. General Motors executives claimed their objective was to send a message to film audiences that their brand would be "alive and well" in 2032 (ironically, General Motors discontinued the brand in 2004).

A more recent example was found in the CBS comedy *How I Met Your Mother*, during which a young couple discussed their future while dining at Red Lobster, one of the show's sponsors. Immediately following that scene was an actual commercial for the seafood restaurant. Another recent example was found on the set of *American Idol*, where judges in the singing competition were seen sipping Diet Coke (one of the program's primary advertisers) in between performances.

Although no one is referring to the trend of increasing numbers of product placements as a "controversy," some television producers object to the practice. In a 2006 interview, producers for the hit programs *ER* and *Law & Order* complained that as serious dramatists, they're concerned about the interference of commercialism into what they believe are products of art. They suggested that product placements are more appropriate for situation comedies, which most viewers take much less seriously. They are also concerned about potential artistic limitations that advertising commitments might place on their work. In a hospital or crime drama, for example, will an automobile manufacturer insist that its product be shown only in a positive light, and never involved in a crash or used in the commission of a crime?

Television producers don't always get it right with product placements. In an episode of the television drama *The West Wing*, a flashback scene showed a character using a pay telephone with the Verizon logo. The scene was said to have taken place in 1997 — three years before the company was created.

Advertising of Controversial Products and Services

Based on decades of Supreme Court cases, neither the federal government nor state governments can prohibit the advertising of legal products or services. Common law states that if a product is legal to manufacture, sell, purchase, or own (or if a service is legal to perform), no government agency or body can declare it illegal to advertise, except in unusual circumstances. That set of exceptions, known as the **Central Hudson Test,** provides that advertising regulation is justified only in cases in which the advertisement is deemed to be inaccurate, deceptive, or misleading; or the regulation is based on government's concern for public health or safety. In both cases, the government bears the burden of proof regarding why the regulation is necessary. In addition, the courts require the government to establish that the proposed law has the potential to achieve the desired result and is narrowly tailored to a specific set of circumstances.

One of the first cases involving the government's attempt to regulate the advertising of a legal product or service occurred in the early 1970s, when officials in Virginia attempted to punish a weekly newspaper for accepting advertising for a New York-based abortion clinic. At the time, a Virginia law prohibited the performing of abortions as well as the advertising of such services, even those provided in other states, where abortion was legal at the time.

A trial court found the newspaper guilty and fined it $500, which was to be reduced to $150 if it promised not accept similar ads in the future. Despite the nominal amount of the fine, the editor of the newspaper appealed, based on what he saw as a publisher's First Amendment right to determine its advertising policy. In 1975, two years after the Supreme Court legalized abortion nationwide in its decision in *Rowe v. Wade,* the court overturned the editor's conviction, this time on First Amendment grounds. The Court determined that the newspaper's publisher had the right to accept advertising for services that were legal at the place where they were performed.

One of the few cases in which the Central Hudson Test has been successfully used to regulate advertising occurred in a 1988 Supreme Court case. The plaintiff in the case was a company that owned casinos on the island of Puerto Rico; the defendant was a company employed by the island's government to regulate casino gambling. The regulatory company had an unusual policy on advertising: casinos could not advertise on the island itself, but could advertise in the mainland United States. After being fined by the company for violating the rule, the casino owners appealed through the court system, and the case eventually reached the Supreme Court. In its decision, the court ruled in favor of the regulatory company, ruling that its advertising policies were legal under the Central Hudson Test because of the potential harm of gambling and its alleged connection to organized crime.

In many other cases, however, the courts have applied the "high burden of proof" principle and ruled that governments were unable to establish a connection between their advertising regulations and the desired effect. In a 1997 case, for example, the Supreme Court overturned a Baltimore city ordinance prohibiting alcohol and tobacco advertising on billboards because the city failed to establish the link between the advertising of those products and underage drinking and smoking. In many cases involving city and county governments and their prohibition of billboards, the courts have ruled that the city's claim of "visual blight" was insufficient grounds to allow such laws to remain in effect.

Many newspapers and television and radio stations decline to sell advertising space or time to adult bookstores and video stores, fortune tellers, firearm sellers, practitioners of alternative forms of medicine, and escort services and massage parlors (or other adult businesses that are allegedly fronts for prostitution). They also reject advertisements regarding employment or investment schemes they suspect might be fraudulent.

Advertising Aimed at Children

In cases in which children are the targets of advertising, the Federal Trade Commission, Federal Communications Commission, and various watchdog groups contend that a higher regulatory standard should apply. One example is the FCC rule regarding the total number of minutes that can be allotted to advertising during children's programming.

Regardless of the content of ads, the FTC and watchdog groups claim that children are "unqualified by age or experience to anticipate or appreciate the possibility that representations may be exaggerated or untrue." The Children's Advertising Review Unit of the Better Business Bureau adds that "younger children have a limited capacity for evaluating the credibility of information they receive; advertisers therefore have a special responsibility to protect children from their own susceptibilities."

Advertising industry executives admit that while their speech may not deserve the same degree of First Amendment protection as political speech, it is not completely unprotected, and the fact that some consumers may not be any taller than the top of the television set does not take away their rights as potential receivers of that information.

Advertisers also claim that it is the responsibility of parents — not the courts or government regulatory agencies — to help children evaluate the credibility of information they receive through the mass media (see Case Study 6-B).

In response to the criticism from numerous consumer watchdog groups, the advertising industry in 2003 discontinued its annual "Golden Marbles" awards program that honored achievement in print and broadcast advertising aimed at children.

Advertising Boycotts

One of the most controversial but least talked about issues in mass communication is the advertising boycott — a business' decision to cancel its advertising with a specific newspaper or television station or network in retaliation for one or more negative news stories. While such boycotts are seldom discussed publicly, case studies in journalism publications indicate that such boycotts occur more often than the general public is aware of. Under federal law, however, advertising boycotts are a violation of anti-trust laws and are investigated by the Federal Trade Commission and U.S. Justice Department.

The most common examples of an advertising boycott are those involving car dealerships that occurred in many communities in the 1990s and early 2000s. Angry at news stories about defective automobiles or stories that provided consumers with information on how to negotiate lower prices for the purchase of their cars, dealerships resorted to canceling their advertising in those publications and on those television stations. In some cases, dealerships worked together to organize the boycotts.

In 1993, the advertising agency employed by the California State Lottery informed the *Sacramento News & Review* that it would no longer advertise in the paper because of an article critical of the lottery. The newspaper did not object to the tactic, only to the lack of advance notice. If the agency had informed the newspaper in advance, its editor said, the paper would have offered lottery officials or representatives of the agency the opportunity to reply to the criticism with its own op-ed piece.

Some advertisers claim that boycotts represent a "last resort" in responding to what they perceive as false, unfair, or damaging news coverage. In a sense, advertising boy-cotts are easier to pursue and much less expensive than libel suits. Newspaper editors and television station owners, however, dispute the "last resort" idea, claiming that most advertising boycotts catch them by surprise. Instead, they prefer that advertisers explore less drastic methods for resolving conflicts, such as requesting the opportunity to respond to negative news stories in the form of op-ed pieces or on-camera rebuttals.

The financial impact of an advertising boycott depends largely on the size of the community. In small towns, where a car dealer or other large company might account for much of the newspaper's advertising revenue, the cumulative effect of a lengthy boycott might be substantial. But in a larger community, newspapers and television stations have enough other advertisers to compensate for the loss of one or a few. In addition, a news-paper or television station that is part of a national chain or network can easily survive the loss of a major advertiser, whereas a local independent newspaper or station might not.

Many advertising boycotts are short-lived, as advertisers quickly realize that they need the newspaper or television station more than the media organization needs the ad-vertising revenue. At worst, it is a lose-lose situation for both parties. Considering the lack of case studies to document the effectiveness of boycotts, some advertisers claim that even though they might not result in a change in news coverage, they cancel their ad-vertising out of principle, stating they will not continue to advertise in a newspaper or on a television station that has treated them unfairly.

The idea of an advertising boycott is not limited to news programming. In the spring of 1978, a nationwide association representing the nursing home industry took offense at an episode of the popular CBS television series *Lou Grant* that focused on the alleged mistreatment of nursing home patients. The American Health Care Association claimed that the problems portrayed in the fictional program were true at one time, but had been resolved a decade earlier. Further, the AHCA claimed, the program might cause undue anxiety for individuals about to enter nursing homes, as well as for their families. When the episode was scheduled to run again that summer, the association contacted more than 200 CBS affiliates and asked them not to carry it. Although none agreed to cancel the program, several added a disclaimer at the beginning of the program that indicated the story line was fictional and should "not be taken literally." The AHCA also contacted the major corporations that advertised during the program and persuaded two of them to can-cel their sponsorships.

Advertisers' Influence on News and Reviews

While most daily newspapers have ethical standards that would prohibit reporters and editors from considering how a news story might affect an advertiser (either positively or negatively), many weekly newspapers and monthly magazines have much looser stand-ards. In the latter cases, advertisers are often able to influence news coverage simply by making significant long-term advertising commitments that guarantee that the publica-tions, which often struggle financially, can remain solvent. Instead of waiting for an advertiser to make threats, editors of weekly newspapers and monthly magazines avoid awkward situations by simply publishing positive stories about advertisers without being prompted. Such influence is difficult to document and seldom discussed among staff writers, but most know without asking that writing negative stories about major advertisers is forbidden.

One example of such influence is found in the "Top 10" lists that travel publications produce. Lists such as the "Top 10 Vacation Destinations in the Southwest" and the "Top 10 Golf Resorts in the Southeast" often imply that committees of staff writers produce the lists in an objective fashion by visiting numerous locations, comparing notes, and then voting to determine the rankings. But on-site visits are seldom part of the process, and a closer examination of the finished product usually shows that the magazine has simply published a list of its top 10 advertisers in that category.

Many working journalists admit in confidential interviews and surveys that their superiors speak publicly about avoiding such ethical temptations, but what they do in practice contradicts their public statements. Television stations and newspaper editors, according to subordinates, often censor their own broadcasts and publications in order to placate major advertisers. That contradiction prompted media critic A. J. Liebling to comment that there was little point in having codes of ethics for journalists and advertising managers unless those codes also applied to publishers and television station owners.

One example is the making of an advertising commitment to a publication in exchange for news coverage — the news source agrees to purchase a minimum amount of advertising, and in exchange to publication produces only positive stories. While the strategy of "buy and ad, get a story" was once common among trade publications, the idea of purchasing advertising space in exchange for news coverage is outdated. Some less-reputable publications may suggest such an arrangement, but those who do are unlikely to be the most respected in a field.

Serious news publications and television stations would never agree to such an arrangement, and most reporters and editors resent the suggestion that major advertisers are entitled to special treatment.

One example of a journalism specialty working hard to overcome accusations of unethical conduct is restaurant reviews. The relationship between restaurant reviewers and a newspaper's advertising department is often misunderstood. Many readers unfamiliar with how the journalism business works may assume that restaurant reviewers tend to write positive reviews about establishments that advertise in their newspaper and ignore those that don't. That belief may stem from the era — journalism historians say the policy was very common in the 1970s — in which restaurant reviews were written by the advertising department. Only restaurants that were major advertisers were reviewed, and the restaurants were always positive. Because so many readers believe that policy is still in place, most restaurant reviews are accompanied by a disclaimer that explains the decisions about which restaurants are reviewed are not influenced by whether or not those restaurants advertise in the newspaper. The statement also advises readers that restaurant critics dine anonymously and pay for their own meals, to counter the incorrect assumption that reviewers get better treatment and/or free meals by identifying themselves to restaurant management.

The problem of advertisers exerting pressure on journalistic decision-makers is not a new one. As far back as 1967, a *Wall Street Journal* survey found that 23 percent of business and financial editors claimed they had been told by upper management to "puff up" positive stories or downplay negative stories about major advertisers. In the early 1990s, a survey of television and radio reporters indicated that 29 percent had received similar instructions from station owners and managers. Two decades later, similar surveys are no longer conducted, or if they are, the results are not publicized. But anecdotal evidence indicates the problem is still there — it's just not talked about.

Textbooks dealing with journalism history and ethics chronicle a number of cases in which journalists lost their jobs for violating the unwritten rules. Examples include reporters fired for writing articles critical of major advertisers and restaurant reviewers who wrote positive reports about establishments that were not advertisers. But such stories need not be published to cause problems. Reporters have seen their stories "spiked" (cancelled) due to advertising concerns, and in extreme cases just suggesting a story idea could cost a reporter his or her job, as editors view such suggestions as lapses in judgment. Most of those anecdotes are from the 1970s and 1980s, but while few newspaper publishers or television station owners would admit it publicly, many reporters contend that such pressure still exists today.

Larger, more reputable newspapers and television stations prevent such problems by erecting figurative "walls of separation" between their news and advertising departments. That means that reporters are instructed not to consult with or discuss stories they are working on with any employees of the advertising department, and restaurant reviewers choose which restaurants to visit without consulting anyone else at the newspaper.

While most daily newspapers and broadcasting outlets adhere to strict policies separating their news and advertising functions, at smaller weekly newspapers, lifestyle magazines, and trade publications, the "wall of separation" is difficult to detect — and is sometimes non-existent. In those publications, it is often difficult for a reader to tell where the news stories stop and the advertising begins.

The narrower the focus of the publication, the more likely it is to see its news content heavily influenced by advertising dollars. Some architectural magazines, for example, have policies that overtly indicate that only advertisers will receive favorable coverage. The editor of one fashion magazine, quoted in a *Wall Street Journal* article, said that "we write about companies that advertise with us . . . that's what magazines do."

Portrayals of Women

Many critics of the advertising industry claim that the ways it portrays women are offensive and often harmful. Pointing to the use of excessively thin models in fashion magazines and television advertising, critics claim that young women and teenage girls exposed to those ads often develop self-esteem problems and are more vulnerable to eating disorders and other unhealthy habits and attitudes.

One such critic is Jean Kilbourne, who has written a number of books and produced a series of videos titled *Killing Us Softly, Still Killing Us Softly, Killing Us Softly 3*, and *Slim Hopes: Advertising and the Obsession with Thinness*. Kilbourne uses hundreds of examples of print and broadcast ads that show women in unnatural and offensive circumstances and stereotype women as being obsessed with their appearance.

In 2010, Kilbourne produced yet another video, *Killing Us Softly 4*, which includes examples from Internet advertising as well as that found in traditional print and broadcast media.

In a book on the sociological implications of advertising, American Association of Advertising Agencies President John Crichton added that consumers should expect advertising to be not only accurate, but also realistic. "Beyond accuracy, the question is often one of perception," Crichton wrote. "It is true that the dress in the advertisement is available in the sizes, colors, and price advertised — but will the dress make the purchaser look like the slim young woman in the ad? Answer: Yes, but only if the purchaser looks like her already."

The Influence of Advertising on Consumer Spending

Many critics of popular culture believe that the American advertising industry manipulates the buying habits of the audience by blurring the lines between what people want and what they need. Some use the example of the child who sees a toy advertised on television and tells his parents that he "needs X." Parents must then correct the misunderstanding by explaining to the child that he or she doesn't need X, he or she simply "wants" it.

The same effect is seen on adults, who critics say are led to believe they "need" a certain car, electronic device, item of furniture, or article of clothing when actually they only "want" it. Professor Theodore Levitt, an economist at the Harvard Business School, once said that consumers do not purchase products, but rather results. "People do not buy quarter-inch drills, they buy quarter-inch holes," he said. "They do not buy soap; they buy cleanliness. They do not buy clothing, they buy appearance." Charles Revlon, the founder of the cosmetics company that bears his name, one said that "in our factory we make cosmetics, in the store we sell hope."

Today, economists and consumer advocates blame the advertising industry's tactics, along with easy access to retail credit cards, with the epidemic of credit card debt and personal bankruptcy that began in the 1990s and continues in the early part of the new century. Consumer advocate Dave Ramsey, author of a number of books and host of a nationally syndicated radio program, blames the advertising industry, as well as the credit card industry, for contributing to the epidemic of over-spending and personal bankruptcy seen in the United States in the 1990s and early 2000s. Ramsey says the advertising and credit card industries conspire to encourage Americans to "spend money they don't have to buy things they don't need to impress people they don't like."

The Myth of "Suggested Retail Price"

The Federal Trade Commission regulates usage of the phrase "manufacturer's suggested retail price" (MSRP) and admonishes retailers not to use those words casually in their advertising. The FTC requires that the MSRP must be determined by the manufacturer rather than the retailer. In some cases, however, retailers use the term with an ast-+erisk and a disclaimer that reads, "this price is only an estimate; no actual products may have been sold at this price."

For Discussion

Case Study 6-A   **Lottery Advertising: What Are the Odds?**

Although seldom the target of legal action, the advertising of state lotteries is often criticized by consumer groups as false or deceptive. Much of the criticism is based on how state lottery agencies use their advertising campaigns to glamorize the new lifestyles of lottery jackpot winners without mentioning the nearly astronomical odds associated with winning the large prizes.

One often-cited statistic regarding lottery odds is that an individual is more likely to be struck by lightning than win a lottery jackpot. The Michigan Lottery spoofed this cliché in one of its advertising campaigns of the 1980s. One television spot showed a man using that comparison to ridicule customers standing in a lottery line at a convenience store. A lightning bolt suddenly drops through the ceiling of the store and strikes him, leaving his clothing smoldering and his hair singed. He steps up to the counter and says to the clerk, "One ticket, please."

Critics of state lotteries claim that the advertising of the games detracts from the work ethic by promoting the idea that the way to get ahead in life is through luck rather than hard work. Many anti-lottery educators point out the mixed messages teenagers receive: in school, they are taught about the importance of hard work, but then they see the lottery advertising that says that all one must do to get rich is buy a lottery ticket.

According to the Council on Compulsive Gambling, fewer than half of state-run lotteries disclose the odds of winning in print advertising, and only 25 percent do so in television ads. Officials typically defend that shortcoming by claiming that there is simply not enough space in print advertising copy, nor is there time in television and radio spots to include such information. In Missouri and a handful of other states, inclusion of lottery odds is mandated by law, but the information flashes on the screen for just a few seconds. In his 1993 article in the *Boston College Law Review*, Professor Ronald J. Rychlak wrote that few lottery ads could pass the Federal Trade Commission's rules that apply to privately run sweepstakes.

Spokespersons for the lottery industry deny the charges that lottery advertising media deceives the public. "Most people play the lottery simply as a form of entertainment," one spokesperson told *The Christian Science Monitor* in 1999. "Not because they expect to take home big bucks. The average person knows the odds of winning the jackpot are extraordinary."

In 1992, outgoing Indiana School Superintendent H. Dean Evans blasted his state's lottery commission for its advertising that showed school children thanking lottery ticket purchasers for supporting their education. He called the ads misleading and in poor taste and asked journalists across the state to imagine "how many children may have come to school hungry or from a house in disarray because a parent has used the family funds to buy lottery tickets."

Under pressure from gambling opponents, some state lotteries have reduced the total volume of advertising or changed their approach. In Pennsylvania, lottery advertising is limited by law to 1 percent of the amount generated in gross sales. Several other states are eliminating the "All You Need is a Dollar and a Dream" and similar themes in their advertising. In other states with similar limitations, officials say that such rules demonstrate that they can "promote the product without over-promising results."

In the late 1990s, the North American Association of State and Provincial Lotteries (NASPL) issued a list of do's and don'ts for advertising campaigns conducted by its members. Among the do's are:

- reflect diversity in audiences;
- promote responsible lottery play;
- provide information about available help for problem gamblers;
- emphasize the fun and entertainment aspect of playing lottery games.

The list of "don'ts" include:

- play on ethnic stereotypes;
- portray product abuse, excessive play, or a preoccupation with gambling;
- encourage people to play excessively nor beyond their means;
- present, directly nor indirectly, any lottery game as a potential means of relieving any person's financial or personal difficulties;
- exhort play as a means of recovering past gambling nor other financial losses;
- promote the lottery in derogation of, or as an alternative to, employment, nor as a financial investment, or a way to achieve financial security;
- denigrate a person who does not buy a lottery ticket or unduly praise a person who does buy a ticket;
- imply that lottery games are games of skill.

Some lottery critics believe, but cannot prove, that lottery advertising is timed to coincide with the delivery of welfare and social security checks, a charge that lottery agencies deny.

Despite the good intentions of state legislatures and groups such as NASPL, misunderstandings in lottery advertising are inevitable. In 1983 in Illinois, for example, the lottery continued to run radio advertisements that encouraged customers to buy tickets in a scratch-off game with a grand-prize of $100,000, even though there was only one such ticket printed and it had already been redeemed.

That scenario was repeated in 2008 when it was reported that the New Jersey Lottery continued to advertise its "Million Dollar Explosion" scratch-off game even after all six of the grand prize tickets were redeemed.

As a result of the negative publicity, New Jersey and several other states revised their lottery marketing policies to either terminate such games after the last of the top prizes had been won or clarify on the tickets the relative availability of secondary prizes.

There are other ethical considerations regarding how lotteries are marketed. As both subjects of news stories and sources of advertising revenue, state lottery agencies often enter into an uncomfortable relationship with the media. Newspapers and television stations profit greatly from lottery advertising and then either intentionally or unintentionally help promote lotteries by glamorizing the lifestyles of the winners and covering drawings and other lottery-related events as news stories, regardless of the minimal news value involved. No one has classified the relationship as quid pro quo, but media ethicists might call it incestuous — or at least an unintended consequence.

- In general, do lottery agencies bear the responsibility of making sure potential lottery customers fully understand the odds associated with purchasing lottery tickets in hopes of winning multi-million dollar jackpots? Or should this be an example of caveat emptor (let the buyer beware)?

- Re-read the last paragraph if this case. Do you agree that television stations that cover lottery-related news stories (such as live drawings and stories that glamorize the lifestyles of new jackpot winners) while their advertising departments are benefiting from lottery advertising are involved in a conflict of interest? (Consider the fact that there are few other positive news stories in which there is also an advertising connection).

Case Study 6-B **Campaign for a Commercial-Free Childhood**

Advertising aimed at children is a frequent target of the Federal Trade Commission and watchdog groups that express concern over the impact that advertising has on children who have not yet learned to be skeptical of commercial messages. In 2000, children's advocates formed the Campaign for a Commercial-Free Childhood (CCFC), a program designed to monitor the advertising industry and encourage more responsible advertising aimed at children.

CCFC specifically targeted food and soft-drink companies for subjecting children to what it called a culture of "rampant consumerism."

In response to the criticism it receives from CCFC and other watchdog groups, the advertising industry — led by executives representing major food producers — formed the Alliance for American Advertising. The alliance claims its mission is to "help advertisers defend their First Amendment rights."

- Should the responsibility for scrutinizing advertising content directed at children lie with the company providing the products, the advertising agency creating the advertising campaigns, the media that carry the advertisements, or the parents of potential audience members?

- What is your reaction to the positions taken by the advocacy groups mentioned in the case?

Case Study 6-C   What Time Does the Movie Really Start?

Although few people would refer to it as a "controversy" or "ethical dilemma," movie audiences often complain that feature films typically begin 20 to 30 minutes after the scheduled time advertised in local newspapers and in other public sources of information. The reason behind the trend is the increased number of movie previews advertisements that precede most feature films.

The criticism comes at a time when movie attendance is at an all-time low and theater income is down. Most theater operators blame the downturn on the national economy and the loss of market share to DVD vending machines, online movie streaming, and the expansion of cable and satellite movie channels. In addition to the loss of income, many theaters have closed — especially the older venues that cannot be retro-fitted with today's modern projection and sound equipment.

Theater operators defend the practice by claiming that showing more commercials and previews of upcoming films provides late-comers the chance to find their seats without walking in front of other patrons or otherwise distracting from the film. Cynical observers, however, believe it is simply the theater owners' desire for the income derived from pre-movie advertising.

In 2004, the president of the National Association of Theater Owners acknowledged that audiences often complain about the commercials, but he did not offer any specific solutions, simply stating that "We get into trouble when we start to look like TV." In 2005, Connecticut State Representative Andrew Fleischmann introduced legislation requiring movie theaters to advertise the actual start of the feature film rather than the start of the previews and commercials. The legislation failed. That same year, Loews Cineplex, one of the major theater chains in the U.S., began including disclaimers in its advertising that "the feature presentation will begin 10 to 15 minutes after the posted time," but audience reactions have been mixed.

- Should this be considered an issue subject to "truth in advertising laws," or looked at as "just one of life's inconveniences"?

- Compared to other forms of alleged advertising deception (such as those involving food and drug products), is this really worthy of the time of the Federal Trade Commission and other advertising regulators and watchdog groups?

Case Study 6-D

Aggressive Fund-Raising, or Deceptive Advertising?

While nonprofit organizations are seldom criticized for the work they do, some are scrutinized for the manner in which they conduct their fund-raising appeals through either paid advertising or telemarketing. While watchdog groups such as the Better Business Bureau Wise Giving Alliance and the American Institute of Philanthropy monitor and evaluate organizations' fund-raising tactics, the news media also raises questions about the process. Three such examples have surfaced in the last decade.

The first category of nonprofit organizations to come under media scrutiny was that of Police Benevolent Associations (PBAs). Most PBAs are organized at the city or county level, and their main purpose is to provide support for the families of law enforcement officers killed in the line of duty. Instead of raising money using volunteers, however, most PBAs hire professional fund-raisers that do the majority of their work using telemarketers. Their fund-raising appeals suggest the money raised will be spent on providing financial support for widows of slain police officers and college scholar-ships for their children. While some of the money does go to that purpose, much of it goes to political activities, such as lobbying in the state legislatures regarding issues of interest to law enforcement and supporting political candidates the associations have endorsed. While some donors may agree with spending money on those other purposes, others may not; and many donors feel misled by the telemarketers' heart-warming stories about widows and children receiving financial support. In addition, many critics object to the PBAs hiring outside firms (which often keep between 25 and 75 percent of the money collected) instead of using volunteers.

Similar criticisms have been launched at AIDS-related charities, many of which are also organized at the local level. Among their chief fund-raising activities are bicycle rides, and many such events are organized by professional firms that keep more than 70 percent of the money raised, leaving less than 30 percent for AIDS-related causes. In contrast, the American Lung Association's annual bike rides, organized entirely by volunteers, raise similar totals but give 60 to 75 percent of the money raised to the organization's causes.

Another category of organizations under recent media scrutiny are those responsible for relief efforts following national disasters. Following the terrorist attacks of September 11, 2001, those organizations executed some of the most successful fund-raising efforts in history, collecting millions of dollars and funding a number of programs to support recovery efforts. Early the following year, however, media reports indicated those organizations had collected more money than they could possibly spend on September 11-related recovery efforts, but the organizations were still using that appeal in their fund-raising.

In their defense, those organizations were spending the excess money to help the victims of hurricanes, tornadoes, and floods — all worthy causes. While critics admitted those other causes were important ones, they believed the tactic of continuing to use images of September 11 victims in the organizations' fund-raising appeals was a dishonest approach. Some even compared it to the bait-and-switch tactic used by some advertisers. In 2005-06, many of those same organizations executed successful fund-raising campaigns to generate money for victims of Hurricane Katrina, but they were later criticized for continuing to use images of hurricane victims in their television spots and other fund-raising appeals long after they had raised more money than they could possibly spend for that purpose.

- If you were a frequent donor to your local Police Benevolent Association and learned that it had turned over its fund-raising operation to a professional fund-raising firm that took 60 percent of what it collected, would that change your opinion of the group? What about the fact that much of the remaining 40 percent goes to political activities rather than helping the widows and children of police officers? Would the fact that at least *some* of the money collected goes to a worthy cause be enough to keep you as a donor?

- What about the AIDS-related charities? Is the fact that at least *some* of the money goes to AIDS-related causes enough to justify the use of an outside fund-raising firm?

- What about the relief agencies that used images of September 11 victims and Hurricane Katrina victims in their fund-raising appeals, but spending that money on other worthy causes? Do you agree with the critics' view that such a tactic is analogous to the bait-and-switch tactics used by some advertisers?

Case Study 6-E   Academic Bait and Switch

The problem of "bait and switch" tactics has long been an ethical issue facing the advertising industry. The term is used in both Federal Trade Commission guidelines and the Code of Ethics of the American Advertising Federation (although the code simply refers to it as "bait advertising") Although the term was initially applied mostly in cases involving consumer products such as home electronics and automobiles, more recently the term has been applied to other situations, including fund-raising (see Case Study 6-D) and even the promotion of colleges and universities.

The latter problem began earning media attention in the mid-1990s when the NBC series *Dateline* produced a detailed report in which it used the term "academic bait and switch" to refer to the way that major universities boast in their recruiting literature and other promotional activities about the credentials of their senior faculty (many of them Nobel and Pulitzer Prize winners) and imply to parents that their children will be taught by those individuals. What the universities don't disclose to parents, however, is those senior faculty members typically teach only graduate students, while the bulk of undergraduate classes — especially those for freshmen and sophomores — are taught by graduate teaching assistants who are just few years older than their students. While student evaluations often indicate the teaching skills of teaching assistants are just as good as (and sometimes better than) those of senior faculty members, the concern is that the universities' advertising is deceptive.

While the *Dateline* segment cited cases of positive student experiences with teaching assistants, it also uncovered cases of students complaining that many teaching assistants lacked basic teaching skills, were not available for assistance outside of class, or lacked the fundamental knowledge of the material necessary to teach it. In extreme cases, *Dateline* reported, teaching assistants in the technical sciences were international students who struggled with the English language, making their lectures nearly indecipherable.

To address concerns of state legislators that too much of the responsibility for undergraduate teaching is relegated to teaching assistants, many universities list a full-time faculty member on the course schedule as the "instructor of record," but still delegate the actual teaching duties to a graduate student. The official university records do not disclose that the professor listed on the course schedule is seldom in the classroom, and in many cases is not even on campus at the time the class meets.

In 2009, *The Chronicle of Higher Education* published a lengthy article along the same lines. Also using the term "academic bait and switch," the *Chronicle* article was written by a professor at a prestigious school who claimed that when he began his career as a graduate teaching assistant, he was assigned to teach freshman English composition classes that he clearly wasn't qualified to teach. "Students attend the university to be taught by experts, not amateurs," he wrote. "Before I set foot on campus, I didn't know that teaching assistants actually taught. I assume that 'teaching assistant' meant 'assisting a teacher.' "

The professor, who was quoted anonymously in order to avoid harming his career, said he received less than a day of training on how to teach his courses, along with encouraging words from his department chair: "look confident."

Many professors and former professors have expressed similar opinions in their books, although most used the term "academic fraud" instead of "bait and switch." As far back as 1988, retired professor Charles J. Sykes cited a joke frequently told about the statue of Abraham Lincoln on the campus of the University of Wisconsin. Lincoln is shown seated in a chair, nearly identical to how he is portrayed at the Lincoln Memorial in Washington, D.C. According to campus lore, the statue of Lincoln rises from the chair every time a senior professor who teaches more than two classes per semester walks by.

On a more serious note, Sykes wrote that, "For parents who pay college costs (especially those who chose a school because they thought their children would actually study at the feet of its highly touted faculty), it has meant one of the biggest cons in history."

One of Sykes' recommendations is that universities should be held to the same truth-in-advertising standards as other advertisers and should be required to disclose in their advertising as well as promotional materials the research-to-teaching ratio of faculty employment contracts and the proportion of courses taught by teaching assistants.

In his 2006 book, *Our Underachieving Colleges*, former Harvard University President Derek Bok wrote that the emphasis on research means that the professors touted in the universities' promotional literature are seldom in the classroom, and that "the real teaching is left to inexperienced graduate students . . . lost in the crowd, many undergraduates finish college without knowing a single faculty member well enough to ask for a letter of recommendation."

- Do you agree with Charles Sykes' suggestion that colleges and universities be held to the same truth-in-advertising standards as other advertisers? If so, would a requirement that universities disclose the research-to-teaching ratio in faculty contracts and the proportion of classes taught by teaching assistants go far enough?

Case Study 6-F   **Joseph Lister and the**
                                      Product That Bears His Name

The problem of manufacturers making false or exaggerated claims about the potential benefits of using their products is nothing new. As far back as 1923, the Lambert Pharmaceutical Company began marketing a new mouthwash it called Listerine, playing on the name of Joseph Lister, an English surgeon and medical researcher known for developing surgical procedures that would limit infections. Lister had nothing to do with the company or any of its products, but many consumers were misled by the product's name.

The company also claimed at the time that Listerine could cure "halitosis" — the medical term for bad breath — when in reality it could only mask the symptoms without addressing the cause. What the advertisements did not mention was that bad breath could be attributed to a number of causes, including poor diet, smoking, gum disease, and diabetes — none of which could be cured by mouthwash.

Similar misconceptions about mouthwash continue today, prompting the American Dental Association to explain on its website that "mouthwashes are generally cosmetic in nature and do not have any long-lasting effect on bad breath."

The product has not seen the end of its legal problems, however. Throughout much of the 20th century, the company claimed that using the product could cure sore throats and reduce the severity of colds. In 1977, it was forced by the Federal Trade Commission to spend more than $10 million on ads to clarify that "Listerine will not prevent colds or sore throats or lessen their severity."

In 2005, a manufacturer of dental floss complained when Pfizer, Listerine's new parent company, claimed that the mouthwash was as effective as dental floss in reducing plaque and gum disease. Fearing a decline in sales of its dental floss, Johnson & Johnson filed suit against Pfizer, claiming that such ads were "false and deceptive" because no tests had been conducted to determine the relative merits of the two products. A federal judge agreed with Johnson & Johnson's claim and ordered Pfizer to withdraw the ad.

- Do you think that misleading advertising has gotten better or worse in recent years?

- Do you think that Federal Trade Commission rules are too strict, just about right, or too loose?

Discussion Problem 6-A   The Case of the Cable Descrambler

You're the advertising manager at your school newspaper. One day you take a break between classes and visit the newspaper office, and waiting for you is the faculty advisor.

He's just received a call from the manager of the local cable television company, which is a major advertiser in the student paper. The manager called to the advisor's attention an ad that another advertiser has placed in the student newspaper. The ad is for a device that enables the user to descramble cable television signals and, essentially, obtain cable television service for free. The ad was placed by an out-of-state company that provided only a post office box, 1-800 telephone number, and Web address. The ad was paid for in advance, and the advertisers' check has already been cashed. The advertiser paid for 12 weeks, and the ad has already run for two.

The cable company insists that you stop carrying the ad and warns that if you don't, the company will cancel its advertising in the student newspaper and may also sue the university for the loss of subscriber revenue. The advisor convenes a meeting that includes you, other student editors, and her. When it's your turn to speak, which of the following recommendations would you make?

a. Cancel the ad immediately, issue a partial refund to the advertiser, apologize to the cable company, and hope that will be enough to prevent further conflict.

b. Allow the ad to run the remaining 10 weeks, since it has already been pre-paid, but promise the cable company you will not renew the ad after that.

c. Inform the cable company that you cannot be responsible for the content of every advertisement that runs in the student newspaper, and one advertiser will not dictate policies regarding what other ads you will accept. You will allow the advertiser to renew the ad if it wishes to. Besides, you claim, it's "just a student newspaper."

d. Suggest that the university attempt to settle the matter without going to court, but insist that the cable company prove damages — a specific dollar amount lost due to local customers using the device to steal cable signals.

Discussion Problem 6-B   Is This Ad Too Good to Be True?

You're the advertising manager at your school newspaper. You accept an ad from an out-of-state company offering "deep discount" spring break travel packages for college students. The students responding to the ad paid for the trips six weeks in advance, but when they arrive at the airport for their trip, they find their airline tickets are worthless, as the flight numbers and other details printed on tickets aren't recognized by the airline's employees or computers. Some of the students then attempt to cancel their hotel reservtions by phone, only to find the names and addresses of the hotel are fictional. They call the company that sold the packages and learn that it has gone out of business.

In the weeks that follow this incident, you're relieved to find out that students' credit card companies provide fraud protection and were able to refund their money. But it did raise the question: To what extent was your student newspaper to blame for accepting the ad? Was it your responsibility to scrutinize the "too good to be true" ad, or is this another case of caveat emptor (let the buyer beware)?

Discussion Problem 6-C   **Advertising Agencies
                                           and Competing Proposals**

You're running a small company, and you're considering hiring an agency to come up with a long-term advertising strategy. You contact four of the largest advertising agencies in town and provide them a request for proposals (RFP). Each agency submits a written response to your RFP and also comes into your conference room to do an in-person presentation.

Agencies A and B submit fairly weak proposals and you eliminate them early in the process. But Agency C and Agency D present an interesting scenario.

Agency C submitted an excellent written proposal and you know it's exactly what your company needs to do. The problem is that when the account executives came to do the in-person presentation, they turned out to be the most obnoxious people you've ever met. You can't picture yourself working with them for the long-term because you fear there would be too many personality conflicts.

Agency D submitted a written proposal that was very ordinary, and at first glance, it appeared to be only slightly better than the proposals from Agencies A and B that you had already rejected. But when you met Agency D's representatives in person, they were very enthusiastic and the chemistry between your employees and their employees was very positive.

Then one of your employees suggests taking the good proposal from Agency C and hiring Agency D to carry it out.

Without consulting an attorney, which of the following do you believe?

a. It is **already illegal** or **should be illegal** for a prospective client to do that.

b. It is **perfectly legal** to do that. Perhaps it is unfair to Agency C, but the agency developed and submitted the proposal at its own risk, and that's just one of the "down sides" associated with being in a competitive business.

c. It may be legal to do that, but it is certainly **unethical** and a lousy way to treat another business.

Discussion Questions

601. Earlier in this chapter you read about the work of feminist scholar Jean Kilbourne, who has produced a series of books and videos critical of how the American advertising industry portrays women in a stereotypical manner. What is the root cause of these stereotypes? Does advertising reflect our attitudes toward women, or does the advertising portrayal influence our attitudes? Should advertising be regulated by the Federal Trade Commission to avoid such negative depictions, or could advertisers claim such depictions, while offensive, are protected by the First Amendment? Could commercials that are offensive to women, or portray them in a stereotypical way, be addressed by any part of the American Advertising Federation Code of Ethics (see Appendix A)? If not, should a new paragraph be added to address this concern?

602. Do you agree with the rationale used to explain the need for product placements (that the value of traditional advertising is diminished because of viewers who skip through or past them)? Does the inclusion of product placements make television pro-grams and movies more realistic? Are the producers of the programs justified in their concern that product placements infringes upon their "art"?

Notes

152   **"The seller sees the house he owns the way"**: Lee Thayer, *Ethics, Morality and the Media: Reflections on American Culture*. New York: Hastings House Publishers, 1980, p. 109.

155   **"or that Danish pastry actually comes from Denmark"**: Randy Bobbitt, *Exploring Communication Law: A Socratic Approach*. Boston: Allyn & Bacon, 2008, p. 246.

156   **new medications must show "fair balance"**: Dennis L. Wilcox, Glen T. Cameron, Bryan H. Reber, and Jaw-Hwa Shin, *Think Public Relations*, Boston: Allyn & Bacon, 2012, p. 198.

162   **"that's what magazines do"**: Edward Spence and Brett Van Heekeren. *Advertising Ethics*. Upper Saddle River, NJ, 2004, p. 88.

162   **"It is true that the dress in the advertisement"**: Thayer, p. 111.

163   **"People do not buy quarter-inch drills"**: Thayer, p. 110.

163   **"in the store, we sell hope"**: Thayer, p. 186.

164   **"few lottery ads could pass Federal Trade Commission rules"**: Randy Bobbitt, *Lottery Wars: Case Studies in Bible-Belt Politics*. Lanham, MD: Lexington Books, 2007, p. 18.

164   **"Most people play the lottery simply"**: Brad Knickerbocker, "The Growing Cost of Gambling." *Christian Science Monitor,* June 7, 1999, p. 1.

164   **"because a parent has used the family funds to buy lottery tickets"**: Bobbitt, *Lottery Wars*, p. 25.

165   **"reflect diversity in audiences"**: Bobbitt, *Lottery Wars*, p. 26.

168   **"We get into trouble when we start to look like TV"**: Ben Steelman, "Is Going to the Movies a Dying Pastime?" *Wilmington Star-News*, June 2, 2005, p. C-30.

171   **"Before I set foot on campus"**: Henry Adams, "Academic Bait-and-Switch." *The Chronicle of Higher Education*, June 16, 2009.

172   **"For parents who pay college costs"**: Charles J. Sykes, *ProfScam*. Washington, DC: Regnery Publishing, 1988, p. 8.

172   **"well enough to ask for a letter of recommendation"**: Derek Bok, *Our Underachieving Colleges*. Princeton, NJ: Princeton University Press, 2006, p. 8.

CHAPTER 7

Ethical Issues in Public Relations

Background

- An employee in a company's public relations department takes a camera to the annual Christmas party and takes photographs of employees in embarrassing situations. The photographs are then published in the January issue of the company's employee newsletter and also on the company's website.

- A company lays off several top executives, many of whom charge the company with gender and age discrimination. After the company successfully defends itself in court against the accusations, it issues a news release which disparages the motives and integrity of the former employees. The former employees then file a libel suit against both the company that issued the news release and the newspaper that quoted the release in its stories.

- A presidential press secretary tells a gathering of print and broadcast journalists that the administration has no plans for U.S. military action in response to a revolution in a South American country, even though he knows that as he speaks, the president and his military advisors are planning to invade the country by air and land.

What is Public Relations?

Public relations is often confused with advertising, marketing, promotion, publicity, propaganda, and other terms dealing with persuasion. But there are several significant differences. There are three characteristics typically found in legitimate public relations campaigns:

Free choice. Members of the audience must be able to freely choose among several actions: adopt the ideas or behaviors being advocated by campaign organizers, adopt the ideas or behaviors of another party involved in the issue, remain committed to their previously held ideas or behaviors, or not take part in the issue at all. The concept of free choice also means there must be no coercion involved. Professional communicators are allowed to be assertive in their work, of course, but in an ethical public relations campaign, the final choice must be up to members of the audience.

Mutual benefit. Both the communicator and the audience must emerge from the transaction with some benefit. A campaign in which only the communicator benefits is more accurately labeled as "manipulation" or "propaganda" rather than true public relations.

Multidisciplinary approach. Instead of working only through the media — an approach typically used in advertising — true public relations campaigns may also apply theories and techniques from fields such as psychology, sociology, and education. For example, a company trying to sell cat litter may find success with traditional advertising and marketing techniques. However, an organization attempting to promote the importance of spaying or neutering cats will have to apply a variety of other communications techniques to be successful.

Despite the emphasis on mutual benefit, public relations professionals serve as advocates for a company, nonprofit organization, or cause. To some degree, the practice of public relations is linked to the First Amendment to the U.S. Constitution and general principles of freedom of expression. Part of a PR professional's job, some observers say, is to help his or her clients or employers exercise their First Amendment rights.

While serving as advocates, public relations professionals also have an obligation to serve the public interest, tell the truth, and focus on the fair resolutions of conflicts rather than attempting to gloss them over. Deane Beman, former commissioner of the PGA Tour, said, "I'm not a style over substance guy. I prefer substance over style. I'm not interested in papering over a problem with PR. I'd rather solve the problem."

A number of notable authors and other public relations experts have attempted to deal with the topic of public relations ethics in their writings and public comments.

In addition to his admission of regret over once working for a tobacco manufacturer, public relations pioneer Edward L. Bernays often addressed the topic of appropriate conduct at professional meetings and on college campuses across the country during the last 20 years of his life. Bernays was often critical of the codes of ethics of the Public Relations Society of America (PRSA) and International Association of Business Communicators (IABC) for their dependence on voluntary compliance.

In *Public Relations: Strategies and Tactics,* a popular textbook for introductory-level public relations classes, authors Dennis L. Wilcox, Phillip H. Ault, and Warren K. Agee describe a practitioner's four ethical obligations: to society and the public interest, to his or her client or employer, to the interests of the public relations profession, and to his or her own personal value system. "In the ideal world, the four would not conflict," they wrote. "In reality, however, they often do."

Confidential surveys of those who work in the field provide some alarming statistics. In one study by *PR Week,* for example, 43.9 percent of respondents reported feeling uncertain about the ethics of a task they were asked to perform, and only 31.1 percent believed the ethical boundaries of their job had been clearly defined. More than 25 percent of the respondents reported having lied on the job, and more than 38 percent said they had exaggerated information about a client or product — and those are just the ones who admitted it.

Legal and Ethical Limitations on the Public Relations Profession

Unlike the advertising industry, the public relations industry is not regulated by state or government agencies. However, individuals practicing public relations, as well as their clients or employers, may still get into legal trouble if they violate laws that apply to individuals and organizations in general. These problem areas include:

Insider trading: Using confidential business information to buy or sell stock in a client's business for personal gain.

Obstruction of justice: Refusing to cooperate with a law enforcement investigation of a client or employer, or taking any other actions that impede such an investigation.

Intellectual property: Using the creative property of an individual or company without permission (covered in more detail in Chapter 10). This includes the complicated legal relationships between employers and freelancers (the legal term is "independent contractors") and the ownership of photographs, written text, video programs, graphic designs, and social media content. Under current law, the permanent rights to work created by an independent contractor revert to the contractor after the employer has used the material one time — unless the two parties sign a legal agreement that assigns permanent rights to the employer.

Defamation: Damaging the personal or professional reputation of an individual or the public perception or financial standing of an organization. While more often associated with journalistic products, defamation can also take place in public relations materials such as news releases and internal publications.

Invasion of privacy: Committing privacy violations such as **false light** (disseminating information that is true but exaggerated or otherwise misleading), **private facts** (disclosure of personal information that is not newsworthy), or **appropriation** (the use of a person's name or image for promotional purposes without permission). Much like defamation, these offenses are more common with journalistic products but can also be found in public relations materials.

Insider trading is covered later in this chapter. Except for obstruction of justice, each of the other issues is covered in more detail in Chapter 10.

Some General Rules

There are two general principles regarding the legal and ethical obligations of public relations professionals:

The practitioner's obligation to the law always takes priority over his or her obligation to a client or employer. This means that public relations representatives must cooperate with law enforcement investigations or other legal matters involving a client or employer, regardless of any confidentiality agreements between the parties.

Communication between public relations representatives and their clients or employers is confidential in a general sense, but not privileged in a legal sense. While professional communicators have a general obligation to maintain the confidences and privacy rights of clients or employers, that does not mean they can claim privilege in a legal proceeding. Unlike doctors and lawyers, who are legally and ethically required to maintain confidentiality with their patients and clients, public relations professionals don't benefit from legal protection. Because they often have information dealing with controversial and potentially illegal activities of their clients and employers, they may be forced to provide that information to courts or government investigators.

Public Relations and the First Amendment

There are many circumstances in which public relations professionals find themselves helping their clients to express their First Amendment rights, but here are the two most common:

Contributions to political candidates and issues campaigns. Because companies often coordinate their contributions to political candidates and issues through their public relations departments, those professionals should be knowledgeable about state and federal laws that affect such contributions.

The Federal Elections Commission and the court system draw a distinction between expenditures and contributions in terms of First Amendment protection. If an individual or organization purchases an advertisement that supports or opposes a candidate or issue, that is considered an **expenditure** and is therefore permitted under the law, with little or no limitations. While individuals may still give money directly to a candidate's campaign, corporations may not; as such a donation would be considered a political **contribution**. In many cases, the courts have expanded the definition of "contributions" to include not only direct cash donations, but also the provision of free or discounted facilities or services or access to mailing lists. The rules regarding contributions to issues campaigns are somewhat looser; companies can contribute to campaigns that support or oppose issues at the state and federal level, but must still disclose the dollar amounts donated.

Except for the prohibition of direct contributions to candidates, profit-making companies have the same status as individuals in terms of how their political activities are regulated. For nonprofit organizations, however, the rules depend largely on the organization's Internal Revenue Service status.

The IRS uses the designation **501** to refer to nonprofit organizations whose primary function is education, philanthropy, health, and similar non-controversial causes. Although they are allowed to express political opinions, they may not openly support or oppose political candidates and are discouraged from supporting or opposing issues except those directly related to their primary purpose.

The designation **527** is used to refer to nonprofit organizations whose primary function is political involvement. These organizations are given more latitude by government regulators and the courts in advocating or opposing candidates or issues. In presidential election campaigns between 2004 and 2012, for example, political journalists and commentators used the term "527 ads" to refer to political ads sponsored by those groups.

The concept of 527 groups is often confused with that of "political action committees," but the two ideas are quite different. A 527 group is an independent entity, while a political action committee (PAC) is a group affiliated with a specific industry, professional association, or labor union.

Regardless of which category such groups fall in, they are required to disclose lists of their members and other financial supporters as well as how they spend their money.

Political advertising, direct mail, and bill stuffers. As mentioned in the previous section dealing with the First Amendment, determining whether communication is classified as political speech or commercial speech depends on its content, not who is speaking. The landmark case in this area was argued before the U. S. Supreme Court in 1978. Prior to that case, the First Amendment right of free speech was considered a right that applied to individuals; the issue of free speech rights for companies and organizations had not been raised. But in the early 1970s, a bank in Boston used its newspaper advertising to communicate to its customers and the public about political issues affecting the banking business. Those ads violated a Massachusetts law, but when the bank appealed its case through the court system, the Supreme Court eventually ruled that political speech is worthy of First Amendment protection regardless of its source. That ruling invalidated the Massachusetts law and set the precedent for four decades of similar decisions.

The same general rule applies to direct mail campaigns and the inserts or "bill stuffers" that electric, telephone, water, and cable companies included with the statements they send their customers. Prior to the 1970s, those materials caused little controversy, as they dealt mainly with non-controversial topics.

In the 1970s and 1980s, however, utility companies created controversy by using those materials to urge customers to vote for or against certain political issues and write their elected government officials to express their views. Many state governments passed laws banning such communication, but when those laws were challenged in the court system, they were declared unconstitutional because they infringed on the companies' First Amendment rights.

Such cases are less common today because of the shift from traditional paper bills delivered by the U.S. Postal Service to systems of online billing and bill-paying, but the cases are still significant because they set precedents regarding the extent to which the First Amendment applies to public relations materials.

Differentiating Between Advertising and Public Relations

The Federal Trade Commission and court system often use the blanket term "commercial speech" to refer to the advertising and public relations industries without drawing a distinction between the two. The obvious exceptions include the cases in the previous section in which speech disseminated by a company is clearly identified as political speech based on its content. But in most cases, the FTC and courts apply rules regarding "truth in advertising" to public relations materials, even though organizations disseminating the materials consider them to be part of their public relations efforts.

Sporting goods manufacturer Nike found itself in such a conflict in 2002-03. The company had been accused of violating child labor standards and condoning "sweatshop" conditions in its overseas factories. The company responded to those criticisms using standard public relations techniques — news releases, letters to newspaper editors, and other forms of public communication that did not resemble advertising in any way. The company also wrote letters to university administrators on campuses where students had called for their institutions to boycott the company, which was a major provider of athletic equipment.

A California-based consumer advocacy group sued the company under the state's truth-in-advertising law. The state's unusual advertising statute not only prohibited companies from disseminating false information (a determination usually left to the Federal Trade Commission), but also allowed individuals to file charges against violators, even though they may not have been personally harmed. The case centered not on whether Nike's statements were true, but whether they were protected as free speech and whether groups not directly affected by the ads should be allowed to pursue such cases.

A California trial court sided with Nike, ruling that its messages aimed at responding to public criticism were statements of opinion rather than commercial messages, and therefore deserved First Amendment protection. The California Supreme Court reversed that decision, claiming that every message a company disseminates is to some degree a commercial message and was therefore not fully protected by the First Amendment.

Nike appealed the decision to the U.S. Supreme Court, and in doing so was publicly supported by numerous other free-speech advocates, including the Public Relations Society of America and the American Civil Liberties Union.

The Court eventually ruled on the second issue — that consumer groups had a right to file claims even if not directly affected by the case — and it sent the case back to the California trial court to be tried again. Before the trial was set to begin, the two parties reached an out-of-court settlement. What was left unsettled, however, was the issue of whether it was appropriate to view advertising and public relations materials in the same light in terms of First Amendment protection.

Public Relations Representatives Working as Lobbyists

When public relations professionals represent clients in advocating or opposing political or regulatory issues at the federal level, they are required to register with the federal government as lobbyists. Most states have similar regulations for public relations professionals working on state-level issues. In most states, the secretary of state or attorney general is the official in charge of the registration process.

If a public relations representative is working in the public relations department at a public utility and wants to meet with state legislators in an attempt to influence public policy, those officials may deny access to them if they are not registered lobbyists.

Registration has been a requirement for full-time political consultants since the early 1900s, but for public relations professionals, the requirement is a newer one. Even if lobbying is only a small part of their job duties, public relations representatives are required to work under the same rules as full-time lobbyists if they represent their clients in legislative matters. Most large public relations firms that deal with legislative issues have at least one of their senior staff members registered.

Legal and Ethical Problems in Investor Relations

Investor relations is a large and complex area of federal law that is subject to frequent change. It is often difficult to keep up with those changes — meaning that when in doubt, public relations representatives should contact their companies' legal departments for guidance. Attorney and public relations expert Frank Walsh wrote in a 1991 book on legal issues in public relations that "there is a great deal for public relations professionals to know, but perhaps the most important thing for them to know is when to talk to the company's attorney."

The two most critical issues in this area are public disclosure and insider trading.

Public disclosure refers to the requirement that information about a publicly held company that may affect how its stock is evaluated (by stockbrokers, analysts, or potential investors) must be released in a manner that is timely, accurate, and in its correct context. Examples include announcements about quarterly or annual earnings, potential mergers and acquisitions, changes in leadership, new products or services, major expansion plans, employee layoffs, pending litigation (as plaintiff or defendant), or a change in credit rating.

The Securities and Exchange Commission has the authority to punish companies that fail to perform up to that expectation, and stockholders can sue companies because the information was not provided in a timely manner, was deemed to be misleading, or was not in its correct context. Analysts suggest that important news be released in the late afternoon or early evening after the stock markets have closed, as opposed to releasing it while the trading floors are open.

The SEC requirement that public relations representatives are responsible for the accuracy of news releases does not mean those representatives must cross-examine their clients in detail about the information they are asked to disseminate, but they should not blindly release questionable information without some level of scrutiny.

Accusations of **insider trading** are a potential problem for public relations professionals who work for publicly traded companies or the agencies that represent them. Owning stock in companies that your public relations agency represents may result in a number of opportunities for conflicts of interest — both real and perceived.

If employees of a company or its public relations agency use inside information to illegally trade that company's stock, they might be in violation of the **Securities and Exchange Act of 1934**, a law dealing with insider trading. An individual becomes an "insider" if he or she is in a position to learn of business information that affects that organization's stock before that information becomes public knowledge. SEC rules prohibit such individuals from purchasing or selling stock until after the information becomes public.

Because of the complexity of SEC rules and the possibility of "honest mistakes" resulting in charges of insider trading, many public relations agencies take the added precaution of prohibiting their employees from owning stock in the companies the agency represents. Even if an agency allows it, it is a bad idea. There are plenty of other good stocks to invest in.

Professional Codes of Ethics

The two major professional organizations serving the profession are the Public Relations Society of America (PRSA), based in New York; and the International Association of Business Communicators (IABC), based in San Francisco. Both organizations provide codes of ethics for their members, and both of those codes have their merits and their shortcomings.

On the positive side, advocates of professional codes claim that they help newcomers by educating them about professional guidelines and sensitizing them to ethical problems in their field. They also provide helpful information that individuals and agencies working in the field can cite in explaining the proper course(s) of action to employers and clients that find themselves in ethical dilemmas.

On the negative side, both codes are subject to the same criticisms:

Vague and imprecise language. Both codes use terms such as "integrity," "channels of communication," and "realistic expectations," but neither code offers any definitions. One of the critics is Donald K. Wright, professor emeritus at the University of South Alabama, who wrote in a 1993 article that the codes "are more cosmetic than anything else . . . They're warm and fuzzy and make practitioners feel good about themselves, but they don't accomplish much. They don't even come close to being meaningful tools for ensuring accountability. They don't achieve what they've set out to do, and most are filled with meaningless rhetoric and are not taken seriously by the majority of those who practice public relations."

Lack of legal consequences. Unlike the codes of other professions (such as law and medicine), adherence to public relations codes is strictly voluntary. Although there are procedures in place for enforcing the codes — the strongest punishment the organizations can apply in cases of violating ethical codes is revoking the individual's membership — both organizations are reluctant to take such action.

Limited scope of application. The ethical codes apply only to those individuals who belong to the organizations. Researchers estimate that in the United States, only about 15 percent of professional communicators who describe their work as "public relations" belong to either PRSA or IABC.

Like most professional codes of ethics, the PRSA and IABC codes are ripe for discussion in the categorical imperative-situational ethics dichotomy (see Chapter 2, pp. 28 and 36). Are the codes written to be interpreted as inflexible, carved-in-stone documents? Or should they be viewed as flexible, make-it-up-as-you-go-along sets of guidelines?

Many traditionalists in the field argue the former — that professional codes are meant to be inflexible and not subject to exceptions. Like many other critics of situational ethics, they claim that a set of rules that is too easily subject to exceptions or multiple interpretations is not a set of "rules" but rather a set of "suggestions." The more cynical among them question the value of such "flexible rules" and contend that if the rules cannot be strictly interpreted and enforced, there's little need to have them.

Others believe the opposite and conclude that "situational ethics is the dominant moral value in the decision-making process in public relations."

More informally, some public relations professionals make decisions based on which course of action is most expedient or "doing what needs to be done" with little or no consideration of the long-term consequences. But public relations theorist and researcher John Marston contends that the "ends justify the means" rationale is inconsistent with public relations ethical principles. In his 1963 book, one of the earliest textbooks to address ethical challenges in public relations, Marston argued that "public relations, like democracy itself, is a way of achieving agreement through understanding and persuasion . . . the way is just as important . . . because democracy itself lives by the road it travels."

The PRSA and IABC codes are reproduced in their entirety in Appendix A, but here are some of the common areas they cover:

1. Serving the public interest. Both codes of ethics state that all public relations activities must be carried out with regard to the best interests of the public. In other documents, the two organizations explain that term "public interest" refers to those rights and privileges granted to Americans by the U.S. Constitution and its amendments.

2. Respecting the "gifts and freebies" policies of the news media. As discussed in Chapter 5, most media outlets and professional associations have strict rules governing what journalists may and may not accept from individuals or organizations which they cover — or may find themselves covering in the future. Similarly, profession-al organizations such as PRSA and IABC have ethical guidelines that regulate the cir-cumstances under which public relations representatives may provide product samples or other items or services that would assist journalists in developing their stories.

Examples of behaviors that violate these guidelines include (1) giving to media rep-resentative gifts of more than nominal value, (2) providing journalists with trips or travel opportunities that are unrelated to legitimate news interests, or (3) attempting to secure media coverage by connecting it to the organization's advertising activities. A Latin term often used in discussing this issue is **quid pro quo**, the translation of which means "something for something." In this context, the term refers to an unethical agreement to swap one product, service, or favor for another, such as the giving of a gift or bribe in exchange for positive news coverage. The practice is common in other parts of the world, but not in the United States — at least not blatantly. The term might apply, however, in cases in which an organization makes an advertising commitment to a news organization in exchange for positive news coverage.

Many media organizations and state and local press associations have guidelines that prohibit reporters from accepting any gift or promotional item, regardless of the cost, if it is not directly related to the story the reporter is researching. A typical policy may use wording such as "cash, the equivalent of cash, or anything that can be easily converted to cash." The latter two phrases would pertain to gift cards or two-for-one coupons for local restaurants or other businesses.

Some other guidelines allow reporters to accept items under a certain dollar amount, calling it a "business courtesy," in order to avoid having reporters offend individuals or organizations they may deal with on a long-term basis. Such guidelines allow journalists to accept items such as T-shirts, keychains, coffee mugs, and similar promotional items.

Many journalists, however, are still reluctant to accept even the most insignificant gift. One Associated Press reporter, responding to a survey, quipped that "If it's worth more than $20, I can't accept it . . . If it's worth less than $20, it's crap and I don't want it." Another reporter, in a column published on the Internet, said that marketing firms, public relations agencies, and other promotional entities should avoid the tradition of giv-ing holiday gifts to reporters who cover their clients and should instead make equivalent donations to local charities. "That might not make headlines," the journalist wrote. "But neither does all the junk they send us."

Journalists often refer to such items as "freebies" or "trash and trinkets." While most are harmless, some demonstrate a lack of taste and judgment. When the movie studio 20th Century Fox wanted to promote the release of *Ravenous*, a 1999 film about cannibalism, publicists sent movie critics boxes of raw steaks. In 2002, romance publisher Harlequin promoted its new book *Fish Bowl* by sending journalists sealed fish bowls containing car-nivorous Siamese fighting fish, a gimmick that drew criticism from animal rights groups.

An important clarification of this provision is that it does not prohibit the reasonable giving or lending of products or services to media representatives who have a legitimate news interest. The emphasis here is on the key phrases *reasonable giving or lending* and *legitimate news interest.*

Examples of allowable behavior would include:

a. Loaning a product to a journalist who has been assigned to write a story or review about that product. Because the product is not being *given* to the journalist, but instead it is being *loaned* for a short period of time, it would be considered "reasonable." Because the writer has been assigned to write the review (most public relations representatives confirm such assignments with an editor), it is considered "legitimate news interest."

b. In cases of consumable products such as toothpaste or mouthwash (a circumstance in which it would be impractical to ask the journalist to return what is left over), the public relations or marketing representative should provide the journalist with only enough of a sample for him or her to make a judgment.

c. Allowing a theater critic to attend the performance of a play would be considered legitimate news interest, although many theater critics, like movie critics and restaurant critics, prefer to do their work anonymously in order to avoid unwanted attention.

d. In limited circumstances, public relations representatives will offer — and travel and entertainment journalists will accept — free airline tickets, hotel rooms, meals, and other expenses associated with their coverage of grand openings of resorts or premieres of major motion pictures.

Of all of these examples, the last one is perhaps the most controversial among public relations professionals and journalists. In the entertainment industry, the popular term is *press junkets*, which are often weekend trips for movie and television critics. In addition to the opportunity to screen an upcoming movie or television pilot far in advance of its public release, critics often receive free hotel rooms and food for the duration of the trip, and in some cases also receive free airline tickets.

In the travel and tourism industry, such trips are called "fam tours" — short for "familiarization tour." The marketing department of the Walt Disney Corporation is a frequent target for criticism, based on the lavish press parties it hosts at Disneyland in California and Walt Disney World in Florida.

The issue is a controversial one for news organizations, and their policies vary. At most major daily newspapers, the policy is "absolutely not." At smaller dailies and weeklies, as well as monthly travel and entertainment magazines, policies may allow for some subsidizing of journalist travel, but only if the travel is approved by an editor and there is an understanding that the journalist is under no obligation — either stated or implied — to write a positive story.

At one time such trips were limited to full-time entertainment critics and travel journalists who had name recognition within their industry, but today, such opportunities are also offered to freelance writers and bloggers who can provide some assurance that their work will be published or posted to a legitimate website. Inexperienced public relations representatives occasionally find themselves victims of "freelance scammers" who falsify their credentials in order take subsidized trips to exotic destinations with no intention of writing or blogging about them. To avoid being scammed, experienced public relations representatives verify freelance writing assignments with editors or check the blogger's track record or other credentials.

In many other cultures, publicists, public relations representatives, and other individuals or groups seeking positive news coverage resort to bribing journalists. The practice is so casual that it is considered analogous to American diners who tip servers and other restaurant employees. While American media ethicists would not approve of such arrangements, observers with a more international perspective hold a different view. "Such customs are not necessarily bad just because they are different," wrote international public relations researchers Philip Seib and Kathy Fitzpatrick in their 1995 book, *Public Relations Ethics.* Other experts fall back on the adage, "When in Rome, do as the Romans do." In their 1994 book, authors James Jaska and Michael Pritchard added that "one should not assume that he or she understands another society's practices well enough to criticize them, let alone try to change them."

3. Releasing truthful information and avoiding intentional deception.

False or deceptive information can influence individuals and groups to make inappropriate decisions and place their own welfare at risk. When they discover the deception and its source, most individuals and organizations will be resentful and will likely become more negative toward the cause than they were before. Whether the deception is intentional or unintentional, professional communicators suffer from damage to their credibility — as well as that of their employers — and typically find such damage difficult to repair.

During military operations, the U.S. military often engages in "disinformation," which is the intentional release of false information in order to deceive or mislead the enemy. While few media organizations would knowingly go along with such a strategy, they sometimes find themselves as accomplices in the deception. When civilian businesses attempt such a strategy, they often find the media unlikely to be fooled into participating in the deception. When reporters catch on to the disinformation, they will not only expose it, but will also be less likely to trust information from that company or nonprofit organization in the future.

When public relations representatives are asked questions that they cannot answer for legal or competitive reasons, they should explain the reason or reasons for the delay and indicate when they might be able to respond. Most reporters will understand and respect the legal reasons, but they will not understand or respect "no comment" or any other form of evasion or deception.

A common example that public information officers and media relations specialists deal with is the amount of information that is appropriate to release to the media about employees or former employees who are part of newsworthy events. Examples of "good news" situations include those in which an employee earns an award, given either by the employer or by a professional organization or industry association, or is elected to a leadership position in an organization. Examples of "bad news" situations include employees who have been crime victims or are suspected of committing crimes on or off company property. Regardless of whether the news is good or bad, public relations professionals should limit the information they give out to the beginning and ending dates of employment, job title, and job description. Public relations representatives should not release information about salary, home address, marital and family relationships, organizational memberships, or job performance.*

---

*Information about government employees is subject to federal and state public records laws and is discussed in more detail in Chapter 10.

4. Preserving confidentiality. In the agency-client relationship, agency employees cannot share information from one client with another client or with anyone else except on a "need to know" basis. In general, agency employees are expected to keep information secret until the client directs them to release it.

An important clarification of the confidentiality principle is that the obligation is in effect *before a formal relationship begins* and extends *beyond the termination of that relationship.* When a client discloses confidential information to an agency (or the agency uncovers information during its research) during preliminary discussions, that information is protected under the confidentiality rule, even if that agency is not hired. Likewise, employees of a corporate public relations department, independent contractors, or agencies representing a client are bound by the confidentiality rule even after the termination of working relationships — regardless of the circumstances under which the relationship ended.

While PRSA and IABC expect agency representatives to honor confidentiality agreements with their clients, such agreements do not prohibit professional communicators from "blowing the whistle" on a client or employer who is doing something illegal or from testifying in court about a client's or employer's illegal activity.

In terms of whistle-blowing or voluntarily providing information to law enforcement or regulatory agencies, this clarification is significant not only for what is says, but what it does not say. While it says public relations representatives *may* report unethical behavior, it does not say that they *must* report it. If a public relations representative wanted to voluntarily provide information about a company doing something illegal, but was not sure if such action was appropriate, he or she could find justification in the professional association's concept of "serving the public interest."

5. Severing relationships with any client or employer if that relationship requires conduct contrary to ethical guidelines. Later in this chapter, public relations veteran Lee Baker provides a scenario about a public relations representative who is reluctant to quit his job over an ethical dispute after remembering that he faces "a $3,000 orthodontist bill, a mortgage, and a wife thinking about divorce."

Because they have greater knowledge of the behind-the-scenes behavior of an organization, employees in the public relations department may find themselves in the uncomfortable position of deciding whether or not to be a whistle-blower. Examples might include having knowledge of a company's record of employment discrimination, insurance fraud, environmental violations, stock market irregularities, or other problems. Although they are protected against employer retaliation by federal laws, potential whistle-blowers must decide whether or not to play that role.

Larry Johnson, author of a number of books about business ethics, claims that companies should reward whistle-blowers rather than attempt to retaliate against them. "No CEO of any honest company would want his or her people to participate in illegal or immoral activities," Johnson contended in his 2003 book, *Absolute Honesty.* "If you see something going on that's not right, your first option is to go to your boss and say, 'this is going on; I can't participate because it's against my values.' If that doesn't work, take it up the chain of command." Addressing the concern that anti-retaliation laws are not foolproof and that being a whistle-blower involves the risk of losing one's job, Johnson wrote, "There will always be risk involved. Only you can make the decision on where you draw the line on what's right and wrong."

6. Avoiding conflicts of interest. Public relations agencies or individual public relations professionals are admonished to not perform work for any client or employer which causes a conflict — real or perceived — with the interests of another client or employer, unless full disclosure is made to and approval is given by all parties involved.

In an agency setting, that means that an agency cannot represent clients that compete against each other. Some agencies hoping to retain two competing clients may attempt to skirt the issue by appointing separate account teams and forbidding them to discuss the details of their work with each other. That idea may sound good in theory, but even if the firm does have separate account executives and attempts in good faith to keep that wall of separation in place, the typical agency has only one art department, one media department, and one research department. The inner workings of a public relations agency do not lend themselves to complete confidentiality within the office.

The conflict of interest principle also prohibits the performance of work for any client or employer which causes a conflict — real or perceived — with the individual's personal interest. One example of this conflict involves an individual who works full-time in the public relations department of a company (or a public relations agency) and performs work as a freelancer in his or her free time. The individual may not accept as a freelance client any company that competes with his or her full-time employer unless both the client and the employer are aware of the situation and both agree to it.

This would also apply to the case of an independent public relations consultant or employee at a public relations agency whose personal interest — such as membership in a special-interest group — is in conflict with the interests of a current client. An example would be a consultant employed by a chemical company while also serving as an officer of an environmental watchdog group. If the watchdog group is involved in litigation against or is otherwise targeting the chemical company, the consultant must either resign his or her position in the watchdog group or cease working for the chemical company or the agency that represents it. As much as he or she may claim the ability to remain neutral, at some point he or she will be caught in the conflict between the two parties and will be forced to choose which loyalty is more important. It is best to make such a decision before the conflict arises.

7. Promising results that are outside of the individual's direct control. It is permissible to guarantee to clients conditions such as quality of service, degree of efforts, or methods utilized, because those are conditions within the control of public relations representatives or agencies. Representatives and agencies can, for example, guarantee their clients that a research project will be executed ethically and responsibly, will use the most up-to-date methods and technology, or will utilize a certain sample size. Agencies cannot, however, guarantee what the results of the research project will reveal. Likewise, an individual or agency cannot promise that the client will be profiled in an industry publication, that a client will see an increase in product sales, or that proposed government legislation will be passed or defeated. Any of those may be listed as objectives, but they cannot be guaranteed because of other intervening variables and the degree to which those results are largely outside the control of the individuals or agencies attempting to accomplish them.

The ethical rule that prohibits agencies from making promises to clients about results is one that some clients find problematic, as they are accustomed to working with other service providers who are able to guarantee their work. But most experienced agency executives know that over-promising simply to win new accounts over their competitors is a bad business practice. When clients fire their agencies, one of the most common reasons for doing so is that the agencies "over-promised and under-delivered."

Current Issues and Controversies

The Challenge of Media Relations

In media relations, the difficulty of meeting media deadlines creates new pressures on the public relations staff. Before the advent of the Internet, media relations specialists had to be concerned with only two deadlines per day — the television deadline (usually late afternoon) and the print deadline (usually early evening for the next day's morning newspaper). Today, however, most newspapers and television stations of any size have corresponding Internet and social media sites that are updated constantly, meaning that with rapidly developing news stories, deadlines occur every hour.

The working relationship between journalists and public relations professionals is one that is interdependent, but not necessarily reciprocal. Even though each side depends on the other, at times the relationship appears to be unbalanced. Corporate public relations representatives depend heavily on the journalists — especially business reporters — to disseminate company information to their external publics. Part of the job of a public relations representatives is to help the journalists do their jobs better, but it is not the responsibility of journalists to assist public relations representatives in carrying out their job duties.

While relationships between journalists and public relations representatives for nonprofit organizations can sometimes be adversarial, the problem is much more serious in the cases of business journalists and corporate public relations representatives.

While they are reluctant to admit it, business reporters depend heavily on information provided by public relations representatives. Without public relations representatives to provide story ideas, publications such as *The Wall Street Journal* and *Business Week* simply could not fill all of their pages. Rebecca Madiera, the public relations director for Pepsico, describes the relationship as being similar to a game of tennis: "You're on opposite sides of the net, but it's the only way to play the game."

Historically, public relations professionals and journalists have a love-hate relationship. While both depend on each other in the execution of their job duties, the working relationship between the two professions is sometimes contentious. Journalists are probably more critical of public relations representatives than the other way around, but many of those criticisms are based not on substance but on conditioning and role expectation. Some of the more cynical journalists say, "I'm a journalist; I'm supposed to hate public relations people. It's in my job description."

A recent survey conducted by a New York-based PR firm indicated that more than 65 percent of journalists distrust public relations professionals, but that 81 percent indicated they need them.

The journalism profession's dependency on public relations materials has increased dramatically in the last two decades, as newspaper, television, and radio news operations trim the size of their staffs. That is especially true in the case of local television news, where news programming has expanded from an hour a day in the 1980s to more than two hours a day in 2014 — but with production staffs remaining the same size or in some cases shrinking.

Major complaints about public relations professionals and their materials include (1) too many unsolicited materials sent by postal mail, electronic mail, and fax; (2) too many follow-up calls and emails, and (3) unfamiliarity with the style, format, or deadlines of the newspaper or television or radio program being approached. In the case of agency personnel providing information on behalf of clients, journalists claim that those communicators are often unable to answer follow-up questions about the products or services being promoted and are unable to connect journalists with helpful sources within the client companies.

Public relations professionals should avoid playing favorites — or appear to be playing favorites — among the media representatives who cover the company or nonprofit organization. The worst example is providing one reporter advance information about an upcoming announcement, thus allowing him or her to break the story ahead of his or her competitors.

An important clarification is that this rule would not prevent a public relations representative from helping a reporter working on an "enterprise story" — one in which the reporter has developed a story idea based on his or her initiative. One example involves the reporter who learns that a major industry publication is about to publish a list of the top 100 executives in a certain field and that a local company employs three of those 100. If the reporter plans to write a story about those three employees and asks for help from the company's public relations representative, that individual should respect the reporter's initiative and is not obligated to share that same information with other journalists unless it is requested.

In politics and government, it is common for reporters to ask for an "exclusive" — an agreement that the journalist will be the first (or sometimes only) person provided with information about a certain topic. That often happens when a reporter learns about the content of an upcoming announcement several days before it is scheduled, and someone on the staff of the politician or government agency asks the reporter to not break the story in advance. In return for "sitting on the story," the journalist is given the first interview with the politician and/or government official involved.

While this practice is common in politics, in corporate or nonprofit public relations work it should be done rarely — perhaps never. The long-term damage to the organization's relationships with other journalists outweighs any short-term benefit that might result.

Here are some of the most common criticisms that journalists cite about their working relationships with public relations professionals:

Public relations representatives limit our access to company officials.
We want to talk to the president of the company, not the PR guy. The president of the company will tell us the truth; the PR guy will just get in the way.

Public relations representatives will stonewall, refuse to release information, and often lie to us. We want the truth and we want it now, but the PR department tries to put off releasing the information and hopes we will go away.

Public relations representatives exaggerate the importance of things that we see as trivial. They over-promote events and products and look at the news media as a source of free publicity.

The Debate over Licensing

Numerous times in the history of the profession, the leaderships of PRSA and IABC have considered the potential for a formal licensing procedure for public relations professionals. The program would be analogous to those in place for other professionals, such as architects and accountants.

Public relations pioneer Edward L. Bernays was the leading advocate for licensing from the late 1950s until his death in 1995. Since his passing, however, no individual or group has stepped forward to advocate licensing with the same level of enthusiasm. If public relations professionals could be licensed, Bernays argued, the program could require more educational preparation (perhaps a specific college degree), enhance the image of the industry, and provide a mechanism for removing from the profession those individuals or agencies found to be incompetent or guilty of dishonest or unethical conduct.

Those opposing the idea counter with two arguments of their own. The first counterargument is that before a formal licensing program could be established, there would have to be a universal definition for public relations — one that all of the major professional groups could agree upon. A second problem is that neither PRSA nor IABC (nor any other professional group) wants the responsibility for setting up the bureaucracy and due process that would be necessary to administer such a program. If the licensing process were to be modeled after those of other organizations, the subsequent increase in office staff would cause membership costs to double or triple, and the legal fees associated with court challenges could increase membership costs even further.

Ethical Dilemmas on the Job

Public relations professionals are often faced with assignments that potentially call for unethical or questionable conduct — or perhaps just appear to. Before making hasty assumptions, the individual should first clarify the assignment or task, clear up any misunderstandings, and then determine whether or not complying with the request would indeed involve an ethical violation.

If the individual finds the answer is "yes," he or she has a number of options. The first is to advise the client or employer that the actions being considered are not only in violation of accepted ethical guidelines, but also not in the best interests of the organization. One way to approach this difficult situation is to provide examples of how similar conduct resulted in negative results for other organizations in the past. Public relations textbooks, especially those used in case studies classes, contain many examples that could be cited. The second strategy is to simply refuse to participate and explain the reasons for doing so. The practicality of this tactic depends on the nature of the relationship between the individual and the client or employer; professionals new to their positions may lack the confidence to do so.

A third option — to be considered only in the most serious circumstances — is to sever relationships with the client or employer in question. The justification for such a drastic step is clear, however. A public relations professional forced to act in a way that conflicts with accepted ethical standards will lose confidence in the client or employer and will therefore be unable to provide appropriate counsel or serve as a credible spokesperson. But in his 1993 book, *The Credibility Factor: Putting Ethics to Work in Public Relations*, Lee W. Baker writes:

When asked to violate ethics by a boss or client, I do not take the arbitrary position that a practitioner should immediately quit, or threaten to. First, that is a bad negotiating technique. Second, it implies that all ethical issues are black and white. Some hard-liners say that we must have the courage to stand by our principles, and if necessary, walk away from a client. But how does an individual with two children in college, a mortgage, a $3,000 orthodontist bill, and a wife thinking about divorce walk away from a high-paying job on a matter of principle?

Robert L. Dilenschneider, former president of Hill & Knowlton, wrote in his book, *Power and Influence: Mastering the Art of Persuasion,* that the public often judges an organization's ethical performance "by comparing what it says to what it does." Another adage used in discussions of business ethics is that "what an organization DOES will shout so loudly that no one will hear what it SAYS."

The bottom line of the two quotes above is that employees, government regulators, journalists, current and potential customers, and current and potential stockholders will compare an organization's actual conduct with what it says about itself in news releases, television interviews, and on its website; the discrepancies will be conspicuous. "I have never seen a truly unethical company elude being found out for long, especially these days," Dilenschneider wrote. "In our trade, we learn about the likely ethics soft spots in a business long before they become public knowledge."

Unethical Practices of <u>Some</u> Public Relations Agencies

Relationships with clients represent an ethical minefield for public relations agencies. Practices for which agencies are sometimes criticized include:

Bait and switch: An experienced senior account executive or agency officer (with local or national name recognition) makes the presentation and lands the account, but then the detail work is assigned to younger, less experienced staffers; the senior executive is never seen again. In another variation, an agency may send one or more attractive young women to make new business proposals to male clients. Those potential clients are likely unaware that once they hire the firm, they are unlikely to ever see those women again, much less have the opportunity to date them. Not only is this an unethical way for public relations agencies to treat potential clients, but also an unethical way for them to treat their own employees.

Churning: Unscrupulous agencies often create unnecessary work or exaggerate the amount of staff time actually involved in a project in order to "pad" the client's bill. Unless the client (or someone in its accounting office) scrutinizes the monthly bill line by line, such padding may go undetected.

Unrealistic expectations: While presenting new business proposals, agency representatives may claim there is more publicity potential in a project than there actually is. They may drop titles of publications such as *The Wall Street Journal* into the conversation in order to land a prospective account, even though the agency representative already knows that such publicity is unlikely.

Staged news conferences and "planted" questions: An agency may have employees pose as reporters at a client's news conference and ask friendly set-up questions to influence the tone of the event, or have them attend a competitor's news conference to ask hostile questions. Even more extreme tactics include gathering information on a client's opponents by infiltrating meetings of the opposition group or posing as college students working on a research project and gathering information by mail, email, or telephone.

Liese L. Hutchison, former associate professor of communication at St. Louis University, suggests that agency owners and managers should insist on high ethical standards for their employees by either adopting the code of ethics of either PRSA or IABC (or developing more specific guidelines of their own), requiring employees to sign the code, inserting the code into requests for proposals, and then setting the example by demonstrating ethical conducts themselves.

News Releases and Manufactured Quotes

Even though the entire content of a news release is seldom used in a news story, reporters often lift "manufactured quotes" (quotes that have been written by the public relations staff but are attributed to others) from the release instead of calling to obtain quotes first-hand.

While some journalists have a policy of not using quotes they suspect may have been manufactured, most accept it as part of their working relationship with public relations professionals and may use them if they are not silly or libelous. When doing so, many journalists will likely use connecting phrases such as *said in a statement released by the company* to indicate that the quotes did not result from an actual interview.

In most cases, public relations representatives ask the client to provide general thoughts about the topic to be discussed, expand on those thoughts to create a more detailed and effective quote, then obtain the client's permission to use the quote in its finished form. A representative who creates a quote and includes it in a news release without the client's approval risks exposing the client to embarrassment, criticism, or a possible defamation lawsuit if the quote includes factual errors.

Dealing with Inaccurate or Misleading Media Coverage

When faced with inaccurate or misleading reporting, public relations representatives for the individuals or organizations involved in the story should carefully think through their responses. Errors in media coverage can be placed in one of four categories:

Defamation. Errors that are defamatory — seriously damaging to the reputation or financial well-being of the organization — should be taken seriously by both parties. These errors might be the grounds for legal action, but this is a decision for the organization's legal department, not the public relations staff.

Serious (but non-defamatory) factual errors. These are errors that affect the audience's understanding of a story and for which there is documentation available to prove their falsity. In these cases, the public relations staff should request the media outlet for a correction or retraction, but should do so in a professional manner and without threats of legal action.

Minor inaccuracies. These are errors that do not affect the audience's understanding of the story. An example of a minor inaccuracy is reporting that a company was founded in 1984 when it was actually founded in 1985, or reporting that the president of the company holds a degree in chemistry when the degree earned was actually in biology. Errors of this type should be ignored, or at most, corrected in a less formal way — simply asking the media organization to correct the information in its clip files or electronic archives (so the error won't be repeated), but not insisting on a published correction.

Subjective errors. An example of a subjective error is a columnist or other opinion writer stating that your company's priority for the coming year is in one area of its operation, when you know it is in a different area. In most cases, errors of this type — while annoying — should be ignored. Unlike reporters, columnists and opinion writers are given considerable leeway by their editors to make assumptions, state opinions, and speculate on topics within their areas of expertise. And when they do so in a way that presents your organization in a bad light, your best response is to do nothing — especially when it is a first-time occurrence.

If the same columnist makes such errors frequently, however, a more appropriate response is to meet formally with the individual to discuss the collective impact of the errors. If the subjective errors are made by multiple columnists, the more appropriate response is to meet with the newspaper's editorial board or television station's news director and/or general manager.

The Debate over Confidentiality and Privilege

Professional codes of ethics require public relations professionals to treat as confidential the majority of the information they exchange with clients. However, this principle does not apply in situations such as being questioned by federal or state law enforcement investigators, testifying in court, or providing a deposition in a legal proceeding.

This is quite different from the practice of law and medicine — lawyers and physicians cannot be required to testify in court against their clients and patients — although many public relations professionals believe they should have the same level of confidentiality.

The rationale for not providing similar legal protection for public relations representatives includes the following factors:

Lawyers and doctors and lawyers work in fields that are well-defined, while public relations is not well-defined. If public relations professionals are given privilege, a company in legal trouble could simply re-draw its organizational chart and claim that all of its employees work in public relations and are therefore immune to subpoenas and other court proceedings.

Granting privilege to public relations professionals may impede important government investigations. As mentioned earlier, public relations representatives often have inside knowledge of matters such as employment discrimination, insurance fraud, stock market irregularities, and environmental damage. They should be required to provide this information because those investigations serve the greater public interest, which the industry codes identify as the most important value.

Compared to the work of lawyers and doctors, the work of public relations professionals is not that important. Individuals facing criminal charges have the constitutional right to legal representation, while patients have a moral right to health care. No one has the constitutional or moral right to public relations advice, however. Opponents of proposals to grant privilege to public relations professionals contend that their work is simply not as important as legal representation or health care.

Those in favor of changing the rules and providing privilege often cite the following factors:

A public relations representative testifying in court against a client or employer is putting his or her career on the line. Whether the testimony is voluntary or mandated by the court, he or she cannot continue to work for the client or employer against whom the testimony was given. He or she should not be put in that awkward position.

Professional communicators deserve the same level of legal protection as lawyers and doctors. Lawyers must have the complete trust of their clients in order to provide competent legal presentation, and doctors must have the complete trust of their patients in order to provide adequate health care. Public relations is no different — clients and employers must have trusting relationships with their outside public relations agencies or employees of the PR department in order for those individuals to provide their best advice or service.

Without privilege, public relations professionals are too vulnerable. Without legal protection, public relations representatives are easy targets for prosecutors, defense attorneys, and government officials who are simply looking for shortcuts rather than doing more thorough investigative work on their own. Shield laws protect journalists; public relations representatives should have similar protection.

Litigation PR

One of the fastest-growing trends within the profession is the phenomenon of law firms hiring public relations agencies to augment their courtroom strategy. Known as **litigation PR**, the law firm's objective is to use public relations techniques to influence public opinion both inside and outside of the courtroom.

Prior to the selection of a jury in a criminal or civil trial, such tactics are often effective in presenting a favorable impression of the defendant to prospective jurors who are following media coverage of pre-trial proceedings. Once the trial is underway, public relations firms are used to measure how the public perceives the media coverage.

Although the technique had already been in use for more than a decade, the idea of using focus groups to help trial lawyers design their courtroom strategies came to the attention of the media and the public during the 1995 murder trial of O.J. Simpson. Forensic Technologies, a California-based research firm, conducted four surveys of Los Angeles residents — potential jurors — to gauge public attitudes toward Simpson during pre-trial proceedings. The company then used two focus groups to help defense attorneys prepare for the juror screening process and determine what qualities they should look for in prospective jurors. During the trial itself, the company conducted additional focus groups, having the participants function as "mock juries" and react to videotaped segments showing the defense lawyers so they could adjust their presentation styles.

Today, many defense attorneys in criminal trials as well as civil trials (such as product liability cases) use focus groups to help them with both jury selection and trial strategy. One of the reasons for their popularity and success is the similarity of the group dynamics involved in focus group discussions led by a moderator and jury deliberations led by a foreperson.

Citing examples from the Simpson trial and other well-publicized cases, an article about the phenomenon in the *New York Times* criticized the process by reporting that "litigation blackmail is being committed in the U.S. every day, aided and abetted by journalists, lawyers, and public relations professionals . . . it is not the function of the press, or of those who disseminate news and information on the fringes of journalism — like talk shows — to allow the merits of individual cases to be argued or promoted outside of due process."

Other critics contend that public relations techniques are being used in ways that the founders of the profession never intended. The technique of leaking information to the media with the intention of influencing potential jurors is one example that the profession's founders, as well as public relations ethicists, would find troubling.

For Discussion

Case Study 7-A   When a PR Firm Could Use a PR Firm

Public relations firms are often criticized when they accept clients involved in controversial public issues. In 1991, for example, Hill & Knowlton was criticized for accepting the assignment of developing an anti-abortion campaign for one of its clients, the United States Catholic Conference. The account was worth an estimated $3 million.

Many of the firm's 1,850 employees objected to the idea, and two felt strongly enough to resign. The employees were angry not only at the concept of the campaign, but also the fact they read about it in the media before hearing it from their own employer. In addition to dealing with the employees' negative reaction, a major Hill & Knowlton client (that the firm declined to identify) canceled its working relationship with the firm.

The irony of the situation was that the firm's president, Robert Dilenschneider, had just published a book on issues management and in practice the firm violated many of the principles espoused in the book. In hindsight, Dilenschneider admitted that the firm did a "very bad job" at handling the controversy.

After months of media criticism, the agency established a policy that any employee who objected to the campaign would not be required to work on it. That was an easy situation to resolve for a large organization such as Hill & Knowlton, a world-wide firm with thousands of employees; it could easily find enough to staff the account. The situation would be far different for a small firm that may have only five or six employees and requires every staff member work on every account.

In 1992, Hill & Knowlton generated controversy again when it represented an international organization called Citizens for a Free Kuwait, the purpose of which was to generate support for the U.S. military action against Iraq after it invaded its tiny neighbor. The firm arranged for a 14-year-old Kuwaiti girl to testify before a congressional committee looking into human rights abuses allegedly carried out by Iraqi soldiers during the conflict. The girl claimed that she had witnessed soldiers taking Kuwaiti infants from their hospital incubators and leaving them on the floor to die.

After it was learned that the stories were exaggerated (and may have been fabricated), the firm was accused of misleading Congress while not disclosing the fact that the girl was the daughter of Kuwait's ambassador to the U.S.

- Were these situations involving Hill & Knowlton handled fairly and ethically? What would you have done differently if you were in a leadership position in the agency?

- What if you were the owner of a small firm fewer than a dozen employees) with a tradition of having every employee involved in every account, and several objected to working on a specific project or for a specific client?

Case Study 7-B   PR for PR

It is not uncommon for members of the media, consumer watchdog groups, and the general public to express skepticism or distrust of the public relations industry. In the previous century much of that reputation was deserved, as practitioners of the profession were caught attempting to deceive the public or mislead the media. Much of the skepticism is based on incidents of the 1920s and 1930s, when industry publicists — the forerunner of today's corporate public relations practitioners — routinely lied to government investigators, the media, and the public while representing companies in times of crisis. Today, that practice is continued by Hollywood publicists and press agents who represent the interests of their clientele by exaggerating the importance of an entertainer's accomplishments, staging phony events, and stonewalling the media's attempts to pursue legitimate news. The image of the profession in the latter half of the previous century led the Public Relations Society of America to hire a full-time public relations officer and develop campaigns to improve the image of the profession — the so-called "PR for PR" approach.

Today, most public relations professionals and communication researchers believe that public perception of the profession is improving. Whether that is the result of the PRSA efforts or simply a coincidence is uncertain. While the perception of exaggeration and deception are waning, one significant criticism of the profession remains — that PR representatives withhold significant information from the media and public. Many public relations experts are advocates within their organizations for honesty and openness, and recent PRSA publications use the term "transparency" to refer to the need for companies to conduct as much of their business as possible in the open.

In addition, many public relations traditionalists object to the casual use of the term "public relations." Too often, they say, the term is used as a synonym for schmoozing, deception, manipulation, distortion, or disinformation. Perhaps the worst offenders are those that refer to what public relations representatives do as "spin." Robert Dilenschneider, former president of Hill & Knowlton, says that use of the term in a public relations context debases the profession and creates the impression that public relations representatives are nothing more than paid liars. "Spin is to public relations what pornography is to art," Dilenschneider wrote in a 1998 guest column in *The Wall Street Journal.*

Criticism of the public relations profession is nothing new. Advice columnist Ann Landers took a jab at the profession in a 1988 column in which she predicted that a high school boy with a reputation for misleading and deceiving his teachers and female classmates "might have a great future in public relations." Members of professional associations such as PRSA and the International Association of Business Communicators (IABC) flooded her mailbox with complaints, prompting her to apologize in a subsequent column in which she also mentioned some of the industry's positive aspects.

As mentioned in Chapter 2, one early critic of the public relations industry was journalism historian Daniel Boorstin, who complained that consumers were at the mercy of powerful corporations using their public relations and advertising budgets to intentionally mislead and exploit the public. Boorstin was followed in the 1980s by Jeff and Marie Blyskal, a husband-and-wife team of consumer advocates and authors of *PR: How the Public Relations Industry Writes the News.* The authors pointed to dozens of examples of news stories based primarily on content of news releases. Unlike later critics, who blame the problem on the newspaper industry, the Blyskals say the fault lies with both the aggressiveness of the public relations industry and the laziness of reporters.

In 1989, consumer advocate Joyce Nelson took a similar stance in her book, *Sultans of Sleaze: Public Relations and the Media.* Nelson claims the primary strength of an organization's public relations function is its ability to operate "under the radar . . . gliding in and out of troubling situations without being noticed" and manipulating public opinion without leaving behind any evidence of its work.

The alternative political magazine *Utne Reader* also scrutinizes the public relations industry. In one 1994 article, it accused the public relations profession of "shaping public life in ways we're not supposed to notice" and commented (incorrectly) that the profession's core principle was that it is "easier to change the way people think about reality than it is to change reality."

Today, among the field's most vocal critics are consumer activists Sheldon Rampton and John Stauber, who authored a 1995 book titled *Toxic Sludge is Good For You: Lies, Damn Lies and the Public Relations Industry,* the title of which indicates its tone. Today, Rampton and Stauber continue their criticism of the field through publishing *PR Watch,* a website that its founders say "calls attention to the misleading and unethical conduct" of some public relations professionals.

The profession also continues to draw harsh words in recent decades from various consumer advocates and other critics.

In her 2005 book, *Bait and Switch: The Futile Pursuit of the American Dream,* author Barbara Ehrenreich tells the story of a professional woman exploring a variety of career options. The author describes public relations as "journalism's evil twin" and writes that "whereas a journalist seeks the truth, a PR person may be called upon to disguise it or even to advance an untruth . . . if your employer, a pharmaceutical company, claims its new drug cures both cancer and erectile dysfunction, your job is to promote it, not to investigate the grounds for those claims."

The profession took its worst beating in 2008 when former White House Press Secretary Scott McClellan published his book, *What Happened,* which chronicled his three years working as the top public information officer in the federal government. The book itself did not create the uproar, but media critics used anecdotes from the book as examples of how public relations professionals "manipulate" the news media and public opinion. CBS News commentator Andrew Cohen said that McClellan's revelations were just the "tip of the iceberg" and that the government's use of "spin" was just one example of how the public relations industry negatively affects society. In his on-air commentary, Cohen said, "Show me a PR person who is accurate and truthful and I'll show you a PR person who is unemployed." Cohen also mocked PRSA's Code of Ethics and its emphasis on accuracy and truth by comparing it to a criminal ring having a creed that included the clause, "thou shall not steal."

Much like they did in the Ann Landers case, PRSA and IABC responded quickly to defend the industry.

- Is it an appropriate use of the organization's time and resources to engage in a "PR for PR" campaign, or is the task simply too big to be realistically addressed?

- If the organization were to engage in such a campaign almost certain to be successful, but would require a substantial increase in the organization's membership dues, would it be worth it to you?

Case Study 7-C   **Another Bad Day at the Office for FEMA**

In October 2007, wildfires swept across southern California, leaving thousands of families homeless and causing billions of dollars in property damage. The Federal Emergency Management Agency (FEMA) planned a news conference at its Washington, D.C. offices to brief reporters on the agency's response to the disaster.

Due to the short notice and other miscommunications, FEMA officials found themselves talking to an empty room. Rather than cancel the briefing, FEMA officials gathered agency employees to pose as journalists and ask softball questions, such as, "Are you pleased with FEMA's response so far?" Reporters were invited to listen to the news conference by telephone but were not allowed to ask questions, and television stations were later given videotaped copies of the news conference without being told that it was staged.

Once the deception was exposed, FEMA claimed it was the idea of one senior administrator, and that the media spokesperson conducting the briefing did not recognize FEMA employees as the "reporters" asking the questions. FEMA Director David Paulison, Homeland Security Secretary Michael Chertoff, and President George W. Bush all condemned the event as "unacceptable."

The fake news conference fiasco came just two years after a much bigger FEMA failure — its response to Hurricane Katrina. The Category 5 storm was one of the most expensive and deadly to hit the mainland United States, coming ashore near New Orleans in late August 2005. The storm killed more than 1,800 people (including those killed on Caribbean islands in the storm's path) and caused $86 billion in property damage.

Communication systems were down, meaning that reporters were at a disadvantage working in damaged and dangerous areas. A series of miscommunications between FEMA, city government officials in New Orleans, and state officials in Louisiana resulted in a lack of information (or sometimes the wrong information) being provided to journalists. Although several parties shared the blame, FEMA took most of the criticism, and critics used the scenario to portray the Bush administration as callous and uncaring toward the people affected. The slow and ineffective response led to the resignation of FEMA director Michael D. Brown.

Following the Katrina and fake news conference fiascos, ongoing news coverage of FEMA highlighted a number of mistakes and oversights, many of them related to unnecessary bureaucracy created by the agency's new organizational structure. FEMA was once an independent agency, but after becoming part of Department of Homeland Security following the September 11, 2001 terrorist attacks, its new leaders were mostly political appointees with little or no previous experience in disaster recovery. Many congressional leaders called for the agency to be removed from underneath the Homeland Security umbrella and once again made an independent agency.

- How does a federal government agency such as FEMA recover from having such an ethical misdeed publicized?

- If you were a journalist covering FEMA and knew about these incidents, would you be skeptical of any information you received from the agency in the future?

Discussion Problem 7-A   **Was That Focus
                                        Group Really Confidential?**

As part of a research project in an advanced public relations class, students organize focus group sessions to gather student perception on the problem of sexual assault on campus. Because of the sensitive nature of the discussions, students are organized into separate groups for men and women. Before the sessions begin, the moderators inform the participants that their identities and their comments would be kept confidential. Each participant fills out a registration card, but moderators assure the group that is only so the students can send them thank-you cards in the mail.

During one of the focus group sessions for female students, several of the participants tell nearly identical stories about a specific downtown bar at which they suspect employees may have spiked their drinks with date-rape drugs. Although none of the women were assaulted as a result, they did recall being nauseated and dizzy for several days.

The women's comments become part of the written record of the session. Several weeks later, when the students prepare their final report, they mention the women's experience but do not elaborate on it. At the end of the semester, the professor who supervised the project submits a copy of the final report to the Dean of Students office, not thinking about the impact of the information related to the date-rape drug.

The Dean of Students notices it, however, and contacts the professor to ask if he will disclose the names of the students participating in the focus group sessions so he can question them, find out which bar they were referring to, and notify local law enforcement.

1. What should the professor do — turn over the names of the students (which means violating the agreement that their identities would remain confidential) or stick to the promise of confidentiality given to the participants at the beginning of the session?

2. Even though information revealed in social science research may be confidential in a general sense, it is not legally protected (such as in cases of doctor-patient privilege or lawyer-client privilege). In this case, does the interest of possibly uncovering illegal activity (such as use of a date-rape drug) take priority over the moderator's promise of confidentiality? Why or why not?

3. Which of the philosophers studied in Chapter 2 might help the professor make this decision?

Discussion Problem 7-B   **Get Your Can to the Game**

You're a student at Enormous State University, and a campus organization you belong to has spent most of the fall semester planning an event to benefit the food bank that helps low-income families in your community. The event, scheduled to take place two weeks before Thanksgiving, involves chapter members working with players from a minor-league baseball team to collect cans of food outside the stadium before a home game. Fans who bring at least two cans of food may exchange them for coupons that give them a discount on tickets for the game. Fans who already have their tickets when they come to the stadium will receive discount coupons for a local restaurant. Fans will also receive one raffle ticket for each can of food they bring.

In addition to providing the discounts, the management of the baseball team allows your group to use its name in promoting the event, provides prizes for the raffle, and helps the group obtain an insurance waiver required by the company that manages the stadium. The afternoon of the game, the team gives the students part of the pre-game program to present the raffle prizes and make a brief announcement explaining the year-round needs of the food bank.

The goals for the event are to:

- generate donations for the food bank;
- create awareness of the year-round needs of the food bank;
- get some practice in event-planning and developing publicity materials;
- generate publicity and recognition for the student organization.

Your faculty advisor helps your group prepare news releases to promote the event. The afternoon of the game, your members are busy collecting cans outside the stadium. The baseball players, who were supposed to be there to help collect cans and sign autographs, are nowhere in sight. Reporters from the local daily newspaper and television station arrive and start to interview the students. Then three baseball players show up, and the reporters cut short their interviews with the students and begin to interview the players.

On the 6 o'clock news that night, the television reporter who was there provides a report that does not mention the students, your student organization, or even the name of your university. Instead, the story consists only of interviews with the baseball players and makes it appear as though they were solely responsible for the food drive. The next morning, the daily newspaper carries a story that includes some quotes from the players, but also quotes the students and gives your organization the majority of the credit for the event.

1. How should your student group respond, if at all, to the television news story that gave all the credit to the baseball players?

2. Which philosophers discussed in Chapter 2 might help you make this decision?

Discussion Problem 7-C   The Golf Weekend

You are the communications manager for a small nonprofit organization. Part of your job is to oversee a variety of publications such as newsletters, annual reports, and other similar items, including oversight of a competitive bidding process involving three local print shops. Unlike other nonprofits, you have a large and generous budget for these publications. Since all of the print shops do similar work in terms of quality and price, you attempt to spread out the jobs in order to be fair to all.

The sales manager for one of the three printing companies invites you to spend a weekend with him and other members of the sales staff (no funny business is implied here) at a golf resort in a neighboring state. Golf fees at the resort are $150 per round, and hotel rooms cost more than $200 per night. The sales manager tells you that all of the golf, accommodations, and meals will be paid for by his company as a business expense.

1. Which of the following courses of action do you take?

    a.   Accept the invitation and show your gratitude by making sure that company is the lowest bidder on all future printing contracts.

    b.   Accept the invitation but inform the sales manager that the competitive bidding process will continue and the work will continue to be spread among the four printers.

    c.   Accept the invitation without saying anything.

    d.   Decline the invitation.

2. Is there a fifth alternative?

3. Which philosophers discussed in Chapter 2 might help you make this decision?

Discussion Problem 7-D   Go Quietly or Else

You are the communications manager for a very visible and well-respected nonprofit organization in a small town, and part of your job is to serve as the primary spokesperson and contact for local media. You report to the executive director, a 75-year-old man who has been in his job for more than 20 years. He reports to a board of directors that is elected by the membership.

You are working in your office one morning when the executive director walks in, accompanied by the chairman of the board of directors. They tell you that the executive director has decided to retire the following month and they want to you draft a news release announcing the retirement and emphasizing his many years of dedicated service and how much his leadership will be missed (this is a small town in which a story such as this would make front-page news).

You begin working on the news release, but later that day you are having lunch with two co-workers who tell you the real story: The executive director has actually been fired from his job, but the board of directors is allowing him to "retire" in order to help him retain his dignity as he makes a graceful exit. As it turns out, the man is showing the first signs of senility and is in failing health. He is loved and respected by everyone in the town, but he is no longer able to do his job and the board of directors, anxious for more vibrant leadership, has told him privately to "go quietly or else." At least that is what your co-workers are telling you.

1. Codes of conduct for the public relations profession specifically prohibit you from disseminating information you know to be false. What do you do?

2. Suppose you have reason to doubt what your co-workers are saying; you believe it may be just speculation on their part. To what extent are you obligated to investigate the accuracy of the story before releasing it to the media? Before you finalize the news release, should you confront the executive director with your suspicions?

3. Which philosophers discussed in Chapter 2 might help you make this decision?

Discussion Problem 7-E   **College Degrees for Sale**

You are the public relations director at Cornerstone College, a private liberal arts college that is struggling financially. One of its most popular programs is one called Bachelor of Independent Studies (BIS), which allows non-traditional students to combine traditional college courses with those in which they get college credit for life experiences such as employment, military service, or community volunteer activities. The program requires that at least 50 percent of the credits be earned through traditional classroom courses, meaning that no more than 50 percent can come from life experience. While local companies recognize the degree for employment credentials, students have not been able to use it for entry into law school and other graduate programs, leading to the perception around the campus and in the community that it is not a "real" degree. The publicity materials you have developed, however, describe it as a legitimate college degree.

You have been called into a meeting in the college president's office. At the meeting are the president, the college's chief fund-raising officer, and several other administrators. The purpose of the meeting is to decide how to recognize a local philanthropist who is about to donate $10 million to the college. The institution is desperate for the money, and though the check has not yet been received, the money has already been earmarked for various building renovations and the expansion of existing academic programs.

The president is unsure how to recognize the donor's generosity. Then the college's fund-raising director makes a suggestion: since the donor recently mentioned in a meeting with college administrators that his life-long dream was to complete the college degree program that he began but never finished 40 years ago, the college should consider his life experience and award him the BIS degree at the commencement ceremonies to take place at the end of the spring semester (about a month away). The fund-raising director points out that this would mean more than just the traditional "honorary degrees" the college hands out to prominent citizens and that it is warranted in this case because of the size of the gift.

The president summons the director of the BIS program to join the meeting. She resists the idea because the man in question would be unable to fulfill the requirement that 50 percent of the work be in the form of traditional classes, and that it is unlikely that his life experience would be sufficient, either.

But the president and the other administrators insist that the college find a way to justify the degree, saying that because of the size of the donation and the college's need for an infusion of cash, the rules can be bent. "Make it happen," the president says. He also rules out alternatives such as an honorary degree and naming a building after the donor.

As the public relations director for the college, you face a dilemma. You have always felt confident in your working relationship with the president, and he has always trusted and followed your advice. But now you are unsure how firm the ground is underneath your feet. Like other college employees, you are aware of the institution's desperate financial circumstances. But you are also concerned about the potential damage to the college's reputation and that of the BIS program. Even though many on campus and in the community consider the BIS as not a "real" degree, you have promoted it as such in your publicity materials and are concerned that the news coverage resulting from the financial gift and awarding of the degree will damage the college's credibility and create the public perception that it is now selling college degrees in exchange for financial contributions.

1. Do you speak up at the meeting, and if so, what do you say?

2. Which philosophers discussed in Chapter 2 might help you make this decision?

Discussion Questions

701. Professional organizations such as the Public Relations Society of America (PRSA) and the International Association of Business Communicators (IABC) have rejected suggestions that they develop a formal licensing program for public relations professionals. Should they reconsider this possibility? If you were a member of one of these organizations, would you support an effort to develop such a program, even if it meant the organization would have to expand its office staff and increase annual membership fees?

702. Public relations ethicist Robert Dilenschneider says that "the public judges an organization's ethical performance by comparing what it says to what it does." Can you think of examples from current or recent news stories?

703. The PRSA and IABC Codes of Ethics (as well as other passages in this chapter) suggest that public relations professionals "sever relationships" with any client or employer if the relationship requires unethical conduct. But author Lee W. Baker, who offers his perspective on this issue on p. 195, disagrees and says that such a rule is impractical. Which side do you take on this issue, and why?

Notes

181 **"I'm not a style over substance guy":** Bill Fields, "Words From the Wise." *GolfWorld*, March 28, 2011, p. 49.

181 **"In the ideal world":** Dennis Wilcox, Philip Ault, and Warren Agee, *Public Relations: Strategies and Tactics.* Boston: Allyn & Bacon, 2002, p. 161.

185 **"There is a great deal for public relations professionals to know":** Frank Walsh, *Public Relations and the Law*. Gainesville, FL: Institute for Public Relations Research, 1991, p. 60.

186 **"not taken seriously by the majority of those who practice public relations":** Donald K. Wright, "Enforcement Dilemma: The Voluntary Nature of Public Relations Codes." *Public Relations Review*, Spring 1993, pp. 13-20.

186 **"the decision-making process in public relations":** Richard Johannessen, *Ethics in Human Communication*. Long Grove, IL: Waveland Press, 2002, p. 72.

186 **"because democracy itself lives by the road it travels":** John E. Marston, *The Nature of Public Relations*. New York: McGraw-Hill, 1963, p. 346.

187 **"It it's worth less than $20":** Dennis L. Wilcox, *Public Relations Writing and Media Techniques*. Boston: Pearson, Allyn & Bacon, 2009, p. 300.

189 **"Such customs are not necessarily bad":** Philip M. Seib and Kathy Fitzpatrick, *Public Relations Ethics*. Fort Worth, TX: Harcourt Brace, 1995, p. 22.

189 **"let alone try to change them":** James A. Jaska and Michael S. Pritchard, *Responsible Communication and Ethical Issues in Business, Industry, and the Professions*. New York: Hampton Press, 1996, p. 101.

190 **"If you see something going on that's not right" and "There will always be risk involved":** Larry Johnson and Bob Philips, *Absolute Honesty*. New York: Amacom, 2003, p. 176.

192 **"You're on opposite sides of the net":** Public Relations Society of America teleconference, "Media Relations." New York: PRSA, 1998.

192 **A recent survey conducted by a New York-based PR firm:** Dennis L. Wilcox, *Public Relations Writing and Media Techniques*. Boston: Pearson, Allyn & Bacon, 2009, p. 272.

195 **"When asked to violate ethics by a boss or client":** Lee W. Baker, *The Credibility Factor: Putting Ethics to Work in Public Relations*. Homewood, IL: Business One Irwin, 1993, pp. 182-183.

195 **"by comparing what it says to what it does" and "In our trade, we learn about the likely ethics soft spots":** Robert L. Dilenschneider, *Power and Influence: Mastering the Art of Persuasion*. New York: Prentice-Hall, 1990, p. 34.

196 **setting the example by demonstrating ethical conducts themselves:** Liese L. Hutchison, "Agency Ethics Isn't an Oxymoron." *Public Relations Tactics*, May 2000, p. 13.

199 **"to allow the merits of individual cases to be argued or promoted outside of due process":** Philip M. Seib and Kathy Fitzpatrick, *Public Relations Ethics*. Fort Worth, TX: Harcourt Brace, 1995, p. 98.

201   **"Spin is to public relations what pornography is to art":** Robert L. Dilenschneider, "Spin Doctors Practice Public Relations Quackery." *Wall Street Journal,* June 1, 1998.

202   **"easier to change the way people think":** Joel Bleifuss, "Flack Attack." *Utne Reader*, January/February 1994, pp. 72-77.

202   **"not to investigate the truth behind those claims":** Barbara Ehrenreich, *Bait and Switch: The Futile Pursuit of the American Dream.* New York: Holt Publishing, 2005, p. 2.

202   **"Show me a PR person who is accurate and truthful" and "thou shall not steal":** "Attacks by CBS Show the Public's Opinion of PR Pros." *PR Week*, June 5, 2008.

CHAPTER 8

Ethical Issues in Political Communication

Background

- The lieutenant governor of a state is running for governor, and his opponent airs television and radio advertisements that link him to the unpopular governor who resigned in disgrace. Using themes such as "more of the same," the opponent wants voters to believe the lieutenant governor is guilty of the same misconduct and unpopular policies as the previous governor, even though there is nothing in the official record to indicate any similarity.

- In a city with only a small Latino population, 62 percent of registered voters responding to an opinion poll indicate they plan to vote for the Latino candidate for mayor in the upcoming election, but on Election Day, his white opponent wins, 52 percent to 48.

- At the request of a statewide gun-rights organization, a state legislature authorizes the Department of Motor Vehicles to issue a "gun rights" specialty license plate. When a political group in favor of gun control asks to have its own "anti-gun" license plate, the legislature refuses to consider it because the plates would be "too controversial."

From a legal standpoint, political communication is regulated to some extent by the Federal Elections Commission and the election laws of individual states, but such laws are often difficult to enforce because of the value that society and the courts place on freedom of expression. Not only are existing laws difficult to enforce, but new laws dealing with political communication are difficult to create. In addition to First Amendment concerns, another reason is the reluctance of state and federal lawmakers to change the system under which they were elected to office in the first place. Most see no reason to change the laws that might make it easier for potential opponents to defeat them in a future election.

Other than the American Association of Political Consultants (AAPC) and the American Association for Public Opinion Research (AAPOR), there are few professional oganizations for individuals involved in political communication.

The AAPC Code of Ethics deals with issues such as fair treatment of clients, colleagues, and opponents; false and misleading attacks; and unfair appeals based on race, religion, and sex. In a separate statement on push polling (described later in this chapter), the AAPC condemns the practice as a "false and misleading tactic" that corrupts and degrades the political process.

The AAPOR has a code of ethics that requires members to maintain high standards for integrity; use only accepted research methodologies for collecting data; be transparent in how they collect, process, and report research results; and reject any assignment that calls for violating any principles of the code. The latter rule specifically mentions sales, fundraising, and political communication as areas in which they may be asked to manipulate their results to fit the preferences of the individuals or organizations paying for the research.

In addition to the AAPC and AAPOR codes, numerous communication textbooks dealing with political communication offer what they call "ethical guidelines." However, these guidelines are even less binding on political communicators than the voluntary ethical codes found in the advertising and public relations industries.

Charles Larson, for example, provides a list of guidelines in his 1992 book, *Persuasion: Reception and Responsibility*. Among his suggestions are that political communicators avoid (1) using false, fabricated, misrepresented, distorted, or irrelevant evidence to support claims; (2) oversimplifying complex ideas; and (3) advocating something they do not believe themselves. Larson points out that few politicians are aware of such voluntary guidelines, and even fewer adhere to them. Using examples from presidential campaigns from the 1970s through the 1990s, Larson reports that politicians of both parties frequently misquote their opponents and experts, exaggerate their own records and those of their opponents, and in many cases make up "facts" to support their claims.

Dennis Gouran, a contributor to a 1976 book edited by Daniel Dieterich, admonishes politicians and political communicators not to (1) manipulate the media into falsely casting issues in a positive light; (2) use overly complex language or euphemisms in order to obscure the truth; or (3) unnecessarily classify government documents that would otherwise be accessible to the public.

During the 1976 election season, the citizens lobbying group Common Cause proposed a set of guidelines for candidates (at the federal, state, and local levels) and their campaign staffs. Unlike the two examples above, the Common Cause guidelines were cast in positive rather than negative terms. According to the guidelines, ethical political communicators (1) provide opportunities for their candidates to engage in unrehearsed communication with voters (today, candidates do so in what they call "town hall forums"), (2) hold frequent news conferences, and (3) limit their advertising to campaign issues rather than personal attacks on the opposition.

Current Issues and Controversies

The Science of Shaping Opinions

In their 1953 book, *Communication and Persuasion,* psychologists Carl Hovland, Irving Janis, and Harold Kelley explained a number of generalizations about persuasion and opinion change that are just as valid today as they were a half century ago. Among them were:

1. Individuals' opinions are more likely to change in the desired direction if conclusions are explicitly stated than if those individuals are left to draw their own conclusions. Some communicators believe that if all of the facts are laid before audience members, they will make the right decisions. The weakness of the latter concept is that even highly intelligent audiences frequently fail to see the implications of the facts unless those implications are laid out.

2. Effects of persuasive messages tend to wear off over time. Even when persuasion is effective, the results are seldom permanent. Repetition is often necessary to drive home certain points.

3. Audience members most in need of hearing a message are least likely to hear it. Parents who attend PTA meetings are mostly those whose children are having the least difficulty in school. Persons who could benefit from social services are the least likely ones to attend public meetings at which those services are discussed. Promoters must therefore use a variety of communication tactics rather than just a limited number.

4. Audience members are more likely to make the desired choice if both sides of an argument are presented instead of only one side. Audiences tend to be skeptical of an individual or organization that tells them only one side of the story and expects them to accept it without questions. A more effective strategy is to explain both sides of an issue, but then explain why one side should be preferred over the other.

Communication ethicist Richard Johannesen offers his own set of guidelines:

1. No public official is immune from criticism for his or her performance.

2. Anyone participating in a political debate has an intellectual responsibility to prepare himself or herself by learning all of the available facts.

3. It is more appropriate to criticize a person's ideas than to criticize the person.

4. It is acceptable to question or criticize a person's motives only after you have completely examined the merits of their arguments.

5. Once you have publicly criticized another person's proposal, you must follow it up by introducing your own alternatives.

The Difference Between Persuasion and Propaganda

The term "persuasive campaign" should not be confused with its less admirable cousin, the "propaganda campaign." By definition, legitimate attempts at persuasion differ from propaganda in several important ways. **Persuasion**, practiced by public relations professionals and more reputable political communicators, is defined as "an effort to gain public support for an opinion or course of action." What is implied in the definition is that the effort is based on truthful and ethical methods. Conversely, **propaganda,** as practiced by unscrupulous political communicators, is "the attempt to have a viewpoint accepted on the basis of appeals other than the merits of the case." Propaganda often uses methods that could be labeled as unethical or manipulative.

Another way of drawing a distinction between the terms is to say that persuasion is based on truth, while propaganda is based on fiction or exaggeration; persuasion is based on consensus, while propaganda tries to set up adversarial relationships or "us versus them" scenarios.

In their 1992 book, *Propaganda and Persuasion,* theorists Garth S. Jowett and Victoria O'Donnell based their definitions of the two terms on the intent of the communicator. Persuasion, according to the authors, is intended to serve the interests of both the persuader and the audience, while propaganda generally serves only the interests of the person acting as its source. Jowett and O'Donnell's view is consistent with the long-standing philosophy of public relations and public information programs producing results that are mutually beneficial or "win-win."

Jowett and O'Donnell's work was an expansion of that done by Columbia University Professor Clyde R. Miller, who founded the Institute for Propaganda Analysis during World War II. At first, the emphasis was to study the use of propaganda in the war in Europe, but he quickly expanded its scope to include the study of propaganda from all sources, including the Ku Klux Klan, other extremist groups, and the American advertising industry.

The institute is still in operation today and identifies — in its publications and on its website — nine common propaganda devices:

Name-calling. The use of emotional labels that are offered in the place of logic or evidence. Examples of labels applied to individuals include "extremist," "radical," "liberal," "fundamentalist," and "racist." Examples of labels applied to ideas include "social engineering," "legislating morality," and "counter-culture." For example, when critics wanted to generate opposition to President Clinton's proposed health care plan in the early 1990s, they did so in part by referring to Clinton and his wife, Hillary, as representing the "counter-culture." Throughout Barack Obama's presidency, critics referred to him and his legislative proposals as "socialist."

In the 1950 Democratic primary for the U.S. Senate seat in Florida, challenger George Smathers resorted to name-calling in his attempt to defeat popular incumbent Claude Pepper. What was unusual about his choice of words was how easily they were misconstrued — which was exactly the effect he was hoping for. In numerous public speeches across the state, Smathers labeled Pepper as a "shameless extrovert" who "practiced nepotism" with his sister-in-law. Even worse than that, Smathers claimed, Pepper and his wife-to-be practiced "celibacy" before they were married, and Pepper's sister was a "known thespian."

In another example of questionable name-calling, republican Richard Zimmer used a fake website to label democratic Robert Torricelli as a "liberal" as the two New Jersey representatives ran for a U.S. Senate seat in 1996. One of Zimmer's television ads showed a man conducting a keyword search on a personal computer and typing in "liberal." That search led to a website labeled "www.lib.toricelli.com," which included a photograph of Torricelli and a summary of his voting record. What was unknown to many viewers was that no such website existed; it was a fictional yet real-looking creation of an advertising agency, as no such site existed anywhere on the "real" Internet.

While the Federal Trade Commission would require a commercial spot attempting the same tactic to include a disclaimer indicating that the website was an artificial representation, the limited degree to which the Federal Elections Commission regulates political advertising meant a similar disclaimer in the Zimmer case was unnecessary.

Glittering generalities. Similar to name-calling. Instead of asking the audience to reject an idea without examining the evidence, a communicator resorting to glittering generalities wants the audience to accept an idea without requiring evidence. What results are generalizations so extreme that receivers disregard the lack of substance behind those appeals. Examples of glittering generalities include "family values," "wasteful spending," and "liberal bias of the press." Other examples are claims that begin with phrases such as "everyone knows that . . . " and "it goes without saying that . . . "

Transfer. The communicator wants the audience to take the authority, sanction, or prestige of a respected idea and apply it to a new idea that the communicator wants the audience to accept. Examples include the use of symbols such as the cross, representing the Christian church; or Uncle Sam, representing patriotism and love of country. If a church publication shows the cross being used to promote helping the poor, it implies that helping the poor is something that Christians should do. If a cartoonist draws Uncle Sam in a manner in which he approves of a proposed new law, it implies that all patriotic Americans should be in favor of it. When car dealers fly enormous American flags over their lots, they are sending subtle messages to potential customers that purchasing a car is "an American" thing to do.

Transfer is often used as a tactic in political races. In the 2008 presidential primary campaign, for example, opponents of Senator Hillary Clinton reminded voters of the policy decisions and scandals associated with her husband, former President Bill Clinton, hoping voters would transfer their distrust of Bill to Hillary. Later, during the general election campaign, opponents of Senator John McCain attempted to link him with the policies of President George W. Bush, hoping voters would transfer their dislike of Bush to McCain.

Bandwagon. In this approach, audiences are encouraged to adopt a certain idea or behavior because "everyone else is doing it" and they "do not want to be left behind."

The marketing profession uses a variation of the bandwagon approach called the "entitlement appeal." That appeal uses marketing messages such as "you want this," "you need this," "you have to have this," and "you deserve this."

Plain folks. This approach suggests that audiences should adopt an idea because it comes from people similar to them or reject an idea because it comes from someone unlike them.

Testimonials. Appeals from influential celebrities or other authority figures whose expertise may be irrelevant to the product being sold or idea being promoted. A common example is the use of professional athletes to endorse companies or products, including those that are unrelated to the sport for which they are known.

Card-stacking. A method in which the communicator stacks the cards in favor of the desired result, often by presenting one-sided evidence or half-truths. For example, critics of a university's athletic program may point out the graduation rate for the school's athletes is only 45 percent (and therefore the athletic program should be eliminated), but not mentioning (or perhaps not knowing) that the graduate rate for non-athletes is only 42 percent.

A more modern term for card-stacking is *spin,* which is often used in a derogatory manner to refer to communication disseminated by public relations professionals.

During the presidency of Ronald Reagan, for example, political advisors frequently arranged for the president to speak to groups of seniors in venues such as senior centers and other gathering places for older Americans. The theme of those speeches was always about Reagan's support for such programs, and that is what was reported in news coverage of the events. But what the reporters seldom mentioned in their stories was that the Reagan administration often advocated reducing or eliminating funding for those programs.

In the mid-1990s, crime statistics released by the U.S. Justice Department indicated that crime rates had dropped in most major categories in the previous decade. Democrats claimed that it was because of the newly introduced crime-fighting initiatives of President Bill Clinton, even though those initiatives had not yet had time to have any effect. Republicans, on the other hand, claimed the decrease in crime rates was due to the "get tough" policies of President Reagan (out of office for more than five years) that were now beginning to take hold. Which side was correct? Neither one. Criminologists attributed the decline in crime rates to changes in demographics. Young men between the ages of 18 and 29 had become smaller in proportion to the population as a whole, and since that demographic category is typically responsible for the majority of criminal activity, the crime rate dropped accordingly.

Scare tactics. Devices intended to influence behavior are common in advertising and political campaigns. A communicator using this tactic typically pairs a negative result with the desired behavior required to avoid it. Examples include television commercials showing an accident scene followed by the suggestion of wearing seat belts, or the scene of a house fire followed by a pitch for smoke detectors.

Perhaps the most outrageous example of scare tactics in a political campaign was found in the 1970 race for governor of Alabama between challenger George C. Wallace and incumbent Albert Brewer. Wallace had already served as governor from 1962 to 1966, but could not run again because of an Alabama law prohibiting a governor from serving consecutive terms. His wife, Lurleen, was elected governor in 1966, but it was widely known during her term that Wallace himself was still running state government. When Lurleen Wallace died mid-way through her term, Brewer, then lieutenant governor, became the state's new chief executive.

Wallace publicly opposed the integration of Alabama's public schools and declared that the state policy was "segregation today, segregation tomorrow, and segregation forever." Political historians claim that the 1970 election season was the last in which candidates could openly appeal to voters' racist attitudes; after that they would have to resort to "code words" such as "militant groups" to refer to African Americans and other minorities.

But in 1970, Wallace believed that such euphemisms were unnecessary. His newspaper, television, and radio ads used themes such as "Don't allow blacks to take over Alabama" and similar warnings designed to appeal to other segregationists. At a time when civil rights groups were advocating the integration of the Alabama Highway Patrol, the Wallace campaign aired a radio spot that opened with ominous background music and police sirens. The announcer then warns, "Suppose your wife is driving home late at night. She is stopped by a highway patrolman. He turns out to be black. Think about it. Elect George C. Wallace."

Euphemisms. Terms intended to obscure or soften the true meaning of behaviors or concepts. Examples include a company referring to employee layoffs as "early retirement opportunities" or the government referring to a tax increase as a "revenue adjustment."

Other Propaganda Techniques

Although not officially part of the IPA list, there are five other argumentative techniques used in political communication: the slippery slope, the false dichotomy, the ad hominem argument, the straw man argument, and stereotyping. All are basically extensions of the "scare tactics" method previously described in that they are based on warning decision-makers (usually voters) of the perceived negative consequences associated with choices to which the persuader is opposed. They are often used in desperation because the persuader has already found more legitimate persuasive techniques ineffective.

The slippery slope. Sometimes called the "thin entering wedge" or "getting the camel's nose inside the tent." This is a technique in which the party who opposes a policy change warns that even the slightest change will open the door to more drastic (and harmful) changes in the future. One example is found in the debate over banning controversial books from school libraries. School officials sometimes decide that it is permissible to remove a controversial book because it is "just one book" and ask "what's the harm?" Civil liberties groups and other opponents of such action claim that once a precedent is established, other less controversial books might be at risk in the future. Another example is found in the debate over state lotteries. In order to counter the position of lottery advocates that such lotteries represent "benign gambling" or "gambling lite," opponents warn that the adoption of state lotteries will open the door to more serious forms of gambling such as casinos, even though there are no cases of state lotteries leading to the adoption of casino gambling.

False dichotomy. An oversimplified or artificial division of a political issue in a way that tells voters or other decision makers that they must choose between the two opposing ideas, with no alternatives possible. Political clichés that represent this idea include "us against them" and "you're either for us or against us." In each presidential election, the false dichotomy is reflected in constant references to "red states" and "blue states."

In many state lottery debates, for example, advocates warned voters that if they did not approve a lottery, the state would be forced to raise taxes on retail sales, property, and income (the pro-lottery campaign in one state used the slogan, "A lottery sure beats a tax increase"). Opinion polls indicate that many voters are influenced by the false dichotomy, even though many lottery opponents and individuals knowledgeable about the budgeting process know that there is little connection between lottery income and revenue generated by taxes.

Many politicians use false dichotomies because they believe voters or other decision-makers can more easily understand issues that involve only two choices, but when they do so they often underestimate the audiences' ability to understand and process complex ideas.

Ad hominem. From the Latin for "argument against the person." This is an extension of both "fear" and "name-calling" and is a method of arguing against an idea by attacking the person who proposes it. Many opponents of proposed spending programs, for example, base much of their persuasive efforts on challenging the motives of the advocates of the plan and referring to them as "reckless liberals" or "tax-and-spend politicians."

Straw man argument. Sometimes called the "straw man fallacy." This is a technique used to persuade the audience to oppose a candidate or an idea based on a premise that is likely false or exaggerated, but also easier to understand. The metaphor is based on the fact that a straw man (a falsehood) is easier to attack and defeat than a real man (a truth). The straw man argument is also known as "reaching for the long-hanging fruit."

Here's a common example: Suppose Candidate A and Candidate B are in a close race, and the biggest difference between their two campaign platforms involves tax reform. Candidate A believes that Candidate B's tax proposals are dangerous and would likely lead to economic chaos if adopted. But he also knows that the issue is so complex that few voters would understand it. Instead of criticizing his opponent's tax plan, he finds another issue on which he and Candidate B disagree and exaggerates or misstates B's position on that issue because he believes voters will be more likely to understand it.

Here's another example: Suppose the city council is considering granting a permit for a national hotel chain to build a new hotel in a rapidly growing commercial district. Owners of existing hotels in the area fear the loss of business, but they know that members of the city council are unlikely to be sympathetic to their financial concerns. Instead of opposing the convention center on those grounds, they argue that the new hotel will generate more traffic and lead to more gridlock.

A real-world example of the straw man argument was seen in the early stages of the 2008 presidential campaign. Opponents of democratic candidate Barack Obama focused public attention on his former pastor, Reverend Jeremiah Wright, who was known for inflammatory comments he made about race relations and other controversial issues. Even after Obama denounced Wright's comments and resigned from his church, opponents continued to publicize those comments and make them a campaign issue because the relationship between Obama and Wright was easier to criticize than other aspects of Obama's campaign.

Stereotyping. A tactic in which a communicator expects members of the audience to make decisions based on overgeneralizations or outdated perceptions. Examples of stereotypes in political communication include republican and conservative politicians being "tough on crime" and always seeking to cut taxes while spending more money on military projects and less on social programs. Democrats and liberals are typically stereotyped as being "soft on crime" and wanting to raise taxes while spending less money on military projects and more on social programs.

Disinformation

As discussed in Chapter 7 (page 189), the U.S. military often engages in "disinformation" in times of war. Both republican and democratic presidential administrations authorize the Pentagon to release false information in order to deceive or mislead an enemy. While few media outlets would knowingly go along with such a strategy, they occasionally are fooled themselves and find themselves as accomplices.

Some governmental spokespersons — including those representing the White House, the Pentagon, and other cabinet departments — object to such tactics. Some go along in order to keep their jobs, but occasionally they feel strongly enough to quit their posts. In 1986, for example, State Department spokesperson Bernard Kalb resigned to protest the disinformation program regarding American military operations in Libya. In his resignation letter, Kalb said that his concern was not just for his own reputation and credibility, but for the "credibility of the United States, the word of America, and what the word of America means."

Problems with Polls

Most political or public opinion polls conducted by major survey research organizations are done using strict protocols, and advances in sampling and polling methodologies allow those organizations to predict the outcome of elections with a high degree of accuracy. There are problems, however.

Weighted samples. In some cases, researchers concerned that some demographic or psychographic groups may have been under-represented in the survey samples chosen may adjust the numbers to provide what they believe will be more accurate results. Although results should never been deliberately "slanted" to show results favorable to a cause, in some cases it is appropriate to "weight" results to provide a more realistic picture. As an example, a company with 500 male employees and 500 female employees might expect that of the 200 employees responding to a morale survey, 100 would be male and 100 female. But what should the researcher do if 150 are male and only 50 are female? For questions in which the gender of respondents is unlikely to affect their answers (such as issues of parking or building cleanliness), the results can be reported as is. But for questions in which the gender of the respondent is likely to affect answers (such as those dealing with sexual harassment, promotion opportunities, building security, or maternity leave policies), the results might be weighted to reflect the gender breakdown of the employees. In the scenario above, women's answers would be multiplied by three, then matched against the responses from male employees and then computed as a percentage. When explaining the results, however, the researcher should provide the results both ways — raw data and based on weighted results — and allow the individual or company requesting the research to decide which data to use. The researcher should then also consider why one group or the other is over-represented or under-represented in the sample and consider it as a possible "red flag" that there may be a larger problem.

Courtesy bias and the "Bradley Effect." One of the factors that may skew the results of any form of opinion research is the tendency of survey respondents or focus group members to offer answers they believe are the "right" answers or those that will not offend the interviewer or other participants. In public relations and marketing research, the phenomenon is known as "courtesy bias." Respondents to non-anonymous surveys and participants in focus groups who know which company is sponsoring the survey or focus group will tend to indicate a preference for that company's products or services, whether that is their true opinion or not. In surveys or focus groups dealing with environmental issues, respondents tend to overstate their participation in recycling programs and their purchase of "green" products because they assume those are the "right" things to say. In media research, respondents often indicate they get their news from the *Wall Street Journal* or National Public Radio in order to appear more sophisticated, even though in truth they may read only tabloid newspapers (or consume no news media at all).

In political polling, the phenomenon of stating a preference for the more popular or progressive candidate, yet voting for someone else, is known as the **Bradley Effect**. It is named for Tom Bradley, the black democratic mayor of Los Angeles who ran for governor of California in 1982. In nearly every poll taken prior to Election Day, Bradley was well ahead of his white republican opponent, and most pundits predicted he would win easily. He lost by less than 1 percent of the vote. The discrepancy between the polling data and Election Day results was attributed to the pollsters' belief that respondents wanted to appear to be progressive and open-minded by indicating they favored the black candidate, when in actuality they had already decided to vote for the white candidate.

In the 2008 democratic presidential primary in New Hampshire, pollsters predicted Illinois Senator Barack Obama would win easily over the only other major candidate in the race, New York Senator Hillary Clinton. They based that prediction on Obama's substantial lead in their polls. But on primary day, Clinton scored a surprising win, and pollsters theorized that the inaccuracy of their polling data may have resulted from New Hampshire voters wanting to look "trendy" by indicating support for the black candidate, even though they had already decided to vote for Clinton. Based on that theory, Obama supporters worried (unnecessarily) that polling data indicating their candidate would win in the general election might be vulnerable to a similar error.

The Bradley Effect is not limited to just candidates; it also surfaces in campaigns based on issues. In a number of elections in southern states in the late 1990s and early 2000s, for example, polling data indicating voter support or opposition to proposed state lotteries were found to be highly unreliable. Pollsters found that respondents indicated support or opposition to the issue in polls and focus groups because of peer pressure or other factors, then voted the opposite way on Election Day.

Push polls. These represent a somewhat recent strategy in political persuasion. Often conducted by telephone, the push poll is designed to appear as a legitimate public opinion poll administered by a neutral source, but is actually a subliminal attempt to influence public opinion by one side or the other in a political debate. A typical push poll question is "Would you be *more likely* or *less likely* to vote for Candidate X if you knew he was accepting illegal campaign contributions from special-interest groups?

Of course, most respondents would say "less likely," but soliciting that answer was not the point of asking the question. If you read the question again, you notice that it never accused Candidate X of doing anything wrong. It merely planted the idea in the mind of the person responding to the question. On Election Day, the respondent may not remember where or how he or she heard about it, but will remember hearing the name of Candidate X and "illegal campaign contributions" in the same sentence.

In a formal statement separate from its Code of Ethics, the American Association of Political Consultants condemns the practice and says that "push polls are not polls at all" and urges the news media and the public to draw distinctions between push polls and legitimate opinion research.

Legitimate polling organizations such as Roper and Gallup are also critical of the method and would never allow their employees to use such a tactic. It persists, however, in every election cycle, even though no candidate will acknowledge authorizing such a tactic as part of his or her campaign.

Associated Press Guidelines for Reporting Research Results

Because of the proliferation of surveys conducted or sponsored by political organizations, special-interest groups, and other parties with an interest in the outcome (and journalists' interest in survey results), the Associated Press provides the following guidelines for journalists who include such results in their print and broadcast stories. The intent of the guidelines is to provide readers and viewers the information necessary to place survey results in their proper context.

Who conducted the poll? Was it done by a professional public opinion research firm, a political candidate's staff, or another organization with an interest in the outcome? Journalists recognize the significance of research conducted by firms such as the Gallup Corporation, the Harris Poll, or Pew Research. The most credible university-based polling organizations include those at Quinnipiac University (Connecticut), Elon University (North Carolina), and Middle Tennessee State University.

Many media outlets are conducting their own opinion research and forming partnerships to share both the costs and the results. Examples include the USA Today/CNN Poll, the NBC News/Associated Press Poll, and the CBS News/Wall Street Journal Poll.

Sample size and how the sample was chosen. A survey with a small sample size is not as reliable as one with a larger sample. The time and place selected to sample is also important. For example, if one were to conduct a survey to determine which sport is more popular — football or baseball — using a sample chosen from a crowd of people leaving a stadium after a football game, that would obviously not be an appropriate sample. That is obviously an exaggerated example, but some researchers draw their samples using methods and locations that are almost as questionable.

Who was in the sample? At the level of absolute certainty, survey research reflects only the opinions of those in the sample; but at the level of probability, the results can be projected onto the larger audience from which the sample was drawn. Many media consumers do not understand the complexity of survey research, so care must be taken when the results are announced.

Methodology. Was the survey conducted by telephone, mail, electronic mail, social media, in-person, or some other method?

Sponsorship, if any. Reporters are skeptical of any poll that is privately sponsored, and for good reason. Reporters may mention those results of privately sponsored research in their stories, but will identify the sponsor so that readers can put the results in context.

Margin for error. A poll's margin for error is determined by a mathematical formula and expressed in a percentage related to the sample size. The larger the sample size, the smaller the margin of error; the smaller the sample size, the larger the margin for error.

Timing. When was the research conducted? Opinions can change overnight. A poll taken the day after a presidential speech is going to give to a different result than one taken a week later. The results of a poll taken the day before a televised debate, party convention, or other political event will likely be quite different from one taken the day after. The results of a survey conducted several days or weeks before a major news event might be quite different from those of a similar survey conducted days or weeks after, even if the connection between the topic of the poll and the nature of the news event was remote. Reporters often combine this detail with margin for error, writing in a story: The poll was taken the week of March 3 and had a margin for error of . . .

How were the questions worded, and in what order were they asked? It is unlikely the exact wording of the questions will appear in the newspaper story, but most polling companies provide reporters with a copy of the questions.

Federal Laws and Supreme Court Cases on Political Advertising

Nonprofit organizations are limited by law in how they support or oppose political candidates and issues. Among the IRS categories are:

501 (c) (3) — Also known as "charities," these organizations may not support or oppose political candidates but may support or oppose political issues as long as that is not their primary purpose.

501 (c) (4) — Also known as "social welfare agencies," these groups may legally support or oppose candidates or issues as long as that is not their primary purpose.

501 (c) (6) — Also known as "business organizations," these groups include chambers of commerce and similar associations. They may legally support or oppose candidates or issues as long as it is done through political action committees for which contributions are voluntary.

527 — These are purely political organizations that are given more leeway in how they spend money and support or oppose political candidates or issues. Although the designation has existed for years, 527 organizations did not become well-known until the 2004 presidential election campaign.

Legal and ethical restrictions on political campaigns have resulted from a plethora of federal laws and court cases. The most important of these laws and cases are:

The Federal Election Campaign Act of 1974. The first attempt to legislate political communication, the FECA resulted from the Watergate scandal of the early 1970s.

One of the significant components of the FECA was the division of political advertisements into two categories: candidate ads and issue ads. Candidate ads were the easiest to define; those were the ads that directly supported or opposed specific candidates for public office. Issue ads were those that appeared to support, oppose, or sometimes merely discuss a controversial public issue, but in some cases they were thinly disguised attempts to promote or oppose candidates by linking them to controversial issues.

A typical issue ad might call attention to Congressman X's record of voting in favor of tax breaks for certain types of companies. The spot might emphasize that the companies that received the tax breaks also violated environmental laws, thus implying that Congressman X favors tax breaks for environmental lawbreakers. Even though the ad may not mention that Congressman X is running for re-election, its intent is obvious.

The primary limitation of issue ads is that they cannot use words or phrases such as *vote for, vote against, elect, support, defeat, reject,* or *Smith for Congress.* This list is sometimes referred to as the "magic words test."

***Buckley v. Valeo* (1976).** This Supreme Court case, which drew a distinction between **contributions** and **expenditures**, is discussed in more detail in Chapter 10. In short, it established the principle that *contributions to candidates* could be limited by law, while *expenditures by candidates* (or anyone else) could not be.

The latter philosophy is based on the presumption that contributions have more potential than expenditures to corrupt the political system.

***Bank of Boston v. Bellotti* (1978).** This Supreme Court case established the general principle that corporations have the same First Amendment rights as individuals to comment on legal, social, and political issues (discussed in more detail in Chapter 10).

Bipartisan Campaign Reform Act of 2002. The BCRA is also known as the McCain-Feingold bill in recognition of the two senators who introduced it: John McCain, a republican from Arizona, and Russ Feingold, a democrat from Wisconsin. The BCRA was aimed at reducing the influence of issue advertising and closing other loopholes. Proponents of the bill hoped it would address the problem of money influencing politics, but instead it only forced politicians and their financial supporters to find ways to circumvent the law.

One such method of circumvention is through the so-called "527 ads." Under the BCRA, such organizations could not sponsor political ads that mention a "clearly identifiable candidate" within 30 days of a primary election or within 60 days of a general election. Within those windows, the organizations' political advertising could refer only to issues and not to candidates.

Another provision of the BCRA was a requirement that political ads on television and radio include an announcement by the candidate such as "I am (name), a candidate for (office), and I approved this message." The rationale was to prevent candidates and parties from broadcasting ads attacking opponents and then denying responsibility. While the law applies only to candidates for national office, many states have passed similar laws for state and local elections.

A conflict tangentially related to the BCRA took place during the 2004 presidential election campaign. A political group supporting the re-election campaign of President George W. Bush sought to restrict the advertising of Michael Moore's documentary film *Fahrenheit 9/11* on the grounds that because the film itself was critical of the Bush Administration, television advertisements promoting the film were themselves politically motivated.

Citizens United filed a complaint with the Federal Elections Commission, stating that to advertise the film within 60 days of the November 3 election would violate the BCRA. The FEC, however, sided with Moore after the filmmaker responded that to limit such advertising would violate his First Amendment rights, as well as the rights of theaters wishing to advertise and show the film and individuals who wanted to watch it.

***Wisconsin Right to Life v. Federal Elections Commission* (2007).** This Supreme Court case nullified several provisions of the BCRA, the most significant being the rules concerning the 30-day and 60-day windows during which corporations and nonprofit groups could not sponsor candidate ads. Corporations and nonprofit organizations may now sponsor such ads at any time, but they are still prohibited from making direct financial contributions to candidate campaigns.

***Citizens United v. Federal Elections Commission* (2010).** In this ruling, the Court reiterated the 2007 ruling that corporations and nonprofit organizations were no longer bound by the 30-day and 60-day windows established by the BCRA. The Court also recommended that the Federal Elections Commission put more emphasis on enforcing disclosure rules that require individuals and groups to disclose the amount of money donated and to which candidate that money was donated (exceptions to disclosure rules are discussed in Chapter 10).

One conservative political group, in arguing for the loosening of regulations regarding advocating or opposing political candidate, pointed out the inconsistency of court rulings that "allow for burning the American flag and wearing profane T-shirts in public, yet don't allow citizens to advocate the election or defeat of a presidential candidate."

Funding of Government Communication Activities

Because of a 1913 law known as the **Gillett Amendment**, government agencies and units cannot spend taxpayer money on promotional activities or legislative advocacy unless they are authorized to do so by law or congressional mandate. The rationale behind the law is to prevent government agencies from spending taxpayer money to implement advertising and public relations campaigns related to political issues in which they have a vested interest. The law does not apply to government agencies and branches of the military and their employment of public information officers, as those functions are authorized by law and there are no conflicts of interest.

Although the Gillett Amendment is a federal law and does not apply to states, many state legislatures have created similar laws restricting the expenditure of state funds. One example is found in the case of state universities that use public money to campaign for increases in financial support from their state legislatures. In essence, a university involveed in such an activity is using taxpayer money to generate more taxpayer money, creating an inherent conflict of interest. Universities wanting to conduct such persuasive activities must therefore do so using privately raised funds.

Recent examples of federal government agencies violating the law include the Department of Education's payment of $240,000 to broadcast commentator Armstrong Williams for promoting the No Child Left Behind Act on his syndicated television and radio programs. During the Bush Administration, the Government Accounting Office (GAO) — an independent agency that reports directly to Congress —determined that other federal government agencies engaged in numerous other promotional activities that violated the law, including payments to newspaper columnist Maggie Gallagher and magazine columnist Michael McManus for their support of a federal program that promoted traditional marriage over cohabitation.

The Bush Administration is not the first presidential administration to violate the Gillett Amendment. In the 1990s, for example, the administration of President Bill Clinton spent more than $128 million on a variety of promotional activities.

Even after the GAO determined that many of the expenditures of both the Bush and Clinton administrations violated the law, prosecutors declined to press charges, despite the complaints of numerous government watchdog groups and members of Congress.

The Influence of Talk Radio

Like many aspects of American political culture, the value and impact of talk radio depends largely on who is making the assessment. Political conservatives, who make up a large percentage of the talk radio audience, view it as a sacred island in what they perceive to be a vast sea of liberally biased media. For them, talk radio is their primary free-speech outlet and their only viable alternative to network and cable television news, National Public Radio, and their favorite liberal-media villain — the *New York Times*. In contrast, many liberals view talk radio as a billion-dollar industry fueled by anger, intolerance, paranoia, and distrust of government.

Beginning in late 1989 and throughout much of the 1990s, talk was the fastest-growing format on the AM radio dial. Today, about 520 AM and FM radio stations across the country have adopted an all-talk format, with nearly all offering a combination of local and nationally syndicated programming. In addition, hundreds of local stations offer talk programming for at least part of their broadcast day, bringing the total number of talk outlets to more than 1,400 and the total audience to more than 100 million. According to Pew Research, approximately 17 percent of Americans listen to talk radio on a regular basis, giving it greater reach than any format other than country music. While trends in politics and popular culture have increased the number of listeners, the growth in the popularity of car telephones (and later hand-held cellular telephones), has increased the number of callers.

A recent study by the Center for American Progress found that more than 90 percent of political talk radio programming is based on conservative viewpoints. The study compiled samples from 257 news and talk stations owned by America's five largest media conglomerates and found that combined, they offered 2,570 hours per week of conservative programming and only 254 hours of programming considered "liberal" or "progressive." Recent polls taken immediately following recent presidential and midterm elections indicate that voters who regularly listen to talk radio voted for republican candidates by a 3-to-1 margin.

In his 2004 book, *The Politics of Misinformation*, political scientist Murray Edelman wrote that most political debate, including that which takes place on talk radio, is based on falsehoods and exaggerations. "All but a small minority of such discussion and claims are based on false beliefs, false information, false premises, and false logic," he wrote. "And whenever one party to a political dispute begins to indulge in misrepresentation, the incentive is strong for all others to do the same." Edelman's assertions raise questions about the role of talk radio hosts — do they allow falsehoods to continue, point out the weaknesses and fallacies of their arguments, or add to them?

"Facts are not terribly key to talk radio," wrote Chris Mondiacs, a political reporter in New Jersey, in a 1992 column. "There are many instances in which talk show hosts seize on an issue without fully understanding it. They come from the perspective of accusing anyone who holds a government office of being corrupt." Media critic Peter Laufer comments that "aspiring talk show hosts find it easier to get on the air if they are willing to adjust reality."

In 2005, the Annenberg Public Policy Center at the University of Pennsylvania conducted an in-depth study of American media and their influence on the political process. One of the startling findings of the study was that almost as many Americans (27 percent) labeled popular host Rush Limbaugh as a "journalist" as they did *Washington Post* Associate Editor Bob Woodward (30 percent).

For much of the last 20 years, conservatives have complained about an alleged "liberal bias of the media." Although academic studies typically find that no such bias exists — claiming that the liberal orientation of working journalists is counterbalanced by the conservative ownership of newspaper chains and television networks — the charge continues to be made by talk radio hosts, conservative watchdog groups, and individual authors who use dubious sampling techniques and anecdotal evidence to support their point.

Many talk radio hosts believe their programs can help remedy that (perceived) liberal bias by offering conservative or libertarian perspectives on politics and current events. Many media critics and watchdog groups, however, say that talk radio has overcompensated for a problem that doesn't exist.

Former Vice President Al Gore called talk radio the "Limbaugh-Hannity-Drudge Axis" (referring to conservative hosts Rush Limbaugh and Sean Hannity and blogger Matt Drudge) and wrote that the "fifth column of the fourth estate is made up of propagandists pretending to be journalists . . . through multiple overlapping outlets covering radio, television, and the Internet, they relentlessly force-feed the American people right-wing talking points and ultra-conservative dogma disguised as news and infotainment."

For Discussion

Case Study 8-A   Cindy Watson vs. the Hog Farmers

Prior to 1995, Cindy Watson was a little-known businesswoman in Rose Hill, North Carolina who never expressed any interest in politics, other than to vote in local, state, and national elections. But when an official of the Duplin County Republican Party asked her to run in a special election to fill a vacant seat in the state legislature, she reluctantly agreed.

When elected, she became the first Republican to represent the heavily democratic Duplin County since the Civil War. Ironically, she had no idea that her work in the legislature would spark another civil war and focus national attention on her small district in southeastern North Carolina.

Shortly after taking office, Watson heard from dozens of her constituents, who complained that waste and stench from area hog farms were causing asthma in children and seniors and that waste was contaminating water wells with bacteria. Large-scale hog farming was the county's biggest business and a major part of the local economy.

By 1997, Watson had joined forces with environmental groups and other legislators to confront the corporate polluters. Watson co-sponsored legislation that would place a temporary moratorium on new pork production operations and require existing companies to phase out the lagoons that collected the waste of 9.3 million hogs. The state had previously tried to pass environmental regulations aimed at curtailing hog industry polluters, but heavy lobbying by the hog industry had always quashed those efforts.

But in 1998, after an accident resulted in the spill of 25 million gallons of hog waste into North Carolina's New River, the people of the state rallied around Watson's proposal, and the legislature passed the law. That's when the hog industry decided that Watson, as well as two other legislators who helped her pass the moratorium, had to be defeated.

Spending more than $2.9 million in the year leading up to the 1998 election, the corporate hog farms — operating under the name Farmers for Fairness (FFF) — saturated the districts of Watson and two other republican legislators with negative ads and push polls. The ads painted the three legislators as being anti-business and exaggerated their positions on a variety of issues unrelated to the hog industry. All three lost their seats to primary challengers, and that November all three seats fell into democratic hands.

The North Carolina Board of Elections began an investigation into the tactics of Farmers for Fairness, during which it called several of the group's political consultants to testify. Several admitted that Watson and the two other legislators had been specifically targeted for defeat, but they also claimed that their tactics were both legal and ethical.

One consultant testified in BOE hearings that FFF was so determined to see the three legislators defeated in the primary that it was willing to risk losing those seats to democrats in the general election. Another consultant said in media interviews that the group was merely exercising its right of free speech — and that the only way it could do so was "to buy it."

In the years following the conflict, Watson became nationally known as a martyr for the problems in the American political system, earning her respect and sympathy from republicans and democrats alike. In 2004, she was presented with the John F. Kennedy Profile in Courage Award for her tenacity in representing the interests of her constituents and standing up to the corporate interests.

- Does reading this story make you more cynical about politics than you already were?

- Are such cases simply a byproduct of free speech that we must tolerate in order to maintain our First Amendment freedoms?

Case Study 8-B   **Taking License with Free Speech**

In the late 1900s and early 2000s, legislatures in several southern states dealt with proposals to offer license plates bearing the slogan "Choose Life" and graphics supporting adoption as an alternative to abortion. In many of the states, abortion-rights groups such as Planned Parenthood and the National Organization for Women (NOW) challenged the plates under the principle of "equal protection," claiming that "when the state creates a forum for the expression of political views, it cannot promote one opinion and deny the forum to opposing opinions."

In 2001, a court in Florida dismissed the first of those suits, claiming that NOW failed to prove the program was unconstitutional.

In October 2004, however, a court in Tennessee ruled that state's "Choose Life" plate violated the constitution because it promoted only one side in the abortion debate and did not allow groups with opposing viewpoints to sponsor their own plates. Lawmakers in Tennessee worried that a strict interpretation of the court ruling might prompt individuals to challenge the appropriateness of the state's other specialty license plates, such as those supporting endangered species and encouraging citizens to protect environmentally sensitive lands, such as the Great Smoky Mountains National Park. In November 2004, a higher court ruled that the state of Tennessee had engaged in "viewpoint discrimination" and declared the license plates unconstitutional. Early in 2005, the U.S. Supreme Court declined to hear the appeal, leaving in place the ruling of the circuit court. While Florida maintains its program of "Choose Life" plates, other southern states have avoided potential litigation by eliminating all potentially controversial license plates.

For the last decade, the Sons of Confederate Veterans (as the name indicates, it consists of descendents of Civil War veterans from southern states), has established "Confederate Heritage" license plates in nine southern states. The license plate programs are part of the group's planned celebration for the 150th anniversary of the beginning of the Civil War. Proceeds will go to restore battlegrounds and other historic sites related to the war.

From 2011 through 2015, challenges to Confederate license plate programs in Mississippi and Texas worked their way through the court system. Mississippi's five-year program calls for honoring a different Confederate leader each year, and the choice of General Nathan Bedford Forrest for the 2014 plate drew the ire of civil rights groups, who pointed out Forrest was also an early founder of the Ku Klux Klan. That case has not yet been decided. In 2015, however, the U.S. Supreme Court ruled that the state government of Texas was not required to establish a Confederate license plate program.

- If you were the governor of a state in which this issue was debated, would you (a) allow only one side in a controversial debate to sponsor license plates, depending on the preference of the legislature; (b) allow both groups to sponsor license plates provided they followed the same guidelines as non-controversial groups; or (c) decide that state license plates should stay out of politics and disallow any political or potentially controversial messages.

- Is there a slippery slope problem in this conflict? Suppose you choose (b) and allowed both sides in the abortion debates to sponsor their own license plates. What if a white supremacist group and other controversial groups wanted their own license plates?

Case Study 8-C

**Violating the Law, or a
Series of Honest Mistakes?**

During the late 1990s and early 2000s, Kevin Geddings was a superstar in the fields of public relations and political communication. Working as a paid consultant, he helped politicians in four southern states create state lotteries to generate money for badly needed educational programs. His work on the North Carolina legislation, however, led to the end of his career.

Shortly after the lottery legislation was approved, Geddings and another consultant, Meredith Norris, were accused of violating North Carolina laws. Geddings had accepted an appointment to the North Carolina Lottery Commission, but in filling out financial disclosure forms, he failed to list his previous business relationship with Scientific Games Corporation (SGC), a potential lottery vendor. SGC had paid Geddings more than $228,000 for his work on lottery campaigns in South Carolina, Tennessee, Oklahoma, and North Carolina. More than $9,000 of that amount changed hands after Geddings was appointed to the commission. In an email that surfaced during the investigation, Geddings had told an employee of his firm to "never acknowledge by phone that Scientific Games is a client."

After his relationship with SGC was revealed, Geddings promised to recuse himself from any votes involving lottery vendors. Commission Chairman Charles Sanders told Geddings that the problem may just be one of "perception," but that more problems would ensue "if another shoe were to drop."

"Mr. Chairman," Geddings reportedly told Sanders, "there is no other shoe."

But Geddings' promises and Sanders' open mind weren't good enough. After several days of intense media scrutiny, Geddings resigned from the lottery commission. A few months later he was indicted by a federal grand jury on charges of "honest services fraud" for not reporting his previous financial arrangement with Scientific Games.

Norris, a former member of the legislative staff, had worked on behalf of Scientific Games without registering as a lobbyist. At one point, according to media reports, Norris arranged a yacht cruise for legislators and SGC executives. Norris denied her role constituted lobbying and instead claimed that she was simply trying to monitor the legislation rather than influence it. Editorial page editors who had raised the original concerns about the potential for lottery-related political corruption felt vindicated. "We told you so" editorials soon appeared in newspapers across the state.

Norris pleaded no contest to the charges she faced and was sentenced to one year of probation. Geddings was convicted and sentenced to four years in prison. Three years into that sentence, the U.S. Supreme Court ruled in an unrelated case that "honest services fraud" applied only to outright bribery and not to conflicts of interest. Based on that ruling, Geddings' lawyers were successful in persuading a federal court to have the balance of his sentence vacated.

After selling his Charlotte firm, Geddings said he's out of the public relations business for good. "No one wants to hire a PR guy who gets as much bad PR as I do," he told a reporter from the *Raleigh News & Observer*.

- Is it fair to require a professional communicator to register as a lobbyist when he or she describes his or her work as "public relations" or "consulting"?

- Should there be a rule stating that registration is required when an individual spends a certain percentage of his or her time in lobbying? If so, what percentage would be appropriate?

Case Study 8-D   **Mixing Entertainment with Politics**

One of the fastest-growing trends in American politics is that of Hollywood celebrities taking sides in political debates and campaigns.

Critics often point out that while the celebrities themselves may be knowledgeable about the campaigns and issues, their fans may not be. Therefore, those critics believe it is inappropriate for celebrities to use their name recognition and appeal to influence the outcome of elections. In their defense, the celebrities point out that as Americans, they are simply exercising their First Amendment rights of free speech.

A large majority of these cases involve liberal celebrities endorsing liberal candidates. Actors including Martin Sheen, Sean Penn, Susan Sarandon, Woody Harrelson, Barbra Streisand, Jane Fonda, Alec Baldwin, and Ed Asner have supported democratic candidates by speaking at campaign events, appearing in television commercials and campaign videos, and endorsing candidates in media interviews.

In 2003, the country trio Dixie Chicks created controversy by making disparaging remarks about President George W. Bush during a concert appearance in England. Although the performers later apologized to the president, they supported his opponent, democrat John Kerry, in the 2004 election, and in subsequent elections continued to support democratic candidates for a variety of federal offices. That prompted political commentator Laura Ingraham to author a book titled *Shut Up and Sing* that was critical of the Dixie Chicks and other entertainers getting involved in politics.

While the majority of entertainers getting involved in politics are doing so from a liberal perspective, some conservatives do so as well. Among the most popular are country singer Toby Keith and actors Gary Sinise and James Woods. When Woods portrayed New York Mayor Rudy Giuliani in a made-for-television movie about the September 11 terrorist attacks, he told television critics that he accepted the role partly due to his admiration for the mayor and partly due to his desire to honor the memories of the firefighters who died in the World Trade Center and the military men and women who died at the Pentagon.

- Do you agree with the critics who say that it is inappropriate for celebrities to use their influence in this way, or with the performers themselves, who claim they are simply exercising their First Amendment rights of free speech?

- To what degree to these endorsements affect your voting decisions?

Case Study 8-E   **Stop Using Our Song!**

When Alaska Governor Sarah Palin took the stage at the Republican National Convention in August 2008 to accept her party's nomination for vice-president, her theme song — "Barracuda" — played in the background. During the campaign, the song, chosen based on Palin's nickname, continued to be used as background music. One legal problem: the rock group Heart, which recorded the song in 1977, still held the copyright and had not given Palin or anyone associated with her campaign permission to use it.

"Sarah Palin's views and values in no way represent us as American women," the group's leader singers, Ann and Nancy Wilson, said in media interviews. No formal legal action was taken, but the Wilsons did ask her to stop using the song. Palin's running mate, Arizona Senator John McCain, was not as lucky. After using the 1980s song "Running on Empty" as his theme music, he was sued by Jackson Browne, the recording artist who still held that copyright.

The "Barracuda" and "Running on Empty" cases are just two examples from a 30-year history of politicians using popular songs as their theme music on the campaign trail and in television commercials.

Other famous cases of musicians rejecting the use of their work in political ads involve Bruce Springsteen, who complained when President Ronald Reagan used snippets of Springsteen's song "Born to Run" in television commercials during his 1984 re-election campaign, and Tom Johnston, who complained when Florida Governor Bob Martinez used more than a minute of Johnston's instrumental work, "Long Train Running," in television commercials during his 1990 re-election bid.

David Byrne of the group Talking Heads sued Florida Governor Charlie Crist for appropriating the group's 1985 hit song "Road to Nowhere" without permission or compensation. Byrne continued to press the suit even after Crist agreed to stop using the song in his 2010 campaign for the U.S. Senate. The spot was never shown on television, but was instead on the campaign's website and YouTube videos associated with the campaign.

During the 2012 presidential campaign, republican vice-presidential candidate Paul Ryan took the stage accompanied by Twisted Sister's 1984 hit, "We're Not Going to Take It." After the band's lead singer Dee Snider complained, Ryan stopped using it.

When he kicked off his 2016 presidential campaign in June 2015, real estate mogul Donald Trump used as background music the Neil Young song "Rockin' in the Free World." Young immediately complained, prompting Trump to stop using it.

Most artists who hear their work used in political campaigns based their complaints not on the lack of compensation or even the lack of permission — just their desire not to have their fans (or anyone else) mistakenly believe they were endorsing a political candidate. Before reaching the point of litigation, many cases are typically resolved when lawyers representing the artists send "cease and desist" letters to the politicians. In nearly every case, the candidates immediately stop using the music, and in many cases also apologize to the copyright holders. Those artists often say that while the apologies are appreciated, the damage is already done because many of their fans will not see the apology.

- Because they are considered political speech rather than commercial speech, should politicians be allowed to use copyrighted material under the legal principle of "fair use"? (see an explanation of fair use in Chapter 10)

- Would your answer change if the political advertisements or campaign videos were required to include a disclaimer on the screen that clarified the artist performing the music is not endorsing the candidate?

Discussion Problem 8   All or Nothing

You're serving on the city council in your community. The local professional football team is threatening to move to another town unless the city builds a new stadium. Your state's constitution allows individual communities to adopt "local option" sales taxes of up to 1 percent, but such taxes (basically raising the sales tax from 6 to 7 percent) must be approved by the voters. The council has proposed adopting the 1 percent tax increase, with all of the proceeds going to build the new football stadium. Before the proposal can make it onto the ballot, however, two unions — one representing school teachers and the other representing law enforcement — come forward to oppose the idea. They provide polling data (that you determine is reliable) showing the proposal to earmark all of the new revenue for the football stadium losing at the polls, 58-42 percent. But when the poll described a hypothetical plan to designate 50 percent of the revenue for the stadium, 25 percent for local schools and 25 percent for the police and fire departments and paramedic service, the proposal would win at the polls, 62-38.

When the city council approaches the owner of the football team with the idea of sharing the revenue from the tax, he rejects the idea and insists that all of the revenue go to stadium construction. "It's all or nothing" he tells the council. He says that his main concern is that once other groups in the community hear about the change in the proposal, they will come forward and demand their own share of the revenue. "Today it's the police and schools, tomorrow it will be libraries and hospitals, then next week it will be the museums and the art galleries . . . it will never stop," he says.

Which propaganda techniques do you recognize in this scenario?

Discussion Questions

801. The First Amendment provides a greater degree of protection for political speech than commercial speech, and therefore the Federal Elections Commission and state governmental agencies find it difficult to regulate political ads, even those that are clearly exaggerated and sometimes false. Should this change? Is there a way to increase the truthfulness of political ads without violating the First Amendment?

802. Of the propaganda techniques listed in this chapter, which have you seen in recent election campaigns or modern-day commercial advertising campaigns?

Notes

214   **advocate something they do not believe themselves** and **rather than personal attacks on the opposition:** Charles Larson, *Persuasion: Reception and Responsibility.* Belmont, CA: Wadsworth Publishing Company, 1992. pp. 37-38.

214   **that would otherwise be accessible to the public:** Dennis Gouran, "Guidelines for the Analysis of Responsibility in Governmental Communication." *Teaching About Doublespeak*, ed. Daniel Dieterich. Urbana, IL: National Council of Teachers of English, 1976.

215   **why one side should be preferred over the other:** Carl Hovland, Irving Janis, and Harold Kelley, *Communication and Persuasion.* New Haven, CT: Yale University Press, 1953, p. 44.

216   **by introducing your own alternatives:** Richard L. Johannesen, Kathleen S. Valde, and Karen E. Whedbee. *Ethics in Human Communication*, sixth edition. Long Grove, IL: Waveland Press, 2008, p. 77.

216   **the person acting as its source:** Garth S. Jowett and Victoria O'Donnell, *Propaganda and Persuasion.* Newbury Park, CA: Sage Publications, 1992, p. 99.

217   **"a known thespian":** Kerwin Swint, *Mudslingers: The Twenty-Five Dirtiest Political Campaigns of All Time.* New York: Union Square Press, 2006, p. 47.

219   **"Elect George C. Wallace:"** Swint, p. 228.

221   **"what the word of America means":** James A. Jaksa and Michael S. Pritchard. *Communication Ethics.* Belmont, CA: Wadsworth Publishing, 1988, p. 131.

226   **'defeat of a presidential candidate":** Jesse Holland and Mark Sherman, "Hillary Movie and Campaign Finance." Associated Press report, September 6, 2009.

227   **"and whenever one party to a political dispute":** Murray Edelman, *The Politics of Misinformation.* New York: Cambridge University Press, 2001, p. 8.

227   **"there are many instances in which talk show hosts":** Mike Hoyt, "Talk Radio: Turning up the Volume." *Columbia Journalism Review,* November/December 1992, pp. 45-50.

227   **"if they are willing to adjust reality":** Peter Laufer, *Inside Talk Radio: America's Voice or Just Hot Air?* New York: Carol Publishing Company, 1995, p. 247.

227   **One of the startling findings:** Randy Bobbitt, *Us Against Them: The Political Culture of Talk Radio.* Lanham, MD: Lexington Books, 2010, p. 13.

228   **"disguised as news and infotainment":** Al Gore, *The Assault on Reason.* New York: Penguin Books, 2007, p. 66.

229   **"to buy it":** Bill Moyers, *Free Speech for Sale.* Video documentary by the Corporation for Public Broadcasting, 1999.

230   **"deny the forum to opposing opinions":** James J. Kilpatrick, "Taking License With Free Speech." Syndicated newspaper column, November 6, 2004.

230   **"never acknowledge by phone," "there is no other shoe,"** and **"No one wants to hire a PR guy":** Randy Bobbitt, *Lottery Wars: Case Studies in Bible Belt Politics.* Lanham, MD: Lexington Books, 2005, p. 185-86.

233   **"Sarah Palin's views":** "Use of 'Barracuda' for Sarah Palin Nets GOP a Heart Attack." *New York Daily News*, September 6, 2008.

CHAPTER 9

Ethical Issues in Workplace Communication

Background

- A student struggling in her college classes confides in her psychology professor and discloses that the recent break-up with her fiancé has caused her grades to slip, and she solicits advice on both the academic side of the issue as well as the psychological side. A few weeks later, the woman's ex-fiance is found murdered, and the student in question is the only suspect. When police learn about the relationship between the student and the professor, they ask the professor to reveal the content of their conversations and turn over the woman's "personal reflection papers" that were written as a class assignment.

- A company's human resources department receives numerous complaints from African American and Muslim employees who claim that co-workers are sending them harassing email messages and constantly quizzing them on their political leanings and church activities. The company responds to the complaints by saying that it is up to the employees to resolve their own conflicts.

- A college student visits his college's career services center for help revising his resume prior to an upcoming job search. When the counselor questions some of the information listed on his preliminary draft, the student admits, "Yes, a lot of that stuff is exaggerated. But everyone does it. If I don't do it, I'm at a disadvantage."

There are no federal or state laws that apply specifically to workplace communication, but laws from other areas, such as those regarding defamation and privacy, may apply. In addition, labor and employment laws regarding workplace issues such as employment discrimination and sexual harassment may have implications for professional communicators. Typical problem areas in workplace communication include harassment of co-workers or subordinates, lying to cover up mistakes, lying to or misleading a superior or subordinate about the status of a project, taking credit for another individual's work, and falsifying expense reports, time sheets, or other financial documents.

There are no professional organizations that deal with all aspects of business communication, but specific aspects of business communication are subject to the ethical codes of organizations such as the Public Relations Society of America (PRSA) and the International Association of Business Communicators (IABC). These codes were discussed in detail in Chapter 7 and are provided in the appendices.

In addition to the PRSA and IABC codes, the two organizations serving the field of personnel administration — the American Society for Personnel Administration (ASPA) and the Society for Human Resource Management (SHRM) — have codes of ethics that cover a variety of issues. ASPA employs a code of ethics that requires its members to (1) maintain truthfulness and honesty, (2) ensure that others receive credit for their work and contributions, (3) guard against conflicts of interest or their appearance, (4) respect superiors, subordinates, colleagues, and the public, and (5) take responsibility for their own errors.

SHRM has a sweeping "code of conduct" that deals with issues such as confidentiality of personnel records, appropriate use of public funds, fairness in the employee recruiting process, and the responsibility of organizations to protect whistle-blowers.

Current Issues and Controversies

Sexual Harassment in the Workplace

While sexual harassment has been a workplace problem ever since men and women began working together centuries ago, the problem became more prevalent in the 1970s and 1980s as increasing numbers of women entered the workplace. The term **sexual harassment** was coined in the 1970s to refer to a variety of offensive behaviors, including unwelcome sexual advances, requests for sexual favors, and other verbal and physical conduct of a sexual nature. Today, sexual harassment is considered one of the major factors in employee turnover and loss of productivity, as well as a major legal issue for employers of any size and type. Despite government figures indicating sexual harassment claims have dropped slightly between 2000 and 2014, organizations still need to take the problem seriously because of both the legal liability and the potential harm to their reputations.

The media focused additional attention to the matter as they pursued two major news stories of the 1990s: the confirmation hearings for Supreme Court Justice Clarence Thomas, whose nomination was threatened by accusations of sexual harassment by a former co-worker; and the events leading to the impeachment of President Bill Clinton, whose affair with a White House intern focused new light on male-female relationships in the workplace.

The landmark court case dealing with sexual harassment was argued in 1986. In *Meritor Savings Bank v. Vinson*, the U.S. Supreme Court ruled that employers bear the responsibility of protecting their employees from sexual harassment and can be found liable for not taking action, even in cases in which management was not aware of the problem.

After that ruling, companies across the country developed formal sexual harassment policies and made them part of written policy manuals and new employee orientation programs.

Those policies, following the lead of court rulings and legal publications, identify two categories of sexual harassment. **Quid pro quo** (from the Latin for "something for something") is the demand by a work supervisor or other superior for sexual favors in exchange for a promotion, salary increase, or other workplace privileges; or the threat to terminate an individual for not complying with the request. **Hostile work environment** is a term used to describe offensive jokes of a sexual nature, repeated remarks regarding a person's body or clothing (even if meant to be complimentary); unwelcome hugging, kissing, or other physical contact; and pornographic images such as screensavers, posters, calendars, or photographs.

Most organizational policies include a formal process that begins with the employee bringing the matter to the attention of a supervisor. If the offending party is the supervisor, the complaint is filed with either the next supervisor on the organizational chart or the human resources office. The purpose of the internal procedure is to resolve the conflict without going to court or generating media attention. Because the litigation process is expensive and emotionally draining for both plaintiffs and defendants, most companies find formal policies are critical to resolving conflicts early in the process.

In extreme cases, however, employers are unable or unwilling to address sexual harassment complaints internally, leaving victims with no other choice than litigation. Once within the court system, such cases are argued in civil court based on laws regarding employment discrimination. Those laws include anti-retaliation provisions that prohibit employers from firing or otherwise retaliating against plaintiffs.

Before going to court, complainants may seek assistance from the Equal Employment Opportunities Commission (EEOC), a federal agency responsible for administering laws involving a variety of employment discrimination issues. While the EEOC cannot provide legal representation or formal legal advice, the agency can be helpful in advising employees regarding the legal process and alternatives to litigation.

While the common perception is that sexual harassment occurs mostly between male supervisors and female subordinates, that is not always the case. The EEOC estimates that each year, 15 to 20 percent of individuals filing sexual harassment claims were male, with alleged perpetrators in those cases being both male and female. Researchers who study the issue also claim that cases of sexual harassment are more often about the exercise of power than the pursuit of sex.

The EEOC points out that in addition to establishing and enforcing policies in cases involving conflicts between employees, companies must also be watchful for cases of harassment in which the perpetrators are customers, clients, or outside vendors or contractors. In cases involving vendors and contractors, company leaders should inform those perpetrators that such conduct is inappropriate, and if necessary, notify the perpetrator's employer. If that fails, employers should be prepared to terminate the business relationship with the offending vendor or contractor.

Sexual harassment violates Title VII of the Civil Rights Act of 1964. In 1991, Congress amended that section of the law to provide stronger financial penalties against companies that fail to protect their employees.

Race, Religion, and Politics in the Workplace

While sexual harassment has been a well-publicized workplace issue for several decades, an increasing number of managers have reported receiving complaints of racial, religious, and political harassment as well.

Racial harassment has been a growing problem since the introduction of the Internet into the workplace in the mid-1990s, with the worst examples being the distribution of offensive jokes and visual images via an organization's email network. The courts and employer policy manuals define racial harassment as "epithets, slurs, negative stereotyping, threats, intimidation, hostile acts, denigrating jokes, or the display or circulation of written or graphic material that denigrates or shows hostility to an individual or group."

In terms of religious and political harassment, simply inquiring about a person's religious beliefs or political affiliations is acceptable, even though such questions might make the person being asked uncomfortable. But just as repeated requests for a date or other attention paid to a co-worker can graduate to sexual harassment if those incidents are both persistent and unwanted, repeated attempts to lure a person into a discussion of religion or politics can also cause problems for both the individual and the employer.

And just as employees have the right to seek protection from their employers in cases of alleged racial or sexual harassment, they also have the right to complain about inappropriate inquiries about religion or politics. Examples include repeated inquiries about church attendance or unwanted invitations to attend someone else's church, persistent inquiries about political affiliations or voting decisions, or intentionally denigrating others for their religious or political beliefs.

The harassment of co-workers and subordinates based on their religious and political beliefs has been a workplace issue for decades, but addressing it had been a low priority for organizational leaders until recently. In the decade following the terrorist attacks of September 11, 2001, the number of Muslim employees reporting cases of harassment increased exponentially.

In cases of religious or political harassment, the courts use the term "hostile work environment" in the same way they use the term in sexual harassment cases. To avoid potential problems, many employers prohibit their employees from wearing campaign buttons on their clothing or displaying campaign posters, literature, and other religious or political materials in their workspaces.

In 2009, home improvement retailer Home Depot required an employee to remove a button reading "One Nation Under God" from his store-issued apron. The employee insisted that he was merely expressing his love for the country and showing support for a family member serving in the military. But the company claimed that despite his intent, the button violated the company's policy about wearing any items on their aprons or personal clothing that advocated a political or religious viewpoint. Because Home Depot is a private employer and not a government agency, the employee had no claim that his First Amendment rights were violated.

Honesty in the Workplace and at School

According to a recent survey by CareerBuilder.com, 19 percent of workers admit to lying the workplace at least once a week. Among the reasons cited were appeasing a customer (26 percent), covering up a project failure or missed deadline (13 percent), to explain tardiness or absence (8 percent), or to sabotage the work of a colleague (5 percent). The same survey revealed that 24 percent of all managers had fired an employee for dishonesty. Other examples of workplace dishonesty include using sick days for reasons other than illness; falsifying time sheets, expense reports, or other internal documents; and spreading gossip about co-workers and superiors.

Another common unethical behavior is lying to potential customers about the company's ability to meet a deadline or achieve some other service-related goal, or lying about the positive qualities of a company's products or services or the negative qualities of a competitor's products or services.

In a 1991 article in *Entrepreneurial Woman*, ethicist Michael Josephson listed several rationale that employees often use to justify dishonest or unethical behavior in the workplace. They include:

False necessity. Employees often believe they are behaving as they do because they feel morally or ethically required to do so. For example, an employee may intentionally sabotage the work of a colleague by telling himself or herself, "that project never should have been approved" or "that's not the right direction for this company" when the actual reason behind the behavior was personal or professional jealousy.

Relative filth. Some employees believe that taking ethical shortcuts is acceptable because other employees or the company as a whole is doing something they perceive as much worse. For example, employees may list on their time sheets a few hours they did not work or add a few fictional expenses to travel reports and justify it in their own minds because they know (or suspect) that other employees falsify their time sheets or expense reports to a greater degree.

In another example, an employee justifies the theft of office supplies by telling themselves "the company wastes so much time on landscaping and repainting the building, it will never miss a few dollars worth of copier paper and paper clips."

Rationalization. Sometimes known as the "big stretch." An employee may justify unethical conduct with flimsy excuses, such as taking a slightly longer lunch hour than is allotted and claiming to make it up by working late that night (whether that actually happens or not), or telling himself or herself, "I'll print out my kid's school project at the office because that printer is nicer than what we have at home, and besides, the company doesn't pay me what I'm worth."

Self-deception. In this scenario, employees (or potential employees) tell a falsehood so many times that they no longer remember whether it is true or false. One common example is the individual who early in his or her career falsified information on a resume, such as claiming to have been captain of the high school football team or recipient of an academic award. Each time the resume is revised, the false information remains, and after multiple revisions, the individual is so comfortable with the information that he or she forgets that it was fictional to begin with.

The ends justify the means. A supervisor may coerce employees to work overtime without compensation in order to reduce or eliminate a backlog in work by saying that if the goal is not accomplished, the department or individual employees will be treated unfavorably in the future. There is actually no substance to the threat, but the supervisor believes the goal of reducing or eliminating the backlog of work was more important than being honest with the subordinates.

In a recent National Business Ethics Survey of more than 3,000 American workers, 10 percent reported feeling pressured to compromise the organization's ethical standards, with the sources of pressure including top management (36 percent) middle management (39 percent) and co-workers (15 percent).

241

More than 65 percent reported encountering a situation that invited ethical misconduct on their parts, while 74 percent reported observing some level of misconduct by others in the organization.

Of those claiming to have observed others' misconduct, only half reported those situations to superiors. The most common reasons given for reporting the unethical conduct were confidence that corrective action would be taken and that "it was the right thing to do." The most common reasons given for non-reporting include fear of retaliation, belief that someone else will report it instead, or skepticism that any corrective action would be taken.

One common source of workplace dishonesty is not current employers, but potential ones. One recent survey found that 80 percent of all resumes received included some level of falsehood. Of those, 60 percent were described as "minor exaggerations that had little impact," 15 percent were described as "outright lies," and 5 percent were described as "real whoppers." Among the most outrageous claims made by candidates in resumes included (1) being a member of the Kennedy family, (2) graduating with degrees not offered by the institution they attended or graduating from universities that did no exist, (3) claiming to have owned a company when the candidate had actually worked in the mailroom or other entry-level position, and (4) claiming military experience dating back to before the individual was born. One reported incident involved an applicant for a journalism position submitting a portfolio of work samples that included an article written by the editor conducting the interview.

Two recent examples of falsification of resumes made national news.

In 2001, newly hired Notre Dame football coach George O'Leary was found to have falsified several critical details on his resume and was forced to resign five days into his job (see Case Study 9-A).

The following year, a journalist writing a profile of Ronald Zarrella, chief executive officer of Bausch & Lomb, found that New York University's School of Business Administration had no record of Zarrella earning an M.B.A. there, as Zarrella claimed on his resume and on the company website. When that news became public, Zarrella submitted his resignation, but it was not accepted by the company's board of directors. Instead, Zarrella forfeited his $1.1 million annual bonus at the end of that year.

Because verifying the information included in resumes and on application forms is time-consuming, most employers wait until the field has been narrowed to a manageable number of candidates and carry out such work only after the candidate has had a successful interview and is under serious consideration. In other cases, employers may wait until a formal offer has been made and accepted, warning the candidate that the offer is "contingent upon a background check."

The background check usually begins by with verifying the information on the resume, and if serious discrepancies are found, most employers will offer the candidate an opportunity to clarify the discrepancies in order to allow for typographical errors or similar mistakes. While some employers may be forgiving, many others are not, especially when they find the deception to be intentional. Many employers report that intentional deception results in a withdrawal of the job offer, even in cases in which the erroneous information was not a factor in the original assessment of the candidate's qualifications.

When such deception is detected, many individuals defend themselves by claiming that "everyone lies on their resume" and that they are at a disadvantage if they don't. But most employers and workplace ethicists disagree. "Widespread lying on resumes doesn't justify your doing the same thing," wrote business ethicist Bruce Weinstein in a 2006 newspaper column. "Even if your friends and co-workers are doing it, it is ethically irrelevant to your own behavior."

Another method that employers use to get a more complete picture of job candidates is checking their "online persona" on social media sites such as Facebook and LinkedIn. Many job placement counselors advise their clients that "if you wouldn't want your grandmother to see it, remove it from your Facebook page." Lewis Maltby, founder of a nonprofit organization that studies workplace privacy issues, adds that "you can't blame HR people for looking at social networking sites because hiring the wrong person is a very expensive mistake." Employers are not legally required to inform candidates of negative hiring decisions based on what they have found on social media sites, and it is unlikely they would do so voluntarily. But even if they did, employment lawyers claim, the candidate would have no legal recourse because the hiring decision was not based on a factor prohibited by federal law, such as age, race, religion, gender, or disability.

One profession taking recent notice of the dishonesty trend is college admissions officers. In surveys, they report that inflated credentials on application forms is a growing problem, and most blame parents who exert excessive pressure on their children to gain admission to their alma maters or other prestigious schools. Among the examples listed in surveys include multiple students from the same high school graduating class claiming they were a valedictorian, captain of the football team, or class president. Other students claim non-existent awards or exaggerate the number of hours spent in volunteer activities. As a result of this trend, many college admissions committees are verifying such claims with references and asking more detailed questions during in-person interviews.

Employee Evaluations and Letters of Recommendation

Since the 1980s, one of the major problem areas in business communication is the issue of employee evaluations and letters of recommendation. Even if they are seen by only a small number of people, documents that criticize individuals' job performances or suitability for employment can be the object of defamation lawsuits filed by the offended parties. Employers are therefore extremely cautious in the words they choose when describing a former employee's job performance or explaining to a third party the reasons for one's termination.

Human resources personnel are also cautious in giving and receiving information (either in writing, telephone, or email) about past or present employees, including letters of recommendation, the results of performance reviews, or other evaluative information. The potential cost of litigation has caused many employers to enforce policies about who can provide information about current and former employees and what kinds of evaluative information can be shared.

Even well-meaning supervisors and former supervisors find themselves in trouble after providing what they believed to be positive letters of recommendation or employment evaluations for current or former employees. Most result from simple misunderstandings, but employees who believe they were not hired by another employer as a result may sue the individual, the company, or both. Because of such legal liability, many companies require work supervisors to write letters of recommendation on personal rather than company stationery and preface them by stating they are providing their opinion and not that of the company as a whole. Other employers prohibit supervisors from writing letters of recommendation or providing employment references in their entirety. In cases in which an employee left the company under negative circumstances, many employers require all evaluative documents to be reviewed by their legal departments before being released.

While cases of being sued for information revealed in response to a reference check are worrisome, a more recent trend is that of employers being sued for what they *did not report.* Examples include not reporting that an individual is a convicted child molester when the prospective employer is an elementary school, or not reporting a former employee's tendency to act violently toward co-workers.

In general, employers providing employment references should follow some basic guidelines:

1. Stay within the scope of the questions being asked. Do not respond to questions that are not asked, especially if your answer would be negative.

2. Be as specific as possible. Avoid ambiguous or vague comments.

3. Don't provide negative information without providing specific examples.

4. Provide only information that is related to the position. Avoid commenting on an individual's family life or health issues unless it is connected to the job for which he or she is applying.

5. If you must provide negative information, consult your company's attorney before doing so.

Salary Negotiations

Negotiating a salary for a new job you've just accepted may be the second-most stressful part of the job search, surpassed only by the initial interview.

In a 2009 article, career coach Todd Bavol offered the following tips for new hires:

1. Do not include a salary history or salary expectation on a resume or in a cover letter. If it is higher than what a prospective employer has in mind, you may disqualify yourself for the job. If it's too low, you might be laying the groundwork for a "low-ball" salary offer. Some companies still require such information on application forms, so candidates may be required to answer questions about salary history. But if the form asks for "salary expectation," indicate a range rather than a minimum amount.

2. Going into the negotiation, have in your mind what you consider your "absolute minimum," but don't disclose it.

3. Don't limit your thinking about compensation to just the salary. Also consider life and health insurance, employer contributions to retirement plans, reimbursement for relocation expenses, and reimbursement for college tuition in the pursuit of a graduate degree or other professional training.

4. Do enough research on the employer and the industry in which it operates to make an educated guess as to what the salary range might be. The salaries of government employees and salary ranges of advertised positions are public information. For private companies, specific salaries are not public, but perusing industry publications or checking with employment agencies or your school's career services office might give you a good idea of what to expect. Remember to factor in the region of the country and the current state of the national economy.

5. Do not mention your own financial obligations in a salary negotiation. Prospective employers are interested in your potential value to the organization — not about your credit card debt, student loan obligations, or your responsibility for family health care expenses.

Which Forms of Workplace Communication Should Be Privileged?

As discussed in Chapter 7, communication between public relations representatives and the individuals for whom they work — either external clients or internal work supervisors — is confidential in a general sense, but not privileged in a legal sense. Unlike the relationship between doctors and patients, lawyers and clients, and (in most states) journalists and their sources, the relationship between public relations representatives and their clients is vulnerable to inquiries by law enforcement investigations, grand jury proceedings, and other legal situations. The same confidential-but-not-privileged rule applies to other forms of professional relationships, including those between clients and architects, accountants, and consultants.

One related issue in this area is the level of confidentiality between college students and their professors. The problem is a growing concern for university administrators, as more students are balancing school, work, and family life and often look to their professors for help in dealing with the stress that results.

When students confide in professors about personal problems that are affecting their academic performance, university policy and common sense dictates that professors have a professional obligation to respect the student's privacy (whether the student requests it or not) and not reveal that information to anyone except on a need-to-know basis. The professsor might discuss the matter with a department chair or colleague as appropriate, but should not casually reveal that information. However, such a conversation is not legally privileged, and if the student is later subject of a criminal investigation, the professor might be subpoenaed to testify or provide information, as well as to provide physical evidence in his or her possession.

One professor who advocates legal protection for student-professor communication is Tod Burke, who teaches criminal justice at Radford University. In a 2001 article in *The Chronicle of Higher Education*, Burke wrote, "As faculty members, our first responsibility is to be advocates for our students . . . a wealth of research shows that one key to freshman year academic survival is the development of strong relationships with faculty. Studies show strong relationships are more likely if students know their conversations with faculty are confidential."

While Burke and other observers believe that student-professor communication should be privileged, opponents of the idea object for several reasons. First, they claim, few professors possess the skills necessary to provide appropriate personal counseling and should instead refer at-risk students to school counselors who have specific training and experience in issues related to college life. The second issue is how (and if) the condition of privilege would apply to school employees other than full-time professors, such as adjuncts and teaching assistants.

If the student were to confide in a psychological counselor employed by the institution, such a conversation would be privileged, much like the conversation between any other client and counselor. But the same exceptions would also apply; the counselor would be allowed to (and in most states, legally required to) notify university administrators and/or law enforcement officials in cases in which students are believed to be a danger to themselves or others. In some states, the obligation to report potential danger is a legal one, but in others it is only an ethical one. There is no "one-size-fits-all" model to deal with such situations, as in most states, both the law and professional ethical codes provide the counselor with the discretion as to whether potential danger should be reported, and to whom.

In cases in which a student confides in a psychology professor who is also a licensed counselor, the professor would likely clarify at the beginning of the conversation as to whether the student is asking the professor to act as an academic counselor or psychological counselor. Most universities have policies prohibiting "dual relationships," meaning that it would be professionally inappropriate for a professor to provide counseling services to a student in his or her class.

Communicating with Disabled Co-Workers and Customers

When a company employs individuals who are disabled, many co-workers are unsure about how to communicate with them. Even well-meaning co-workers can offend disabled colleagues through comments and actions.

Despite their advocacy for laws such as the Americans with Disabilities Act, many persons with disabilities do not seek special treatment; they desire only to be treated on an equal basis with others. Some are offended by what they perceive as an artificially sympathetic or patronizing attitude of persons without disabilities. As one example, some object to the modifier "challenged," such as descriptions of persons as "mentally challenged" or "physically challenged." A person who uses a wheelchair, for example, might look at a set of concrete steps and say, "That's not a challenge — that's an impossibility." On a 1990s television sitcom, an adult who never grew beyond the height of four feet was complaining to another character about the patronizing attitude of some persons of standard height. "Do you mean when they bend over to talk to you?" the other character asked. The reply: "No, I mean when they *pick you up* to talk to you."

Advocacy groups for the disabled caution against using negatively charged words and phrases when speaking with or about disabled employees or writing about them in company publications. Examples of terms to avoid include "crippled" (*disabled* is the preferred term), "suffers from," "victim" (write *person with cerebral palsy*, not *cerebral palsy victim*), and "wheelchair bound" (call the person a *wheelchair user* instead; few people are truly bound to a wheelchair; they use it mainly for transportation).

Other suggestions include:

1. If a hearing-impaired individual is accompanied by an interpreter, always speak to the individual, not the interpreter.

2. If a person is missing his or her right arm or if the right arm is a prosthetic, wait for him or her to offer to shake hands. Most individuals in that situation will offer their left hand, but wait for them to make the first gesture.

3. If you offer assistance to a blind person, wait until the offer is accepted. If you offer to accompany a blind person to a location within your building, he or she will likely extend an arm and wait for you to take it.

4. Treat disabled persons with the same respect and dignity as the non-disabled. Do not speak down to them or address them by first name unless you address others the same way.

5. Do not touch a person's wheelchair or other artificial device. Most individuals using wheelchairs consider it as part of their body.

6. If a person has a speech impediment, listen carefully and resist the temptation to finish sentences for them. If you do not understand, do not pretend that you do; politely ask them to repeat what they have said.

7. If you inadvertently make a potentially insensitive remark while speaking with a disabled person, do not be embarrassed. Examples include "Gotta run," "See you later," or "Did you hear . . ." Offer an apology only if the person appears to have been offended. That is unlikely, as many disabled persons are accustomed to such casual remarks.

8. To get the attention of a hearing-impaired person, tap him or her on the shoulder or wave to get his or her attention. When speaking with a hearing-impaired person, speak slowly (but not excessively so) and keep your hands away from your face so the individual can read your lips.

9. When speaking to someone in a wheelchair, find a chair to sit in so you will be at the same eye level. If no chairs are available, do not lean over to speak with them.

Employer Monitoring of Employee Email and Web Activity

While the government is unwilling or unable to regulate communication over the Internet, that is not the case with private industry. Employers often monitor incoming and outgoing email traffic on company-owned computer networks. Court rulings, in supporting their right to do so, have stated that companies own all of the information contained on those computer networks.

Not only are employers trying to prevent the unauthorized release of company information, but they are also attempting to limit other forms of communication that may result in lawsuits involving libel, privacy, or sexual or racial harassment. In a recent survey conducted by the American Management Association, more than two-thirds of companies responded that they routinely monitor the email communication of their employees as well as monitor the websites they visit — both the work-related and non-work-related. News reports indicate that online coverage of major weekday sporting events such as the NCAA basketball tournament and Master's golf tournament result in employees using their computers to follow those events during working hours, thus affecting Web access for other employees.

But the most serious problem involves legal liability. Experts in the fields of both law and technology point out that when individuals use their employers' computer equipment and Internet access to vent in cyberspace, their bulletin board postings and electronic mail postings are not as private as they might believe.

In an effort to prevent employees from engaging in libelous speech or otherwise exposing the company to legal liability, many large employers are monitoring employee email traffic and hiring outside consultants to develop systems for determining the origin of anonymous postings to industry bulletin boards. "If you work at a Fortune 500 company, chances are good your email has been reviewed at least once," says Joan Feldman, founder of the Seattle-based Computer Forensics Inc., which helps companies track their employees' illegal or unethical use of company-owned technology.

While some free-speech and privacy advocates claim that employer monitoring of email violates the rights of employees, recent news stories provide the best evidence of the dangers that companies face by not doing so. When federal investigators looking into allegations of financial wrongdoing at Enron in 2003 gained access to archived computer files, for example, they found pornography, racial comments, offensive jokes, and other material in employee email that would have exposed the company to lawsuits if it had been detected before the company dissolved.

Despite the potential danger involved in not monitoring employee email, many companies are still reluctant to do so. One factor is the cost, which for companies with large numbers of employees may be substantial. Another factor is trust — employers simply prefer to trust their employees and respect their privacy. Many companies in this category wait until they have "probable cause" or other suspicions before snooping in email files.

One such incident occurred at the *Toledo Blade*, one of Ohio's largest daily newspapers, in 2006. Wanting to determine which staff member sent an anonymous email criticizing the newspaper's Pulitzer Prize entry to the organization administering the competition, the management hired a private investigator. Following preliminary evidence, the investigators confiscated the company-owned laptop computer of a reporter and used a computer forensics expert to analyze its hard drive. The newspaper fired the reporter, who had sent the anonymous email through his personal Yahoo account, but using the company-owned laptop. Following the incident, however, the company reverted to its policy of not monitoring employee email except in extreme circumstances.

Court rulings have consistently found that because they are providing the technology, employers are free to conduct such monitoring, and employees do not have a legitimate claim that their privacy has been invaded. That ruling assumes, however, that employers are doing so for a legitimate purpose such as protecting company assets or preventing the transmission of material that is sexually or racially offensive, is harassing, or violates copyright law. Courts would be more sympathetic to the employee if he or she is able to prove that the monitoring is unrelated to legitimate purposes or is voyeuristic in nature.

For Discussion

Case Study 9-A   **The (Bad) Luck of the Irish**

On December 9, 2001, the University of Notre Dame announced it has found the perfect man to fill its football coaching vacancy. Fifty-five year old George O'Leary, the head coach at Georgia Tech, was popular and successful, and his Irish-Catholic ancestry came as a bonus. The new job looked like a good fit as well for O'Leary, a life-long football coach who had worked his way up through the coaching ranks and had coveted the Notre Dame head coaching position for more than a decade.

Just a few days after his introductory news conference, the deal began to unravel when sports journalists looking into O'Leary's background discovered inaccuracies on his resume, including a master's degree from a university that did not exist. O'Leary had also claimed a playing record that included earning three letters at the University of New Hampshire, when in fact he had not played in one game.

His new employer initially supported O'Leary when the discrepancies became public, and O'Leary assured Notre Dame officials that there was nothing else they needed to know. When further background checks found that O'Leary had falsified other credentials as well, the school asked for and received his resignation on December 13.

"Due to a selfish and thoughtless act many years ago, I have personally embarrassed Notre Dame, its alumni and fans," O'Leary said in a statement released by Notre Dame. "The integrity and credibility of Notre Dame is impeccable and with that in mind, I will resign my position as head football coach."

Notre Dame athletic director Kevin White released a statement as well, commenting that, "George has acknowledged inaccuracies in his biographical materials, including his academic background . . . I understand that these inaccuracies represent a very human failing; nonetheless, they constitute a breach of trust that makes it impossible for us to go forward with our relationship."

Ara Parseghian, the former Notre Dame coach who led the Fighting Irish for more than a decade, added that, "I can't understand how you could go all those years and not catch or correct it."

Within days, many sports journalists reported that college football and basketball coaches around the country were "checking their bios in their schools' media guides and on the websites" to make sure they were accurate. Meanwhile, the O'Leary affair provided plenty of material for public discussion. Many callers to sports talk radio programs said the incident simply validated or increased their already negative perception of big-time college athletics. Outside of the sports world, many individuals quoted in media stories said it was "no big deal" because "everyone lies on their resume."

After spending two seasons as an assistant coach for the Minnesota Vikings, O'Leary returned to college football in 2004 as head coach at the University of Central Florida.

- Who is responsible for the embarrassment experienced by Notre Dame — O'Leary (for providing false information on his resume) or the university (for not verifying the details of his resume before the hiring)?

- Do you agree with the opinion of those who said the incident validated or increased their already negative opinion of college sports?

Case Study 9-B   Riley Weston's Little White Lie

In the late 1990s, Hollywood fell in love with Riley Weston. As a writer for the WB Network's hit show *Felicity*, Weston was hailed as a "child prodigy," and *Entertainment Weekly* called her an "up-and-coming 19-year-old" and named her to its list of the "100 Most Creative People in Entertainment." There was only one problem: she wasn't 19; she was 32. Several years earlier, because the best acting roles in television were for teenage girls, she began listing her birth year as 1979 on employment applications. She had also legally changed her name to conceal her previous acting roles playing teenage girls in the early 1980s — when she really was a teenager.

Weston continued the deception continued as she transitioned from acting to writing. Believing that no one would take her seriously as a writer of young-adult television programs and movie screenplays, she continued to present herself as a teenager.

Her real identity and age were revealed after a background check found the social security number she provided belonged to a much older woman — Weston's previous identity. Shortly thereafter, her network contract expired and was not renewed, and Disney Films withdrew its $500,000 offer to write a screenplay.

Weston admitted the deception and apologized to her fans, but railed against the double-standard and Hollywood's obsession with youth. "If I were getting a job in any other industry, would anyone care how old I am?" she asked reporters.

Today, Weston is an actress (portraying women closer to her real age), singer, voice-over performer, and novelist. Her first book, *Before I Go*, was published in 2006.

- Does the frustration of dealing with what Weston called "Hollywood's double standard and obsession with youth" justify her deception?

- Is this a case of the ends justifying the means?

- Is there a tendency to excuse what Weston did by saying that it's "just show business"?

Discussion Problem 9-A   Competing Loyalties

Your best friend is an executive with a major consumer products company. You work for the same company, but in a different department, and while you occasionally see your friend at work, you see her more often socially.

Your friend is successful in her job and well thought-of among her superiors, subordinates, and peers, but a competitor has offered her a better job that will increase her salary and benefits while requiring her to relocate to a different city. Your friend is open to the idea of a job change, but says she is leaning toward keeping her current job because she has family and friends in the area, owns a house that she likes, and believes the current employer is one that she would like to work for until retirement. The competing company has given your friend one week to decide about the job offer. You are the only person outside of your friend's family that knows about the situation.

You are one of the few employees invited to a meeting at which you are briefed on the company's secret plan for reorganization. The plan includes a number of options, with most of them including eliminating several departments, consolidating others, and terminating about a quarter of the workforce. Nothing is definite, but regardless of which parts of the plan are implemented, it appears that your friend will be one of the employees let go.

At the beginning of the meeting and again at the end, you are reminded that the content of the meeting is to remain confidential and that you are not allowed to discuss it, either with co-workers, family members, friends, or anyone else.

1. Do you tell your friend about what you know so she can factor that into her decision? Is your loyalty in this case to your friend or to your employer?

2. What philosophers or philosophies from Chapter 2 would help you make this decision?

Discussion Problem 9-B

**Harry and Sally's Letters
of Recommendation**

Dr. I. C. Waterboyle is an award-winning chemistry professor at Enormous State University. This morning he received an email from Harry, a former student, asking for a letter of recommendation for a job with a new chemical firm coming to town. Attached to the email is a job description for the position. Dr. Waterboyle remembers Harry as an average student who made mostly C's and did only the minimum amount of work to get by. He does not respond to the email, but instead moves it to a folder labeled "to do later." He intends to write the letter, but is too busy to do it today.

The next day, Dr. Waterboyle is at Shoppalott Mall and runs into Sally, a former student who once worked for him as a research assistant. He remembers her as an excellent student and research assistant who made all A's. They talk mainly about what is happening with the university's football team, and neither mentions anything about Sally's career or the new company.

When he arrives at his office, Dr. Waterboyle starts to write the letter for Harry, but then has a thought: Sally, who may or may not know about the new chemical company, would be a much better fit for the job (based on the job description) than Harry.

1. What should Dr. Waterboyle do?

   a. Write the letter for Harry because he asked for it, and even though he may not be the best fit, he should protect the confidential nature of the communication and reward him for his initiative in finding and pursuing the job opportunity.

   b. Contact Sally and ask if she is interested in the job. If she is, he will write the letter for her only. If she is not interested, he should write the letter for Harry.

   c. Write letters for both former students and let the company decide which one is best.

   d. He should not write the letter for Harry if he does not have confidence in him, regardless of what he does for Sally.

2. Would you answer change if Dr. Waterboyle had responded to and promised to write the letter for Harry before he ran into Sally? What if Sally had asked Dr. Waterboyle if he knew of any jobs in the area?

3. Which of the following interests should Dr. Waterboyle be most concerned with?

   a. Rewarding Harry for his initiative in locating the job opportunity.

   b. Rewarding Sally for being a much better student.

   c. Helping the chemical company hire the better candidate.

   d. Protecting his reputation and that of the university for the success or failure of its graduates.

Discussion Problem 9-C   Traveling on Company Business

You're traveling on company business and spend three nights in a business-oriented hotel, charging expenses to your personal credit card. Your employer's procedure for business travel is for employees to save their receipts from hotels, rental car agencies, and restaurants and submit them for reimbursement upon returning to the office. Upon checking out of the hotel, you fill out a guest survey card in which you complain about several problems with your room, including leaky plumbing, a broken thermostat, poor reception on the television, and difficulty with the wireless Internet access.

You submit your receipts to the company's travel department and within a few days are reimbursed for your total travel expenses of $800. The following day you get an email from the hotel manager apologizing for the problems with the room and notifying you that a refund in the amount of $125 (the cost of one night's stay) will be posted to your credit card.

1. Do you report this to your employer and pass along the refund?

2. Which of the philosophers or concepts discussed in Chapter 2 might help you make this decision?

Discussion Problem 9-D   The Reverse Reference Call

A few months ago, you changed jobs. Although you are happy in your new job and it has turned out to be better than your old one, you are still bothered by the negative circumstances under which you left your previous employer. While there were several positive aspects to the old job, they were outweighed (in your opinion) by the negatives, which included sexual harassment (affecting several of your co-workers, but not you) and a lack of advancement opportunities for women and minorities. Now that several months have gone by and you're enjoying the new job, you've decided to put the experience behind you and get on with your career.

One day at your new job you receive a phone call from a person who is a finalist, but has not yet been offered, your job at the old company. She asks you for your candid assessment of the company and the people who work there.

1. What do you say?

   a. Tell the whole story — positives and negatives.

   b. Tell the person only the positives.

   c. Tell the person only the negatives.

   d. Decline to volunteer information, but agree to answer specific questions.

   e. Decline to answer; it's not your business.

2. Which of the philosophers or concepts discussed in Chapter 2 might help you make this decision?

Discussion Problem 9-E   Overheard at the Coffee Shop

You're a professor at Enormous State University, and you're in the campus coffee shop reading today's newspaper. While trying to avoid the appearance of eavesdropping, you can't avoid overhearing a conversation between two university staff members (not professors) talking about a specific candidate for student government president. The conversation is mostly about the student's alleged drug and alcohol use, past problems with eating disorders, and sexual behavior. At one point, one of the individuals in the conversation, speaking loud enough for others in the coffee shop to hear, says she can't believe the university would "allow such a drunken slut to represent the university."

You become even more concerned when you realize the student being talked about is a student in your class, a highly thought-of student in your department, and a friend of your daughter. You believe you know the woman well enough to know the accusations are false.

1. What do you do?

    a. Take the two employees aside and advise them their conduct is inappropriate and offensive.

    b. Speak to the employees' supervisor about their inappropriate and offensive conduct.

    c. Contact the university office in charge of supervising the student body election, under the reasoning that such gossip interferes with the fair election process.

    d. Contact the student and offer to serve as a witness if she chooses to file a formal complaint or sue for slander.

    e. Some combination of a, b, c, and/or d.

    f. Do nothing; it's not your business.

2. Which of the philosophers or concepts discussed in Chapter 2 might help you make this decision?

Discussion Problem 9-F   **At the Mall, No News Is Good News**

At a major shopping mall in your community, business has been slowing declining for several years. The two anchor stores are doing an average amount of business, but the smaller stores in between are struggling because of the reduced number of customers. The movie theatres inside the mall have closed, along with a major restaurant and half of the vendors in the food court.

Owners of the struggling stores blame the problems on the physical condition of the mall, including the failure of the management company to upgrade the heating, air conditioning, and plumbing systems. In addition, the company has reduced the number of security guards it employs, even after an increase in the number of assaults and vehicle break-ins in the parking lot.

A business reporter for the local newspaper is developing a lengthy investigative story about conditions at the mall. Along with a photographer, he spends an afternoon walking around the mall and interviewing store managers and other employees. Representatives of the management company refuse to be interviewed, however. A few days after the story is published, several of the store managers and employees quoted in the newspaper are fired by their companies, which were informed by the mall management company about a clause in their leases that reads, "Employees of mall stores are prohibited from criticizing the management company in media interviews or any other public venue." That development generates another newspaper story that is critical of both the management company (for having such an unusual clause in its leases) and the companies that fired the employees (for not contesting the clause and protecting the rights of their employees).

1. Does the clause in the lease violate the employees' First Amendment rights?

2. If you were the public relations representative advising the companies that leased space in the mall, what would your advice be?

3. If you were the public relations representative advising the mall management company, what would your advice be?

Discussion Questions

901. Does "religious harassment" and "political harassment" warrant the same concern on the part of employers as cases of racial and sexual harassment? Because most expressions of religious or political beliefs are protected by the First Amendment (while sexual comments and advances are clearly not), is there a potential for this being a Constitutional issue?

902. The landmark case in the area of sexual harassment was argued in 1986. In your opinion, has the problem gotten better or worse in the three decades since that case was argued?

Notes

240   **Other examples of workplace dishonesty:** Amy Joyce, "When Do Workplace Lies Cross the Line?" *The Washington Post,* April 16, 2008.

241   **In a 1991 article in *Entrepreneurial Woman*:** Alison Bell, "What Price Ethics?" *Entrepreneurial Woman,* January/February 1991, p. 68.

242   **One reported incident:** "Ten Tall Tales Told on Resumes." CNN.com, August 13, 2008.

242   **his $1.1 million annual bonus:** David Callahan, *The Cheating Culture: Why More Americans are Doing Wrong to Get Ahead.* New York: Harcourt, 2002, pp. 12-13.

242   **"Even if your friends and co-workers are doing it":** Bruce Weinstein, "Lying on Your Resume Isn't Part of the Game." Syndicated newspaper column, November 18, 2006.

243   **"hiring the wrong person is a very expensive mistake":** Phyllis Korkki, "Is Your Online Identity Spoiling Your Chances?" *New York Times*, October 10, 2010, p. 8.

243   **As a result of this trend:** Mary Beth Marklein, "Is There Any Truth to Today's Resumes?" *USA Today,* February 6, 2003, p. 1-A.

244   **In a 2009 article:** Todd Bavol, "Salary Negotiation is a Tricky Business." *Northwest Florida Business Climate,* May 2009, pp. 14-15.

245   **"As faculty members, our first responsibility":** Tod Burke, "Should Student-Professor Communication be Privileged?" *The Chronicle of Higher Education,* December 2001.

247   **"If you work at a Fortune 500 company":** "More Companies Monitor Employee E-Mail." Associated Press report, March 11, 2002.

249   **"Due to a selfish and thoughtless act many years ago":** "Academic, Athletic Irregularities Force Resignation." ESPN News, December 14, 2001.

249   **"George has acknowledged inaccuracies":** "O'Leary Admits Resume is False, Quits Irish." *New York Daily News,* December 15, 2001.

249   **"I can't understand how could go all those years":** "O'Leary Out at Notre Dame After One Week." SportsIllustrated.com, December 14, 2001.

CHAPTER 10

When Ethical Issues Become Legal Issues

The First Amendment and Political Speech

What the Amendment Says (and Doesn't Say)

The First Amendment to the U.S. Constitution reads:

> *Congress shall make no law respecting an establishment of religion, or prohibiting the free exercise thereof; or abridging the freedom of speech, or of the press; or the right of the people peaceably to assemble, and to petition the government for a redress of grievances.*

In order to fully understand the First Amendment, you must first consider the following ways in which it has been interpreted and sometimes misinterpreted:

1. A common misconception is that the First Amendment exists only for journalists, and only journalists can benefit from it. When James Madison wrote the First Amendment in 1791, he wasn't thinking about journalists as much as he was thinking about the ordinary citizen on the street. He did include a clause about freedom of the press, but historians believe that he was more concerned about freedom of speech in general — the right of citizens to express opinions on political and social issues — than the rights of the journalism profession.

2. The First Amendment is not just for the benefit of people or organizations that want to disseminate information — it's also for the benefit of the people who want or need to receive that information. Even if you never work in journalism or broadcasting, write a letter to the editor, work in the entertainment industry, or stand in front of the city council and make a political speech, you still benefit from the

First Amendment because you are a potential receiver of information provided by others.

The Supreme Court has made this point several times in recent cases dealing with the rights of advertisers. The court has ruled that the First Amendment protects not only the rights of the advertisers to send information — but also the rights of consumers to receive that information if they choose to.

3. The First Amendment cannot be superseded by state or local laws or government actions. Because of the Fourteenth Amendment's "equal protection" clause, an individual's national citizenship takes priority over his or her citizenship of a state, county, or city. Therefore, no state or local law can invalidate or take priority over a federal law or constitutional right.

In cases involving freedom of expression, the equal protection clause means that because the federal government cannot restrict one's free-speech rights, neither can a state, county, or city government or agency.

Many states have free-speech clauses in their constitutions, but most simply reinforce rights already guaranteed by the federal constitution.

4. Many provisions of the First Amendment are not supported by public opinion. When communication researchers conduct surveys on freedom of speech, they consistently find that the public tends to support free speech as an abstract concept, but not in the specific cases such as those involving flag-burning, pornography, or other matters dealing with decisions of taste.

In the years following the September 11, 2001 terrorist attacks, support for First Amendment freedoms such as the rights of individuals to criticize the government and the rights of journalists to scrutinize American military operations overseas dropped dramatically. More recent surveys indicate support for the First Amendment has rebounded somewhat.

The First Amendment Center at Vanderbilt University conducts an annual "State of the First Amendment" survey regarding public understanding of and support for the First Amendment. The survey question showing the most change in the last 15 years asks individuals if they agree or disagree with the statement, *The First Amendment goes too far in the rights it guarantees.* The following table indicates how responses changed significantly between 1999 and 2002 (with the events of September 11 being the intervening variable), but have rebounded since:

	agree	disagree
2014	38	57
2010	17	79
2006	18	76
2002	49	47
1999	28	67

The 2014 results are those of a telephone poll commissioned by the First Amendment Center and conducted by Gallup, Inc., in May 2014, with a sample size of 1,006 individuals aged 18 and older. The margin for error was plus or minus 3.2 points. Similar questions, methodology, sample sizes, and margins for error applied to previous surveys. Copyright 2014 the First Amendment Center. Used by permission.

Two questions not asked on the 2014 version of the survey dealt with offensive song lyrics and burning the American flag as a form of political protest. Between 1999 and 2010, the percentage of responses indicating support for musicians choosing to sing offensive lyrics in public increased from 56 to 68 percent. On the issue of flag-burning, surveys indicated the number of responses in favor of a law prohibiting such speech dropped from 51 to 38 percent between 1999 and 2010.

Levels of Speech

Most types of speech can be classified as either obtrusive or non-obtrusive (or unobtrusive). **Obtrusive speech** means the material is forced onto others or cannot be easily avoided. Examples include communication that occurs in a public place and is amplified by a megaphone. **Non-obtrusive speech** is that which occurs in times, places, and manners that make it easy to avoid. Examples include forms of entertainment found in an indoor movie theater or video rental store.

The majority of speech falls somewhere between the two extremes. Examples include broadcasting or outdoor advertising. While some would argue that both are obtrusive (and the Supreme Court has ruled that television and radio have the *potential* to be obtrusive), they are easier to avoid than some of the examples listed above.

What Does the First Amendment Really Mean?

For the first 180 years of its existence, the First Amendment's free speech clause was looked at in a context of dissemination, meaning that it dealt almost exclusively with the rights of communicators to speak or publish. It wasn't until the latter half of the twentieth century that three other aspects of the free speech clause were debated: the First Amendment *right of confidentiality*, the First Amendment *right of access*, and the First Amendment *right of editorial control*.

Right of confidentiality refers to the media's claim that they have the right to protect the identity of their sources. As of 2014, 41 states and the District of Columbia have **shield laws** that protect this privilege, but the right is not absolute. In numerous cases, the courts have ruled that a state's shield law does not allow reporters to protect the identity of their sources in cases in which the needs of law enforcement outweighed the reporters' right to protect their confidential relationships. In states without shield laws, courts have the option of recognizing a broader, common-law concept called **journalistic privilege**, which in essence provides journalists with protection only in the case being decided.

Because of the inconsistency in the degree of protection that the 42 shield laws provide, and the fact that nine states have no shield laws at all, Congress has on occasion debated the potential for a national shield law that would provide uniform protection and take priority over all state shield laws. The most recent debate took place in 2008, but no laws to that effect were passed.

Right of access is the media's claim that they should have nearly unlimited access to news events and locations. The courts agree that as a general principle, the media must have access to news events and locations in order to do an effective job of gathering news. But the courts have also ruled that such rights can be limited in certain situations involving judicial procedure and the safety and privacy of trial witnesses and crime victims. The courts have also ruled that journalists cannot have unlimited access to the sites of automobile accidents, airplane crashes, or other dangerous situations. The latter rulings are based on concern for the privacy of accident victims and the potential for journalists and photographers to interfere with the work of emergency personnel (this issue is discussed in more detail later in this chapter).

Right of editorial control refers to the media's claim that in addition to their right to disseminate information, they also has the right to determine what information they *do not disseminate*. One example is found on the newspaper editorial page. While most newspapers do a good job of publishing a balance of letters to the editor and often invite outside experts to submit guest editorials (a more complex version of a letter to the editor), they are under no legal obligation to do so.

In terms of advertising, courts have ruled that the right of editorial control means that media outlets have the right to deny advertising space or time to companies whose products or services they view as harmful to society or too controversial. Many major television networks, as well as local stations, for example, have policies of not accepting advertising for controversial products such as firearms, alcoholic beverages, fireworks, or contraceptives; or businesses such as adult bookstores and video stores, massage parlors, escort services, or abortion clinics. The principle of providing media outlets with this leeway dates back to the country's founding. In the late 1700s, for example, newspaper publisher Benjamin Franklin quipped that his newspaper "was not a stagecoach with seats on it for everyone."

The same rules do not apply to political advertising on television and radio, however, because of Federal Elections Commission and Federal Communications Commission rules about candidates' access to advertising.

The Hierarchy of First Amendment Protection

Legal scholars who follow the decisions of the U.S. Supreme Court have found that certain types of expression consistently get treated in certain ways. Those patterns, while not foolproof, do provide some degree of predictability as to the outcome of cases. One of the most common ways those patterns are expressed is known as the "hierarchy of First Amendment protection," which includes nine forms of communication arranged on three tiers: those deserving the highest level of protection, those deserving some degree of protection but not protection that is absolute, and those that deserve no Constitutional protection whatsoever.

At the highest level of protection — nearly absolute — are categories referred to as political speech and religious expression. **Political speech** is defined as "news or opinion about government or public affairs." **Religious expression** is any communication related to a person's spiritual beliefs, or lack thereof. Like any other form of speech, political speech and religious expression can be spoken, written, published, or broadcast; and may take the form of leaflets, posters, or public oratory.

At the middle level on the hierarchy are forms of speech that receive some (but not absolute) protection. Those forms of expression include **commercial speech** (truthful advertising and most public relations materials), **hate speech,** (defined in the following section), and **non-obscene sexual expression** (entertainment of a sexual nature that does not meet the definition of obscenity).

At the bottom of the hierarchy are forms of expression that receive no protection at all — **defamation, false advertising, fighting words,** and **obscenity.**

HIGHEST LEVEL OF PROTECTION	Political speech Religious expression
SOME PROTECTION, BUT NOT ABSOLUTE	Commercial speech Hate speech Non-obscene sexual expression
NO PROTECTION	Defamation False advertising Fighting words Obscenity

Clarifications on the First Amendment Hierarchy

Is corporate advertising political or commercial speech? Many forms of communication are difficult to categorize, as they may contain elements of both political and commercial speech. When the courts must decide if a specific communication is political speech or commercial speech, they do so based on content — not on who is speaking or in what format. For example, private companies often use paid advertising to encourage voters to approve or reject issues at the ballot box. But just because the company is a commercial interest doesn't automatically make it commercial speech — the company still has the right of political speech, and the fact that the company had to pay to put it in the form of an advertisement does not disqualify it from being political speech.

The government and the courts do not consistently recognize the difference between advertising and public relations, however. The Federal Trade Commission — the government agency responsible for enforcing truth-in-advertising laws and other forms of advertising regulation — often looks at public relations materials as though they were simply a variation of advertising and uses the blanket term "commercial speech" to refer to both forms of communication. The court system also does not recognize the distinction, unless the public relations materials clearly address political issues, in which case they qualify for a higher degree of First Amendment protection.

Hate speech vs. fighting words. The categories of hate speech and fighting words are commonly confused, but are quite different in the eyes of the court system. **Hate speech** is defined as hostile (but non-violent) speech aimed at a group of people (not specific individuals) based on race, religion, ethnicity, sex, or sexual orientation. **Fighting words** are direct personal insults made against a specific person or persons in their presence, those words "which by their very utterance inflict injury or tend to incite an immediate breach of the peace." The First Amendment, the courts have ruled, "does not protect a speaker who eggs his audience on to commit a violent act, whether against himself or against others."

Commercial speech vs. false advertising. Commercial speech — a euphemism for truthful advertising and most forms of communication used by public relations professionals — receives some degree of First Amendment protection because, while not as important as political speech (such as journalism), it is nevertheless a source of consumer information.

How does the government regulate advertising and not violate the First Amendment? Tobacco companies are not allowed to advertise their products on television or billboards located in certain areas of the community. The Federal Communications Commission enforces rules about the advertising on television and radio, and the FTC enforces rules about advertising in general. The U.S. Postal Service enforces rules about direct mail advertising. City and county governments enforce rules about the size, location, and content of outdoor advertising.

While truthful advertising receives some (but not absolute) protection, false advertising receives no protection (see Chapter 6).

Obscenity vs. non-obscene sexual expression. The terms **pornography** and **obscenity** are often confused, but they are quite different in the eyes of the courts and federal regulators. **Pornography** is an artistic term rather than a legal term. In most cases, it falls under the category of **non-obscene sexual expression** — meaning that the government can regulate it, but cannot prohibit it altogether.

In several cases, the Supreme Court has referred to pornography as being "protected speech, but only marginally so" and as speech that deserves a place "on the outer fringes of First Amendment protection." **Obscenity** is a legal term used to refer to material of a sexual nature that is so offensive that it deserves no Constitutional protection.

How does the government regulate non-obscene sexual expression without violating the First Amendment? City and county governments have zoning rules regarding the location of adult businesses. Publishers of adult magazines must abide by postal regulations about how they are mailed. Many states also have rules about the sale of adult material to minors.

The Supreme Court and Political Speech

When considering cases involving political speech, there are six guidelines the Supreme Court follows that are nearly absolute.

Strict scrutiny. Also called "heavy burden of proof," **strict scrutiny** refers to the court's tendency to place the burden of proof on the government to explain why it needs to restrict speech, as opposed to a citizen's obligation to explain why his or her speech should not be restricted.

A state legislature may have good intentions when it attempts to prohibit controversial forms of expression such as pornography, exhibitions of hate speech, and flag-burning (as a form of political protest), but when those laws are challenged, lawyers defending the statutes will likely be unable to prove to the satisfaction of the court that the state's interest in limiting speech outweighs the First Amendment values at stake.

Content neutrality. The principle of **content neutrality** means that government restrictions on speech cannot be based on content, but can be based on the **time, place, and/or manner** of the speech.

3/23

Dr. B said
3 categories

Although the concept of time, place, and manner was used in free speech cases in the 1930s, it is more commonly associated with a 1941 case. A religious group in New Hampshire staged a parade through a downtown area without the necessary city permit, and the group's leaders were promptly arrested. Claiming that the requirement to secure a permit violated three of its First Amendment rights — speech, religion, and assembly — the group appealed the convictions. Prosecutors claimed that parade permits were necessary — not to decide who could have a parade and who couldn't — but so local officials could know about the parade ahead of time in order to provide security personnel and trash pickup and to prevent problems caused by two or more groups wanting to have a parade at the same time. The Supreme Court agreed, and in issuing the decision, used a term that would become a major principle in First Amendment cases for the next seven decades (and probably beyond) — that of "time, place, and manner." The case is significant because it reaffirmed what the Supreme Court had stated in previous cases: that free speech rights are not absolute and that "reasonable" restrictions were permissible.

Over the next 70 years, a number of similar court rulings have been based on the same principle. In making such rulings, the courts often differentiate between a **traditional public forum** (a location where controversial speech is common) and a **limited public forum** (a location where controversial speech might be encountered, but conditions demand that it be limited).

Most traditional public forums take one of three forms:

Physical forums include the National Mall in Washington D.C. (historically, the scene of political protests for decades) or other locations where individuals or groups often carry protest signs or distribute literature.

Passive forums include bulletin boards in public places and the newspaper editorial page.

Electronic forums include Internet discussion groups, blogs, electronic mail distribution lists, and social networking programs such as Facebook and Twitter.

Examples of limited public forums include airport terminals, public libraries, and other places where political and religious activity can be limited. Courts sometimes use the term **non-public forum** to refer to prisons, military bases, and other government-supervised venues where expression can be limited with little or no recourse.

The courts have ruled that at shopping centers and malls, individuals and groups have the right of political speech, even though those locations are private property. The controversies in this area began in the 1960s when groups opposing the Vietnam War attempted to distribute literature at shopping centers across the country. In a landmark case involving a shopping center in Portland, Oregon, the Supreme Court determined that the management of the shopping center had the right to limit speech that took place on the property as long as the rules were fair and treated all groups equally; it could not allow one group to protest while denying the same right to groups expressing opposing viewpoints. Following that ruling, many state legislatures adopted laws in the 1970s (that are still applied today) that prohibit shopping center owners from banning political speech, based on the principle of "equivalent function." Because those shopping centers were gathering places for large numbers of people, they were the equivalent of public places in terms of free speech protection. While shopping center owners retained the right

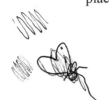

to prohibit commercial speech and any behavior that endangers the shopping center's customers or employees, they cannot interfere with the peaceful distribution of literature that is political in nature. Collectively, these state laws are known as **equivalent function rules** or **rules of quasi-public places**.

Even though the laws are inconsistent with its ruling in the Oregon case, the Supreme Court has ruled that equivalent function rules are constitutional because they expand free-speech rights rather than limit them.

Today, many sports stadiums and arenas have similar problems because while they are publicly owned, they are often leased to private interests for events. In those circumstances, most "equivalent function" rules would allow the party leasing the stadium or arena to regulate commercial speech but not political speech.

Overbreadth and vagueness. The courts generally uphold laws limiting speech that serve legitimate objectives, but they require those laws to be as narrow and specific as possible. The courts generally invalidate laws that are too open-ended or based on terms that are too difficult to define.

The Supreme Court describes such laws as "over-inclusive" or **overbroad** or **vague.** While the two terms are sometimes lumped together, they are actually different legal concepts. "Overbreadth" refers to those laws that the Supreme Court finds to be in violation of the First Amendment because they restrict speech more than necessary.

"Vagueness" refers to laws that the Supreme Court finds to be in violation of the First Amendment because they are so loosely written that potential speakers would not know ahead of time that such speech was prohibited.

Conduct vs. speech. The Supreme Court generally upholds laws and lower court rulings restricting a person's conduct, but strikes down those that attempt to limit speech or expression. Two opposing cases in this area are a 1968 case that involved a war protestor burning his draft card and a 1989 case involving a protestor burning the American flag as a form of political protest.

In the draft card case, the court ruled that government had the right to prosecute the individual for burning his draft card because the charge was "destruction of government property" and was not related to his motives in protesting the war.

Twenty-one years later, the Supreme Court made the opposite ruling regarding flag burning, determining that it was political speech rather than conduct and fell within the individual's First Amendment rights. Justice William Brennan, writing the majority opinion, made three significant points: (1) the Court cannot find something illegal just because it is objectionable or distasteful; (2) expression of dissatisfaction with the government is at the core of the First Amendment; and (3) the country is strong enough to withstand this type of critical speech.

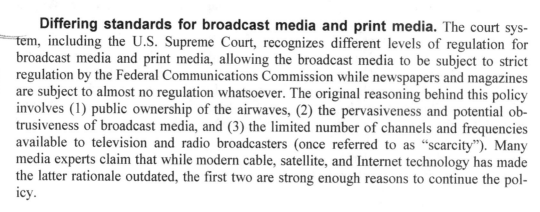

Differing standards for broadcast media and print media. The court system, including the U.S. Supreme Court, recognizes different levels of regulation for broadcast media and print media, allowing the broadcast media to be subject to strict regulation by the Federal Communications Commission while newspapers and magazines are subject to almost no regulation whatsoever. The original reasoning behind this policy involves (1) public ownership of the airwaves, (2) the pervasiveness and potential obtrusiveness of broadcast media, and (3) the limited number of channels and frequencies available to television and radio broadcasters (once referred to as "scarcity"). Many media experts claim that while modern cable, satellite, and Internet technology has made the latter rationale outdated, the first two are strong enough reasons to continue the policy.

Compelled speech. The Supreme Court has ruled that just as the First Amendment does not allow the government to limit an individual's right to speak, it also means that individuals or organizations cannot be required to participate in speech to which they object. The first conflict of this nature was a 1943 case in West Virginia in which the Supreme Court ruled that school children could not be required to recite the Pledge of Allegiance if their families' religious beliefs forbade it.

It was a 1977 case, however, which set the modern standard for similar cases. A New Hampshire couple objected to the state motto, "Live Free or Die," on their car license plate. They covered the slogan with masking tape and were charged by the state of New Hampshire with defacing the plate. When the case was appealed to the Supreme Court, the court ruled in favor of the couple on two grounds: first, because of strict scrutiny (the state failed to prove that the couple's actions were harmful); and second, because the couple was simply "opting out" of speech to which they objected.

Since that ruling, many other compelled speech cases have resulted in similar rulings. Government employees cannot be required to sign pledges to support or oppose a political philosophy. Physicians working in government-run health clinics cannot be required to counsel patients against abortion. In a 1995 case, the Supreme Court ruled that a private association organizing a community parade could not be required to include in the parade those groups to which the association objected. In terms of advertising, both print media and broadcast media have the right to refuse commercial advertising without stating a reason.

In the 1980s, the Court applied the compelled speech rule to the manner in which labor unions and professional organizations collect money from their members and spend it to support political candidates and issues to which some members objected. As a result of such cases, the Federal Elections Commission and many state governments have enacted laws requiring groups to segregate the money they collect from members into required contributions (that may not be spent on political activities) and voluntary contributions (that may be spent on political activities).

In the 1990s, the Supreme Court considered whether the compelled speech rule applied in cases in which college students objected to how their student activity fees were used to fund campus activities (such as student newspapers or athletics) in which they had no interest or student organizations involved in controversial causes. The Court ruled in favor of universities, rejecting the students' "compelled speech" claims.

In the early 2000s, the Court applied the compelled speech rule to conflicts that began when the U.S. Department of Agriculture and other government agencies attempted to force agricultural companies to contribute to special funds that would be used to promote those products through media campaigns. In those cases, the Court ruled in favor of the agricultural companies and determined they should not be required to fund the promotional programs.

Prior Restraint vs. Punishment After the Fact

Government regulation of speech takes two forms: prior restraint and punishment after the fact.

Prior restraint (commonly called "censorship") is a legal term referring to the actions of a government agency or official to cut off speech at the source or stop it before it is spoken, published, or broadcast. That principle is inconsistent with the libertarian philosophy that allows for complete freedom of expression.

Punishment after the fact is based on the philosophy of English legal scholar William Blackstone (see Chapter 2, p. 27), who believed that not even the most controversial forms of speech should be prohibited. Much like libertarians such as John Milton, Blackstone believed that citizens should be able to hear all points of view and decide for themselves what was true and what was false, and what was important and what was trivial. Blackstone applied one caveat to the libertarian philosophy, however — that speakers, writers, and publishers must stand behind their words and be prepared to accept responsibility for whatever harm was caused. As a result, those individuals could be prosecuted under appropriate laws such as those involving copyrights, defamation, or obscenity. Paraphrased, Blackstone might have said, "think before you speak" and "think before you publish." Today, the principle of not allowing for censorship, but allowing instead for punishment after the fact, is known as the **Blackstonian Doctrine.**

Copyrights and Trademarks

The Basics of Intellectual Property

Copyrights and trademarks are part of a larger area of law known as **intellectual property**, a term that refers to the rights of individuals and organizations to protect their creative products. In the United States, intellectual property law is grounded in Article I, Section 8, Clause 8 of the Constitution, which seeks to "promote the progress of science and the useful arts, by securing for limited times to authors and inventors the exclusive right to their respective writings and discoveries."

The four areas of intellectual property law recognized at the federal level are copyrights, trademarks, trade secrets, and patents. In many states, trade secrets are also protected by state law.

Trade secrets and patents are of primary interest to company attorneys and engineers and seldom affect the work of professional communicators. While an organization's attorneys are also primarily responsible for protecting its copyrights and trademarks, professional communicators should still be knowledgeable of the basics of the law and assist the organization in protecting those assets.

Copyright refers to the legal protection for creative works such as internal and external publications, research reports, videos, and material appearing on a website. A **trademark** provides protection for an organization's name or logo, or that of a product or service.

Copyright Basics

History of copyright law. American copyright law has been expanded over the years to cover art prints, music, photographs, and paintings. In addition to being revised to cover different forms of expression, copyright laws have also been expanded to include all of the various recording methods that have been developed, including phonograph records, motion picture film, audio tape, video tape, computer software, compact disks, and digital video disks.

The first specific copyright law was enacted by Congress in 1790, and major revisions were enacted in 1909, 1976, and 1998. Elements of all three revisions are still in effect today and are discussed later in this section.

Copyright eligibility. Ideas cannot be copyrighted, but a fixed or tangible expression of an idea, such as that expressed in a film, video, drawing, photograph, or piece of fiction or non-fiction writing, can be. Although it may not be in a fixed form to the same degree as material printed on paper or recorded on tape or film, much of the content found on the Internet is eligible for copyright protection (and in most cases is protected).

A copyright deals only with ownership; it has nothing to do with truth, quality, or social value. One could publish a magazine with content consisting entirely of falsehoods, and it would still be eligible for a copyright (the potential for libel claims would be a separate problem). The same rule applies to quality and taste; the copyright office makes no judgments about how good or how bad the product is. A poorly written novel or movie script or tasteless pornographic film is nonetheless eligible for copyright protection.

One criteria the courts use to determine eligibility for copyright protection is the amount of originality or creativity that was involved in the development of the work. The **originality and creativity principle** was the deciding factor in several major Supreme Court cases involving conflicts between intellectual property law and the First Amendment. The basic principle is that the more originality and creativity involved in the creation of a work, the greater amount of copyright protection it receives. The courts generally rule that facts are not "created" but only "discovered," and therefore a simple presentation of facts, without any creative arrangement or interpretation, is not deserving of copyright protection.

Example: If a history professor writes a book about the Civil War that is only a chronological presentation of known facts — without interpretation or commentary on those facts — it would not receive much copyright protection. But if the author presents those same facts about the Civil War and then adds some opinion, interpretation, or commentary, that increases the amount of copyright protection because the author has expended more effort. If the author then uses the Civil War as the backdrop for a historical novel — starting with known historical facts and adding fictional characters and dialogue — it receives even more protection because of the greater degree of creativity and effort involved.

Generally, fiction gets more protection than non-fiction. Collections of facts have very little protection, so companies that compile mailing lists, telephone directories, and computer databases find it difficult to protect them because of court rulings that no special effort, creativity, or skill is involved in compiling them.

Copyright notice. The copyright notice consists of three parts: the copyright symbol (or the word "copyright"), the year of completion, and identification of the copyright holder. Examples:

© 2015 Kendall-Hunt Publishing

copyright 2015 Kendall-Hunt Publishing

In order for a work to receive full copyright protection, the holder must submit a form to the government and pay a small fee. For most items, two copies must be submitted — one for the copyright office to keep on file, and the other to be on file at the Library of Congress. Although a work is copyrighted once it is in a fixed form and registration is not required, such action is still recommended and is legally advantageous (the concept of an "unregistered" or "common law copyright" is discussed later in this chapter).

Length of copyright protection. Under current law, copyright protection for work created by an individual lasts for 70 years past the life of the creator. For work created by an organization, copyright protection lasts for 120 years after its creation or 95 years after its first usage, whichever comes first. If copyright ownership changes through sale or inheritance, the original date of the material's creation still applies.

Prior to passage of the Sonny Bono Copyright Term Extension Act of 1998, each of those time periods was 20 years shorter. The new terms now apply retroactively to works created prior to 1998.

Public domain. Works deemed to be in the **public domain** can be used by others without permission or compensation. Public domain applies to four categories of work:

1. Products for which the copyright has expired, including songs such as "Here Comes the Bride," "Pomp and Circumstance," patriotic marches, and church hymns. A common misconception is that the song "Happy Birthday to You" is in the public domain, but it is not. Warner Communications holds the copyright, which expires in 2030.

2. Products that hold social, cultural, or scientific significance, such as the Bible, the Constitution, the Declaration of Independence, the music and lyrics to "The Star-Spangled Banner," the design for the American flag, or the Periodic Table of the Elements that appears in most chemistry textbooks.

3. Works that are so basic as to have no significant value, such as a calendar, a height/weight chart, or an alphabetical list of state capitals.

4. Documents produced by the federal government. Research reports or other works created by private parties using government funding may be copyrighted, but not government documents such as census reports, economic data, or similar materials.

Proving a copyright claim. An individual or organization that believes that another party has violated copyright law can file a claim of **infringement.** In order to have a successful claim, the plaintiff must prove (1) access (the fact that the defendant had to opportunity to copy the material), and (2) substantial similarity between the two items in question. "Access" is important to prove because it helps to negate one of the common defenses — coincidence. It is often easy for a defendant to claim that the similarity is a coincidence, and difficult for the plaintiff to prove that it was not.

The term *copyright infringement* (a legal term) is often confused with *plagiarism* (an ethical term), but the terms are not interchangeable. If a newspaper reporter takes a wire service story, changes only a few words and then submits it to his newspaper under his byline, he has committed both the legal offense of copyright infringement (for which the wire service could sue the newspaper), and the ethical offense of plagiarism, for which he could be reprimanded by his newspaper. If a student borrows generously from a book in the public domain without proper citation, he or she has not violated copyright law, but is still guilty of plagiarism. Even if a student (or any other individual) acknowledges the source of the work, he or she may still be guilty of copyright infringement if the amount of the material borrowed from the copyrighted work exceeds the provision of fair use (explained on the following page). In other words, attribution or citation is not a defense in copyright infringement cases.

Copyright Act of 1909. The most important component of the 1909 revision is the **works for hire doctrine**, which deals with copyright conflicts between organizations and employees. In short, the doctrine states that products created as part of an employee's assigned work duties belong to the employer and not to the employee.

In the case of freelancers or independent contractors, the rights to their work revert to them after the first usage, unless a written agreement or contract with a "works for hire" clause has been signed by both parties.

Copyright Revision Act of 1976. The 1976 revision of copyright law introduced two concepts that had not been addressed in previous copyright laws: (1) unregistered copyright (sometimes called a common law copyright) and (2) fair use. Both concepts are at the heart of many copyright cases debated today.

Unregistered or "common law" copyright refers to the rights of individuals and organizations to protect their creative works without having formally registered them with the U.S. Copyright Office. Prior to this revision of the law, authors and publishers could not claim copyright infringement for materials that had not been formally registered. While registration is still recommended and is legally advantageous, it is no longer absolutely required. Under the principle of unregistered copyright, an author's work is legally protected as soon as it is completed. A common law copyright gives the copyright holder the right to prevent unauthorized use of his or her work, but not the right to recover financial damages, for which the copyright must be formally registered.

The most common examples of the unregistered copyright principle being applied are in the cases of photographs taken for a model's portfolio or actor's press packet, works of fiction or poetry submitted in amateur writing competitions, and proposals for creative projects such as movie screenplays or television pilots.

Fair use is a set of exemptions in the copyright law that allows for the usage of copyrighted materials for certain nonprofit purposes. The three categories of fair use are (1) news reporting and criticism, (2) classroom teaching and academic research, and (3) parody.

The *news reporting and criticism* provision means that journalists may use "brief and reasonable" excerpts from copyrighted works in published or broadcast news stories without permission. Book reviewers, television critics, and movie critics may also do so. There is no definition for what constitutes "brief" and "reasonable," but since most news stories and reviews are beneficial to the work rather than harmful, this element of fair use is seldom challenged.

The category of *classroom teaching and academic research* has generated mild controversies for decades and affects educators at all levels, from kindergarten through graduate school. The fair use provision allows educators to copy portions of books and periodicals for distribution to students. The rule also applies to broadcast television programs (except those shown on a pay-per-view basis) used in the classroom. Fair use does not apply to computer software.

The main limitations of fair use are that copies must be reasonable in number, not sold for profit, and used for brief periods of time. The 1976 law did not define terms such as "reasonable in number" and "brief periods of time," meaning each case is decided on its own merits.

The concept of *parody* refers to cases in which one work may resemble another, but is different enough to avoid confusion among the audience, such as when entertainers write and perform songs that are similar to better-known works but change the lyrics for the purposes of humor. Courts have ruled that such parodies are not copyright infringement because there is no financial loss suffered by the copyright holder and there is no impact on the potential market for the performer's original material. In addition, parodies are generally protected against copyright infringement cases because many take the form of commentary or criticism and therefore have First Amendment value.

Digital Millennium Copyright Act of 1998. This was first major revision of copyright law since 1976. The DMCA had two main purposes: (1) to address cyberspace issues and (2) to bring U.S. copyright laws into closer alignment with those of other countries. Advocates of the law included lobbyists representing movie producers, television producers, music publishers, and Internet service providers.

The DMCA has two main components:

The **circumvention rule** made it illegal to manufacture or sell software that breaks the encryption codes used in computer-based communication. Advocates of the law said that this rule was not necessary because of technology that existed at the time, but because of what technology might be developed in the future.

The **limited liability rule** relieved online service providers from the responsibility for copyright infringement that takes place on their networks, meaning that ISPs are not required to be the "copyright police." This provision includes, however, a **notification clause** that requires ISPs to remove copyrighted material upon request of the copyright holder. It also provided ISPs with immunity from liability when they remove copyrighted material.

In the same session in which it passed the DMCA, Congress also lengthened the term of copyright extension by 20 years (see details previously in this chapter). The law was named the **Sonny Bono Copyright Term Extension Act** to honor the late musician-turned-congressman who advocated the legislation.

Recent and Ongoing Issues in Copyright Law

Challenges to copyright extension. In 2003, the Sonny Bono Copyright Term Extension Act (CTEA) was challenged by Internet service providers, librarians, and other parties seeking access to copyrighted materials that were originally scheduled to move into the public domain in the near future. In a case that eventually reached the U.S. Supreme Court, the plaintiffs claimed that in adding 20 years to the length of copyright protection, the CTEA was inconsistent with the language of the constitutional origins of copyright law, which used the phrase "limited times." As one example, plaintiffs used the Disney character Mickey Mouse, for which the copyright was set to expire in 2003 but under the new law would continue to be protected until 2023. They also pointed to examples of popular music of the early 1900s that they felt did not deserve further copyright protection.

The Supreme Court, however, ruled that the law was valid and that the new copyright terms were constitutional. Although two dissenting justices argued that the new law might "inhibit new forms of dissemination," the majority ruled that it was not the role of the Court to "second-guess congressional determination and policy judgments of this order" and that the CTEA was not an "impermissible exercise of congressional power." It also determined that the "fair use" provision of copyright law provided the public with sufficient access to protected materials.

Freelance writers and online databases. In the mid-1900s, the National Writers Union and other groups representing freelance writers challenged the policies of the *New York Times* and several other publications, claiming the publications should be required to compensate freelance writers under the "subsequent usage" principle when their work is re-published in electronic databases, which often compensate the publications but not the authors.

When the complaint reached the court system, lower-court rulings sided with the publishers, agreeing with their claim that the electronic versions were simply "revisions" and not subsequent uses of the material. The Supreme Court, however, ruled in favor of the freelancers in 2001. Many of the publications involved in the suit had been selling the database rights for more than 20 years and realized that attempting to retroactively compensate the writers would be problematic, so instead they agreed to withdraw the materials from the databases. In addition, most publishers began requiring freelance journalists to sign "works for hire" agreements that assigned all rights to the publications.

Contributory infringement. Previously applied only to trademark law, the term **contributory infringement** is now applied to copyright law as well. In this case, a contributory infringer is analogous to a criminal accomplice in that he or she does not directly participate in the copyright infringement, but contributes to the violation by providing the method or opportunity.

The first technology for which the principle was applied was coin-operated photocopiers. In the 1970s, when advances in technology caused the price of making photocopies to fall dramatically, publishers of books and magazines worried about the potential loss of business and hoped that the principle of contributory infringement might help them pursue legal action against the public libraries, post offices, grocery stores, or other venues where the photocopiers were located. A series of court rulings, however, ruled that the liability for copyright infringement fell upon the person making the copies, not the company that manufactured the machine or the party that housed it.

In the 1980s, courts made the same rulings in cases involving home video recorders, determining that the responsibility for copyright infringement fell on the person making the copies, not the manufacturers of the equipment.

In the late 1990s and early 2000s, the courts made similar rulings in cases involving the downloading of recorded music. After losing several contributory infringement cases against companies such as Napster, Kazaa, and Grokster, the music industry developed low-cost programs by which customers could legally download music onto portable devices. While music companies still attempt to halt illegal downloads, most concentrate their legal efforts only in the most outrageous cases.

Trademarks

A **trademark** is a legal protection for an organization's name or logo, or that of one of its products or services. Congress established the basis for federal trademark law in 1946 through passage of the **Lanham Act**. The purposes of trademark law are to (1) allow companies a process by which they can discourage imitators and to (2) protect consumers from being confused by similar company names, product names, logos, or advertising characters.

After an initial registration period of five years, a trademark must be renewed every 10 years. Unlike copyrights, which have a finite term, trademarks can be renewed in perpetuity as long as they are still used. A trademark can be lost if its owner fails to use it for a period of two years or longer, or if the term becomes commonly used for similar products. Many companies actively protect their trademarks and take action when journalists (or anyone else) uses those terms generically. Companies such as Xerox, Coca-Cola, and Kleenex, for example, object when their brand names are used to refer to photocopiers, soft drinks, or facial tissues in a general sense.

One specific measure they take is to remind journalists and other parties that the names of their products should always be capitalized rather than lower-cased. While their defensiveness appears unnecessary to some, those companies are simply trying to avoid losing their trademarks in the same way that trademark owners have lost the rights to terms such as *aspirin, band-aids, cornflakes, cellophane, yo-yo,* and *linoleum.* The popularity of consumer electronic devices will likely represent the next challenge to companies attempting to protect their trademarks, as brand names such as *iPhone, iPod, Bluetooth, TiVo,* and *OnStar* may soon become generic terms for similar devices offered by competing companies.

Around the world, the most recognized corporate trademarks include the Nike swoosh, McDonald's arches, the Macintosh apple, and the Olympic rings. In addition to their names and logos, companies also obtain trademark protection for fictional characters that appear on their packaging and in their advertising, such as Tony the Tiger, Ronald McDonald, the Jolly Green Giant, Uncle Ben, Aunt Jemima, the Keebler Elves, Mr. Clean, Betty Crocker, and the Geico Gecko.

Included in trademark law is the concept of a **service mark,** which allows a company or nonprofit organization to protect the name of an intangible concept. A bank, for example, may offer senior customers a special bank-account option and call it a "Silver Savings" account. The service mark would prevent a competing bank from using the name "Silver Savings" to describe its program, but it would not prohibit another bank from offering a similar program under a different name.

Two common complaints in trademark cases are "likelihood of confusion" and "trademark dilution." The term **likelihood of confusion** is applied in cases in which the intentional or unintentional similarity between company or product names or logos creates the false impression that there is an affiliation or endorsement between the two parties. The term **trademark dilution** is applied in cases in which an older, more established company claims that its reputation is harmed by another party's intentional use of a similar name, logo, or other image — usually producing a negative result.

Because litigating trademark cases requires a high burden of proof and involves considerable legal costs, many trademark holders decline to take action except in the most extreme cases. In 2003, for example, lingerie retailer Victoria's Secret pursued a trademark dilution case against an independently owned retail store selling lingerie, pornography, and sex toys under the name Victor's Little Secrets. The larger company lost, however, as the court ruled that few consumers would be misled by the similar names and the alleged damage to its reputation would be difficult to quantify.

In both likelihood of confusion and trademark dilution cases, many other potential plaintiffs are reluctant to take action against non-controversial parties and in other situations in which there is no potential harm to their reputations. For example, the International Olympic Committee holds a trademark on the word "Olympics," but does not enforce it against organizations holding events such as the "Special Olympics" and "Senior Olympics." Likewise, in the 1990s the *Wall Street Journal* declined to take action against a community business organization in Tennessee that titled its newsletter the *Small Street Journal* and used a nameplate similar to that of the national newspaper.

Intellectual Property Issues in the International Marketplace

When the international marketing of books became more common in the late 1800s, it raised the issue of how one nation's copyright laws could be enforced in other countries. Most of the world's industrialized nations agreed on a set of rules called the **Berne Convention for the Protection of Literary and Artistic Works**, a set of rules that requires member countries to respect the copyright laws of other countries without requiring copyright holders to file copyright applications in every country in which a work was distributed.

The United States did not join the convention at first, and throughout much of the 1900s, American book publishers freely republished the work of European authors without compensation to the copyright holders. In the 1980s, American book publishers, movie studios, and music producers realized they were no longer just the perpetrators of copyright infringement but also the victims, so they persuaded the U.S. Congress to join the Berne Convention in 1989.

Today, enforcement of intellectual property law in the global marketplace is a constant challenge for American companies and is part of nearly every trade agreement. One of the most significant of those agreements is the General Agreement on Tariffs and Trade (GATT), passed in 1996, which included an intellectual property provision that was similar to those of the Berne Convention, but applied to a greater number of countries. The rules also applied to trademarks, which are slightly different from copyrights but not covered by the Berne Convention.

Specific problem areas addressed by GATT include music, movies, and computer software, protected by copyright law; clothing, handbags, and jewelry, protected by trademark law; and prescription drugs and sports equipment, covered by patent law. The worst offenders are found in China, Russia, and countries in Eastern Europe and Latin America. Governments in those countries attempt to enforce the rules, but large black markets continue to flourish around the world.

Libel and Privacy

The Basics of Libel Law

Libel is a legal term that refers to the defamation of a person or organization in published or broadcast form. Traditionally, libel law has dealt mostly with mass media outlets such as newspapers, magazines, television, and radio, but recently, courts have attempted, with various degrees of success, to apply libel and privacy laws to the Internet.

The Media Law Resource Center (previously known as the Libel Defense Resource Center) conducts annual studies of libel and privacy litigation nationwide and issues reports that track individual cases as well as overall trends. In recent years, those reports have contained both good news and bad for the news media. The good news is that the total number of cases has gradually decreased over the last 30 years, and the successful defense rate has gradually improved and now exceeds 50 percent (up from 37 percent in the 1980s). The successful defense rate is slightly higher if one considers the number of cases that are reversed on appeal in favor of the media organizations.

The bad news is that in cases won by the plaintiffs, damage awards are increasing exponentially. According to the MLRC, the average jury award in libel and privacy cases won by plaintiffs is approximately $2.85 million. Many publishers and broadcasters have learned that it is often more practical to settle libel claims out of court. Even though the dollar amount paid to the plaintiff is considerably lower, legal fees may still cost an additional $100,000 or more.

A recent example of the trend in large damage awards was the $220.72 million judgment for the plaintiffs a 1997 case in which a Houston-based stock brokerage firm sued the *Wall Street Journal* for libel. Even though the award was overturned on appeal in 1999, the amount of the original trial court judgment is still a record.

The potential cost of libel litigation, as well as the damage to a journalist's reputation and that of his or her employer, are serious concerns for the journalism business and related professions. Journalists and the attorneys who defend them use the term **chilling effect** to refer to the reluctance of journalists and their employers to pursue aggressive or investigative journalism for fear that even the slightest reporting error may result in a multi-million dollar libel suit.

Categories of Libel

There are six major categories of libel:

1. False accusation of a crime. Because of the potential damage to the reputation of a person or organization based on factual errors, crime news is the most heavily edited and scrutinized material published in a newspaper or broadcast on radio or television. Editors require reporters to double-check and sometimes triple-check police reports and court records to ensure accuracy. Suspects are often identified as specifically as possible, including their middle names, ages, addresses, and occupations.

Journalists and other professional communicators should be cautious when using verbs such as *arrested, arraigned, charged, accused,* and *questioned,* as well as legal terms used to classify crimes, such as *burglary, robbery, theft, larceny, rape, sexual assault, murder, homicide,* and *manslaughter.* Each of those terms has a formal legal definition and they should not be used casually or interchangeably. Another precaution that journalists and other professional communicators should take is to use only those terms found in law enforcement documents and court records and not assume that a certain term applies when it has not been used by any official source.

2. False criticism of personal character, habits, or obligations. This could include false claims of promiscuity, dishonesty, cruelty, mental illness, alcoholism, drug abuse, contagious or sexually transmitted diseases, gambling habits, or poor parenting skills. Journalists and other professional communicators should be cautious about the casual use of slang terms or other "red flag" words that may result in libel suits. These include terms such as *deadbeat dad, computer hacker, welfare mother, junkie, adulterer, addict, sex offender, sexual predator, terrorist, drug abuser, town drunk, peeping Tom, slumlord, compulsive gambler, slut, scam artist,* or *ex-convict.* Adjectives requiring caution include *fraudulent, unethical, corrupt, bankrupt,* and *promiscuous.*

Some metaphors that on the surface might appear to be nothing more than hyperbole have the potential to create legal problems if there is a strong negative connotation attached to them. Examples include referring to labor union leaders of as "a gang of thugs using Mafia tactics" or accusing the leader of an environmental group of "pimping for the treehuggers."

3. False criticism of professional performance or competence. News stories or other published documents about physicians accused of performing unnecessary surgeries or over-billing insurance companies are ripe for libel suits if the accusations turn out to be false. And of course, the term *malpractice* should always be used with caution.

4. False criticism of business performance or financial standing. News stories or other published documents that report that a company is in financial trouble, is the target of a lawsuit, or is under government investigation will likely result in a libel suit if the information later proves to be false.

5. Product disparagement. Also known as **trade libel**, this involves criticism of a product rather than an individual or company. Two recent product disparagement cases are worth noting. The first case involved television talk show host Oprah Winfrey, who successfully defended herself against a lawsuit filed by an industry group whose product was criticized on her show. The second case involved a consumer protection publication that defended itself against accusations that it libeled a product about which it published a negative review. While both Winfrey and the magazine were successful in defending themselves, in each case they spent considerable money on legal fees and a great deal of time assisting their attorneys in preparing their cases.

6. False criticism of political or religious beliefs or affiliations. Examples include incorrectly labeling someone as a communist or atheist. These examples vary by state, however. Even though some state defamation laws still list such accusations as potentially libelous, many plaintiffs find it difficult to prove harm. In many states, courts have ruled that racial or ethnic slurs, as well as general name-calling, do not damage a person's reputation and are therefore not grounds for a libel suit.

Components of Libel

In order to have a successful libel claim, a plaintiff must prove six factors:

1. Defamation. Defamation is defined as "communication which has the tendency to so harm the reputation of another as to lower him in the estimation of the community or to deter third persons from associating with him." Defamation does not include embarrassment or hurt feelings.

2. Harm. This element is sometimes included as part of the "defamation" factor and is sometimes listed separately. Generally, "harm" or "damages" refers to injury to a person's reputation, financial condition, or emotional well-being.

3. Identification. In order to have a strong libel claim, a person must be identified directly rather than indirectly. A person mentioned by name can obviously make a successful claim of identification. But if a news story makes a reference to a "high-ranking city official" or "a university administrator," that's not specific enough to constitute identification.

Group libel refers to actions taken by individuals claiming they were defamed by criticisms of a group. The validity of a group libel claim depends on two factors: the size of the group (the larger the group, the less likely the courts will rule in favor of the plaintiff) and the likelihood that an individual would be harmed by libelous information concerning the group. Examples of statements with the potential of sparking group libel cases are that "all lawyers working for firm X are incompetent" or that "all professors at a university Y are convicted criminals."

4. Communication. Once referred to as "publication" because it applied mainly to print journalism, the broader term is more commonly used today because it also applies to broadcast journalism as well as cyberspace. Three parties must be involved in a successful libel action: the publishing or broadcasting entity, the victim, and a third person who can identify the victim. Newspapers and magazines are considered to have *published* if one or more copies are circulated. Radio and television stations are considered to have *communicated* when they air a broadcast. In the case of alleged libel on the Internet, *communication* takes place when a third party has access to the information. In most states, libel laws provide a statute of limitations of one or two years, meaning that plaintiffs have that period of time after that material is communicated to file their complaints with the appropriate court.

5. Fault. The two levels of fault are **negligence** (sometimes called "sloppy reporting") and **actual malice** (also called "reckless disregard for the truth"). Examples of negligence include relying on untrustworthy sources, failure to seek additional information from the person or organization that is the subject of the story, failure to allow that person or organization to respond, failure to check dubious facts, or the failure to read (or the misreading of) pertinent supporting documents. Examples of malice include knowing for certain that a story is false (or having strong suspicions that it might be false), but publishing or broadcasting it without further investigation or fact-checking.

6. Falsity. Generally, plaintiffs in libel cases bear the burden of proving that the published or broadcast information is false. Minor errors, such as incorrect spelling, dates, or similar details that do not affect the audience's understanding of a story, cannot be the basis for a defamation suit.

The Nature of Libel Plaintiffs

Libel plaintiffs fall into one of the following categories: (1) living persons and (2) organizations (businesses or nonprofit associations). Common law provides three general rules concerning certain types of plaintiffs which, in most cases, do not have legitimate libel claims:

Government units and agencies. In a democratic society, courts have determined, journalists and other citizens have the right to criticize their city, county, state, and federal government, and those government units and agencies cannot be defamed as a result. Although most such criticism would otherwise be protected against libel action by the "fair comment" defense (explained in the following section), common law has provided this additional layer of protection. Individual government employees can sue, however, but only on their own behalf.

Libels of omission. Individuals who believe they should have been mentioned in a positive news story (but were left out) have the right to ask the newspaper or magazine to correct the omission, but do not have grounds for a libel action. Examples include a newspaper story that lists students at the local high school who earned academic awards or college scholarships, or a story that lists all of the citizens of the community who earned awards for military service. While those individuals might claim they were offended by the oversight, the courts have ruled that such omissions are not libelous.

Libel of the dead. The issue of whether family members or other interested parties can sue for libel on behalf of a deceased person varies by state. Only a few state libel statutes allow family members of a deceased person to sue for libel under a concept known as "desecration of memory." Most state laws specify that when individuals die, the right to sue for libel dies with them. Some states do not permit family members to initiate a libel suit after the death of the defamed person, but do allow them to continue a libel suit filed by the individual before his or her death.

Defenses Against Libel Claims

There are three defenses commonly used in libel cases; defendants need to establish only one in order to successfully defend their stories.

1. Truth. If the media organization can prove what it published or broadcast is true, the suit is often thrown out altogether, regardless of other conditions. Terms such as "truth" or "falsity" refer to the details that form the core of the story.

2. Fair comment and criticism. Also known simply as "opinion." The courts have defined an "opinion" as an expression that cannot be proven true or false. Although the U.S. Supreme Court has ruled in numerous cases that there is "no such thing as a false opinion," the fair comment defense actually originated with a New York state court. In a 1930 case, that court ruled that "everyone has a right to comment on matters of public interest and concern, provided they do so fairly and with an honest purpose . . . such comments or criticisms are not libelous, however severe in their terms."

Today, the fair comment and criticism defense exists to allow journalists, commentators, or the general public (acting as individuals or organizations) the right to fairly criticize (1) public officials for their performance in office, and (2) businesses for the quality of their products and services or the performance of their employees. Because they fall into the category of opinion writing, reviews of restaurants, books, films, plays, recorded music, and concerts are also protected under the concept of fair comment because they are based largely on the opinion of the person writing the review. Reviewers and critics can add another layer of fair comment protection by listing examples to support negative reviews. In a 1994 case, for example, the *New York Times* successfully defended a book review in which it described an author's work as "sloppy journalism." Instead of using the term without explanation, the reviewer provided examples of the author's journalistic techniques in order to support the criticisms.

Privilege. Under most circumstances, speakers addressing governmental meetings or legal proceedings cannot be guilty of libel, nor can a reporter quoting them. The rationale for the privilege defense is that both public officials and private citizens speaking at public meetings should be able to do so without fear of being sued, and that journalists should be able to report on what was said. Despite this common law protection, libel suits are often filed based on comments made, but the courts typically side with the defendants unless there is overwhelming evidence that the journalist intentionally misquoted or exaggerated the individual's comments.

There are three other defenses employed in defamation cases, but they are not recognized by all courts:

The **wire service defense** provides limited protection for newspapers or other media outlets that publish or broadcast defamatory information based on wire service reports. In order to successfully use this defense, four conditions must be met: (1) the wire service is a reputable one, (2) the defendant did not know the story was false, (3) there were no indicators in the story (i.e. "red flags") in the story to raise suspicions of possible falsity, and (4) the defendant did not alter the material to a substantial degree.

Neutral reportage, an extension of the privilege defense, refers to the rights of journalists to report information gathered in situations other than governmental and legal proceedings, such as interviews, even if they suspect the comments might be false. Most courts that recognize it have established three qualifications: (1) the matter must be one of public interest, (2) the information must be from a credible source, and (3) the journalist must allow the criticized party the opportunity to respond.

Rhetorical hyperbole is a defense in which a defendant claims that a statement is so clearly an exaggeration that no reasonable member of the audience would believe it to be true. Examples are statements such as "your mother's so fat that...."

In a 1988 case, for example, a well-known television evangelist sued a national magazine over an ad parody that suggested that he had sex with his mother and addressed his congregation while drunk. A trial court ruled the material was not libelous because the accusations in it were "so outrageous that no reasonable person would have believed them."

Private Figures vs. Public Figures

Whether the plaintiff is a private figure or public figure determines the level of fault he or she is required to establish. Private figures have to prove only negligence or sloppy reporting, while public figures must show actual malice or "reckless disregard for the truth." About one-third of all of libel cases are filed by public figures, mostly persons in elected or appointed government positions, professional sports, or the entertainment industry.

There are three types of public figures:

1. All-purpose public figures. These individuals are a "celebrities" whose names are "household words." These includes public officials, well-known professional athletes, and entertainers. Generally, all aspects of such a person's life are public.

2. Limited or "vortex" public figures. These individuals are public figures only when they are involved only in a specific event, issue, or controversy. The limited public figure label applies in cases in which (1) the issue or controversy in which the individual is involved began before publication of the allegedly libelous material and (2) the individual is voluntarily participating in or attempting to resolve the issue or controversy.

3. Involuntary public figures. These individuals do not seek the spotlight but instead are thrust into it, such as witnesses to well-publicized crimes or other individuals involved in news stories by circumstance.

Major corporations and nonprofit organizations are often considered the equivalent of public figures for libel purposes. When making that determination, the courts take a number of factors into consideration, including size, name recognition, pervasiveness of its advertising, and involvement in political and social issues.

The most famous libel case in the history of American journalism is *New York Times v. Sullivan* (1964). It is significant for several reasons, the most important of which was the creation of the **actual malice rule** that drew a distinction between public officials and private figures and required public figures to meet the higher burden of proof in libel cases.

The Sullivan case was a byproduct of the civil rights movement of the 1960s. It began when the police commissioner in Montgomery, Alabama was criticized in a *New*

York Times advertisement, paid for by a national civil rights group, which accused him and his department of misconduct in dealing with protestors. It was one of the first widely known cases of alleged libel taking the form of an advertisement; prior to this case, libel was typically thought of as something that occurred within the context a news story.

The commissioner sued the *Times* for libel and won an initial judgment of $500,000. That judgment was overturned by the Supreme Court, which ruled that because of his public figure status, the target of the ad was required to prove not only that the accusations were false, but that the newspaper knew of their falsity before publishing them. The commissioner could prove the former but not the latter.

In its unanimous decision, the court determined that to allow public officials to prevail in defamation cases would create a chilling effect and limit the media's First Amendment right to scrutinize the performance of public officials. The court did not define what a public official was in the *Sullivan* case, but in later cases, it defined a public official as anyone who is "elected to a public office or who participates in policy development."

In addition to creating the actual malice rule, the Court determined in the *Sullivan* case that in many situations, alleged libel was a natural byproduct of free speech and should be tolerated as something that results from the "heated exchange of public debate." As a result, the burden of proof in libel cases was shifted from the defendant to the plaintiff.

In the decade that followed the *Sullivan* ruling, state and federal courts ruled that because of the traditional First Amendment protections given the press, public figures are obligated to accept public scrutiny and criticism as part of their positions and should be successful in their libel claims only in extreme cases — i.e., actual malice.

In later cases, the courts expanded the actual malice rule to cover not only public officials, but also public figures — a category that would include entertainers, athletes, and individuals campaigning for public office or speaking on controversial public issues.

Despite the history of public figures losing libel cases because of being unable to prove actual malice, such cases are not impossible to win. In cases throughout the 1970s, 1980s, and 1990s, public officials and political candidates have won libel cases against the media. Those cases, while rare, have established that public officials and candidates for public office — once thought to be almost "libel-proof" — could indeed be successful in libel actions if their evidence was strong enough to prove actual malice.

Limitations and Clarifications Regarding the "Fair Comment" Defense

There are two common misconceptions about the fair comment defense.

The first misconception is that fair comment is an airtight defense. Common law states that fair comment protection applies to any expression of an opinion that is based on facts. Once a writer or commentator provides a series of facts, whatever opinion he or she then presents to the audience is protected. But if he or she presents information that later proves to be false, and the error invalidates the opinion, the writer or commentator has lost fair comment protection. Many court rulings in fair comment cases paraphrase the adage that says, "Every man has a right to his own opinion, but no man has the right to his own facts."

Editors of newspaper opinion pages report that many of the original versions of letters to the editor they receive might be found libelous in court because of factual errors. Before publishing the letters, editors will either correct or omit the errors or offer the writers the opportunity to revise their submissions.

The second misconception is that in order to be protected, material must appear on the newspaper editorial page or, in the case or broadcasting, somehow labeled as "opinion." While placement on the editorial page or overtly identifying material as "opinion" is legally advantageous, it is not absolutely necessary. Opinion writing in the form of political columns, movie reviews, concert reviews, book reviews, and restaurant reviews are generally protected, even if they appear in other sections of the newspaper. In many cases, however, publishers and broadcasters can provide their work products with an additional layer of fair comment protection by attaching labels such as "opinion," "analysis," or "commentary."

SLAPP Suits

A **SLAPP suit** (Strategic Litigation Against Public Participation) is one in which a company or other organization seeks to discourage an individual or group from criticizing it publicly by suing for libel, or threatening to. Examples include real estate developers filing suits against environmental advocacy groups to discourage those groups from criticizing the developers in media interviews or publicity campaigns.

When threats are carried out, those lawsuits are seldom successful, in many cases because defendants are successful in claiming a "fair comment" defense. In addition, judges and juries are usually sympathetic to defendants because such cases are often cast in a "David and Goliath" context — large corporations acting like neighborhood bullies by attempting to intimidate concerned and well-meaning private citizens or nonprofit groups. Knowing the potential costs of providing a defense, however, many targets of such suits are intimidated enough to halt their criticisms before the cases get too far along.

Because SLAPP suits are considered threats to free speech, some state governments have attempted to discourage them by applying the malice rule. Other states enact laws that require unsuccessful plaintiffs to pay the legal fees of defendants, and in extreme cases defendants can collect compensatory damages if the actions of the plaintiffs are found to be excessive.

Although the term was coined in the 1980s, the concept actually goes back to the 1960s, when major chemical companies attempted to intimidate environmental author Rachel Carson. Her 1962 book, *Silent Spring*, documented the impact of agricultural chemicals on the environment and captured the attention of scientists, researchers, educators, physicians, and politicians. Major chemical companies, many of whom were mentioned in the book, first attempted to silence Carson by threatening to boycott sponsors purchasing advertising time during television interview programs on which she was a guest. When that failed, they threatened to sue her for libel if she mentioned those companies on talk shows, in public appearances, or in subsequent books. No lawsuits were ever filed, and Carson wrote several more books critical of the chemical industry.

The Basics of Privacy Law

Courts recognize four areas of privacy law: false light, private facts, appropriation, and intrusion.

False light. The presentation of a person in a news story or other medium in a manner that may not be inaccurate per se, but is exaggerated or misleading. It is different from libel because instead of claiming financial loss or serious harm to reputation, plaintiffs base their claims on embarrassment or humiliation — damage that is less tangible, yet in the eyes of plaintiffs, easier to claim.

Private facts. This term refers to the details of one's life that (a) would be highly offensive to a reasonable person, and (b) is not of legitimate interest to the public. In most states, common law specifies that private facts are those concerning one or more of the following aspects of a person's life:

1. Mental and emotional condition, including grief
2. Physical health
3. Love and sexual relationships, including sexual orientation
4. Decisions regarding procreation and contraception
5. Family relationships
6. Victimization of a violent or sexual crime
7. Association memberships and affiliations
8. Religious beliefs or church membership
9. Financial matters
10. Academic records

Private facts cases are different from libel cases in three respects:

1. While libel cases deal with falsehoods, private facts cases deal with information that is basically truthful.

2. Unlike a libel plaintiff, who must prove loss to financial standing or reputation, a private facts plaintiff sues for shame, humiliation, and mental anguish. In other words, libel claims are based on how others view the plaintiffs, but private facts cases deal with how the plaintiffs view themselves.

3. Unlike libel defendants, the defendants in private facts cases cannot use "truth" as a defense.

There are three common defenses that journalists use in private facts cases:

Newsworthiness. The newsworthiness defense includes two assumptions: first, that when a person leaves his or her home, he or she forfeits the expectation of privacy; and second, once a person becomes newsworthy, he or she remains newsworthy for life. The latter principle applies to persons falling into the category of "all purpose public figures" (as found in libel law), such as former presidents of the United States, Hollywood celebrities, and well-known professional athletes. Therefore, stories related to the health and financial standing of such individuals are generally immune from private facts suits.

Because the notion of newsworthiness is subjective and varies from one media outlet to the next, the courts are fairly generous in allowing them to determine for their own purposes what is newsworthy and what is not.

Public domain. News in the public domain includes that which has been previously published, broadcast, or is generally known; takes place at a public event; is contained in a government document; or is announced at a government meeting. In order to be considered in the "public domain," the information must also be accurate and legally obtained. The public domain defense is based on the principle that anything that the public can see or hear, by extension, can also be covered in the media.

Consent. Information disclosed during an interview or otherwise revealed voluntarily cannot be subject of a private facts case. Once it is given, consent cannot be withdrawn.

In addition to common law principles regarding privacy, students at colleges and universities have additional rights under the **Family Educational Rights and Privacy Act** (FERPA), which limits the types of information an educational institution can release about them without their permission. For example, when a student is the victim or alleged perpetrator of a well-publicized crime or a university athlete has been suspended from competition, journalists often ask university officials for information regarding that student's mental or physical health, academic performance, or disciplinary history. Under FERPA (as well as a university's own student records policy), most of that information cannot be released to the media and is available to other university officials on a need-to-know basis.

Appropriation. This term refers to the use of a person's name, image, voice, or likeness for commercial purposes without permission and/or compensation. Although not considered as damaging to a person's reputation as libel or false light, plaintiffs nonetheless claim that being a victim of appropriation results in two forms of harm. First, an entertainer's fans or a politician's supporters may think less of him or her if they erroneously believe he or she has endorsed a controversial company, product, or cause. Second, a celebrity who generates income from product endorsements could claim financial loss because one company is getting for free the benefit of an endorsement that other companies are paying for.

Truth is not a defense in appropriation cases. A photograph can be taken and used for news purposes without the subject's permission, but the same photograph cannot be used for advertising or promotion.

As the result of a 1992 case, the courts expanded the "image and likeness" concept to include a person's voice. Recording artist Bette Midler sued the Ford Motor Company and its advertising agency, Young & Rubicam, after they produced a commercial using another performer imitating Midler's voice and performing one of her songs. Because Midler was widely associated with the song and the voice was so similar to hers, the court ruled in Midler's favor, determining that appropriating a person's voice is the equivalent of using his or her photograph, image, or other likeness.

Laws of appropriation do not apply in cases of **parody,** which is the portrayal of a person that (1) is done for purposes of entertainment or humor (such as in editorial cartoons or television comedy skits), (2) does not attempt to deceive the audience, and (3) does not involve financial gain. In the Midler case, the defendants were unable to use the parody exception because of their intent to deceive the audience into believing that it was actually Midler performing the song.

Intrusion. Intrusion can take one of two forms: physical or electronic. Physical intrusion, also known as trespassing, is the unauthorized entry into a home or business. In many cases, entering a home or business by misrepresentation or deception (see examples in Chapter 5) might be considered trespassing by the courts. Electronic intrusion includes the use of hidden cameras, recording devices, or other electronic means to invade someone's privacy (also covered in Chapter 5).

Intrusion is often an issue in how celebrities are pursued by the media in public places. Helping shield celebrities from tabloid photographers is seldom a priority for local law enforcement, and celebrities who hire private bodyguards often find confrontations between them and tabloid photographers lead to larger publicity problems.

Anti-paparazzi laws are often discussed (and sometimes passed) at the state and federal levels, but are difficult to enforce because of the media's First Amendment right to gather news.

Libel and Privacy Law Applied to Non-Journalistic Products

The majority of libel and privacy litigation is based on the content of news stories, but also vulnerable are photographs, captions, headlines, and advertisements. Libel can also take place in news releases, internal publications, and other public relations materials. One notable example of the latter is a 1979 case in which a U.S. senator was sued by a researcher because of defamatory comments in the senator's news releases and newsletters. There were no public relations professionals directly involved in the case, but it caught their attention because it involved materials commonly used in the public relations profession.

News releases. While the writers of news releases must follow the same rules as journalists with respect to libel, they also benefit from some degree of First Amendment protection. In addition to "truth," courts often consider the "fair comment" defense (customarily applied to editorials and other forms of opinion writing) and apply it to opinions expressed in news releases.

The fair comment defense has been successful in several major libel cases based on information and opinions included in news releases. In one case, a public relations agency representing an alcoholic beverage company claimed "fair comment" when it was sued by a former employee of the company. The company had sued the former employee for violating a confidentiality agreement, and when the company won the suit, the public relations firm issued a news release explaining the grounds for the legal action. The former employee claimed he was defamed in the news release, but the court ruled in favor of the company, finding that all statements in the release were either factual (as based on the findings of the court in the initial case) or were protected as fair comment.

The New York Supreme Court ruled in favor of the New York Yankees in a libel suit filed by a replacement umpire who worked several of the team's games when Major League Baseball's regular umpires were on strike. The news release quoted the team's owner as calling the man a "scab" who "had it in" for the Yankees and "misjudged" plays. The release added that the man did not "measure up to American League standards" and criticized his decision to eject two Yankees players from a game.

A state civil court ruled in favor of the umpire, but the New York Supreme Court overturned, exam-ining the news release and determining that, like in the previous case, all of its com-ponents were statements of either fact or opinion, both of which were protected.

Internal publications and websites. Internal publications such as employee newsletters and magazines often cause legal problems for organizations because the courts tend to apply libel and privacy law to those publications. Many companies have been sued by their employees for either libel or invasion of privacy because of de-famatory or embarrassing information in internal publications. Complicating the privacy problem is the fact that while legal concepts such as "private facts" and "false light" ap-ply, the privacy defenses commonly used by professional journalists (such as "news-worthiness") do not.

In numerous cases, courts have ruled that news releases and employee newsletters are "tools of the trade" and are not eligible for the "newsworthiness" defense; nor are they eligible for the same level of First Amendment protection as newspapers and other media. Therefore, companies that allow defamatory or embarrassing information to be published in company newsletters or other internal publications can be sued by offended employees affected and cannot claim "newsworthiness" or "press freedom" as a defense.

Professional communicators who are responsible for producing an organization's publications or maintaining its website should be familiar with how appropriation law pertains to the photographs they choose for those publications.

For non-employees, the rule is simple: Organizations may not use a person's name, photograph, image, likeness, or voice to promote the company or endorse a product or service unless that person provides his or her consent in writing. If a public official, pro-fessional athlete, show business personality, or other celebrity attends a company's event and a member of the communications staff takes photographs of the event, it is safe to use those photographs in the company newsletter or other publication provided they are presented in their correct context: the individual attended the company's event and mingled with and/or signed autographs for employees. But the company cannot use those photographs in print or broadcast advertisements to promote that company's products or services without written permission of the individual involved.

Nonprofit organizations must also be careful when using photographs of celebrities to endorse their causes. When a celebrity attends an event and consents to photographs, that consent should be looked upon as a short-term endorsement. Just because he or she ag-rees to be photographed and does not object to those photographs being published in the next issue of the newsletter (or posted for a brief period of time on the organization's website) does not mean those photographs can be used in perpetuity. Most celebrities who agree to attend such events will insist on written agreements that spell out for how long and for what purposes their photographs may be used.

For employees, the rules are even simpler. Organizations may not use their names, photographs, images, likenesses, or voices to endorse a product or service unless they provide their consent in writing. However, companies that frequently use photographs of employees in their internal publications or advertisements often have new employees sign consent forms as a condition of employment so they will not have to do them individual-ly at the time they are used. This process also gives the public relations departments con-sent to provide photographs to the media when employees earn recognition within the company or industry.

In many cases, courts will recognize the concept of "implied consent," meaning that if a photographer asks an individual or group of people to pose for a photograph and explains that it is for the employee newsletter, written permission from the individuals being photographed is not required. But if the photographs are candid or not posed, it is better to obtain written permission.

Minors cannot give consent to having their photograph used. When employees bring their children to a company event, the public relations department must have the parents' written permission to use their photographs in company publications or on websites.

Access to Information

Who Owns Information?

"Access to Information" refers to the rights of journalists to be at the location of news events, and the rights of both journalists and ordinary citizens to attend meetings of governmental bodies and to examine government records. The issue of "access" is an important one for public relations professionals because they often find themselves having to make decisions regarding media access to locations and events, public access to records, and whether or not federal and state laws apply to certain situations.

At the federal level, Congress makes laws pertaining to access to federal meetings and records, while state legislatures make laws concerning such access at the state, county, and city levels. At all levels of government, some amount of secrecy is legitimate, but some cases provide obvious examples of abuse.

The majority of federal and state laws do not differentiate between media access and public access. Any meeting that is open to the general public must also be open to the media, and any public records that may be examined by members of the general public may also be examined by journalists. Government officials may provide *greater* access to the media, but may not provide *less* access.

Many states have either government agencies or private watchdog groups that provide assistance to journalists or individual citizens who believe a state or federal agency is not in compliance with open meetings or open records laws. The enforcement power of state agencies, typically called the "Freedom of Information Bureau" (or similar title) varies greatly. In some states, their power is limited to providing advice or helping individuals or groups file their complaints; while in other states, these agencies have the power to investigate cases and bring formal charges against alleged offenders.

Access to News Events and Locations

The legal system has always struggled to strike a balance between the rights of journalists to gather news and the needs of government agencies, the courts, the military, law enforcement, and emergency personnel to conduct their work without interference. The most contentious examples of this conflict are courtrooms, military installations, prisons, and crime and accident scenes. Even though the first three are examples of government property, they are not in the same category as other federal buildings.

Courtrooms. Judges have broad authority to regulate the number and position of courtroom cameras and can require the media to use a pool system. In some cases, judges may close the courtroom for pre-trial proceedings to protect the privacy of witnesses or victims or to avoid damaging pre-trial publicity.

Military installations. When visiting military installations, journalists are customarily accompanied by public affairs officers, and photographers are limited in how they may photograph aircraft, ships, weapons complexes, and electronic devices.

Prisons. Reporters visiting a prison are assigned escorts and must abide by strict rules concerning where they can go and to whom they may speak. When these rules are challenged, the courts typically support the rights of prison management to maintain order, determining that prisons are unique settings and that prison officials may make reasonable "time, place, and manner" restrictions on media tours and interviews. The courts have historically rejected the media's First Amendment claims and determined that journalists do not have the right to go any place where the public could not go.

Crime and accident scenes. The courts generally side with law enforcement and emergency services personnel in their attempts to restrict media access to crime and accident scenes, based on the importance of preserving evidence, protecting the privacy of victims, and avoiding interference with the work of law enforcement personnel or emergency medical workers.

Two cases decided in separate state courts 10 years apart established that a journalist's access to certain news locations such as accident scenes — even those on public property — can be limited in the interest of public safety and the privacy rights of injured individuals. In 1979, a state court in New Jersey rejected the "First Amendment right of access" claim of a newspaper photographer who was not allowed to take close-up photographs of an automobile accident because his actions violated a state law that made it illegal to "obstruct or interfere with matters involving law enforcement or public safety." In 1989, a state court in Wisconsin rejected a similar "access" claim made by a local television news crew when it was not allowed to shoot close-up video at the scene of an airplane crash.

Even though the rulings in the above cases came from state courts and are therefore binding only in those states, they have since been cited in numerous similar cases in other states.

While law enforcement officials have the right to limit media access to such scenes, many agencies will cooperate with journalists and photographers by establishing an "outer perimeter" and "inner perimeter" at the scenes of crimes or accidents. While the public would be required to remain beyond the outer perimeter, professional journalists and photographers may be allowed to approach the inner perimeter with the understanding that they must not interfere with the investigation and must respect the privacy rights of the injured.

Access to Public Meetings

The Government in the Sunshine Act, passed by Congress in 1976, requires approximately 50 federal agencies, commissions, and boards to meet in public. The term is based on a famous quote by Supreme Court Justice Louis Brandeis, who in addressing the issue of government corruption, stated that "sunlight is the best disinfectant."

Most states have similar laws that apply to meetings of state, county, and city governmental bodies within those states. Collectively, such laws are known as **sunshine laws,** although most states have specific titles for their laws, such as the Florida Government in the Sunshine Law, the North Carolina Open Meetings Law, and the West Virginia Open Governmental Proceedings Act.

In most states, private organizations such as chambers of commerce and business development councils are subject to open meetings laws and open records laws when they receive a portion of their funding from local tax revenue, grants, or other government sources.

Public officials attempting to circumvent public meetings laws by discussing issues by telephone conference calls, electronic mail exchanges, or text messaging have found little success. In many states, the courts have ruled that open meetings laws apply to all such forms of electronic communication, even when government officials use their personal computers or other communication devices. In addition to email messages being subject of open meetings laws, in most states they are also subject to open records laws (covered in the following section). In many communities, public officials are able to enjoy the convenience of telephone conference calls while still conforming to public meetings laws by allowing the public to listen in on those calls through toll-free telephone numbers.

Generally, a journalist can attend any meeting that is open to the general public. Most governmental bodies can apply exemptions, however, such as meetings during which the discussion of certain topics may compromise law enforcement investigations, affect contractual negotiations, or be harmful to the privacy of individuals involved, such as health matters and hiring/firing decisions. In most states, open meetings laws do not apply to jury deliberations or meetings of grand juries and parole boards.

When only a portion of a meeting is closed, it is referred to as **executive session.** During a school board meeting, for example, the board may go into executive session numerous times to discuss security matters (such as the type of alarm system to purchase for a school building), discuss pending real estate transactions, or negotiate labor agreements with teachers' unions. They also declare "executive session" when disciplining a teacher or making a hiring/firing decision regarding principals or other school administrators. In such instances, the media and members of the public are required to leave the room, with only the officials, participants providing information, subjects of the discussions, and their attorneys remaining in the room.

Most states have open meetings laws that allow such discussions to be held in private, but require that final votes be taken in public.

The term "executive session" is not applied uniformly in all states. In some states, the legislatures have abandoned the idea of a general executive session rule and instead provide lists of narrowly defined exemptions. Even if meetings are closed, written minutes or audio or video recordings of those meetings are subject to public records laws.

In most states, public meetings laws require governmental bodies to meet in locations with adequate seating for the number of people expected to attend and do not allow bodies to meet at facilities connected to organizations with discriminatory policies, such as private country clubs. In many communities, school boards and city councils schedule their meetings in the evening in order to allow for greater public attendance, but they are not required to do so.

Once a public meeting has been scheduled, the body is required to post an official notice through the local media and appropriate websites. That responsibility is usually assigned to the local government's public relations or public information office. The notice must include the time and place of the meeting as well as the agenda items expected to be announced. If a topic arises during the meeting that was not on the announced agenda, the body may discuss it but may not take any action until the following meeting.

In some states, open meetings laws require governmental bodies to allow public comment at meetings. In other states, governmental bodies do so voluntarily, but usually only when dealing with the most controversial issues.

If decisions are made or actions taken during a meeting that are later found to be in violation of a public meetings law, journalists and private citizens may file lawsuits, and courts may render the decisions or actions void. In those cases, most states allow those same bodies to hold **cure meetings** to discuss the issues and vote again — this time in accordance with the law. A cure meeting can restore any decisions or actions voided by the court, but it does not absolve the officials from their liability for the original violation of the law. The penalty for government officials who violate public meetings laws varies greatly by state. On one extreme is the warning or "slap on the wrist," and on the other extreme (for repeated violations) are fines, prison sentences, or removal from office.

In some cases, individuals or media organizations that are successful in gaining access by winning their cases against governmental bodies receive as part of the judgment the reimbursement of their legal costs involved in filing their complaints.

Access to Public Records

At the federal level, most government documents are open for review by the media and general public under a 1967 law called the **Freedom of Information Act** (FOIA). Journalists or other persons denied access to documents subject to the FOIA (i.e. not included in its exemptions) file their complaints with the nearest Federal District Court. If the court agrees with the request, it issues a **writ of mandamus,** which is a legal document ordering the appropriate agency or government employee to comply with the FOIA request.

One of the rationales for the FOIA is that it helps journalists fulfill their role as watchdogs on government as they uncover waste, fraud, and corruption. Recent examples include the investigation into problems at the Federal Emergency Management Agency, which failed to prevent millions of dollars in fraud resulting from the use of FEMA relief checks following a series of hurricanes in Florida; and revelations about mismanagement, incompetence, and patient neglect at Walter Reed Army Hospital. In both cases, it is unlikely that the fraud and mismanagement would have been exposed if journalists had not uncovered it using the FOIA.

Many states have public records statutes that provide public and media access to documents maintained by the state as well as county and city governments and agencies. At those levels, the state attorney general is the public official in charge of enforcement, so individuals denied access must appeal to that office. If successful, the attorney general will issue a writ of mandamus. When legal action is required for journalists to gain access to records, plaintiffs can often recover legal fees in the same manner they would following open meetings conflicts.

At all levels of government, agencies are allowed to charge "reasonable fees" for making photocopies. Many state laws allow agencies to charge "extensive use" fees if the amount of staff time involved in locating or photocopying records is unusual.

The Freedom of Information Act and its Exemptions

The FOIA includes the following exemptions, and many state public records laws include similar provisions:

1. National security. This exemption, often abused, prevents many documents from being disclosed.

2. Agency rules and practices. This exemption allows government agencies to protect information on procedures such as long-term planning, purchasing, and employee hiring and training. The rationale for this exemption is that the disclosure of such rules might assist outsiders in circumventing those rules.

3. Statutory exemptions. This exemption covers materials that have been declared secret by acts of Congress.

4. Confidential business information. Government agencies customarily protect sensitive information pertaining to contractors working on joint projects in order to prevent competitors from using the FOIA to obtain access.

5. Executive privilege. This exemption, also known as "agency memoranda," protects internal documents such as working drafts, policy statements, proposals, and investigative reports. The rationale for the exemption is that government employees need to communicate with each other and share ideas and suggestions that go into the decision-making process without concern that those documents might one day become public. Federal courts that have evaluated FOIA cases dealing with this exemption have ruled that the public has a right to know what policies a government agency has adopted, but not the details of the behind-the-scenes work involved in the development of those policies.

6. Personnel and medical files. Sometimes referred to as the "privacy exemption," this protects all personnel files of federal government employees, but state laws vary. In the case of federal officials, only their salaries are public information.

7. Law enforcement investigative records. These records are protected while the investigation is in progress, but some details are released after the cases are closed.

8. Information about financial institutions. This exemption prevents the release of communication between banks and credit unions and the government agencies that regulate them.

9. Information about geological test sites. The purpose of this exemption, which is seldom challenged, is to prevent land speculators and other persons from learning about the success or failure of drilling experiments and what valuable natural resources may have been discovered.

10. Critical infrastructure. This exemption, the most recent addition to the FOIA, protects documents related to electricity, communications and computer systems, transportation networks, water supplies, and other matters that if released, might provide useful information to terrorists. When first proposed, this exemption was criticized by media organizations and civil liberties groups as "vague and overbroad" because of the potential for abuse by government officials using it to protect non-sensitive information. Over such objections, however, the exemption was passed into law as part of the Homeland Security Act of 2002.

If a document includes both exempt and non-exempt information, the agency is allowed to redact (delete) the exempt information from any copies released.

A notable case in which the courts upheld an FOIA exemption was in a 1990 conflict between the *New York Times* and the National Aeronautics and Space Administration. The newspaper learned of the existence of an audio recording containing cockpit conversations aboard the space shuttle Challenger in the minutes before it exploded on January 28, 1986, killing the seven astronauts aboard. Because NASA is a government agency, the newspaper claimed the recording to be subject to the FOIA. NASA declined the newspaper's request based on the privacy exemption, claiming that it did not want to subject the families to the trauma of knowing the tape had become public. The trial court ruled the privacy exemption did not apply because it was not contained within a personnel file or medical file. NASA appealed to a Circuit Court, which ruled that NASA could exempt the tapes under the privacy clause because of the emotional distress it would cause the astronauts' families.

State Public Records Laws

Much like federal law, state public records laws do not differentiate between media access and public access. Governmental bodies can provide the media with *greater* access to meetings and records, but cannot provide them with *less* access.

Although most journalists would identify themselves as journalists when requesting records, they (or anyone else) cannot be required to do so and cannot be required to explain the reason behind their requests.

In most states, public records laws establish a hierarchy or "retention value" that determines for what length of time records must be kept. On one extreme, written telephone messages or "pink slips" may be discarded once they have been received by the person for whom they were intended. On the other extreme, public records such as meeting minutes or the records of real estate transactions may be required to be retained for several years or in perpetuity. The retention value is based on the content of the record, not the format (paper vs. electronic) in which it was recorded.

Laws require government bodies and agencies to allow access to records, but do not require them to create documents that do not already exist. If a journalist or member of the general public asks for a list of all city employees making a salary of more than $50,000 per year, for example, the city is not required to create such a list. It is only required to provide the salary information for all of its employees; it would be up to the individual requesting the information to trim the list to suit his or her interests.

Laws regarding access to personnel records vary greatly by state. On one extreme, some state laws require only names, job titles, salaries, and starting dates to be made public. On the other extreme are state laws that require nearly every aspect of a person's file to be public information, with only the most private details (such as Social Security numbers, medical histories, or information concerning family members) exempted. The home addresses of most law enforcement officers are also protected, along with employees' participation in employee assistance programs or other health-related programs.

Following the 2001 death of race car driver Dale Earnhardt during the Daytona 500, newspapers in Florida clashed with members of the Earnhardt family over access to photographs taken during the driver's autopsy. The prevailing law in Florida at the time required that autopsy records be public, but it did not specifically address the issue of the accompanying photographs. Media organizations sought access to the photographs as part of their investigation into the safety equipment available to race car drivers. While the Earnhardt family obtained an injunction prohibiting release of the photographs, the Florida Legislature passed the Dale Earnhardt Family Privacy Act that would permanently prohibit such access on the basis of preserving family privacy. While the law applies only within the state of Florida, the rationale behind it is likely to be cited in similar cases in other states in the future.

Soon after the law was passed, media organizations challenged it on First Amendment grounds, but a state appeals court determined that it was constitutional. When the Florida Supreme Court refused to hear the case on further appeal, the ruling of the appeals court stood.

The media organizations announced their intentions to appeal to the U.S. Supreme Court, but dropped the issue after the Court ruled in an unrelated case that death-scene photographs of Vince Foster, a member of President Clinton's White House staff who committed suicide in 1993, were exempt under the Freedom of Information Act's law enforcement exemption. The rationale for the ruling was that the public interest in seeing the photographs was outweighed by the family's privacy interests.

Two recent areas of public records law concern whether the names of state lottery winners should be part of the public record and whether or not the audio tapes from 911 telephone calls should be available to the media and the public. As of early 2015, court cases have not produced consistent rulings on either question.

As more police departments provide officers with "body cameras" to record traffic stops and other interactions with the public, the next legal question to be addressed is whether or not those videos would be subject to public records requests.

For Discussion

Discussion Problem 10-A   **Roadside Memorials**

Your state legislature is considering a law restricting "roadside memorials" (usually a combination of crosses, signs, flowers and other decorative objects) at the sites of highway fatalities. The proposed law would prohibit them from the medians altogether and require them to be at least 30 feet from the sides of the road. The legislators who introduced the proposed law claim they create a distraction for drivers. Family members who have established the memorials claim the law would violate their First Amendment rights. Which side are you on? What legal principles from the First Amendment section of this chapter could you cite?

Discussion Problem 10-B **Who Owns What the Professor Says . . . or What the Students Write Down?**

You're an administrator at Enormous State University. Across the street from the university is an off-campus bookstore that has established a side business in which it pays students in certain classes to submit copies of lecture notes they have taken in class, which store employees then copy and sell to other students. Faculty members are complaining to you about the practice, claiming that their intellectual property rights are being violated. The owner of the bookstore, however, claims the practice is acceptable because (a) the students in question are legitimately registered for those classes (as opposed to outsiders not authorized to be in the room), and (b) his claim that the notes, once committed to paper, become the property of the student, not the professor. What kind of policy would you put in place, and how would your policy conform to current intellectual property law?

Discussion Problem 10-C **Libel in the Student Newspaper**

You're the faculty advisor for the student newspaper at Enormous State University. In a recent issue, the newspaper published a controversial article based on student complaints about older faculty members whose best teaching days are behind them. While no specific faculty members were identified, the article did mention certain academic departments in which complaints were more common, and in most cases the examples provided made it easy to guess which faculty members were being referred to. The article generated a number of letters to the editor on both sides of the issue. One student-written letter mentioned a specific faculty member by name and referred to him as a "senile old man." Could that be libelous? What if the student agreed to re-write the letter and changed that phrase to read, "too old to be an effective teacher"?

Discussion Questions

1001. If a "vote of confidence" were to be taken on the First Amendment today, would the American people vote to keep it or abolish it? Provide examples to support your answer.

1002. Do you agree with the distribution of the various types of expression found on the First Amendment hierarchy? If you had the opportunity to revise the model, what changes would you make?

1003. By providing some degree of First Amendment protection to controversial forms of speech such as flag-burning, hate speech, and non-obscene sexual expression, the Supreme Court is in effect determining that they have some social value. What social values do you think the Supreme Court has in mind when it makes those determinations?

1004. What is your opinion of the "challenges to copyright extension" issue described on p. 273? Is the current length of copyright protection too long, too short, or just about right?

1005. Should an employee be able to sue his or her employer for libel or invasion of privacy for damaging or embarrassing information published in the company newsletter or on the company's website? Why or why not?

If your answer is yes, should the damage award be comparable to that resulting from a libel judgment against a daily newspaper?

1006. One common analogy used to describe libel law is that of "journalistic malpractice" — just as a medical malpractice suit is sometimes a patient's best recourse against an incompetent or unethical physician, a libel suit is sometimes a news subject's best recourse against an incompetent or unethical journalist. Some critics of the journalism profession say that analogy of "journalistic malpractice" is appropriate because it causes journalists to be more careful in their work, and therefore the "chilling effect" is beneficial. Agree or disagree?

1007. Do you agree with the differing levels of fault required for public figures as opposed to private figures? Should those different standards be modified or should they continue?

1008. Do you agree with journalists' claims that they should have "First Amendment right of access" to accident scenes such as airplane crashes and automobile accidents?

1009. Consider the case of public interest in the results of autopsies preformed on deceased celebrities (see the Dale Earnhardt case, p. 294). Which side of this issue are you on?

1010. Some of the most recent controversial cases in the area of public records laws deal with media access to the recordings of 911 calls. Those in favor of media access claim those recordings should be covered under state public records laws and that the media need access in order to investigate claims that 911 operators are not well-trained, are occasionally rude to callers, and their mistakes sometimes result in the loss of life. Opponents, however, claim that 911 recordings capture individuals at emotionally difficult times and should be protected under the privacy exemption. Which side are you on?

Notes

262   **"not a stagecoach with seats on it for everyone":** Frank Luther Mott, *American Journalism.* New York: MacMillan, 1950, p. 55.

263   **Hate speech is defined as:** Randy Bobbitt, *Exploring Communication Law.* Boston: Allyn & Bacon, 2008, p. 24.

263   **"an immediate breach of the peace":** *Chaplinksy v. New Hampshire,* 315 U.S. 568 (1942).

263   **"whether against himself or others":** *Nelson v. Streeter,* 16 F.3d 145 (1994).

265   **"time, place, and manner":** *Cox v. New Hampshire,* 312 U.S. 569 (1941).

265   **"to groups expressing opposing viewpoints":** *Lloyd Corporation v. Tanner,* 407 U.S. 551 (1972).

266   **that such speech was prohibited:** *Houston v. Hill,* 482 U.S. 451 (1987).

266   **not related to his motives in protesting the war:** *United States v. O'Brien,* 391 U.S. 367 (1968).

266   **Justice William Brennan, is writing for the majority:** *Texas v. Johnson,* 491 U.S. 310 (1989).

267   **The first conflict of this nature:** *West Virginia State Board of Education v. Barnette,* 319 U.S. 624 (1943).

267   **"opting out" of speech to which they objected:** *Wooley v. Maynard,* 430 U.S. 705 (1977).

267   **student organizations involved in controversial causes:** *University of Wisconsin System v. Southworth,* 120 S.Ct. 1346 (2000).

267   **promote those products through media campaigns:** *United States Department of Agriculture v. United Foods,* 533 U.S. 405 (2001). See also: Gina Holland, "Farmers Have a Beef with Paying for Ads." Associated Press report, December 9, 2004.

273   **provided the public with sufficient access to protected materials:** *Eldred v. Ashcroft,* 537 U.S. 186 (2003). See also: Daniel Gross, "Of Mice and Men." *Attache,* February 2002, pp. 13-15. Joan Biskupic, "Copyright Case to Determine Use of Classic Culture." *USA Today,* October 9, 2002, p. 5-A.

273   **ruled in favor of the freelancers in 2001:** *New York Times Company v. Tasini,* 533 U.S. 483 (2001).

273   **the machine or the party that housed it:** This concept was addressed in *Williams & Wilkins v. United States,* 487 F.2d 1345 (1975); *Basic Books v. Kinko's Graphics Corporation* 758 F.Supp. 1522 (1991), as well as the fair use provision of the Copyright Revision Act of 1976.

274   **not the manufacturer of the equipment:** *Sony Corporation v. Universal City Studios,* 464 U.S. 417 (1984).

274   **after losing several contributory infringement cases:** *A&M Records v. Napster,* 239 F.3d 1004 (2001) and *Recording Industry Association of America v. Napster,* 284 F.3d 1091 (2001).

275   **alleged damage to its reputation would be difficult to quantify:** *Mosely v. Victoria's Secret,* 537 U.S. 418 (2003).

276 **the amount of the original trial court judgment remains a record:** *MMAR Group v. Dow Jones & Company*, 187 F.R.D. 282 (1999).

277 **whose product was criticized on her show:** *Texas Cattlemen's Association v. Winfrey*, 212 F.3d 598 (1998).

277 **The second case involved:** "Sharper Image Slapped by Consumers' Union." *Crisis Counselor*, December 1, 2004. David Kravets, "Judge Tosses Sharper Image Lawsuit Against Consumer Reports." Associated Press report, November 10, 2004.

278 **deter third persons from associating with him:** *The Restatement of Torts*, second edition. St. Paul, MN: American Law Institute, 1979.

280 **"however severe in their terms":** *Hoppner v. Dunkirk*, 172 N.E. 139 (1930).

280 **in order to support the criticisms:** *Moldea v. New York Times*, 22 F.3d 310 (1994).

281 **"were so outrageous that no reasonable person would have believed them":** *Hustler v. Falwell*, 485 U.S. 46 (1988).

281 **The most famous libel case in history:** *New York Times v. Sullivan*, 376 U.S. 254 (1964).

282 **if their evidence was strong enough to prove actual malice:** Cases in which public officials have won defamation cases, which illustrate that "no one is libel proof," include *Goldwater v. Ginzburg*, 414 F.2d 324 (1969); *Harte-Hanks Communications v. Connaughton*, 491 U.S. 657 (1989); and *Turner v. KTRK*, 38 S.W. 2d 103 (2000).

285 **photograph, image, or other likeness:** *Midler v. Young & Rubicam*, 849 F.2d 460 (1992).

286 **"a buzzing insect, hovering, darting, stinging":** Randy Bobbitt, *Exploring Communication Law*. Boston: Allyn & Bacon, 2008, p. 149.

286 **in the senator's news releases and newsletters:** *Hutchinson v. Proxmire*, 443 U.S. 11 (1979).

286 **were protected as fair comment:** *Karp v. Hill and Knowlton*, 12 Media L. Rep. 2093 (1986).

287 **both of which were protected:** *Parks v. Steinbrenner*, 12 Media L. Rep. 2200 (1986).

289 **any place where the public could not go:** *Procunier v. Pell*, 417 U.S. 817 (1974) and *Saxbe v. Washington Post*, 417 U.S. 843 (1974).

289 **"obstruct or interfere with matters involving law enforcement or public safety":** *State v. Lashinsky*, 81 N.J. 1 (1979).

289 **at the scene of an airplane crash:** *City of Oak Creek v. King*, 436 N.W. 2d 285 (1989).

290 **"sunlight is the best disinfectant":** Louis Brandeis, "What Publicity Can Do." *Harper's Weekly*, December 20, 1913, p. 92.

293 **because of the emotional distress it would cause the astronauts' families:** *New York Times v. National Aeronautics and Space Administration*, 782 F.Supp. 628 (1990).

APPENDIX A

Ethical Codes

American Advertising Federation Code of Ethics

Truth. Advertising shall tell the truth, and shall reveal significant facts, the omission of which would mislead the public.

Substantiation. Advertising claims shall be substantiated by evidence in possession of the advertiser and advertising agency prior to making such claims.

Comparisons. Advertising shall refrain from making false, misleading, or unsubstantiated statements or claims about a competitor or his/her products or services.

Bait Advertising. Advertising shall not offer products or services for sale unless such offer constitutes a bona fide effort to sell the advertising products or services and is not a device to switch consumers to other goods or services, usually higher priced.

Guarantees and Warranties. Advertising of guarantees and warranties shall be explicit, with sufficient information to apprise consumers of their principal terms and limitations or, when space or time restrictions preclude such disclosures, the advertisement should clearly reveal where the full text of the guarantee or warranty can be examined before purchase.

Price Claims. Advertising shall avoid price claims which are false or misleading, or saving claims which do not offer provable savings.

Testimonials. Advertising containing testimonials shall be limited to those of competent witnesses who are reflecting a real and honest opinion or experience.

Taste And Decency. Advertising shall be free of statements, illustrations or implications which are offensive to good taste or public decency.

American Society of Newspaper Editors Statement of Principles

ASNE's Statement of Principles was originally adopted in 1922 as the "Canons of Journalism." The document was revised and renamed "Statement of Principles" in 1975.

PREAMBLE. The First Amendment, protecting freedom of expression from abridgment by any law, guarantees to the people through their press a constitutional right, and thereby places on newspaper people a particular responsibility. Thus journalism demands of its practitioners not only industry and knowledge but also the pursuit of a standard of integrity proportionate to the journalist's singular obligation. To this end the American Society of Newspaper Editors sets forth this Statement of Principles as a standard encouraging the highest ethical and professional performance.

ARTICLE I — Responsibility. The primary purpose of gathering and distributing news and opinion is to serve the general welfare by informing the people and enabling them to make judgments on the issues of the time. Newspapermen and women who abuse the power of their professional role for selfish motives or unworthy purposes are faithless to that public trust. The American press was made free not just to inform or just to serve as a forum for debate but also to bring an independent scrutiny to bear on the forces of power in the society, including the conduct of official power at all levels of government.

ARTICLE II — Freedom of the Press. Freedom of the press belongs to the people. It must be defended against encroachment or assault from any quarter, public or private. Journalists must be constantly alert to see that the public's business is conducted in public. They must be vigilant against all who would exploit the press for selfish purposes.

ARTICLE III — Independence. Journalists must avoid impropriety and the appearance of impropriety as well as any conflict of interest or the appearance of conflict. They should neither accept anything nor pursue any activity that might compromise or seem to compromise their integrity.

ARTICLE IV — Truth and Accuracy. Good faith with the reader is the foundation of good journalism. Every effort must be made to assure that the news content is accurate, free from bias and in context, and that all sides are presented fairly. Editorials, analytical articles and commentary should be held to the same standards of accuracy with respect to facts as news reports. Significant errors of fact, as well as errors of omission, should be corrected promptly and prominently.

ARTICLE V — Impartiality. To be impartial does not require the press to be unquestioning or to refrain from editorial expression. Sound practice, however, demands a clear distinction for the reader between news reports and opinion. Articles that contain opinion or personal interpretation should be clearly identified.

ARTICLE VI — Fair Play. Journalists should respect the rights of people involved in the news, observe the common standards of decency and stand accountable to the public for the fairness and accuracy of their news reports. Persons publicly accused should be given the earliest opportunity to respond. Pledges of confidentiality to news sources must be honored at all costs, and therefore should not be given lightly. Unless there is clear and pressing need to maintain confidences, sources of information should be identified.

These principles are intended to preserve, protect and strengthen the bond of trust and respect between American journalists and the American people, a bond that is essential to sustain the grant of freedom entrusted to both by the nation's founders.

Associated Press Sports Editors Ethical Guidelines

1. The newspaper pays its staffers way for travel, accommodations, food and drink.

    (a) If a staffer travels on a chartered team plane, the newspaper should insist on being billed. If the team cannot issue a bill, the amount can be calculated by estimating the cost of a similar flight on a commercial airline.

    (b) When services are provided to a newspaper by a pro or college team, those teams should be reimbursed by the newspaper. This includes providing telephone, typewriter or fax service.

2. Editors and reporters should avoid taking part in outside activities or employment that might create a conflict of interest or even the appearance of conflict.

    (a) They should not serve as an official scorer at baseball games.

    (b) They should not write for team or league media guides or other team or league publications. This has the potential of compromising a reporter's disinterested observations.

    (c) Staffers who appear on radio or television should understand that their first loyalty is to the paper.

3. Writers and writers' groups should adhere to APME and APSE standards: No deals, discounts or gifts except those of insignificant value or those available to the public.

    (a) If a gift is impossible or impractical to return, donate the gift to charity.

    (b) Do not accept free memberships or reduced fees for memberships. Do not accept gratis use of facilities, such as golf courses or tennis courts, unless it is used as part of doing a story for the newspaper.

    (c) Sports editors should be aware of standards of conduct of groups and professional associations to which their writers belong and the ethical standards to which those groups adhere, including areas such as corporate sponsorship from news sources it covers.

4. A newspaper should not accept free tickets, although press credentials needed for coverage and coordination are acceptable.

5. A newspaper should carefully consider the implications of voting for all awards and all-star teams and decide if such voting creates a conflict of interest.

6. A newspaper's own ethical guidelines should be followed, and editors and reporters should be aware of standards acceptable for use of unnamed sources and verification of information obtained other than from primary news sources.

   (a) Sharing and pooling of notes and quotes should be discouraged. If a reporter uses quotes gained secondhand, that should be made known to the readers. A quote could be attributed to a newspaper or to another reporter.

7. Assignments should be made on merit, without regard for race or gender.

Guidelines can't cover everything. Use common sense and good judgment in applying these guidelines and adopting local codes.

Copyright 2008 Associated Press Sports Editors. Used by permission.

College Media Advisers Code of Ethical Behavior

The adviser is a journalist, educator and manager who is, above all, a role model. Because of this, the adviser must be beyond reproach with regard to personal and professional ethical behavior; should encourage the student media advised to formulate, adhere to and publicize an organizational code of ethics; and ensure that neither the medium, its staff nor the adviser enter into the situations which would jeopardize the public's trust in and reliance on the medium as a fair and balanced source of news and analysis.

The Adviser's Professional Code. Freedom of expression and debate by means of a free and vigorous student media are essential to the effectiveness of an educational community in a democratic society. This implies the obligation of the student media to provide a forum for the expression of opinion — not only those opinions differing from established university or administrative policy, but those at odds with the media staff beliefs or opinions as well.

Student media must be free from all forms of external interference designed to regulate its content, including confiscation of its products or broadcasts; suspension of publication or trans-mission; academic personal or budgetary sanctions; arbitrary removal of staff members or faculty; or threats to the existence of student publications or broadcast outlets. In public institutions, the law is quite clear on guaranteeing broad freedom of expression to the students. In private institutions, media advisers should aid in developing governing documents and working with administrative guidelines which foster a free and open atmosphere for students involved in campus media work, if such freedoms do not currently exist.

Students should be made mindful of their obligation to avoid real and apparent conflicts of interest. They must be held to clear local policies in that regard.

Advisers, in addition to adhering to their code of ethics, should encourage the media they   advise have established and published codes that apply to the student staffs and conform to nation-ally established and accepted journalistic norms regarding professional behavior, conflict of interest, acceptance of gifts and services, honesty and integrity.

Advisers, in these roles as professionals, must ensure that they have or gain the skills and education requisite to teach all aspects of the media they advise.

The Adviser's Personal Code. The ultimate goal of the student media adviser is to mold, preserve and protect an ethical and educational environment in which excellent communication skills and sound journalistic practice will be learned and practiced by students. There should   never be an instance where an adviser maximizes quality by min-imizing learning. Student media should always consist of student work.

Faculty, staff and other non-students who assume advisory roles with student media must remain aware of their obligation to defend and teach without censoring, editing, directing or producing. It should not be the media adviser's role to modify student writing or broadcasts, for it robs student journalists of educational opportunity and could severely damage their rights to free expression. Advisers to student media must demonstrate a firm dedication to accuracy, fairness, facts and honesty in all content of the medium.

Since there is no clear line between student media content and student media operations, ethical prohibitions against interference in content also apply to interference in student media operations in areas such as story assignments, decisions on inclusion or exclusion of content, staff selection, source selection, news and advertising acceptability standards, and most budgetary decisions. Using arbitrary policies, production guidelines or financial constraints to limit student decision making is no more ethical than rewriting or changing editorial content or influencing the physical appearance of media.

Advisers should be keenly aware of the potential for conflict of interest between their teaching/advising duties and their roles as university staff members and private citizens. It is vital that they avoid not only actual but apparent conflicts of interest. The publicity interests of the university and the news goals of the student media are often incompatible. Advisers should be aware of becoming the publicity focus of organizations to which they belong or for activities in which they are participating.

Advisers cannot expect student staff to respect their own ethical guidelines if advisers believe themselves exempt from strict ethical behavior. The requirements for ethical behavior extend to all operations for student media, not just the news or information function.

Perceptions of favoritism in the purchasing of services and equipment or granting of contracts can be just as damaging to credibility as perceived favoritism in news judgment. This is particularly true when offers of unrelated equipment or services are made in return for giving business to vendors. A clear policy that applies to all members of the student media operation should be communicated to all potential vendors.

The Adviser's Obligations. Membership in College Media Advisers, Inc. signifies acceptance of this code and a willingness to abide by its tenets.

The organization will support those members who adhere to this code and thereby become victims of pressure or negative action from university administrators. This may involve formal censure of the offending institution of higher education.

Copyright 2008 College Media Advisers. Used by permission.

International Association of Business Communicators Code of Ethics

Preface. Because hundreds of thousands of business communicators worldwide engage in activities that affect the lives of millions of people, and because this power carries with it significant social responsibilities, the International Association of Business Communicators developed the Code of Ethics for Professional Communicators. The Code is based on three different yet interrelated principles of professional communication that apply throughout the world. These principles assume that just societies are governed by a profound respect for human rights and the rule of law; that ethics, the criteria for determining what is right and wrong, can be agreed upon by members of an organization; and, that understanding matters of taste requires sensitivity to cultural norms.

These principles are essential:

Professional communication is legal.

Professional communication is ethical.

Professional communication is in good taste.

Recognizing these principles, members of IABC will:

Engage in communication that is not only legal but also ethical and sensitive to cultural values and beliefs;

Engage in truthful, accurate and fair communication that facilitates respect and mutual understanding;

Adhere to the following articles of the IABC Code of Ethics for Professional Communicators.

Because conditions in the world are constantly changing, members of IABC will work to improve their individual competence and to increase the body of knowledge in the field with research and education.

Articles

1. Professional communicators uphold the credibility and dignity of their profession by practicing honest, candid and timely communication and by fostering the free flow of essential information in accord with the public interest.

2. Professional communicators disseminate accurate information and promptly correct any erroneous communication for which they may be responsible.

3. Professional communicators understand and support the principles of free speech, freedom of assembly, and access to an open marketplace of ideas and act accordingly.

4. Professional communicators are sensitive to cultural values and beliefs and engage in fair and balanced communication activities that foster and encourage mutual understanding.

5. Professional communicators refrain from taking part in any undertaking which the communicator considers to be unethical.

6. Professional communicators obey laws and public policies governing their professional activities and are sensitive to the spirit of all laws and regulations and, should any law or public policy be violated, for whatever reason, act promptly to correct the situation.

7. Professional communicators give credit for unique expressions borrowed from others and identify the sources and purposes of all information disseminated to the public.

8. Professional communicators protect confidential information and, at the same time, comply with all legal requirements for the disclosure of information affecting the welfare of others.

9. Professional communicators do not use confidential information gained as a result of professional activities for personal benefit and do not represent conflicting or competing interests without written consent of those involved.

10. Professional communicators do not accept undisclosed gifts or payments for professional services from anyone other than a client or employer.

11. Professional communicators do not guarantee results that are beyond the power of the practitioner to deliver.

12. Professional communicators are honest not only with others but also, and most importantly, with themselves as individuals; for a professional communicator seeks the truth and speaks that truth first to the self.

Enforcement and Communication of the IABC Code of Ethics. IABC fosters compliance with its Code by engaging in global communication campaigns rather than through negative sanctions. However, in keeping with the sixth article of the IABC Code, members of IABC who are found guilty by an appropriate governmental agency or judicial body of violating laws and public policies governing their professional activities may have their membership terminated by the IABC executive board following procedures set forth in the association's bylaws.

IABC encourages the widest possible communication about its Code.

The IABC Code of Ethics for Professional Communicators is published in several languages and is freely available to all: Permission is hereby granted to any individual or organization wishing to copy and incorporate all or part of the IABC Code into personal and corporate codes, with the understanding that appropriate credit be given to IABC in any publication of such codes.

The IABC Code is published on the association's web site. The association's bi-monthly magazine, *Communication World*, publishes periodic articles dealing with ethical issues. At least one session at the association's annual conference is devoted to ethics. The international head-quarters of IABC, through its professional development activities, encourages and supports efforts by IABC student chapters, professional chapters, and regions to conduct meetings and workshops devoted to the topic of ethics and the IABC Code. New and renewing members of IABC sign the following statement as part of their application: "I have reviewed and understand the IABC Code of Ethics for Professional Communicators."

As a service to communicators worldwide, inquiries about ethics and questions or comments about the IABC Code may be addressed to members of the IABC Ethics Committee. The IABC Ethics Committee is composed of at least three accredited members of IABC who serve staggered three-year terms. Other IABC members may serve on the committee with the approval of the IABC executive committee. The functions of the Ethics Committee are to assist with professional development activities dealing with ethics and to offer advice and assistance to individual communicators regarding specific ethical situations.

While discretion will be used in handling all inquiries about ethics, absolute confidentiality cannot be guaranteed. Those wishing more information about the IABC Code or specific advice about ethics are encouraged to contact IABC World Headquarters (One Hallidie Plaza, Suite 600, San Francisco, CA 94102 USA; phone, +1 415.544.4700; fax, +1 415.544.4747).

Online News Association Mission Statement

Inspiring innovation and excellence among journalists to better serve the public. The Online News Association is an association composed largely of professional online journalists. The Association has more than 1,200 professional members, that is, members whose principal livelihood involves gathering or producing news for digital presentation. The membership includes news writers, producers, designers, editors, photographers and others who produce news for the Internet or other digital delivery systems, as well as academic members and others interested in the development of online journalism. ONA also administers the prestigious Online Journalism Awards.

OUR VISION:

ONA is a leader in the rapidly changing world of journalism; a catalyst for innovation in story-telling across all platforms; a resource for journalists seeking guidance and growth, and a champion of best practices through training, awards and community outreach.

OUR VALUES:

We believe that the Internet is the most powerful communications medium to arise since the dawn of television. As digital delivery systems becomes the primary source of news for a growing segment of the world's population, it presents complex challenges and opportunities for journalists as well as the news audience.

Editorial Integrity: The unique permeability of digital publications allows for the linking and joining of information resources of all kinds as intimately as if they were published by a single organization. Responsible journalism through this medium means that the distinction between news and other information must always be clear, so that individuals can readily distinguish independent editorial information from paid promotional information and other non-news.

Editorial Independence: Online journalists should maintain the highest principles of fairness, accuracy, objectivity and responsible independent reporting.

Journalistic Excellence: Online journalists should uphold traditional high principles in reporting original news for the Internet and in reviewing and corroborating information from other sources.

Freedom of Expression: The ubiquity and global reach of information published on the Internet offers new information and educational resources to a worldwide audience, access to which must be unrestricted.

Freedom of Access: News organizations reporting on the Internet must be afforded access to information and events equal to that enjoyed by other news organizations in order to further freedom of information.

Public Radio News Directors Inc. Code of Ethics

Public Radio News Directors Inc. is committed to the highest standards of journalistic ethics and excellence. We must stand apart from pressures of politics and commerce as we inform and engage our listeners. We seek truth, and report with fairness and integrity.

Independence and integrity are the foundations of our service, which we maintain through these principles:

Truth. Journalism is the rigorous pursuit of truth. Its practice requires fairness, accuracy, and balance. We strive to be comprehensive. We seek diverse points of view and voices to tell the stories of our communities.

Fairness. Fairness is at the core of all good journalism. We gather and report the news in context, with clarity and compassion. We treat our sources and the public with decency and respect. Our reporting is thorough, timely and avoids speculation.

Integrity. The public's faith in our service rests on our integrity as journalists. Editorial independence is required to ensure the integrity of our work. We identify the differences between reporting and opinion. We guard against conflicts of interest — real and perceived — that could compromise the credibility and independence of our reporting. We are accountable when conflicts occur. We disclose any unavoidable conflicts of interest.

Public Relations Society of America Member Code of Ethics

This Code applies to PRSA members. The Code is designed to be a useful guide for PRSA members as they carry out their ethical responsibilities. This document is designed to anticipate and accommodate, by precedent, ethical challenges that may arise. The scenarios outlined in the Code provision are actual examples of misconduct. More will be added as experience with the Code occurs.

The Public Relations Society of America (PRSA) is committed to ethical practices. The level of public trust PRSA members seek, as we serve the public good, means we have taken on a special obligation to operate ethically.

The value of member reputation depends upon the ethical conduct of everyone affiliated with the Public Relations Society of America. Each of us sets an example for each other — as well as other professionals — by our pursuit of excellence with powerful standards of performance, professionalism, and ethical conduct.

Emphasis on enforcement of the Code has been eliminated. But, the PRSA Board of Directors retains the right to bar from membership or expel from the Society any individual who has been or is sanctioned by a government agency or convicted in a court of law of an action that is in violation of this Code.

Ethical practice is the most important obligation of a PRSA member. We view the Member Code of Ethics as a model for other professions, organizations, and professionals.

PRSA Member Statement of Professional Values

This statement presents the core values of PRSA members and, more broadly, of the public relations profession. These values provide the foundation for the Member Code of Ethics and set the industry standard for the professional practice of public relations.

These values are the fundamental beliefs that guide our behaviors and decision-making process. We believe our professional values are vital to the integrity of the profession as a whole.

ADVOCACY: We serve the public interest by acting as responsible advocates for those we represent. We provide a voice in the marketplace of ideas, facts, and viewpoints to aid informed public debate.

HONESTY: We adhere to the highest standards of accuracy and truth in advancing the interests of those we represent and in communicating with the public.

EXPERTISE: We acquire and responsibly use specialized knowledge and experience. We advance the profession through continued professional development, research, and education. We build mutual understanding, credibility, and relationships among a wide array of institutions and audiences.

INDEPENDENCE: We provide objective counsel to those we represent. We are accountable for our actions.

LOYALTY: We are faithful to those we represent, while honoring our obligation to serve the public interest.

FAIRNESS: We deal fairly with clients, employers, competitors, peers, vendors, the media, and the general public. We respect all opinions and support the right of free expression.

PRSA Code Provisions

FREE FLOW OF INFORMATION

Core Principle: Protecting and advancing the free flow of accurate and truthful information is essential to serving the public interest and contributing to informed decision making in a democratic society.

Intent: To maintain the integrity of relationships with the media, government officials, and the public. To aid informed decision-making.

Guidelines: A member shall:

Preserve the integrity of the process of communication.

Be honest and accurate in all communications.

Act promptly to correct erroneous communications for which the practitioner is responsible.

Preserve the free flow of unprejudiced information when giving or receiving gifts by ensuring that gifts are nominal, legal, and infrequent.

Examples of Improper Conduct Under this Provision:

A member representing a ski manufacturer gives a pair of expensive racing skis to a sports magazine columnist, to influence the columnist to write favorable articles about the product.

A member entertains a government official beyond legal limits and/or in violation of government reporting requirements.

COMPETITION

Core Principle: Promoting healthy and fair competition among professionals preserves an ethical climate while fostering a robust business environment.

Intent: To promote respect and fair competition among public relations professionals. To serve the public interest by providing the widest choice of practitioner options.

Guidelines: A member shall:

> Follow ethical hiring practices designed to respect free and open competition without deliberately undermining a competitor.
>
> Preserve intellectual property rights in the marketplace.

Examples of Improper Conduct Under This Provision:

> A member employed by a "client organization" shares helpful information with a counseling firm that is competing with others for the organization's business.
>
> A member spreads malicious and unfounded rumors about a competitor in order to alienate the competitor's clients and employees in a ploy to recruit people and business.

DISCLOSURE OF INFORMATION

Core Principle: Open communication fosters informed decision making in a democratic society.

Intent: To build trust with the public by revealing all information needed for responsible decision making.

Guidelines: A member shall:

> Be honest and accurate in all communications.
>
> Act promptly to correct erroneous communications for which the member is responsible.
>
> Investigate the truthfulness and accuracy of information released on behalf of those represented.
>
> Reveal the sponsors for causes and interests represented.
>
> Disclose financial interest (such as stock ownership) in a client's organization.
>
> Avoid deceptive practices.

Examples of Improper Conduct Under this Provision:

> Front groups: A member implements "grass roots" campaigns or letter-writing campaigns to legislators on behalf of undisclosed interest groups.
>
> Lying by omission: A practitioner for a corporation knowingly fails to release financial information, giving a misleading impression of the corporation's performance.

A member discovers inaccurate information disseminated via a Web site or media kit and does not correct the information.

A member deceives the public by employing people to pose as volunteers to speak at public hearings and participate in "grass roots" campaigns.

SAFEGUARDING CONFIDENCES

Core Principle: Client trust requires appropriate protection of confidential and private information.

Intent: To protect the privacy rights of clients, organizations, and individuals by safeguarding confidential information.

Guidelines: A member shall:

Safeguard the confidences and privacy rights of present, former, and prospective clients and employees.

Protect privileged, confidential, or insider information gained from a client or organization.

Immediately advise an appropriate authority if a member discovers that confidential information is being divulged by an employee of a client company or organization.

Examples of Improper Conduct Under This Provision:

A member changes jobs, takes confidential information, and uses that information in the new position to the detriment of the former employer.

A member intentionally leaks proprietary information to the detriment of some other party.

CONFLICTS OF INTEREST

Core Principle: Avoiding real, potential or perceived conflicts of interest builds the trust of clients, employers, and the publics.

Intent: To earn trust and mutual respect with clients or employers. To build trust with the public by avoiding or ending situations that put one's personal or professional interests in conflict with society's interests.

Guidelines: A member shall:

Act in the best interests of the client or employer, even subordinating the member's personal interests.

Avoid actions and circumstances that may appear to compromise good business judgment or create a conflict between personal and professional interests.

Disclose promptly any existing or potential conflict of interest to affected clients or organizations.

Encourage clients and customers to determine if a conflict exists after notifying all affected parties.

Examples of Improper Conduct Under This Provision:

The member fails to disclose that he or she has a strong financial interest in a client's chief competitor.

The member represents a "competitor company" or a "conflicting interest" without informing a prospective client.

ENHANCING THE PROFESSION

Core Principle: Public relations professionals work constantly to strengthen the public's trust in the profession.

Intent: To build respect and credibility with the public for the profession of public relations. To improve, adapt and expand professional practices.

Guidelines: A member shall:

Acknowledge that there is an obligation to protect and enhance the profession.

Keep informed and educated about practices in the profession to ensure ethical conduct.

Actively pursue personal professional development.

Decline representation of clients or organizations that urge or require actions contrary to this Code.

Accurately define what public relations activities can accomplish.

Counsel subordinates in proper ethical decision making.

Require that subordinates adhere to the ethical requirements of the Code.

Report ethical violations, whether committed by PRSA members or not, to the appropriate authority.

Examples of Improper Conduct Under This Provision:

A PRSA member declares publicly that a product the client sells is safe, without disclosing evidence to the contrary.

A member initially assigns some questionable client work to a non-member practitioner to avoid the ethical obligation of PRSA membership.

PRSA Member Code of Ethics Pledge

I pledge:

To conduct myself professionally, with truth, accuracy, fairness, and responsibility to the public; To improve my individual competence and advance the knowledge and proficiency of the profession through continuing research and education; And to adhere to the articles of the Member Code of Ethics 2000 for the practice of public relations as adopted by the governing Assembly of the Public Relations Society of America.

I understand and accept that there is a consequence for misconduct, up to and including membership revocation.

And, I understand that those who have been or are sanctioned by a government agency or convicted in a court of law of an action that is in violation of this Code may be barred from membership or expelled from the Society.

Copyright 2000 Public Relations Society of America. Used by permission.

Rebecca Blood's Code of Weblog Ethics

Weblogs are the mavericks of the online world. Two of their greatest strengths are their ability to filter and disseminate information to a widely dispersed audience, and their position outside the mainstream of mass media. Beholden to no one, weblogs point to, comment on, and spread information according to their own, quirky criteria.

The weblog network's potential influence may be the real reason mainstream news organizations have begun investigating the phenomenon, and it probably underlies much of the talk about weblogs as journalism. Webloggers may not think in terms of control and influence, but commercial media do. Mass media seeks, above all, to gain a wide audience. Advertising revenues, the lifeblood of any professional publication or broadcast, depend on the size of that publication's audience. Content, from a business standpoint, is there only to deliver eyeballs to advertisers, whether the medium is paper or television.

Journalists — the people who actually report the news — are acutely aware of the potential for abuse that is inherent in their system, which relies on support from businesses and power brokers, each with an agenda to promote. Their ethical standards are designed to delineate the journalist's responsibilities and provide a clear code of conduct that will ensure the integrity of the news.

Weblogs, produced by nonprofessionals, have no such code, and individual webloggers seem almost proud of their amateur status. "We don't need no stinkin' fact checkers" seems to be the prevailing attitude, as if inaccuracy were a virtue.

Let me propose a radical notion: The weblog's greatest strength — its uncensored, unmediated, uncontrolled voice — is also its greatest weakness. News outlets may be ultimately beholden to advertising interests, and reporters may have a strong incentive for remaining on good terms with their sources in order to remain in the loop; but because they are businesses with salaries to pay, advertisers to please, and audiences to attract and hold, professional news organizations have a vested interest in upholding certain standards so that readers keep subscribing and advertisers keep buying. Weblogs, with only minor costs and little hope of significant financial gain, have no such incentives.

The very things that may compromise professional news outlets are at the same time incentives for some level of journalistic standards. And the very things that make weblogs so valuable as alternative news sources — the lack of gatekeepers and the freedom from all consequences — may compromise their integrity and thus their value.

There is every indication that weblogs will gain even greater influence as their numbers grow and awareness of the form becomes more widespread. It is not true, as some people assert, that the network will route around misinformation, or that the truth is always filtered to widespread awareness. Rumors spread because they are fun to pass along. Corrections rarely gain much traction either in the real world or online; they just aren't as much fun.

There has been almost no talk about ethics in the weblog universe: Mavericks are notoriously resistant to being told what to do. But I would propose a set of six rules that I think form a basis of ethical behavior for online publishers of all kinds. I hope that the weblog community will thoughtfully consider the principles outlined here; in time, and with experience, the community may see the need to add to these rules or to further codify our standards. At the very least, I hope these principles will spur discussion about our responsibilities and the ramifications of our collective behavior.

Journalistic codes of ethics seek to ensure fairness and accuracy in news reporting. By comparison, each of these suggestions attempts to bring transparency — one of the weblog's distinguishing characteristics and greatest strengths — into every aspect of the practice of weblogging. It is unrealistic to expect every weblogger to present an even-handed picture of the world, but it is very reasonable to expect them to be forthcoming about their sources, biases, and behavior.

Webloggers who, despite my best efforts, persist in their quest to be regarded as journalists will have a special interest in adhering to these principles. News organizations may someday be willing to point to weblogs (or weblog entries) as serious sources, but only if weblogs have, as a whole, demonstrated integrity in their information gathering and dissemination, and consistency in their online conduct.

Any weblogger who expects to be accorded the privileges and protections of a professional journalist will need to go further than these principles. Rights have associated responsibilities; in the end it is an individual's professionalism and meticulous observance of recognized ethical standards that determines her status in the eyes of society and the law. For the rest of us, I believe the following standards are sufficient:

1. Publish as fact only that which you believe to be true. If your statement is speculation, say so. If you have reason to believe that something is not true, either don't post it, or note your reservations. When you make an assertion, do so in good faith; state it as fact only if, to the best of your knowledge, it is so.

2. If material exists online, link to it when you reference it. Linking to referenced material allows readers to judge for themselves the accuracy and insightfulness of your statements. Referencing material but selectively linking only that with which you agree is manipulative. Online readers deserve, as much as possible, access to all of the facts — the Web, used this way, empowers readers to become active, not passive, consumers of information. Further, linking to source material is the very means by which we are creating a vast, new, collective network of information and knowledge. On the rare occasion when a writer wishes to reference but not drive traffic to a site she considers to be morally reprehensible (for example, a hate site), she should type out (but not link) the name or URL of the offending site and state the reasons for her decision. This will give motivated readers the information they need to find the site in order to make their own judgment. This strategy allows the writer to preserve her own transparency (and thus her integrity) while simultaneously declining to lend support to a cause she finds contemptible.

3. Publicly correct any misinformation. If you find that you have linked to a story that was untrue, make a note of it and link to a more accurate report. If one of your own statements proves to be inaccurate, note your misstatement and the truth. Ideally, these corrections would appear in the most current version of your weblog and as an added note to the original entry. (Remember that search engines will pull up entries without regard to when they were posted; once an entry exists in your archives, it may continue to spread an untruth even if you corrected the information a few days later.) If you aren't willing to add a correction to previous entries, at least note it in a later post. One clear method of denoting a correction is the one employed by Cory Doctorow, one of the contributors to the Boing Boing weblog. He strikes through any erroneous information and adds the corrected information immediately following. The reader can see at a glance what ~~Bill~~ Cory originally wrote and that he has updated the entry with information he feels to be more accurate. (Do it like this in HTML: The reader can see at a glance what <strike>Bill</strike> Cory originally wrote and that he has updated the entry with information he feels to be more accurate.)

4. Write each entry as if it could not be changed; add to, but do not rewrite or delete, any entry. Post deliberately. If you invest each entry with intent, you will ensure your personal and professional integrity. Changing or deleting entries destroys the integrity of the network. The Web is designed to be connected; indeed, the weblog permalink is an invitation for others to link. Anyone who comments on or cites a document on the

Web relies on that document (or entry) to remain unchanged. A prominent addendum is the preferred way to correct any information anywhere on the Web.

If an addendum is impractical, as in the case of an essay that contains numerous inaccuracies, changes must be noted with the date and a brief description of the nature of the change.

If you think this is overly scrupulous, consider the case of the writer who points to an online document in support of an assertion. If this document changes or disappears — and especially if the change is not noted — her argument may be rendered nonsensical.

Books do not change; journals are static. On paper, new versions are always denoted as such. The network of shared knowledge we are building will never be more than a novelty unless we protect its integrity by creating permanent records of our publications.

The network benefits when even entries that are rendered irrelevant by changing circumstance are left as a historical record. As an example: A weblogger complains about inaccuracies in an online article; the writer corrects those inaccuracies (and notes them!); the weblogger's entry is therefore meaningless — or is it? Deleting the entry somehow asserts that the whole incident simply didn't happen — but it did. The record is more accurate and history is better served if the weblogger notes beneath the original entry that the writer has made the corrections and the article is now, to the weblogger's knowledge, accurate.

History can be rewritten, but it cannot be undone. Changing or deleting words is possible on the Web, but possibility does not always make good policy. Think before you publish and stand behind what you write. If you later decide you were wrong about something, make a note of it and move on.

I make a point never to post anything I am not willing to stand behind even if I later disagree. I work to be thoughtful and accurate, no matter how angry or excited I am about a particular topic. If I change my opinion in a day or two, I just note the change. If I need to apologize for something I've said, I do so.

If you discover that you have posted erroneous information, you must note this publicly on your weblog. Deleting the offending entry will do nothing to correct the misinformation your readers have already absorbed. Taking the additional step of adding a correction to the original entry will ensure that Google broadcasts accurate information into the future.

The only exception to this rule is when you inadvertently reveal personal information about someone else. If you discover that you have violated a confidence or made an acquaintance uncomfortable by mentioning him, it is only fair to remove the offending entry altogether, but note that you have done so.

5. Disclose any conflict of interest. Most webloggers are quite transparent about their jobs and professional interests. It is the computer programmer's expertise that gives her commentary special weight when she analyzes a magazine article about the merits of the latest operating system. Since weblog audiences are built on trust, it is to every weblogger's benefit to disclose any monetary (or other potentially conflicting) interests when appropriate. An entrepreneur may have special insight into the effect of a proposed Senate bill or a business merger; if she stands to benefit directly from the outcome of any event, she should note that in her comments. A weblogger, impressed with a service or product, should note that she holds stock in the company every time she promotes the service on her page. Even the weblogger who receives a CD for review should note that fact; her readers can decide for themselves whether her favorable review is based on her taste or on her desire to continue to receive free CDs.

Quickly note any potential conflict of interest and then say your piece; your readers will have all the information they need to assess your commentary.

6. Note questionable and biased sources. When a serious article comes from a highly biased or questionable source, the weblogger has a responsibility to clearly note the nature of the site on which it was found. In their foraging, webloggers occasionally find interesting, well-written articles on sites that are maintained by highly biased organizations or by seemingly fanatical individuals. Readers need to know whether an article on the medical ramifications of first trimester abortion comes from a site that is pro-life, pro-choice, or strongly opposed to medical intervention of all kinds. A thoughtful summation of the Israeli-Palestinian conflict may be worth reading whether it is written by a member of the PLO or a Zionist — but readers have the right to be alerted to the source.

It is reasonable to expect that expert foragers have the knowledge and motivation to assess the nature of these sources; it is not reasonable to assume that all readers do. Readers depend on weblogs, to some extent, for guidance in navigating the Web. To present an article from a source that is a little nutty or has a strong agenda is fine; not to acknowledge the nature of that source is unethical, since readers don't have the information they need to fully evaluate the article's merits.

If you are afraid that your readers will discount the article entirely based on its context, consider why you are linking it at all. If you strongly feel the piece has merit, say why and let   it stand on its own, but be clear about its source. Your readers may cease to trust you if they discover even once that you disguised — or didn't make clear — the source of an article they might have evaluated differently had they been given all the facts.

Society of American Business Editors and Writers Revised Code of Ethics

Statement of Purpose:

As business and financial journalists, we recognize we are guardians of the public trust and must do nothing to abuse this obligation.

It is not enough that we act with honest intent; as journalists, we must conduct our professional lives in a manner that avoids even the suggestion of personal gain, or any misuse of the power of the press.

It is with this acknowledgment that we offer these guidelines for those who work in business and financial journalism:

Personal investments and relationships. Avoid any practice that might compromise or appear to compromise objectivity or fairness. Never let personal investments influence content. Disclose investment positions to your superior or directly to the public. Disclose personal or family relationships that might pose conflicts of interest. Avoid active trading and other short-term profit-seeking opportunities; as such activities are not compatible with the independent role of the business journalist. Do not take advantage of inside information for personal gain.

Sources: Insure confidentiality of information during the reporting process, and make every effort to keep information from finding its way to those who might use it for gain before it is disseminated to the public. Do not alter information, delay or withhold publication or make concessions relating to news content to any government.

Gifts and favors: In the course of professional activity, accept no gift or special treatment worth more than token value. Accept no out-of-town travel paid for by outside sources. Carefully examine offers of freelance work or speech honoraria to assure such offers are not attempts to influence content. Disclose to a supervisor any offer of future employment or outside income that springs from the journalist's professional activities or contacts. Accept food or refreshments of ordinary value only if absolutely necessary, and only during the normal course of business.

Editorial Integrity: Publishers, owners, and newsroom managers should establish policies and guidelines to protect the integrity of business news coverage. Regardless of news platform, there should be a clear delineation between advertising and editorial content. Material produced by editorial staff should be used only in sections, programming or pages controlled by editorial departments. Content, sections or programming controlled by advertising departments should be distinctly different from news sections in typeface, layout and design. Advertising content should be identified as such. Promising a story in exchange for advertising or other considerations is unethical.

Using outside material: Using articles or columns from non-journalists is potentially deceptive and poses inherent conflicts of interest. This does not apply to content that is clearly labeled opinion or viewpoint, or to submissions identified as coming directly from the public, such as citizen blogs or letters to the editor. Submissions should be accepted only from freelancers who abide by the same ethical policies as staff members.

Technology: Business journalists should take the lead in adapting professional standards to new forms of journalism as technologies emerge and change. The business journalist should encourage fellow journalists to abide by these standards and principles.

Society of Professional Journalists Principles and Standards of Practice

Preamble

Members of the Society of Professional Journalists believe that public enlightenment is the forerunner of justice and the foundation of democracy. The duty of the journalist is to further those ends by seeking truth and providing a fair and comprehensive account of events and issues. Conscientious journalists from all media and specialties strive to serve the public with thorough-ness and honesty. Professional integrity is the cornerstone of a journalist's credibility. Members of the Society share a dedication to ethical behavior and adopt this code to declare the Society's principles and standards of practice.

Seek Truth and Report It

Journalists should be honest, fair and courageous in gathering, reporting and inter-preting information. Journalists should:

- Test the accuracy of information from all sources and exercise care to avoid inadvertent error. Deliberate distortion is never permissible.

- Diligently seek out subjects of news stories to give them the opportunity to respond to allegations of wrongdoing.

- Identify sources whenever feasible. The public is entitled to as much infor-mation as possible on sources' reliability.

- Always question sources' motives before promising anonymity. Clarify con-ditions attached to any promise made in exchange for information. Keep promises.

- Make certain that headlines, news teases and promotional material, photos, video, audio, graphics, sound bites and quotations do not misrepresent. They should not oversimplify or highlight incidents out of context.

- Never distort the content of news photos or video. Image enhancement for technical clarity is always permissible. Label montages and photo illustra-tions.

- Avoid misleading re-enactments or staged news events. If re-enactment is necessary to tell a story, label it.

- Avoid undercover or other surreptitious methods of gathering information except when traditional open methods will not yield information vital to the public. Use of such methods should be explained as part of the story

- Never plagiarize.

- Tell the story of the diversity and magnitude of the human experience boldly, even when it is unpopular to do so.

- Examine their own cultural values and avoid imposing those values on others.

- Avoid stereotyping by race, gender, age, religion, ethnicity, geography, sexual orientation, disability, physical appearance, or social status.

- Support the open exchange of views, even views they find repugnant.

- Give voice to the voiceless; official and unofficial sources of information can be equally valid.

- Distinguish between advocacy and news reporting. Analysis and commentary should be labeled and not misrepresent fact or context.

- Distinguish news from advertising and shun hybrids that blur the lines between the two.

- Recognize a special obligation to ensure that the public's business is conducted in the open and that government records are open to inspection.

Minimize Harm

Ethical journalists treat sources, subjects and colleagues as human beings deserving of respect. Journalists should:

- Show compassion for those who may be affected adversely by news coverage. Use special sensitivity when dealing with children and inexperienced sources or subjects.

- Be sensitive when seeking or using interviews or photographs of those affected by tragedy or grief.

- Recognize that gathering and reporting information may cause harm or discomfort. Pursuit of the news is not a license for arrogance.

- Recognize that private people have a greater right to control information about themselves than do public officials and others who seek power, influence or attention. Only an overriding public need can justify intrusion into anyone's privacy.

- Show good taste. Avoid pandering to lurid curiosity.

- Be cautious about identifying juvenile suspects or victims of sex crimes.

- Be judicious about naming criminal suspects before the formal filing of charges.

- Balance a criminal suspect's fair trial rights with the public's right to be informed.

Act Independently

Journalists should be free of obligation to any interest other than the public's right to know. Journalists should:

- Avoid conflicts of interest, real or perceived.

- Remain free of associations and activities that may compromise integrity or damage credibility.

- Refuse gifts, favors, fees, free travel and special treatment, and shun secondary employment, political involvement, public office and service in community organizations if they compromise journalistic integrity.

- Disclose unavoidable conflicts.

- Be vigilant and courageous about holding those with power accountable.

- Deny favored treatment to advertisers and special interests and resist their pressure to influence news coverage.

- Be wary of sources offering information for favors or money; avoid bidding for news.

Be Accountable

Journalists are accountable to their readers, listeners, viewers and each other. Journalists should:

- Clarify and explain news coverage and invite dialogue with the public over journalistic conduct.

- Encourage the public to voice grievances against the news media.

- Admit mistakes and correct them promptly.

- Expose unethical practices of journalists and the news media.

- Abide by the same high standards to which they hold others.

APPENDIX B

Sources / For Further Reading

General

Alger, Greg, and Jessica Burnette-Lemon. "Ethics in the Real World." *Communication World*, March-April 2006, pp. 28-29.

Allen, Anita. *The New Ethics: A Tour of the 21ˢᵗ Century Moral Landscape*. New York: Miramax Books, 2004.

Callahan, David. *The Cheating Culture: Why More Americans are Doing Wrong to Get Ahead*. New York: Harcourt, 2004.

Dobrin, Arthur. *Ethics for Everyone: How to Increase Your Moral Intelligence*. New York: John Wiley & Sons, 2002.

Elliott, Deni, ed. *Responsible Journalism*. Beverly Hills, CA: Sage Publications, 1986.

Jaksa, James A., and Michael S. Pritchard. *Communication Ethics: Methods of Analysis*. Belmont, CA: Wadsworth Publishing, 1988.

Johannesen, Richard L., Kathleen S. Valde, and Karen E. Whedbee. *Ethics in Human Communication*, sixth edition. Long Grove, IL: Waveland Press, 2008.

Knowlton, Steven R. *Moral Reasoning for Journalists*. Westport, CT: Praeger, 1997.

Olen, Jeffrey. *Ethics in Journalism*. Englewood Cliffs, NJ: Prentice Hall, 1988.

Rieder, Rem. "Race to be First Becomes Race to be Wrong." *USA Today*, April 19, 2013, p. 2-B.

Swain, Bruce. *Reporters' Ethics*. Ames, IA: Iowa State University Press, 1978.

Thayer, Lee. *Ethics, Morality, and the Media: Reflections on American Culture*. New York: Hastings House Publishers, 1980.

Wallace, Mike, and Beth Knobel. *Heat and Light: Advice for the Next Generation of Journalists*. New York: Three Rivers Press, 2010.

Weston, Anthony. *A 21ˢᵗ Century Ethical Toolbox*. New York: Oxford University Press, 2001.

Chapter 1: Why a Book About Communication Ethics?

Benedetto, Richard. "Pessimistic Media Have Made America Cynical." Syndicated newspaper column, January 5, 1993.

Byrne, John A. "Can Ethics be Taught?" *Business Week*, April 6, 1992, p. 34.

Freedman, Samuel G. "Caught Concocting the Facts? No Problem — Fame Will Ensue." *USA Today,* July 6, 1998, p. 13-A.

Grossman, Lev. "The Trouble With Memoirs." *Time*, January 23, 2006, pp. 59-61.

Johnson, Peter. "Trust in Media Keeps on Slipping." *USA Today*, May 28, 2003.

Kristof, Nicholas. "A Necessary Good Slap in the Face." Syndicated newspaper column, April 16, 2005.

Meyer, Philip. *Ethical Journalism: A Guide for Students, Practitioners, and Consumers.* Lanham, MD: University Press of America, 1987.

Mitroff, Ian I., and Warren Bennis. *The Unreality Industry: The Deliberate Manufacturing of Falsehood and What it is Doing to Our Lives.* New York: Carol Publishing Group, 1989.

Murray, Steve. "Facts Don't Make the Best Stories." *Atlanta Journal-Constitution*, February 4, 2006.

Peyser, Marc. "The Ugly Truth." *Newsweek*, January 23, 2006, pp. 62-64.

Pitts, Leonard. "Celebrities and Politicos Take the Truth Out for a Spin." Syndicated newspaper column, May 30, 2007.

Rawe, Julie. "A Question of Honor." *Time*, May 28, 2007, pp. 59-60.

Rice, Pat. "The Internet is Making Newspapers Better." *Northwest Florida Daily News,* June 10, 2007, p. 8-F.

Samuelson, Robert J. "Long Live the News Business." *Newsweek*, May 28, 2007, p. 40.

"Schools for Scandal." *USA Today*, May 2, 2007, p. 17-A.

Sedensky, Matt. "Report Says Journalists are High on Ethics List." Associated Press report, May 7, 2005.

Shepard, Alicia C. "Legislating Ethics." *American Journalism Review*, January/February 1994, pp. 37-41.

Sutel, Seth. "Circulation Declines for Top U.S. Newspapers." *Wilmington Star-News*, May 3, 2005, p. 5-A.

"The State of the News Media 2007." Project for Excellence in Journalism, 2007.

"Too Much Celebrity News, Too Little Good News." Pew Research Center report, October 12, 2007.

Vanderkam, Laura. "When Truth Masquerades as Fiction." *USA Today,* January 17, 2006.

Weinstein, Bruce. "Lawful, Ethical Behavior Don't Always Correlate." *Northwest Florida Daily News*, August 19, 2006, p. 3-D.

Chapter 2: Philosophical Influences on Communication Ethics

Bagdikian, Ben H. *The Media Monopoly.* Boston: Beacon Press, 1992.

Bobbitt, Randy. *A Big Idea and a Shirt-Tail Full of Type: The Life and Work of Wallace F. Stovall.* Tampa, FL: Hillsborough County Historical Society, 1995.

Finlayson, James Gordon. *Habermas: A Very Short Introduction.* New York: Oxford University Press, 2005.

Fletcher, Joseph. *Situational Ethics: The New Morality* Philadelphia: Westminster Press, 1966.

Kurtz, Howard. *The Media Circus: The Trouble With America's Newspapers.* New York: Random House, 1994.

Leslie, Larry. *Mass Communication Ethics: Decision-Making in a Post-Modern Culture.* Boston: Houghton Mifflin, 2004.

Nelson, Joyce. *Sultans of Sleaze: Public Relations and the Media.* Monroe, ME: Common Courage Press, 1989.

Chapter 3: Journalism, Broadcasting, and Entertainment: Content Issues

Bivens, Thomas H. *Mixed Media: Moral Distinctions in Advertising, PR, and Journalism.* Mahwah, NJ: Lawrence Erlbaum Associates, 2004.

Boortz, Neal. *Somebody's Gotta Say It.* New York: Harper Collins, 2007.

Bozell, Brent, and Brent H. Baker, eds. *And That's The Way It Isn't: A Reference Guide to Media Bias.* Alexandria, VA: Media Research Center, 1990.

Bugeja, Michael J. *Living Ethics: Developing Values in Mass Communication.* Boston: Allyn & Bacon, 1996.

"The Dominance of News Coverage." Associated Press report, April 28, 2007.

"Editorial Cartoon Draws Political Ire." Associated Press report, December 11, 2004.

Fallows, James. *Breaking the News: How the Media Undermine American Democracy.* New York: Pantheon Books, 1996.

Fedler, Fred. *Media Hoaxes.* Ames, IA: Iowa State University Press, 1989.

Foreman, Gene. *The Ethical Journalist.* Malden, MA: Wiley-Blackwell Publishing, 2011.

Glassner, Barry. *The Culture of Fear.* New York: Basic Books, 1999.

Goldberg, Bernard. *Arrogance: Rescuing America from the Media Elite.* New York: Warner Books, 2003.

Goldberg, Bernard. *Bias: How the Media Distorts the News.* New York: Harper Collins, 2003.

Headlines and Soundbites: Is That The Way it Is? Cronkite-Ward Videos, 1995.

Hernandez, Debra Gersh. "Conservative Group Targets 'Liberal' Media." *Editor & Publisher,* July 6, 1996, pp. 24+.

Iyengar, Shanto, and Richard Reeves. *Do The Media Govern? Politicians, Voters, and Reporters in America.* Thousand Oaks, CA: Sage Publications, 1997.

Jacquette, Dale. *Journalistic Ethics: Moral Responsibility in the Media.* Boston: Pearson Prentice Hall, 2007.

Kallen, Stuart A. *Media Bias.* San Diego: Greenhaven Press, 2004.

Kurtz, Howard. *Media Circus:The Trouble With America's Newspapers.* New York: Random House, 2004.

Hernandez, Debra G. "Conservative Group Targets Liberal Media." *Editor & Publisher,* July 6, 1996, pp. 24+.

Huberty, Robert. "Want Good Press? Tighten Standards." Syndicated newspaper column, June 19, 2003.

Jamieson, Kathleen Hall, and Paul Waldman. *The Press Effect.* New York: Oxford University Press, 2003.

Jarvik, Elaine. "Critic Says Media Guilty of Bias But No Conspiracy." *Deseret Morning News,* October 16, 2007.

Klaidman, Stephen. *Health in the Headlines.* New York: Oxford University Press, 1991.

Lawrence, Jill. "New Yorker Cover Art Draws Wrathful Reaction." *USA Today*, July 15, 2008, p. 6-A.

Limburg, Val E. *Electronic Media Ethics.* Boston: Focal Press, 1994.

"Lines Blur as Journalism Heads Back to the Future." *USA Today*, November 10, 2010, p. 8-A.

Lipton, Lauren. "Get Real!" *Los Angeles Times*, March 19, 1991.

Lovgren, Stefan. "CSI Effect is Mixed Blessing for Real Crime Labs." *National Geographic News,* September 23, 2004.

Montgomery, Kathryn. "The Political Struggle for Prime Time." In *Media, Audience, and Social Structure,* Sandra J. Ball-Rokeach and Muriel G. Cantor, ed. Thousand Oaks, CA: Sage Publications, 1986.

"NAACP Buries the N-Word." Associated Press report, July 10, 2007.

Page, Clarence. "New Yorker Cover Could Spur a Frank Debate." Syndicated newspaper column, July 18, 2008.

Parker, Kathleen. "Today's 'Diversity' Demands Sameness of Thought." Syndicated newspaper column, September 22, 2007.

Poniewozik, James. "The Decency Police." Article 19 (pp. 118-121) in *Mass Media*, 13th edition (Joan Gorham, ed.). Dubuque, IA: McGraw-Hill, 2007.

Proffitt, Jennifer M. "An Ethical Analysis of the News Coverage of the Columbine Shootings." Association for Education in Journalism and Mass Communications Southeastern Colloquium, Spring 2001.

Rice, Pat. "The Internet is Making Newspapers Better." *Northwest Florida Daily News,* June 10, 2007, p. 8-F.

Roane, Kit R. "The CSI Effect." *U.S. News & World Report*, April 25, 2005.

Rosenberg, Howard. *Not So Prime Time: Chasing the Trivial on American Television.* Chicago: Ivan R. Dee Publishing, 2004.

Sadler, Roger L. *Electronic Media Law*. Thousand Oaks, CA: Sage Publications, 2005.

Schiff, Stacy. "Too Many Can't Tell Fact From Fiction." Syndicated newspaper column, June 19, 2003.

Schudson, Michael. "How News Becomes News." *Media Critic,* Vol. 2, No. 4 (Summer 1995), pp. 76-85.

Schudson, Michael. *The Sociology of News*. New York: W.W. Norton and Company, 2003.

Shaw, David. "Skepticism's Not Unpatriotic." Syndicated newspaper column, date unknown.

Shoemaker, Pamela J., and Stephen D. Reese. *Mediating the Message: Theories of Influence of Mass Media Content.* White Plains, NY: Longman Publishing, 1996.

Smolla, Rodney. *Suing the Press*. New York: Oxford University Press, 1986.

Spence, Edward, and Brett Van Heekeren, *Advertising Ethics*. Upper Saddle River, NJ: Pearson Prentice Hall, 2004.

"The State of the News Media 2007." Project for Excellence in Journalism, 2007.

Stossel, John. "Reporters Should be More Skeptical of Scare Stories." Syndicated newspaper column, March 26, 2007.

Sullivan, Will. "Shock Jocks in Dry Dock." *U.S. News and World Report*, May 18, 2007, p. 42.

Toplin, Robert Brent. "Spirit of Censorship Hits CBS." *Wilmington Star-News,* November 8, 2003, p. 11-A.

Valente, Mickie. "Television Presents Awful Career Models." *The Tampa Tribune*, July 22, 1992.

Wasserman, Edward. "The High Price of Prude." *Miami Herald,* August 20, 2006.

Chapter 4: Journalism, Broadcasting, and Entertainment: Personnel Issues

Aldrich, Leigh Stephens. *Covering the Community: A Diversity Handbook for the Media.* Thousand Oaks, CA: Pine Forge Press, 1999.

Borchers, Timothy A. *Persuasion in the Media Age*. Boston: McGraw Hill, 2002.

Braxton, Greg. "NAACP: With Fall Sitcom Lineup, Major Networks Fail on Diversity." *Los Angeles Times*, June 17, 2006.

Davis, Geena. "Children's Media Skew Gender." *USA Today*, May 2, 2007, p. 19-A.

Halldin, Bill. "Who Reports on Reporters?" *The Tampa Tribune*, October 27, 1991, p. 1-D.

Kurtz, Howard. *Hot Air: All Talk All the Time*. New York: Times Books, 1996.

"Lines Blur as Journalism Heads Back to the Future." *USA Today*, November 10, 2010, p. 8-A.

"Out of Focus, Out of Synch." Report by the National Association for the Advancement of Colored People, 2008.

Puente, Maria. "Disgrace, Dishonor, Infamy: They're Not So Bad Anymore." *USA, Today*, May 22, 2003, p. 1-A+.

Shapiro, Leonard. "Rulings Are For Officials, Not Reporters." *Washington Post*, October 18, 2005.

Shepard, Alicia C. "Legislating Ethics." *American Journalism Review*, January/February 1994, pp. 37-41.

Texeira, Erin. "Remaking Hollywood: Colorblind Casting Challenges Racial Assumptions." Associated Press report, June 23, 2005.

Yu, Roger. "Anchor Blasted for Clinton Donation." *USA Today*, May 14, 2015.

Chapter 5: Journalism, Broadcasting, and Entertainment: Policy Issues

Alderman, Ellen, and Caroline Kennedy. *The Right to Privacy*. New York: Alfred A. Knopf, 1995.

Fitzgerald, Mark. "Naming Alleged Rape Victims." *Editor & Publisher*, December 23,1995, p. 9.

Gartner, Michael. "Naming the Victim." *Columbia Journalism Review*, July/August 1991.

Hansen, Kathleen A., and Nora Paul. *Behind the Message: Information Strategies for Communicators*. Boston: Pearson, 2004.

Johnson, Peter. "Dateline Roots out Predators." *USA Today*, February 15, 2006, p. 9-B.

Johnson, Roy S. "None of Our Business." *Sports Illustrated*, April 20, 1992, p. 82.

Killenberg, George M. *Before the Story: Interviewing and Communication Skills for Journalists*. New York: St. Martin's Press, 1989.

Kurtz, Howard. *The Fortune Tellers: Inside Wall Street's Game of Money, Media, and Manipulation*. New York: The Free Press, 2000.

Lemann, Nicholas. "Amateur Hour" Journalism Without Journalists." *The New Yorker*, August 7, 2006, p. 44.

Limburg, Val E. *Electronic Media Ethics*. Boston: Focal Press, 1994.

Olen, Jeffrey. *Ethics in Journalism*. Englewood Cliffs, NJ: Prentice-Hall, 1988.

Radolf, Andrew. "Junket Journalism." *Editor and Publisher*, October 18, 1986, pp. 16-17.

Reddick, DeWitt C. *The Mass Media and the Student Newspaper*. New York: Wadsworth Publishing, 1985.

Sauber, Richard. "Reporters, Promises, and Sources." Syndicated newspaper column, April 16, 2006.

Seligman, Mac. "Travel Writers' Expenses: Who Should Pay?" *Public Relations Journal*, May 1990, pp. 27-34.

Shafer, Jack. "Eichenwald's Weird Checkbook Journalism." *Slate*, March 8, 2007.

Shaw, David. "Public Figures, Private Lives." Chapter 1 in *Journalism Today: A Changing Press for a Changing America.* New York: Harper's College Press, 1977.

Stevens, Mitchell. *Broadcast News.* New York: Holt, Rinehart and Winston, 1986.

Stone, Gerald. *Examining Newspapers: What Research Tells Us About America's Newspapers.* Newbury Park, CA: Sage Publications, 1987.

Chapter 6: Ethical Issues in Advertising

Amos, Denise L. "Banishing the Bimbo." *St. Petersburg Times*, February 23, 1992, p. 1-I.

"Are Automobile Dealers Editing Your Local Newspaper?" *Consumer Reports*, April 1992, p. 208.

Bauder, David. "Product Placement Concerns Producers of Major TV Series." Associated Press report, May 21, 2006.

Bobbitt, Randy. *Lottery Wars: Case Studies in Bible-Belt Politics.* Lanham, MD: Lexington Books, 2007.

Boddewyn, J.J. *Advertising Self-Regulation and Outside Participation.* New York: Quorum Books, 1988.

Bok, Derek. *Our Underachieving Colleges: A Candid Look at How Much Students Learn and Why They Should be Learning More.* Princeton, NJ: Princeton University Press, 2006.

Cauchon, Dennis. "Lottery Tickets Under Fire." *USA Today*, June 30, 2008, p. 3-A.

"Coming to a Theatre Near You: Truth in Advertising." News release from the office of Connecticut Rep. Andrew M. Fleischmann, January 14, 2005.

Daniel, Douglass K. *Lou Grant: The Making of TV's Top Newspaper Drama.* Syracuse, NY: Syracuse University Press, 1996.

Fisher, Marc. *Something in the Air: Radio, Rock, and the Revolution That Shaped a Generation.* New York: Random House, 2007.

Garrison, Renee. "Dangerous Images: Kilbourne Doesn't Buy Into Sexist Stereotypes." *The Tampa Tribune*, March 7, 1992, p. 1-D.

Jackson, Brooks, and Kathleen Hall Jamieson. *UnSpun: Finding Facts in a World of Disinformation.* New York: Random House, 2007.

Kilbourne, Jean. *The Naked Truth: Advertising's Image of Women.* New York: Ballantine Books, 2004.

Knickerbocker, Brad. "The Growing Cost of Gambling." *Christian Science Monitor*, June 7, 1999, p. 1.

Moore, Roy L., Ronald T. Farrar, and Erik L. Collins. *Advertising and Public Relations Law.* Mahwah, NJ: Lawrence Erlbaum Associates, 1998.

Parsons, Allen. "Advertising and Editorial Are Separate for a Reason." *Wilmington Star-News,* March 5, 2005, p. 1-B.

"Rosenfield Says Pressure Scared Sponsors." *Variety*, March 1, 1978, p. 65.

Spence, Edward, and Brett Van Heekeren. *Advertising Ethics.* Upper Saddle River, NJ: Prentice-Hall, 2004.

Steelman, Ben. "Is Going to the Movies a Dying Pastime?" *Wilmington Star-News*, June 2, 2005, p. 30-E.

Thayer, Lee. *Ethics, Morality and the Media: Reflections on American Culture.* New York: Hastings House Publishers, 1980.

Voorheis, Mike. "OK, Advertisers, Have I Got a Deal For You." *Wilmington Star-News,* June 15, 2006, pp. 1-D+.

Chapter 7: Ethical Issues in Public Relations

"Attacks by CBS Show the Public's Opinion of PR Pros." *PR Week*, June 5, 2008.

Baker, Lee W. *The Credibility Factor: Putting Ethics to Work in Public Relations.* Homewood, IL: Business One Irwin, 1993.

Berger, Bruce K., and Bryan H. Reber. *Gaining Influence in Public Relations: The Role of Resistance in Practice.* Mahwah, NJ: Lawrence Erlbaum Associations, 2006.

Bergman, Eric. "The Ethics of Not Answering." *Communication World*, September/October 2005, pp. 16-19.

Berkman, Robert I., and Christopher A. Shumway. *Digital Dilemmas: Ethical Issues for Online Media Professionals.* Ames, Iowa: Iowa State University Press, 2003.

Bivins, Thomas H. "Applying Ethical Theory to Public Relations." *Journal of Business Ethics,* Vol. 6 (1987), pp. 195-200.

Bleifuss, Joel. "Flack Attack." *Utne Reader*, January/February 1994, pp. 72-77.

Blyskal, Jeff, and Marie Blyskal. *PR: How the Public Relations Industry Writes the News.* New York: William Morrow and Company, 1985.

Bobbitt, Randy, and Ruth Sullivan. *Developing the Public Relations Campaign: A Team-Based Approach.* Boston: Allyn & Bacon, 2005.

Botan, Carl. "Ethics in Strategic Communication Campaigns: The Case for a New Approach to Public Relations." *The Journal of Business Communication*, April 1997, pp. 188-201.

Brown, Carolyn J. "Editorial Ethics and the Public Relations Practitioner." *Northwestern University Journal of Corporate Public Relations,* Winter 1991, pp. 32-36.

Brown, David H. "A Funny Thing Happened on the Way to the Forum on Ethics." *Public Relations Quarterly*, Spring 1986, pp. 20-23.

Curtin, Patricia A., and Lois Boynton. "Ethics in Public Relations." *Handbook of Public Relations,* Ed. Robert Heath. Thousand Oaks, CA: Sage Publications, 2001, pp. 411-421.

Day, Kenneth D., Qingwen Dong, and Clark Robins, "Public Relations Ethics." *Handbook of Public Relations,* ed. Robert Heath, pp. 403-409. Thousand Oaks, CA: Sage Publications, 2001.

Dilenschneider, Robert L. *Power and Influence: Mastering the Art of Persuasion.* New York: Prentice-Hall, 1990.

Dilenschneider, Robert L. "Spin Doctors Practice Public Relations Quackery." *The Wall Street Journal,* June 1, 1998.

Drinkard, Jim. "Public Relations: Selling an Idea With Distortion and Lies." *Charleston Gazette-Mail,* April 17, 1994, p. 4-B.

Edelman, Daniel J. "Ethical Behavior is Key to Field's Future." *Public Relations Journal,* November 1992, p. 32.

"The Ethics of Keeping Secrets." *Communication World,* August/September 1999, pp. 31-40.

Fox, James F. "Public Relations: Some Ethical Guidelines." *Ethics, Morality and the Media,* ed. Lee Thayer. New York: Hastings House, 1979.

Garneau, George. "Ethics Debate Reprised." *Editor & Publisher*, October 19, 1991, pp. 14-15.

Goodell, Jeffrey. "What Hill and Knowlton Can Do For You That It Couldn't Do For Itself." *New York Times Magazine,* Sept. 9, 1990, p. 44+.

Gower, Karla K. *Legal and Ethical Restraints Considerations for Public Relations.* Prospect Heights, IL: Waveland Press, Inc., 2008.

Hamilton, Seymour. "PR Ethics, From Publicity to Interaction." *Public Relations Quarterly,* Spring 1986, pp. 15-19.

Hutchison, Liese L. "Agency Ethics Isn't an Oxymoron." *Public Relations Tactics,* May 2000, p. 13.

Johnston, Jo-Ann. "Investors, Executives are More Wary of Corporate Fraud in Wake of Scandals." *The Tampa Tribune,* July 28, 2003.

Landler, Mark. "When a PR Firm Could Use a PR Firm." *Business Week,* May 14, 1990, p. 44.

Larson, Charles. V. *Persuasion: Reception and Responsibility.* Belmont, CA: Wadsworth Publishing, 1992.

Leyland, Adam. "One Out of Four Pros Admit Lying on Job." *PR Week,* May 1, 2000, p. 1.

Lordan, Edward L. *Essentials of Public Relations Management.* Chicago: Burnham, Inc., 2003.

Mallinson, Bill. *Public Lies and Private Truths: An Anatomy of Public Relations.* London: Cassell Publishing, 1996.

Martinson, David L. "How Should the PR Practitioner Respond When Confronted by Unethical Behavior?" *Public Relations Quarterly,* Summer 1991, pp. 18-21.

Marston, John. *The Nature of Public Relations.* New York: McGraw-Hill, 1963.

McElreath, Mark P. *Managing Systematic and Ethical Public Relations.* Madison, WI: Brown & Benchmark, 1993.

Moore, Roy L., Ronald T. Farrar, and Erik L. Collins. *Advertising and Public Relations Law.* Mahwah, NJ: Lawrence Erlbaum Associates, 1998.

Nelson, Joyce. *Sultans of Sleaze: Public Relations and the Media.* Toronto: Between the Lines Press, 1989.

Parsons, Patricia. *Ethics in Public Relations: A Guide to Best Practice.* Philadelphia: KoganPage, 2008.

Pratt, Cornelius. "Public Relations: The Empirical Research on Practitioner Ethics." *Journal of Business Ethics,* Vol. 10 (1991), pp. 229-236.

Raabe, Steve. "Public Relations Industry Tackles Image Problems." *The Denver Post,* April 12, 2008.

Rothenberg, Randall. "The Age of Spin." *Esquire,* December 1996, pp. 70+.

Seib, Philip and Kathy Fitzpatrick. *Public Relations Ethics.* Ft. Worth, TX: Harcourt Brace, 1995.

Seligman, Mac. "Travel Writers' Expenses: Who Should Pay?" *Public Relations Journal,* May 1990, pp. 27-34.

Shell, Adam. "Disinformation Not Justified in Corporate World." *Public Relations Journal,* February 1992, p. 8.

"Spin is Not the Job of PR." *O'Dwyer's PR Services Report,* January 1997, p. 6.

Springin, Karen, and Annetta Miller. "Doing the Right Thing." *Newsweek,* January 7, 1991, pp. 42-43.

Stacks, Don W. "A Quantitative Examination of Ethical Dilemmas in Public Relations." *Journal of Mass Media Ethics,* 1989, pp. 53-67.

Stauber, John, and Sheldon Rampton. *Toxic Sludge is Good For You: Lies, Damn Lies, and the Public Relations Industry.* Monroe, ME: Common Courage Press, 1995.

Stern, Gabriella, and Joann S. Lubin. "New Ethics Policy at GM Regulates Giving and Receiving." *Detroit Free Press,* June 6, 1996.

Stewart, Sally. *Media Training 101: A Guide to Meeting the Press.* Hoboken, NJ: John Wiley & Sons, 2004.

Swann, Patricia. *Cases in Public Relations Management.* Boston: McGraw Hill, 2008.

Vargas, Ann. "Liar, Liar, PR on Fire." *PR Week,* May 1, 2000, pp. 18-19.

"Ways to Avoid Ethical Problems." *Public Relations Journal,* June 1993, p. 9.

Weingarten, Gene. "I Fought PR, and PR Won." Syndicated newspaper column, January 15, 2006.

Weissman, Jerry. *In the Line of Fire: How to Handle Tough Questions When it Counts.* Upper Saddle River, NJ: Prentice Hall, 2005.

Wessel, Harry. "Workplace Ethics Issues Take Center Stage Again." *The Orlando Sentinel,* May 21, 2003.

Wilcox, Dennis L., Glen. T. Cameron, Bryan H. Reber, and Jae-Hwa Shin. *Think Public Relations.* Boston: Allyn & Bacon, 2012.

Williams, Dean. "Blurred Standards." *Communication World,* August/September 2002, pp. 34+.

Williams, Dean. "Un-Spun: Ethical Communication Practices Serve the Public Interest." *Communication World,* April/May 2002, pp. 27-35.

Witmer, Diane F. *Spinning the Web: A Handbook for Public Relations on the Internet.* New York: Longman Publishing, 2000.

Wright, Donald K. "Enforcement Dilemma: The Voluntary Nature of Public Relations Codes." *Public Relations Review,* Spring 1993, pp. 13-20.

Chapter 8: Ethical Issues in Political Communication

Alexander, Alison, and Janice Harrison. *Taking Sides: Clashing Views on Controversial Issues in Mass Media and Society*, seventh ed. New York: McGraw-Hill, 2003.

Altman, Alex. "A Brief History of the Bradley Effect." *Time*, November 3, 2008, p. 26.

"Auditors Say Bush Violated Law by Buying News Coverage." New York Times News Service, October 1, 2005.

Bleile, Paul. "PR and Propaganda: Were Do You Draw the Line?" *Communication World*, June/July 1998, pp. 26-28.

Bobbitt, Randy. *Lottery Wars: Case Studies in Bible Belt Politics*. Lanham, MD: Lexington Books, 2005.

Bobbitt, Randy. *Us Against Them: The Political Culture of Talk Radio*. Lanham, MD: Lexington Books, 2010.

Borchers, Timothy A. *Persuasion in the Media Age*. Boston: McGraw Hill, 2002.

Clarke, Tori. *Lipstick on a Pig: Winning in the No-Spin Era*. New York: Free Press, 2006.

Combs, James E., and Dan Dimmo. *The New Propaganda*. New York: Longman, 1993.

"Confederate Group Fights for State Specialty Plates." *USA Today,* May 10, 2011, p. 3-A.

Elliott, Stuart. "A Paid Endorsement Ignites a Debate in the Public Relations Industry." *New York Times*, January 12, 2005.

Gouran, Dennis. "Guidelines for the Analysis of Responsibility in Governmental Communication." *Teaching About Doublespeak,* ed. Daniel Dieterich. Urbana, IL: National Council of Teachers of English, 1976.

Holland, Jessie J., and Mark Sherman. "Hillary Movie Puts Campaign Finance Limits at Risk." Associated Press report, September 6, 2009.

Hovland, Carl, Irving Janis, and Harold Kelley. *Communication and Persuasion.* New Haven, CT: Yale University Press, 1953.

Jackson, Brooks, and Kathleen Hall Jamieson. *Un-Spun: Finding Facts in a World of Disinformation.* New York: Random House, 2007.

Jamieson, Kathleen Hall. *Dirty Politics: Deception, Distraction, and Democracy.* New York: Oxford University Press, 1992.

Johnson-Cartee, Karen S., and Gary A. Copeland. *Strategic Political Communication.* Lanham, MD: Rowman and Littlefield, 2004.

Jowett, Garth S., and Victoria O'Donnell. *Propaganda and Persuasion.* Newbury Park, CA: Sage Publications, 1992.

Kilpatrick, James J. "Taking License With Free Speech." Syndicated newspaper column, November 6, 2004.

Kurtz, Howard. *Spin Cycle: Inside the Clinton Propaganda Machine.* New York: Free Press, 1998.

Lakoff, George. *Don't Think of an Elephant: Know Your Values and Frame the Debate.* White River Junction, VT: Chelsea Green Publishing, 2004.

Larson, Charles U. *Persuasion: Reception and Responsibility.* Belmont, CA: Wadsworth Publishing Co., 1992.

Moyers, Bill. *Free Speech for Sale.* Video documentary by the Corporation for Public Broadcasting, 1999.

O'Brien, Timothy. "Spinning Frenzy: P.R.'s Bad Press." *New York Times,* February 13, 2005.

"Payments to Commentator Raise Ethical Concerns." Dennis L. Wilcox and Glen T. Cameron, *Public Relations: Strategies and Tactics.* Boston: Pearson Publishing, 2006, p. 501.

Press, Bill. *Spin This: All the Ways We Don't Tell the Truth.* New York: Pocket Books, 2001.

Rampton, Sheldon, and John Stauber. *Weapons of Mass Deception.* New York: Penguin Group, 2003.

Samples, John. "Stop Funding Government PR." Syndicated newspaper column, February 7, 2005.

Sharp, Tom. "Tennessee, Other States Draw Boundaries for 'Choose Life' Plates." *USA Today,* October 7, 2004.

Shepard, Alicia C. "Legislating Ethics." *American Journalism Review,* January/February 1994, pp. 37-41.

Swint, Kerwin. *Mudslingers: The Twenty-Five Dirtiest Political Campaigns of All Time.* New York: Union Square Press, 2008.

Walsh, Kenneth T. "Political Ads: Good, Bad, and Ugly." *U.S. News & World Report,* January 28, 2008, p. 53.

Chapter 9: Ethical Issues in Workplace Communication

"Academic, Athletic Irregularities Force Resignation." ESPN News, December 14, 2001.

Bavol, Todd. "Salary Negotiation is a Tricky Business." *Northwest Florida Business Climate,* May 2009, pp. 14-15.

Bell, Alison. "What Price Ethics?" *Entrepreneurial Woman,* January/February 1991, p. 68.

Bennett, Jessica. "What You Don't Know Can Hurt You." *Newsweek,* December 17, 2007, p. 10.

Burke, Tod. "Should Student-Professor Communication Be Privileged?" *The Magazine of Radford University,* December 2001, p. 46.

Drummond, Mike. "Efforts to Monitor Employees' Email Costly, Prickly." McClatchey Newspapers Syndicate, August 6, 2006.

Ferrell, O.C., John Fraedrich, and Linda Ferrell. *Business Ethics.* Boston: Houghton Mifflin Company, 2005.

Guffey, Mary Ellen. *Business Communication: Process and Product.* Cincinnati: Southwestern College Publishing, 2000.

Joyce, Amy. "When Do Workplace Lies Cross the Line?" *The Washington Post*, April 16, 2006.

Marklein, Mary Beth. "Is There Any Truth to Today's Resumes?" *USA Today*, February 6, 2003, p. 1-B.

"O'Leary Admits Resume is False, Quits Irish." *New York Daily News*, December 15, 2001.

"O'Leary Out at Notre Dame After One Week." SportsIllustrated.com, December 14, 2001.

Policinksi, Gene. "At Work, Free Speech Isn't Always Free." Syndicated newspaper column, November 3, 2009.

Singer, Gilbert. "Sexual Harassment: It Won't Go Away on its Own." *The Magazine of Northwest Florida Business*, August 2008, pp. 20-21.

"Ten Tall Tales Told on Resumes." CNN.com, August 13, 2008.

Weinstein, Bruce. "Lying On Your Resume Isn't Part of the Game." Syndicated newspaper column, November 18, 2006.

Chapter 10: When Ethical Issues Become Legal Issues

Alderman, Ellen, and Caroline Kennedy. *The Right to Privacy*. New York: Alfred A. Knopf, 1995.

Associated Press Stylebook and Libel Manual. New York: Associated Press, 2008.

Bobbitt, Randy. *Who Owns What's Inside the Professor's Head? Universities, Faculty, and the Battle Over Intellectual Property*. Lewiston, NY: Edwin Mellen Press, 2006.

Bobbitt, Randy, and Ruth Sullivan. *Developing the Public Relations Campaign: A Team-Based Approach*. Boston: Allyn & Bacon, 2009.

Brown, Charlene J., and Bill F. Chamberlin. *The First Amendment Reconsidered: New Perspectives on the Meaning of Freedom of Speech and Press*. New York: Longman, 1982.

Carter, T. Barton, Juliet L. Dee, Martin J. Gaynes, and Harvey L. Zuckman. *Mass Communications Law in a Nutshell*. St. Paul, MN: West Publishing, 1994.

Chamberlin, Bill, and Kent Middleton. *The Law of Public Communication*. White Plains, NY: Longman Publishing Group, 2010.

Colino, Stacey. "Long Arm of the Lawsuit SLAPPS at Dissenters." *In These Times*, March 28-April 3, 1990, pp. 11+.

Devol, Kenneth S. *Mass Media and the Supreme Court*. New York: Hastings House, 1990.

Dill, Barbara. *The Journalist's Handbook on Libel and Privacy*. New York: Macmillan, 1986.

Finn, Michael. "Trademark Tribulations." *American Journalism Review*, September 1993, pp. 44-51.

Fraleigh, Douglas M., and Joseph S. Tuman, *Freedom of Speech in the Marketplace of Ideas*. New York: St. Martin's Press, 1987.

Gilbert, Steven W., and Peter Lyman. "Intellectual Property in the Information Age." *Change*, May/June 1989, pp. 23-28.

Gower, Karla K. *Legal and Ethical Restraints Considerations for Public Relations*. Prospect Heights, IL: Waveland Press, Inc., 2008.

Kaiser, Robert G. "Because You Should Know: Governments Try to Hide What's Embarrassing." *The Washington Post*, June 25, 2006, p. 7-E.

McManis, Charles R. *Intellectual Property Law in a Nutshell*. St. Paul, MN: West Publishing, 1993.

Report on Trials and Damages. Media Law Resource Center, 2010.

Scott, M. M. "Intellectual Property Rights: A Ticking Time Bomb in Academia." *Academe,* May-June 1998, pp. 22-26.

Sharpe, Jo Ellen Meyers. "Whose Copyrights?" *Editor & Publisher*, February 14, 1998, pp. 14-15.

"Should Lottery Winners be Kept Secret?" *USA Today*, January 4, 2013, p. 4-A.

Sneed, Don, Tim Wulfemeyer, and Harry W. Stonecipher. "Public Relations News Releases and Libel: Extending First Amendment Protections." *Public Relations Review*, Vol. 17, no. 2 (1991), pp. 131-144.

Walsh, Frank. *Public Relations and the Law*. Gainesville, FL: Institute for Public Relations Research and Education, 1991.

Subject Index

ABC News, 88, 89
ABC Sports, 61
ABC Television Network, 63
Abelard, Peter, 22-23
Abortion, 90, 158, 230
Absolute Honesty, 190
Absolutism, 35
Academic records, 284-85
Access to information, 288-294
Accident scenes (media access to),
Accuracy in Media, 55
Actual malice rule, 279, 281-82
Ad hominem, 220
Adams-Wade, Nora, 143
Adler, John, 137
Adobe Corporation, 135
Advertising boycotts, 159-60
Advertising industry, 151-73, 183-84, 264
Afghanistan, 94, 142
African American journalists, 92
African Americans, 53, 218-19
Agee, Warren K., 180
Agency-client relations (public relations), 191,
  195-96, 197-99
Agenda-setting, 56
AIDS and AIDS charities, 56, 62, 64, 65, 115,
  138-39, 169
Alabama Highway Patrol, 219
Alcoholic beverages, 262
Alda, Alan, 95, 232
Alger, Dean, 6
Alliance for American Advertising, 167
Amedure, Scott, 58
America, 32
American Advertising Federation, 3, 36, 152,
  171, 301
American Association for Public Opinion
  Research, 213-14
American Association of Advertising Agencies,
  151-52, 153, 162
American Association of Political Consultants,
  213-14

American Civil Liberties Union, 184
American Dental Association, 173
American flag, 261, 266, 270
American Foundation for Suicide Prevention,
  114
American Health Care Association, 160
American Idol, 157
American Institute of Philanthropy, 169
American Lung Association, 169
American Management Association, 247
American Red Cross, 50
American Society for Personnel Administration,
  238
American Society of Media Photographers, 135
American Society of Newspaper Editors, 3, 84,
  92, 106, 302-03
Americans with Disabilities Act, 246
Amos n' Andy, 53
Amoss, James, 72
Amtrak, 73
Amusing Ourselves to Death, 41
Anheuser-Busch, 52
Annenberg Public Policy Center, 227
Anonymous sources (see confidential sources),
  117
Anti-paparazzi laws, 113
Appropriation, 110, 181, 285-86, 287-88
Aquinas, Thomas, 23
Aramony, William, 12
Areopagatica, 26
Aristotle, 19, 21-22
Arnold, Oren, 33
Arrogance, 55
Ashe, Arthur, 138-39
Asian journalists, 92
Asner, Ed, 232
Associated Press Sports Editors, 304-05
Associated Press Stylebook, 121
Associated Press, 91, 94, 121, 141, 187, 223
At the Center of the Storm, 127
Atlanta Braves, 62
Atlanta Public School System, 13

Atlas Shrugged, 34
Atomic Energy Act (of 1954), 130
Ault, Phillip H., 180
Aunt Jemima, 274
Auto mechanics, 14
Automobile license plates, 230

Bacon, Francis, 24-25
Bagdikian, Ben, 6, 40-41, 122
Bait and Switch (book), 202
Bait and switch (in advertising), 152, 171, 301
Bait and switch (in public relations), 195
Bait and switch (interviewing technique), 120
Baker, Lee W., 190, 194-95
Baldwin, Alex, 232
Baltimore, city of, 7
Bamberger, Michael, 91, 98
Bandwagon, 217
Bangles, 68
Bank of America, 52
Bank of Boston v. Bellotti, 225
Bankers, 14
Barnacle, Mike, 94
"Barracuda," 233
Barron, Jerome, 7
Baudrillard, Jean, 32-33, 41
Bavol, Todd, 244-45
Bay of Pigs, 130
Beast, The, 123
Before I Go, 250
Behavioral advertising, 152
Beman, Deane, 180
Benedetto, Richard, 9
Bennett, William, 12
Bentham, Jeremy, 29-30
Bergen, Edgar, 68
Bernays, Edward L., 180-94
Berne Convention, 275-76
Bernstein, Carl, 117
Berry, Justin, 127
Better Business Bureau, 169
Better Crocker, 274
Bias, 55
Bible, 142-43, 270
Biden, Joe, 63, 88
bin Laden, Osama, 143
Bipartisan Campaign Reform Act, 225
Bissinger, H. G., 95-96
Black, Don,
Blackstone, William, 27, 268

Blackstonian Doctrine, 27, 268
Blair, Jayson, 10, 94
Blogs and blogging, 26-27, 188, 265, 319-22
Blood, Rebecca, 319-22
Bluetooth, 274
Bly, Nellie, 96, 122
Blyskal, Jeff and Marie, 201
Bok, Derek, 172
Bok, Sissela, 38-39
Bono, Sonny, 113
Book publishing, 275
Book reviews, 280, 283
Boorda, Jeremy, 116
Boorstin, Daniel, 40, 201
"Born to Run," 233
Boston Bruins, 95
Boston College Law Review, 164
Boston Globe, 87, 88, 90
Bowl Championship Series, 91
BP oil spill,
Bradlee, Ben, 122
Bradley Effect, 221-22
Bradley, Bert, 36
Bradley, Tom, 221-22
Brandeis University, 38
Brandeis, Louis, 290
Brando, Marlon, 157
Brauchli, Marcus, 7-8
Breakthrough, 88
Breath of the Gods, The,
Brennan, William, 266
Brewer, Albert, 218
Bribery, 31
British Petroleum, 129
Broadcast News, 120-21
Broussard, Paul, 115
Brown & Williamson Tobacco, 157
Brown University, 35, 100
Brown, Hub, 140
Brown, Michael, 203
Browne, Jackson, 233
Bryant, Kobe, 113
Buckley v. Valeo, 225
Budweiser, 53
Burden of proof, 264
Burke, Tod, 245
Bush, Barbara, 60
Bush, George H.W., 10
Bush, George W., 10, 60, 96, 109, 127, 136, 137, 142, 203, 217, 225, 226, 232
Bush, Jeb, 109

Bush, Jenna, 60
Bush, Noelle, 109
Business executives, 14
Business Week, 192
Byrne, David, 233

Cable News Network (CNN), 126, 127, 141, 142
Cable television, 8
California Highway Patrol, 94
California State Lottery, 160
California Supreme Court, 184
Cambodia, 93
Campaign for a Commercial-Free Childhood, 167
Campari Liquer, 57
Capital punishment, 28
Car salespeople, 14
Card-stacking, 218
CareerBuilder.com, 240
Carlin, George, 68
Carson, Rachel, 283
Carter, Jimmy, 122
"Case of the Lying Husband, The," 32
Castro, Fidel, 135
Categorical imperative, 28-29, 35, 36, 38
Catholic Church, 23, 25, 66
Caveat emptor, 153
CBS News, 4, 10, 54, 87, 94, 125, 126, 142, 129, 137, 202
CBS News/Wall Street Journal Poll, 223
CBS Radio Network, 75
CBS Sports, 61
CBS Television Network, 68, 160
Celebrity Apprentice, 63
Cellular telephones, 8
Center for American Progress, 227
Center for Integration and Improvement of Journalism, 53
Central Asia Institute, 94
Central Hudson Test, 158
Challenger (space shuttle), 293
Charlotte Observer, 50
Checkbook journalism, 24, 126-27
Cheers, 157
Chertoff, Michael, 203
Chevrolet Motor Company, 157
Chicago Tribune, 122-23
Child abuse, 91
Child pornography, 126-27
Chilling effect, 2, 276

Christian Science Monitor, 164
Chronicle of Higher Education, 171, 245
Churning, 195
Cianfrani, Henry, 85
Circumvention rule, 272
Citizen journalism, 70
Citizens for a Free Kuwait, 200
Citizens United v. Federal Elections Commission, 226
Citizens United, 226
City council meetings, 290-91
Civil Aeronautics Board, 153
Civil Disobedience, 22
Civil Rights Act (of 1964), 239
Civil rights, 218-19, 239
Civil War, 61, 228, 230, 269
Clarifications, 132-33, 142-43
Clergy, 14
Cleveland Plain Dealer, 122
Clinton Global Initiative, 88
Clinton, Bill, 12, 60, 88, 108, 127, 216, 217, 226, 238, 294
Clinton, Chelsea, 60
Clinton, Hillary, 88, 216, 217, 222
Cobain, Kurt, 115
Coca-Cola, 274
Cochrane, Elizabeth Jane (Nellie Bly), 122
Cognitive dissonance, 56
Cohen, Andrew, 202
Colbert, Stephen, 73
Colgate-Palmolive, 155
College football, 41-42, 218
College Media Advisors Code of Ethical Behavior, 306-07
College sports, 41-42, 218, 285
Columbia Journalism Review, 85-112
Columbia University, 126, 143, 216
Columbine High School, 60, 126
Commercial speech, 262-64
Common Cause, 214
Common law copyright, 271
Common newsroom, 7
Communication and Persuasion, 215
Communication law, 1, 259-94
Communist Party, 31
Compassionate decision-making, 27
Compelled speech, 267
Complete Works of Nellie Bly, The, 122
Computer Forensics Inc., 247
Concert reviews, 280, 283
Conde Naste Traveler, 128

Confederate Heritage license plates, 230
Confidential sources, 117-19, 305
Confidentiality, 119, 181, 190, 187-98, 201-02,
    309
Conflicts of interest, 85-91, 190-91, 316-17,
    321, 323, 326
Consent, 285
Content neutrality, 264-66
Contraceptives, advertising of, 262
Contributions to political campaigns, 182, 225
Contributory infringement, 273-74
Cooke, Janet, 10, 93
Cookies, 152
Coors Brewing, 53
Copyright Law (of 1909), 271
Copyright Revision Act (of 1976), 272-72
Copyrights, 268-75
Cornell University, 35
Corporation for Public Broadcasting, 55
Corrections and correction policies, 131-35,
    142-43
Cosell, Howard, 61
Council on Compulsive Gambling, 164
Couric, Katie, 137
Courtesy bias, 221-22
Courtrooms, 289
Cox Doctrine, 111-12
Cox, James, 87
Credibility Factor, The, 194-95
Credit cards, 163
Crichton, John, 151-52, 162
Crime and accident scenes, 289
Crime rates, 218
Crist, Charlie, 233
Critical infrastructure exemption to FOIA, 293
Criticism of traditional media, 9-11
Crossing Jordon, 65, 76
CSI Effect, 65, 76-77
CSI Miami, 76
CSI New York, 76
CSI, 65, 76-77
Cultural relativism, 31
Cumulative effects theory, 48
Cure meetings, 291
Current Issues in Higher Education,

Da Vinci Code, The, 66
Dale Earnhardt Family Privacy Act, 294
Dallas Morning News, 143
Dallas Times-Herald, 116

Danson, Ted, 157
Dateline, 50, 124-25, 131, 142, 161, 171
Day care providers, 14
Daytona 500 (race), 294
Death of Outrage, The, 12
Deceptive advertising, 152-56
Declaration of Independence, 270
Deer Hunter, The, 116
Defamation, 133, 181, 196, 262, 276-283
Democratic Party, 87
Demolition Man, 157
Department of Homeland Security, 203
Department of Housing and Urban Develop
    ment, 153
DePaulo, Bella, 39
Desecration of memory, 279
Detroit Lions, 95
Dewey, John, 34
Dieterich, Dennis, 214
Digital manipulation of photographs, 135-37
Digital Millennium Copyright Act, 272
Digital video disks, 269
Dilenschneider, Robert L., 195, 199-200, 201
Direct response advertising, 152
Disinformation, 221
Disney Films, 250
Disneyland, 128, 188
District of Columbia, 261
Diversity, 91-93
Dixie Chicks, 232
DNA testing, 76
Dockers, 157
Dog-fighting, 131
Donaldson, Sam, 89
Double-dipping, 89-90
Downloading music, 273-74
Downs, Thomas M., 73
Drudge Report, 228
Drudge, Matt, 228
Drunk driving, 56, 63, 97
Duckett, Melinda, 116-17, 140
Duke University, 13
Duke, David, 71-72
Duplin County Republican Party, 228
Durkheim, Emile, 30-31. 34
Dwyer, R. Budd, 114-15

Earnhardt, Dale, 294
East Oregonian, The, 143
eBay, 128

Edelman, Murray, 227
Editorial cartoons, 58-59
Editorial control, 262
Edwards, Edwin, 71-72
Efron, Edith, 54-55
Ehrenreich, Barbara, 95-96, 202
Eichenwald, Kurt, 126-27
Electronic (traditional) forums, 265
Electronic mail, 152, 247, 265
Elon University, 223
Employee evaluations, 243-44
Employer standards, 2-3
Ends justify the means, 24, 38, 240
Enron, 248
Entertainment Weekly, 250
Entrapment, 124
Entrepreneurial Woman, 241
Environmental Protection Agency, 153
Equal Employment Opportunities Commission, 239
Equal protection clause, 260
Equivalent function rules, 266
ER, 157
Errors, correcting, 131-35, 142-43
Escambia County (Florida), 64
ESPN, 65
ET: The Extraterrestrial, 157
Ethics, definition of, 1
Eubank, Bill, 141
Euphemisms, 219
European influences, 22-33
Evans, H. Dean, 164
Executive privilege, 292
Executive session, 290
Expenditures in political campaigns, 182, 225

Facebook, 152, 243, 265
Fahrenheit 9/11, 225
Fair comment, 279, 280, 282-83
Fair use, 271-72
False advertising, 154-56, 262, 264
False dichotomy, 219-20
False light, 110, 181, 284
Falwell, Jerry, 57
Family Educational Rights and Privacy Act (FERPA), 285
Family influence on decision-making, 2
Farmers for Fairness, 228-29
Federal Communications Commission, 6, 47, 48, 67-70, 153, 159, 217, 262, 264

Federal Election Campaign Act, 224
Federal Elections Commission, 153, 182, 213, 225, 226, 262, 267
Federal Emergency Management Agency, 203, 291
Federal Radio Commission, 47, 48, 68
Federal Reserve Board, 35
Federal Trade Commission, 152-56, 159, 163, 164, 167, 171, 173, 183-84, 263, 264
Feingold, Russ, 225
Feldman, Joan, 247
Felicity, 250
Fellini, Federico, 113
Fields, Virginia, 136
Fighting words, 262
Firearms, advertising of, 159, 262
Fireworks, advertising of, 262
First Amendment, 4-5, 25, 35, 62, 64, 130, 159, 180, 182-83, 213, 230, 232, 240, 254, 259-294, 302
First Amendment Center, 260-61
First Amendment hierarchy, 263
First Amendment right of access, 261-62
First Amendment right of confidentiality, 261
First Amendment right of editorial control, 262
Fish Bowl, 187
Fitzpatrick, Kathy, 189
Flag-burning, 261, 266
Fleeting expletives, 69
Fleischmann, Andrew, 168
Fletcher, Joseph, 20, 36
Flickr, 70
Flight attendants, 66
Flight Plan, 66
Florida Government in the Sunshine Law, 290
Florida Supreme Court, 294
Florida-Georgia football game, 63
Flynt, Larry, 57
Fonda, Jane, 136, 232
Food and Drug Administration, 153, 155-56
Food Lion, 123
Ford Motor Company, 285-86
Foreman, Laura, 85
Forensic Technologies, 198
Forrest Gump, 65-66
Forrest, Nathan Bedford, 230
Foster, Vince, 294
Fountainhead, The, 34
Fourteenth Amendment, 260
Fox News, 64
Fox Television Network, 65

Frankel, Max, 90
Franklin, Benjamin, 262
Free speech clause, 261-67
Freebie policies, 127-29, 187-89, 304, 323
Freedom of Information Act, 291-93
Freelance writers, 188, 273
French, Thomas, 95
Frey, James, 16
Friday Night Lights, 95-96
Fried, Charles, 39
Friedman, Milton, 35
"Fuck," use of term, 122

Galella, Ron, 113
Gallagher, Maggie, 226
Gallup Inc., 223, 260
Gallup Poll, 14-15, 222, 223, 260
Gannett News Service, 9
Garner, James, 157
Gartner, Michael, 112
Gay rights, 53, 91
"Gay," use of term, 64
Geddings, Kevin, 231
Geico Gecko, 274
General Accounting Office, 226
General Agreement on Tariffs and Trade, 275
General Motors, 131, 142, 157
Georgia Technological Institute (Georgia Tech),
    248-49
Gibson, Mel, 62
Gillett Amendment, 226
Giuliani, Donna Hanover, 86
Giuliani, Rudolph, 56-57, 86, 232
Glass, Stephen, 10, 94
Glittering generalities, 217
God, 25
Goldberg, Bernard, 55
Golden Marbles, 159
Golden Mean, 21, 111
Goldstein, Tom, 126
Good Morning America, 71
Google and Gmail, 152
Gore, Al, 228
Gouran, Dennis, 214
Government Accounting Office, 226
Government in the Sunshine Act, 290
Grace, Nancy, 116-17, 141
Grade school teachers, 14
Grand Forks, North Dakota, 15
Great Smokey Mountains National Park, 230

Greek philosophers, 19-21
Greenhouse, Linda, 90
Greenspan, Alan, 35
Grey's Anatomy, 63
Grokster, 274
Group libel, 277
Guantanamo Bay, 142-43
Gulf of Mexico, 129
Gulf War Did Not Happen, The, 32-33
Gulf War, 32-33, 260

Hannity, Sean, 54, 228
"Happy Birthday to You," 270
Harassment, 238-40
Harding, Tonya, 57, 126, 137
Harding, Warren G., 3, 87
Harlan, John, 31
Harlequin Publishing, 187
Harrelson, Woody, 232
Harris Poll, 223
Hart, Gary, 108
Hart, Kevin, 41-42
Hart, Philip, 153
Harvard Business Review, 86
Harvard Business School, 163
Harvard University, 36, 64
Hate speech, 262-63
Hawthorne Effect, 95
Health care debate, 253
Heart, 233
"Here Comes the Bride," 270
Hill & Knowlton, 195, 199-200, 201
Hispanic journalists, 92
Hitler, Adolph, 135
Hobbes, Thomas, 25
Hobby, William P. Jr., 87
Hog farming, 228-29
Holliday, George, 70
Home Depot, 240
Home video recorders, 274
Homeland Security Act (of 2002), 293
Horowitz, David, 62, 64
Horrow, Rick, 93
Hostile work environment, 239
Houston Post, 87
Hovland, Carl, 215
How I Met Your Mother, 157
How the Grinch Stole Christmas, 136
Human resources departments, 239, 243
Humphrey, Hubert H., 54

Hurricane Katrina, 53, 169, 203
Hustler, 57
Hutchins Commission, 5-6, 92
Hutchins, Robert M., 5
Hutchison, Liese L., 196
Hyper-reality, 32-33

"I'll Be Home for Christmas," 59
Ifill, Gwen, 88
Illinois Lottery, 88, 165
Immersion journalism, 94-95, 100
Implied consent, 288
Imus, Don, 63, 75
Indecency (television), 67-70
Independent contractors, 271, 273
Indianapolis Star, 131
Infringement (copyright), 271, 273
Ingraham, Laura, 232
Ingram, Timothy, 123
Insider trading, 181, 184
Institute for Propaganda Analysis, 216-19
Intellectual property, 181, 268-70
Internal publications, 287-88
Internal Revenue Service, 182, 224-25
International Association of Business Commu-
    nicators, 3, 180, 185-86, 187, 190, 194, 196,
    201-02, 238, 308-10
International War Crimes Tribunal, 31
Internet service providers, 272
Internet, 6, 7, 8, 9, 26-27, 152, 217, 265, 272
Interviewing, 119-22
"Introducing Objectivism," 35
Intrusion, 110, 186
Involuntary public figures, 281
iPod, 274
Iran-Contra scandal, 12
Iraq War, 136
Iredell County, North Carolina, 59

Jackson, Janet, 68
Janis, Irving, 215
Jaska, James, 189
Jefferson, Thomas, 26
Jenny Jones Show, The, 58
Jessie James and the Midgets, 63
JFK, 65
Jocose lies, 23
Johannesen, Richard, 215
John F. Kennedy Profile in Courage Award, 229

Johnson & Johnson, 173
Johnson, Ervin "Magic," 138-39
Johnson, Larry, 190
Johnson, Roy, 138-39
Johnston, Tom, 233
Jolly Green Giant, 274
Jones, Christopher, 93
Josephson, Michael, 241
Journalism education, 11
Journalistic privilege, 261
Jovanovic, Dave, 114
Jowett, Garth S., 215
Judges, 14, 289
Jungle, The, 95
Junior League of Greater Fort Lauderdale, 89
Junkets, 127-29, 188
Kaczynski, Ted, 130
Kalb, Bernard, 4, 221
Kansas City Star, 75
Kant, Immanuel, 22, 28-29, 35, 36, 38
Kazaa, 274
Keebler Elves, 274
Keith, Toby, 232
Kelley, Harold, 215
Kennedy, Edward, 112-13
Kennedy, John F., 11-12, 65, 70, 108
Kerner Commission, 92
Kerrigan, Nancy, 57, 126, 137
Kerry, John, 136, 232
Khmer Rouge, 93
Kierkegaard, Soren, 22, 30
Kilbourne, Jean, 162
Killing Us Softly video series, 162
King, Martin Luther Jr., 22
King, Rodney, 70-71, 126
Kleenex, 274
Klein, Tammy, 76
KNBC-TV, 140
Knobel, Beth, 129
Koran, 142
Kroc, Joan and Ray, 10
KTLA, 70
Ku Klux Klan, 71-72, 216, 230
Kurtz, Howard, 85, 88, 110, 139
Kuwait, 200

La Dolce Vita, 113
Lambert Pharmaceuticals, 173
Landers, Ann, 85, 202
Lanham Act, 274

Larry King Live, 71, 127
Larson, Charles, 214
Law & Order, 65, 76, 157
Lawyers, 14
Lee, William E., 6
Leno, Jay, 60, 73
Letterman, David, 59-60
Letters of recommendation, 243-44
Letters to the editor, 282
Leviathan, The, 25
Levitt, Theodore, 163
Lewinsky, Monica, 108, 126
Lewis, Jerry, 61
Libel Defense Resource Center, 276
Libel defenses, 57
Libel of the dead, 279
Libel, 57, 276-283
Libels of omission, 279
Liberal bias of media, 54-55, 227-28
Libertarianism, 5, 26-27, 268
Liberty University, 100
Library of Congress, 270
Licensing (public relations), 194
Lichter, Robert, 54
Liebling, A. J., 161
Life, 70
Likelihood of confusion, 275
Limbaugh, Rush, 54, 64, 227-28
Limited liability rule, 272
Limited public figures, 281
Limited public forum, 265-66
Lincoln Memorial, 171
Lincoln, Abraham, 135, 171
LinkedIn, 243
Lippmann, Walter, 39-40
Lister, Joseph, 173
Listerine, 173
Litigation PR, 198-99
Little People of America, 63
Lobbyists, 14, 184
"Long Train Running," 233
Los Angeles Clippers, 52
Los Angeles County Sheriff's Office, 76
Los Angeles Kings, 52
Los Angeles Times, 52, 54, 67, 121
Lott, Trent, 62
Lotteries, 54, 164-66, 219, 222, 231
Lou Grant, 160
Louisville Courier-Journal, 135
Lowe, Herbert, 92
Lowes Cineplex, 168

Lying: Moral Choice in Public and Private Life, 38
Machiavelli, Niccolo, 24
MacIntosh, 274
MacKinnon, Catherine, 6
Madiera, Rebecca, 192
Madison, James, 259
Magic bullet theory, 48
Magic words test, 225
Major League Baseball, 287
Malice, 279, 281-82
Malpractice, 277
Maltby, Lewis, 243
Manufactured quotes, 196
Manufacturer's suggested retail price, 163
Margaret, Ann, 137
Margin for error, 223
Marion Star, 87
Marketplace of ideas, 6, 26-27
Markstein, Gary, 59
Marquis, Josh, 76
Marston, John, 186
Martin Luther King Jr. Holiday, 61
Martin, Roland, 110
Martinez, Bob, 233
Master's Golf Tournament, 62, 247
Matrix, The, 33
McCain, John, 88, 109-110, 217, 225, 233
McCarthy, Charlie, 68
McClellan, Scott, 202
McCombs, Max, 56
McDonald's, 10, 52, 274
McManus, Michael, 226
McNamara, Robert, 130
McVeigh, Timothy, 145
Media Access Project, 110
Media Circus, The, 85
Media competition, 8
Media convergence, 7
Media Law Resource Center, 276
Media Monopoly, The, 40-41
Media ownership, 6, 40-41
Media relations, 193-99
Media Research Center, 55
Media ride-alongs, 125, 140
Meiklejohn, Alexander, 35
Meritor Savings Bank v. Vinson, 238-39
Miami Herald, 12
Michigan Lottery, 164
Mickey Mouse, 273
Middle Tennessee State University, 223

Middleton, Kent, 6
Midler, Bette, 285-86
Military installations, 289
Military officers, 15
Mill, John Stuart, 5, 26, 29-30
Miller Brewing, 53
Miller, Brownie and Dave, 140
Miller, Clyde, 216-19
Million Little Pieces, A, 16
Milton, John, 5, 26-27
Milwaukee Journal-Sentinel, 59
Minimal effects theory, 48
Minneapolis Star-Tribune, 57
Minnesota Vikings, 249
Miss Teenage America Pageant, 58
Mitchell, John, 130
Monday Night Football, 61
National Council on Adoption, 65
Mondiacs, Chris, 227
Monkey Business, 108
Monroe, Marilyn, 115
Moonlighting, 89-90
Moore, Michael, 225
Mortenson, Greg, 94
Mothers Against Drunk Driving, 63
Movie reviews, 280
Movie starting times, 168
Mr. Clean, 274
MSNBC, 63, 75, 88
Muckrakers, 5
Murdoch, Rupert, 59
Murphy, Ian, 123
Murphy, Wendy, 76
Murrah Federal Building, 145
Murrow, Edward R., 4
Muscular Dystrophy Association, 61
Music downloading, 274
Muslims, 240
Mussolini, Benito, 175
My Life, 127
Myers, Chris, 137

Nachman, Jerry, 112
Name-calling, 216
Napster, 274
Nation, The,
National Aeronautics and Space Administration, 293
National Association for the Advancement of Colored People, 53, 93

National Association of Black Journalists, 92
National Association of Broadcasters, 36, 48-49, 69
National Association of Theater Owners, 168
National Basketball Association, 52
National Business Ethics Survey, 241
National Cable Television Association, 69
National Center for Health Statistics, 115
National Collegiate Athletic Association, 66, 247
National District Attorneys Association, 76
National Football League, 65, 109, 156
National Football League Players Association, 65
National Geographic, 136
National Guard, 10
National Hockey League, 52
National Mall, 265
National News Council, 134
National Organization for Women, 230
National Public Radio, 55, 64, 135, 222
National security exemption, 292
National Writers Union, 273
Natural Law Doctrine, 23
Navy Seals, 143
NBC News, 10, 61, 74, 112, 124, 131, 142, 171
NBC News/Associated Press Poll, 223
NBC Television Network, 50, 68, 73, 96
NBC Universal, 88
NCAA Basketball Tournament, 247
NCAA Women's Basketball Tournament, 75
Negligence, 277
Nelson, Joyce, 202
Neutral reportage, 280-81
New Hampshire license plate, 267
New Jersey Lottery, 165
New Orleans, city of, 53, 203
New Republic, 10, 39, 94
New River, 228
New York Magazine, 56-57
New York Mets, 62
New York Post, 59, 88, 112, 126
New York Supreme Court, 287
New York Times Company, 128
New York Times v. Sullivan, 282
New York Times, 10, 16, 54, 85, 86, 90, 93, 94, 122, 126-28, 128, 130, 199, 273, 280, 281-82, 293
New York University, 240
New York World, 5
New York Yankees, 59-62, 287

New Yorker, 59-93
News conferences, 196
News look-alikes, 62-63
News releases, 67, 193, 196, 286-87
News Twisters, The, 64
Newsday, 92
Newspaper editorials, 262
Newspaper readership, 8
Newspaper reporters, 15
Newsstand, 142
Newsweek, 137, 142-43
Newsworthiness defense, 284, 287
Newton Tab, 87
Nickel and Dimed, 95-96
"Nigger," use of term, 63
Nightline, 71
Nike, 157, 183-184, 274
Nixon, 65
Nixon, Richard, 54
No Child Left Behind, 226
Nobel Prize for Literature, 31
Non-obscene sexual expression, 262-64
Non-obtrusive speech, 261
Nonprofit organizations, 287
Non-public forums, 265
Norris, Meredith, 231
North American Association of State and Pro-
    vincial Lotteries, 165
North Carolina Board of Elections, 229
North Carolina Lottery Commission, 231
North Carolina Lottery, 231
North Carolina Open Meetings Law, 290
Northwest Florida Daily News, 55
"Not for attribution," 119
Notification clause, 272
Nowak, Lisa, 57
Nurses, 15
Nursing home operators, 15

O'Donnell, Victoria, 216
O'Leary, George, 12, 242, 248-49
Oakland Athletics, 143
Obama, Barack, 59, 88, 216, 220, 222
Obama, Michelle, 59
Objectivism, 35
Obscenity, 1, 67, 262, 264
Obstruction of justice, 181
Obtrusive speech, 261
Off/on the record, 118-19
Oklahoma City bombing, 145

Oklahoma Lottery, 231
Olbermann, Keith, 88
Oldsmobile, 157
Olympics and Olympic rings, 274, 275
Ombudsmen, 55, 134-35
On background, 119
On deep background, 119
On Liberty, 29-30
Onassis, Jackie Kennedy, 113
Online databases, 273
Online journalism, 8
Online News Association, 311
OnStar, 274
Open-source journalism, 70
Operation Tailwind, 142
Oprah Winfrey Show, 16, 277
Originality and creativity rule, 269
Orlando International Airport, 57
Our Underachieving Colleges, 172
Overbreadth and vagueness, 266
Oxford University, 25

Pakistan, 94
Palin, Bristol, 59-60, 109-10
Palin, Sarah, 59-60, 88, 109-10, 233
Paparazzi, 113
Paper Lion, 95
"Paradise Lost," 26
Parents Television Council, 70
Parent-Teachers Associations, 86, 215
Parker, Kathleen, 64
Parody (appropriation), 285-286
Parody (copyright), 272
Parseghian, Ara, 249
Parsons, Allen, 127-28
Passive (traditional) forums, 265
Paulison, David, 203
Penn, Sean, 232
Pennsylvania Lottery, 165
Penny press, 5
"Pentagon Papers," 130
Pentagon, 232
People for the Ethical Treatment of Animals, 57
Pepper, Claude, 216-17
Pepsico, 192
Periodical Table of the Elements, 270
Permian High School, 96
Persuasion defined, 216
Persuasion: Reception and Responsibility, 214
Perverted Justice, 50

Pew Research Center, 8, 223, 227-28
Pfizer, 173
PGA Tour, 180
Pharmacists, 15
Philadelphia Inquirer, 85
Photocopiers, 273
Photograph selection, 21, 111
Photographs, manipulation of, 135-37
Photoshop, 135
Physical (traditional) forums, 265
Physicians, 15
Pitts, Leonard, 12
Pittsburgh Steelers, 217
Plagiarism, 271
Plain folks, 217
Planned Parenthood, 230
Plato, 19-21
Playmakers, 65
Pledge of allegiance, 267
Plimpton, George, 169
Police Benevolent Associations, 169
Police officers, 15, 169
Policinski, Gene, 139
Political action committees, 183
Political advertising, 262-66, 213-22, 224-26
Political candidates, 87-88
Political communication, 213-250
Political contributions, 182-83
Political correctness, 61-64
Political harassment, 240
Political speech, 213-50, 262-68
Politicians, 14
Politics of Misinformation, The, 227
Pollitt, Katha, 112
Polls and polling data, 219, 221-24
"Pomp and Circumstance," 270
Pornography, 5, 7, 31, 127, 264
Portfolio, 127
Postman, Neil, 41
Power and Influence, 195
Powerful effects theories, 48
PR Week, 180
PR: How the Public Relations Industry Writes the News, 201
Pragmatism, 34
Presidential election (of 1968), 54
Presidential election (of 1984), 233
Presidential election (of 2004), 144
Presidential election (of 2008), 88, 109-110, 222, 233
Presidential election (of 2012), 182, 233

Presidential election (of 2016), 188, 233
Prime Time Live, 123
Princess Diana, 113, 126
Principle of veracity, 38-39
Printer's Ink statutes, 153
Printer's Ink, 153
Prinze, Freddie Sr., 115
Prior restraint, 27, 267
Prisons, 289
Pritchard, Michael, 189
Privacy law, 284-88
Privacy of news subjects, 23, 38, 58, 106-11, 138-40, 181, 284-88
Privacy, 11
Private facts, 110, 181, 284-85
Private figures, 281-82
Private Lessons, 68
Privilege (confidentiality), 182,197-98, 245-46, 261
Privilege (libel defense), 280
Product disparagement, 277
Product placements, 156-58
Profanity, 68-70, 121-22
Progressive, The, 130
Propaganda and Persuasion, 216
Propaganda, 216-20
Prostate cancer, 57
Prostitution, 159
Proxmire, William, 153
Pseudo-events, 40
Public Broadcasting Service, 55, 88
Public disclosure, 185
Public domain (copyright), 270
Public domain (privacy defense), 285
Public figures, 108-110, 281-82
Public journalism, 34
Public meetings, 288, 290-91
Public Opinion, 39
Public Radio News Directors Code of Ethics, 312
Public records, 289, 291-94
Public Relations Ethics, 189
Public relations industry, 13, 67, 179-203, 231
Public Relations Society of America, 3, 36, 180, 184, 185-86, 187, 190, 194, 196, 201-02, 238, 313-18
Public Relations: Strategies and Tactics, 180
Public service journalism, 50-51
Puerto Rico, 158-59
Pulitzer Prizes for Journalism, 10, 248
Pulitzer, Joseph, 5

Punishment after the fact, 267-68
Push polls, 222

Quid pro quo, 127, 187, 239
Quinnipiac University, 223
Quotations, 121-22, 196

Race, 111, 240
Racial harassment, 240
Radcliffe University, 38
Radford University, 245
Radio Act (of 1927), 48
Radio talk shows, 227-28
Radio Television Digital News Association, 3,
    48-49, 66, 84, 106-07
Raleigh News & Observer, 231
Rampton, Sheldon, 202
Ramsey, Dave, 163
Rand, Ayn, 34-35
Random House, 16
Rap music, 75
Rape victims, 29, 111-13
Rapid Shave, 155
Rather, Dan, 10, 87, 142
Ravenous, 187
Rawls, John, 36-38
Readbacks, 120
Reagan, Nancy, 65
Reagan, Ronald, 12, 65, 137, 218, 233
Reagans, The, 65
Reason to Live, A 116,
Reasonable consumer standard, 155
Rebecca Blood's Code of Weblog Ethics,
    319-22
Red flag words, 277
Red Lobster, 157
Reddick, DeWitt C., 133
Reed, Alastair, 93
Reich, Robert, 87
Relativism, 31
Religious expression, 240, 262
Republican National Committee, 65, 136
Republican National Convention (2008), 233
Republican Party, 55
Restaurant reviews, 161, 280
Resumes, 12, 242
Retractions, 133-35, 142-43
Revlon, Charles, 163
Rhetoric, 19, 21

Rhetorical hyperbole, 281
Rice, Donna, 108
Rice, Pat, 55
Richards, Michael, 63
Right of access, 261
Right of editorial control, 262
Rivera, Geraldo, 87
"Road to Nowhere," 233
Roberts, Cokie, 89
Rocker, John, 62
Rockford Files, The, 157
"Rockin' in the Free World," 233
Rodriguez, Alex, 59
Rolling Stone, 143
Romantic period, 22
Ronald McDonald, 274
Roose, Kevin, 100
Roper Poll, 222
Rosenbaum, Alissa Zinovievna (Ayn Rand),
    34-35
Rotary Club, 33-34, 86
Rothman, Stanley, 54
Rousseau, Jean-Jacques, 27
Rowe v. Wade, 158
Royko, Mike, 122-23
Rules of quasi-public places, 266
Rumsfield, Donald, 127
"Running on Empty," 233
Russell, Bertrand, 34
Russian Revolution, 34-35
Rutgers University, 75
Ryan, Paul, 233
Rychlak, Ronald J., 164
Ryder trucks, 145

Sacramento News & Review, 160
Salary negotiations, 244-45
Sample sizes, 223
Samuelson, Robert J., 7
San Francisco Chronicle, 91
San Francisco State University, 53
Sanders, Charles, 231
Sarandon, Susan, 232
Sartre, Jean-Paul, 31-32
Savage, Michael, 87
Saving Private Ryan, 69
Scare tactics, 218-19
Schmitz, Jonathan, 58
School board meetings 290-91
School libraries, 219

Schweitzer, Albert, 31
Scientific Games Corporation, 231
Scientific method, 24
Second-hand smoke, 56
Secret Government, The,
Securities and Exchange Act, 88, 185
Securities and Exchange Commission, 185
Segregation, 218-19
Seib, Philip, 189
Self-Made Man, 96
Senior Olympics, 275
September 11 terrorist attacks, 54, 66, 126, 169,
    203, 232, 240, 260-61
Service marks, 274
Sexual harassment, 238-39
Sexual orientation, 284
Sharpton, Al, 75
Shaw, David, 54, 122
Shaw, Donald, 56
Sheen, Martin, 232
Shield laws, 261
Shopping centers and malls, 265-66
Shut Up and Sing, 232
Siamese fighting fish, 187
Silent Spring, 283
Simpson, O.J., 137, 198-99
Simulacra and Simulation, 32, 33
Sinclair, Upton, 5, 95
Sinise, Gary, 232
Situation Ethics: The New Morality, 36
Situational ethics, 36
60 Minutes, 4, 94
SLAPP suits, 283
Slim Hopes, 162
Slippery slope, 4, 219
Small Street Journal, 275
Smathers, George, 216-17
Smith, Doug, 138-39
Smith, Kevin, 123
Smith, Patricia, 94
Smith, Ron F., 2
Smith, William Kennedy, 112-13
Smoking Gun, The, 16
Snider, Dee, 233
Snipes, Wesley, 157
Snyder, "Jimmy the Greek," 61
Social contract, 25
Social media, 243
Social responsibility theory, 5
Social Security, 9
Society for Human Resource Management, 238

Society of American Business Editors and
    Writers, 323
Society of Professional Journalists, 3, 6, 36, 48-
    49, 52, 84, 106, 110, 123, 324-26
Socrates, 19-20
Socratic dialogue, 20
Sonny Bono Copyright Term Extension Act,
    270, 272, 273
Sons of Confederate Veterans, 230
South Carolina Lottery, 231
South of Heaven, 95
Speaking and consulting fees, 89
Special Olympics, 275
Speech codes, 63-64
Spin (use of term), 12
Sponsored news, 51-52
Sports Illustrated, 58, 91, 96, 98, 138-39
Sports stadiums, 266
Springsteen, Bruce, 233
St. Louis Post-Dispatch, 156
St. Louis Rams, 156
St. Louis University Hospital, 156
St. Louis University, 196
St. Louis, city of, 11
St. Petersburg Times, 90, 95
Staged photographs, 131
Stalin, Joseph, 135
Stallone, Sylvester, 157
Staples Center, 52
Star Trek: Deep Space Nine, 143
"Star-Spangled Banner, The" 270
State lotteries, 54
State of the First Amendment Survey, 260-61
State public records laws, 293-94
Stauber, John, 6, 202
Stephanopoulus, George, 88
Stephens, Mitchell, 128
Stereotyping, 52-54, 137, 220
Stern, Howard, 68
Stewart, Jon, 73
Stewart, Potter, 1
Stock market, 88
Stone, Oliver, 65
Stossel, John, 56
Strategic litigation against public participation
    (SLAPP) suits, 283
Straw man argument, 220
Streisand, Barbra, 232
Strict scrutiny, 264
Student journalists, 306-07
Student records, 285

Subjection of Women, The, 30
Suicide, 114-17, 125, 141
Sultans of Sleaze, 202
Summers, Lee, 64
Sunshine laws, 290
Super Bowl, 68-69
Sykes, Charles J., 171-72
Syracuse University, 141

Taco Bell, 54
Taliban, 94
Talk radio, 227-28
Talking Heads, 233
Tampa Tribune, 114
Tarbell, Ida, 5
Taylor, Herbert J., 33-4
Television ratings, 69
Television reporters, 15
Television talk shows, 89
Television, 8
"Ten Days in a Madhouse," 122
Tenet, George, 127
Tennessee Lottery, 231
Tennessee Tribune, 144
Testimonials, 218, 301
Texas Air National Guard, 142
Thailand, 93
Theory of Justice, 360
Thin entering wedge, 219
Thomas, Chris, 97
Thomas, Clarence, 238
Thompson-French, Mary Ann, 143
Thoreau, Henry David, 22
Three Cups of Tea, 94
Thurmond, Strom, 62
Timberlake, Justin, 68
Time, 137
Time, place, and manner, 264-66
Times-Picayune (New Orleans), 71-72
TiVo, 274
"To Catch a Baby Broker," 124
"To Catch a Car Thief," 124
"To Catch a Predator," 50, 124-25
"To Catch an Identify Thief," 124
Today Show, 71, 74
Toledo Blade, 248
Tony the Tiger, 274
Torricelli, Robert, 217
Town hall forums, 214
Toxic Sludge is Good For You, 202

Toyota, 89
Trade libel, 277
Trademark dilution, 275
Trademarks, 274-75
Traditional public forum, 265-66
Traditional retail advertising, 152
Transfer, 217
Transit advertising, 152
Travel & Leisure, 128
Travel magazines, 128-29, 161
Tropicana, 135
Trump, Donald, 233
Truth-in-advertising, 154-56, 165-66, 168, 169-70, 171-73, 263
TV Guide, 56, 66, 137
Twain, Mark, 11
Twentieth Century Fox, 187
Twisted Sister, 233
Twitter, 152, 265

U.S. Congress, 6, 55, 67, 68, 200, 226, 272, 273, 275, 288
U.S. Constitution, 180, 187, 259, 270
U.S. Copyright Office, 269, 271
U.S. Department of Agriculture, 267
U.S. Department of Education, 226
U.S. Department of Homeland Security, 203
U.S. Department of Housing and Urban Development, 153
U.S. Department of Justice, 6, 130, 159, 218
U.S. Department of State, 221
U.S. Department of Transportation, 156
U.S. Navy Seals, 143
U.S. News & World Report, 76
U.S. Postal Service, 154, 183, 264
U.S. Secret Service, 125
U.S. Senate, 108, 217, 233
U.S. Supreme Court, 1, 26, 38, 57, 68, 90, 126, 155, 158, 183-84, 224-26, 230, 238-39, 264, 265, 266, 273, 277, 280, 282, 290, 294
Unabomber, 130
Uncle Ben, 274
Uncle Sam, 217
Under-age drinking, 131
United Airlines, 52
United States Catholic Conference, 199-200
United Way, 12
University of Alabama, 65
University of California at Santa Barbara, 39
University of California, 41

University of Central Florida, 2
University of Chicago, 5-6
University of Florida, 60-63
University of Georgia, 63
University of Konigsberg, 28
University of Nevada, 41
University of New Hampshire, 249
University of Notre Dame, 12, 242, 248
University of Oregon, 41
University of Pennsylvania, 227
University of South Alabama, 186
University of Virginia, 143
University of Wisconsin, 35, 136, 171
Unlikely Disciple, The, 100
Unobtrusive speech, 261
Unregistered copyright, 271
Upton, Lauren Caitlin, 58
USA Today, 16, 64, 92, 138-39
USA Today/CNN Poll, 223
Utilitarianism, 29-30
Utne Reader, 202

Vanderbilt University, 260
Vassar University, 94
Veil of ignorance, 36-38
Venditte, Pat, 143
Verizon, 158
Viacom, 79-80
Victor's Little Secrets, 275
Victoria's Secret, 275
Video news releases, 66-67
Vietnam War, 11-12, 31, 54, 136, 142
Vincent, Ned, 96
Vincent, Norah, 96
Virgil, Mike, 58
Virginia Polytechnic Institute (Virginia Tech),
    10, 61, 74
Voluntary Madness, 96
Voter registration and turnout, 144

Wag the Dog, 33
"Walk Like an Egyptian," 68
"Walk With an Erection," 68
Walker, Scott, 123
Wall Street Journal, 93, 161, 162, 192, 195,
    201, 222, 275, 276
Wall Street scandals, 12
Wallace, George C., 218-19
Wallace, Lurleen, 218-19

Wallace, Mike, 4, 7, 129
Walsh, Frank, 185
Walt Disney Corporation, 128, 188, 273
Walt Disney World, 128, 188
Walter Reed Army Hospital, 291
Warner Communications, 270
Washington Monthly, 123
Washington Post, 7, 10, 88, 93-94, 117, 122,
    130, 227
Washington University, 39
Washington, Isaiah, 63
Watchdog role of media, 4, 5
Watergate, 4, 12, 224
Watson, Cindy, 228-29
"We're Not Going to Take It," 233
Weblog ethics, 319-22
Weighted samples, 221
Weinstein, Bruce, 28, 242
Welch, Jack, 86
Wellman, Carl, 39
Wenner, Jann, 143
West Virginia Open Governmental Proceedings
    Act, 190
West Wing, The, 158
West, Mae, 68
Weston, Riley, 250
Wetlaufer, Suzy, 86
WFLA-TV, 97
WGBH-TV, 87
What Happened, 202
When the Game is on the Line, 93
"White lies," 23, 38
White, Kevin, 248
Whitehead, Alfred North, 20
Whitlock, Jason, 75
Who's Your Daddy, 65
Wie, Michelle, 98
Wilcox, Dennis L., 180
Wild Bunch, The, 157
Williams, Armstrong, 226
Williams, Juan, 64
Williams, Robin, 115
Williams, Walter, 64
Wilmington Star-News, 127-28
Wilson, Ann and Nancy, 233
Wilson, Woodrow, 153
Winfrey, Oprah, 16, 137, 277
Wire service defense (libel), 280
Wisconsin Right to Life v. FEC, 225
Woods, James, 232
Woods, Tiger, 62

Woodward, Bob, 117, 227
Workplace communication, 237-50
Works for hire doctrine, 271
World Trade Center, 126, 232
World War I, 3
World War II, 30-31
World Wide Web, 7, 8, 74, 247, 287-88
WRAZ-TV, 65
Wright, Donald K., 186
Wright, Jeremiah, 220
Wright, Robert C., 73
Writ of mandamus, 291

Xanax, 109
Xerox, 274
Xhosa, 27

Young & Rubicam, 285-86
Young, Bob, 87
Young, Neil, 233
Young, Yolanda, 92
YouTube, 71, 75, 233

Zapruder, Abraham, 70-71
Zarrella, Ron, 242
Zimmer, Richard, 217
Zoeller, Fuzzy, 62
Zulu, 27

BOOKS BY RANDY BOBBITT

A Big Idea and a Shirt-Tail Full of Type

Developing the Public Relations Campaign
(co-authored with Ruth Sullivan)

Who Owns What's Inside the Professor's Head?

Lottery Wars

Exploring Communication Law

Decisions, Decisions

Us Against Them

From Barnette to Blaine